This England

Politics, culture and society in early modern Britain

General Editors

PROFESSOR ANN HUGHES
PROFESSOR ANTHONY MILTON
PROFESSOR PETER LAKE

This important series publishes monographs that take a fresh and challenging look at the interactions between politics, culture and society in Britain between 1500 and the mid-eighteenth century. It counteracts the fragmentation of current historiography through encouraging a variety of approaches which attempt to redefine the political, social and cultural worlds, and to explore their interconnection in a flexible and creative fashion. All the volumes in the series question and transcend traditional interdisciplinary boundaries, such as those between political history and literary studies, social history and divinity, urban history and anthropology. They thus contribute to a broader understanding of crucial developments in early modern Britain.

This England

Essays on the English nation and commonwealth
in the sixteenth century

PATRICK COLLINSON

Manchester
University Press
Manchester and New York

distributed exclusively in the USA by Palgrave Macmillan

The right of Patrick Collinson to be identified as the author of this work has been
asserted by him in accordance with the Copyright, Designs and Patents Act 1988.

Published by Manchester University Press
Oxford Road, Manchester M13 9NR, UK
and Room 400, 175 Fifth Avenue, New York, NY 10010, USA
www.manchesteruniversitypress.co.uk

Distributed in the United States exclusively by
Palgrave Macmillan, 175 Fifth Avenue,
New York, NY 10010, USA

Distributed in Canada exclusively by
UBC Press, University of British Columbia, 2029 West Mall,
Vancouver, BC, Canada V6T 1Z2

British Library Cataloguing-in-Publication Data is available

Library of Congress Cataloging-in-Publication Data is available

ISBN 978 0 7190 9025 7 paperback

First published by Manchester University Press in hardback 2011

This paperback edition first published 2013

The publisher has no responsibility for the persistence or accuracy of URLs for any external or third-party
internet websites referred to in this book, and does not guarantee that any content on such websites is, or will
remain, accurate or appropriate.

Printed by Lightning Source

Contents

List of abbreviations

Add., Additional
BL, British Library
NA, The National Archives

Acknowledgments

The essays in this collection mark a transition in my interest from the religion of Post-Reformation England to its political and cultural imagination, as reflected in the sense of where England stood in respect of its past. A sense that the English monarchy, especially in the reign of Elizabeth, contained within it a kind of unofficial republic, the national commonwealth, to which a loyalty was owed which in certain circumstances overcame all other loyalties, was expressed in my article 'The monarchical republic of Elizabeth I', first published in the *Bulletin of the John Rylands University Library of Manchester* in 1987, delivered as my inaugural lecture at the University of Sheffield in 1985, and republished in my *Elizabethan Essays*, in 1994. This piece has gained a certain notoriety, reflected in the publication in 2007 of *The Monarchical Republic of Early Modern England: Essays in response to Patrick Collinson*, edited by John F. McDiarmid. Less familiar is my Ralegh Lecture for 1991, 'The Elizabethan exclusion crisis and the Elizabethan polity', partly because of the relative inaccessibility of the *Proceedings of the British Academy*. I am grateful to the Academy for permission to republish the piece on this occasion. 'Servants and citizens: Robert Beale and other Elizabethans' continued these perceptions. It was originally given as a Joan Henderson Lecture at St Mary's College, Twickenham, in 2004. The late Joan Henderson was a very old friend of the Institute of Historical Research, which was where I was reared, and an authority on that political polymath, Robert Beale. The lecture was repeated at a seminar at the institute, arranged by Professor Pauline Croft. My thanks are due to Dr Maria Dowling of St Mary's College, to Professor Croft of Royal Holloway, University of London, and to the editor of *Historical Research*, the institute's journal, for encouraging this essay and for its initial publication. I am equally indebted to *Historical Research* for permission to republish my 2002 Creighton Lecture, 'Elizabeth I and the verdicts of history', and a plenary lecture to the Anglo-American Conference of Historians, 'The politics of religion and the religion of politics in Elizabethan England', in 2006. 'Pulling the strings: religion and politics in the progress of 1578' carries the same theme into the context of East Anglia at a critical moment in its political and religious history, and a determining moment in the virginal reign of Queen Elizabeth I. The volume of essays in which it appeared grew out of work undertaken at the University of Warwick on John Nichols's seminal *Progresses and Public Processions of Queen Elizabeth*, originally published between 1788 and 1823, on which

I, with many other scholars, have been engaged. My thanks to the editors of the volume and to Oxford University Press for permission to republish.

The title of the book has its origins in a set of lectures given at the University of Richmond, Virginia, in 1999: 'This England: the consummation of English nationhood in the long sixteenth century', which are digested in the Introduction to this volume. I am grateful to the University of Richmond for the privilege of serving as Douglas Southall Freeman Visiting Professor, and to the editorial team of the *Douglas Southall Freeman Historical Review* for publishing the lectures in 1999. The remaining essays in this collection reflect an increasing interest in the historical consciousness of English men and women in the sixteenth century, set in an increasing engagement with the literary culture of the English Renaissance. This was ventilated in a somewhat polemical engagement with so-called New Historicism in lectures given in Bangor, Geneva, Pasadena, Wellington and Zurich. My historiographical concerns were the theme of a special subject which I taught in the University of Cambridge from 1989 to 1996, 'Perceptions and uses of the past in sixteenth-century England'. I am grateful to the resourceful students who took part in that enterprise. They needed to be strongly motivated, since at the onset I had all too little knowledge of the subject myself. My way in was by way of the rhetoric of historical judgment expressed in so many Elizabethan and Jacobean sermons, reflected here in 'Biblical rhetoric: the English nation and national sentiment in the prophetic mode', originally offered as a paper at a conference at the University of California, Los Angeles; and in 'Truth, lies and fiction in sixteenth-century Protestant historiography', which was delivered at a conference on the imagination in early modern Britain, held at the Woodrow Wilson Centre in Washington, DC.

More and more those interests focused on that remarkable monument to the Protestant and historical consciousness of Post-Reformation England, the *Acts and Monuments* of John Foxe and his many collaborators, always popularly known as 'The Book of Martyrs'. In the early 1990s the British Academy began to fund a major research enterprise on Foxe's Book of Martyrs, later supported by the Arts and Humanities Research Board, which has now resulted in a variorum edition of the four editions of the book published in Foxe's lifetime. The amount of scholarly endeavour devoted to every conceivable aspect of this huge book, by David Loades and above all Thomas Freeman and their many assistants, take one's breath away. I served as a chairman of the British Academy Committee for a number of years. The growing knowledge of Foxe in context appeared in a series of symposia of the papers given at a series of conferences. My own 'John Foxe and national consciousness' was delivered to the third of these gatherings held at the State University of Ohio, Columbus, in 1999. But Foxe was shared in my interests by a growing interest in the stamp placed on Elizabethan historiography by William Camden. 'One of us? William Camden and the making of history' was the Camden Society Centenary Lecture, included in a conference on Camden held by the Royal Historical Society at Camden's own Westminster School. I am grateful to the society and to Palgrave Macmillan for the permission to republish that piece, together with 'William Camden and the anti-myth of Elizabeth'. This collection concludes with an account of the nostalgic antiquarianism of John Stow, republished by permission of the Cambridge University Press.

I have been unwell for the whole duration of the preparation of this volume, which means that I am especially indebted to the general editors of the series for taking on tasks which would normally have fallen to me. And I have been well looked after by Emma Brennan, the commissioning editor for the series.

Patrick Collinson

Introduction

This England: race, nation, patriotism

'This England', as everyone knows, is Shakespeare: 'This blessed plot, this earth, this realm, this England'. The rolling and rising cadences across a dozen lines build up to that blunt, but emotionally charged, 'this England', which Shakespeare elsewhere called 'this dear, dear land'. And again: 'This England never did, nor never shall | Lie at the proud foot of a conqueror | But when it first did help to wound itself ... | Come the three corners of the world in arms | And we shall shake them. Naught shall make us rue | If England to itself do rest but true.'[1] Shakespeare being Shakespeare, those ringing stanzas still have the capacity to move, and they have resonated with episodes in the history of the centuries to come, to the extent that whatever they may have meant, in the 1590s, becomes irrelevant. But patriotism has now all but vanished from our culture, except in the painted faces of those following the so-called beautiful game, and at the more unacceptable fringes of our politics. For myself, I look back to a different person, the not quite teenager who, in the 1940s, sang along with everyone else: 'There'll always be an England', with the punch line, 'If England means as much to you as England means to me.'

So my subject is far from fashionable. As a historian of the sixteenth century, do I even have a subject? Social and political scientists, with their eyes fixed on modernising processes, and engaged in a series of arguments with the ghost of Karl Marx, deny that national sentiment packed any political punch before the era of revolution and steam. We shall return to this spectre. Meanwhile historians of the British Isles have decided that they ought to be just that. The only proper object of their attention is not England but the whole package – England, Wales, Scotland and Ireland – and their business a holistic study of what John Pocock has instructed us to call 'the Atlantic Archipelago'. This phrase seems to suggest the Azores and has little chance of catching on outside academic preciosity, but one justification for it is that we can't talk about 'the British Isles' for fear of offending the Irish, who refer instead to 'these Islands'. To write about English history on its own is now a piece of political incorrectness. But we face conceptual complications the moment we travel north of Watford and face up to the fact that 'these Islands' embraced a lot of territory, much of it far to the north and west of Watford, and a number of languages and ethnic identities which, in the course of the sixteenth and seventeenth centuries, found themselves for the most part gathered within the jurisdiction of three kingdoms. These, after 1603, shared one king, who, in his primary function as king of England, only occasionally visited his Scottish kingdom and never, ever, went to Ireland. So these seventeenth-century British kings, like most other early modern monarchs, ruled over multiple monarchies in which some of the constituent parts were more equal than others. This was almost the norm, nation states being rare exceptions.[2]

In the case of 'these Islands', the kingdoms once unified (in a limited sense) under one crown proceeded to bounce off one another like billiard balls. But for events in Scotland and Ireland, there would have been no English Civil War. Now we talk of the War in (or of) the Three Kingdoms. These interactive British Wars are one reason for the current fixation on 'the British Problem', or 'the new British history', since no subject has more engaged the attention of our early modern historians than what we used to call the English Revolution. But historians do, after all, live as much in their own times as in their books and articles, and another reason for the new fashion is the process of European unification, which puts on the line all Europe's constituent identities and, in the case of the United Kingdom, the nature of the union itself.

Now to look out on this complex scene with a vision which stops at Watford is myopic. Yet to try to look at it from no particular standpoint is as impossible a game as three-dimensional chess. So the 'new British history' no sooner invented itself than it had to admit that it had a problem. National history is easier to write, and to teach. Some Irish and Scottish historians are deciding that their first responsibility is to their own national histories after all, and they suspect their English colleagues of using 'Britishness' as a cunning vehicle for a new kind of historical imperialism, so-called British history being not much more than an enriched English history.[3]

What in all this of English nationhood? Out of the seventeenth century emerged and expanded something called Britain, its inhabitants sometimes called Britons, who proceeded to construct a British Empire (no one ever called it an English Empire), a joint enterprise which engaged Welsh, English and Scots as partners, and the Irish as, mainly, victims. England was in the driving seat of this new enterprise, and the English have always assumed, and still do, that for British you may read English, and vice versa. So it has been up to the others, the Welsh, the Scottish and the Irish, to assert their own distinctive nationhoods within 'these islands', which in the early twentieth century led to the creation of a secessionist Irish state and, within the Union, a separate northern Irish state, and which brought us, at the cusp of the Millennium, to the first Scottish Parliament for 300 years, which may or may not lead to a secessionist state, and, a new invention, a Welsh Assembly. The English, insofar as they are noticing, may demand something of the same sort.

However, they are not at all sure what it is to be English. Sometimes it seems that the English have never felt the need to define themselves. Never use the word never. They defined themselves repeatedly: in the eighth century A.D., when a monk called Bede wrote *The Ecclesiastical History of the English People*, when such a thing hardly existed outside his own powerful imagination. They defined themselves as the Anglo-Saxon monarchy, which some say was the first nation state in history.[4] And at that time to say that they were English was as much as to say that they were not Welsh, 'the foreigner', the Welsh calling themselves 'i Cymru'. They defined themselves eloquently in the fourteenth century, which saw the incessant and nation-defining wars with France, and the emergence, or rather re-emergence, three centuries after the Norman Conquest, of English as a major vernacular literature. It has been said that it was in the fourteenth century that God became an honorary Englishman.[5] And above all they defined themselves in the long sixteenth century, the pattern and paradigm for this newly invented nationhood the Biblical narratives of Israel and Judah, with the frequently repeated 'God is English', one of those true words spoken in jest.[6] There were difficulties in equating state and nation in other parts of 'these islands', indeed in imagining, or pretending, that there was a nation at all. In the Middle Ages there was already a Scottish state (or kingdom at least), but no Scottish nation, only four or five linguistic groups with almost nothing in common, as was famously said of Italy, no more than a geographical expression. The Welsh, to this day divided amongst themselves, could only recognise each other as Welsh when they confronted that other which was England.[7] So even more with Ireland, which might never have imagined itself to be Ireland without the invasive Anglo-Normans, and the aggressive, colonising Elizabethan English, the intense Catholicism of their nationhood since the sixteenth century the consequence of tragic and violent encounters with English Protestants. Before the sixteenth century there was a rich Gaelic civilisation which extended from the northwest of Scotland to the southwest of Ireland, but the politics of this other world were radically decentralised, and there was no articulated, let alone organised, Irish nation.[8] So there are senses in which the various nationhoods of 'these islands' depended upon and derived from English nationhood. Once constructed, the nations of 'these islands' have proved tough and durable. From 1801 to 1921, they were amalgamated in a single state with one Parliament, and that Union, minus the Republic of Ireland, still for the moment endures. But there has never been a British nation.

So I make no apology for my subject. Rather, I find it odd that three collections of essays on almost all aspects of the early modern British question, published in 1995, 1996 and 1998,[9] all omit this one aspect: not a single essay on English nationhood, the English self-consciousness of being English. It appears that if English nationhood continues to retain any scholarly mileage, it is not with the new British historians but with those who read English literature. What a pity, said Professor Marilyn Butler, in her inaugural lecture as Professor of English Literature at Cambridge. We don't have that problem. For if people are relieved not to have to learn about English history, they are unlikely to lose interest in Shakespeare, who belongs, as Ben Jonson said, not to an age but to all time, and to the whole world.

In 1567, a Member of the English House of Commons rose to his feet and said this: 'I tell you, Master Speaker, that I speake for all England, yea, and for the noble English nation, who in times past (with noe small honour) have daunted and made the proudest nations aghast.'[10] I cannot justify that man's claim to speak for all England (although it's of the greatest significance that he thought that he could), and nor can I pretend that 'all England' was capable of speaking for itself. Let us admit that we might as well not bother looking for very much practical patriotism in sixteenth-century England. Even 1588, the year of the Spanish Armada which Shakespeare must have had in mind when he wrote 'come the three corners of the world', was not 1914, nor yet 1940. We know, if only from Shakespeare, that common soldiers were not uncompromising patriots. Those who opted for a military career were just as likely to serve other countries, other princes, as their own native country.

Shrewsbury, on the Welsh borders, contained the largest school in Elizabethan England. In 1581, its 360 boys 'marched bravely' in battle order with their generals, captains, drums, trumpets and ensigns, declaring 'how valiantly they would fight and defend their country'.[11] One Shrewsbury alumnus was Sir Philip Sidney, who presently became a national icon when he died of a war wound at Zutphen. But to offset Sidney we have Sir William Stanley. Stanley too fought with distinction at Zutphen. But a few months later he was appointed governor of another Dutch town, Deventer, in charge of a garrison of Irish soldiers. Stanley was a Catholic himself, the brother of a Jesuit priest. Presently, he surrendered his city to the Spaniards and all the troops entered the service of the King of Spain. Later, Stanley headed an English legion which was meant to take part in the Spanish invasion of his own country. If Stanley too was a kind of national patriot, he was a different kind of patriot from the schoolboys of Shrewsbury.[12] This might be dismissed as neither here nor there. England in the 1580s was a divided society, which had not been the case a hundred years before. Yet the case of Sidney and Stanley suggests that we are looking for a rather different kind of patriotism from anything in more recent generations.

PATRIOTISM

We are looking instead for a culturally constructed nationhood, England as an inspired nation.[13] The extent of this imagination cannot be measured, although the popularity in the 1590s of history plays tells us something, at least about London. But its depth and intensity can. The crudest and most basic form of expressed nationhood was no doubt that sense of the other which our parliamentary speaker uttered when he spoke of the whole English nation daunting and making 'aghast' the proudest nations. Traditionally that meant the French. When John Aylmer, a future bishop of London, wrote in 1559 that God was English, he meant that God was not French, and his book came out in the closing weeks of a war which had lasted off and on for two hundred years. He exhorted his readers, as if they were Muslims, to fall flat on their faces before God seven times a day, thanking him that they had been born Englishmen, not French peasants, not to speak of France's allies, what Aylmer called the 'piddling' Scots.[14] With the Elizabethan age of ever wider expansion, the horizons of otherhood expanded. In a book called *The Glory of England* (1615), the journalist Thomas Gainsford compared his native land with China, India and Turkey. 'My joy exceedeth for not being a native amongest them.' 'O happy England! O happy people! O happy London!'[15] By then Englishmen could read a huge book by Richard Hakluyt called *The Principall Navigations of the English Nation*, a powerfully imagined account of an English maritime empire which did not yet exist, except as an idea.

Nurse Cavell would certainly have said that xenophobia is not enough. If we want to look beyond competition and dislike of the other for cultural evidence of imagined nationhood, we have to look to law, language, literature and religion, all in their various ways related to the past, partly remembered, partly imagined. No one will be surprised to learn that the laws of England, the essence of what John Pocock called 'The Ancient Constitution', were of fundamental importance for a sense of English nationhood. One face of 'England' was legal memory. This topic will not be dealt with in this volume. I am no legal historian, and can only refer the reader to Alan Cromartie's *The Constitutionalist Revolution: An essay on the history of England, 1450–1642* (Cambridge, 2006). But, even though my qualifications in linguistics are not much stronger, language we must discuss. Again, the faculty of language seems to be located in the brain very close to the area of memory. *Sensus Grammaticus, sensus historicus.*

LANGUAGE

Experts on national sentiment and nationalism disagree on many things. We shall come back to this. But many would agree that of all the factors making for a sense of nationhood, a shared language, expressing itself in a written vernacular literature, and a shared religious identity are among the most powerful. Language is the strongest bond of nationality, linguistic diversity the greatest obstacle to the formation and sustenance of nation states. But even language is not enough. The imagining is quasi-religious and often derives from religion itself. According to the Irishman, Conor Cruse O'Brien, nationalism is bound to be a religious thing, 'holy nationalism', 'since any nationalism which failed to inspire reverence would not be an effective binding force'; while Adrian Hastings believed that 'the Bible provided, for the Christian world at least, the original model of the nation. Without it ... it is arguable that nations and nationalism, as we know them, could never have existed.' But the anthropologist Ernest Gellner, if he were alive to read it, would raise an eyebrow at this, and he regarded O'Brien as 'intellectually autistic'.[16]

But in the case of sixteenth-century England, we need not waste much time in discussing whether it was language or religion which were the most important force making for an enhanced national self-consciousness, since religion and linguistic imperatives were effectively fused, thanks to the Protestant Reformation, and thanks above all to one man, William Tyndale, and to the New Testament which he translated and began to print, in Germany, in 1525.[17] Of course Tyndale did not invent English as a literary language. It was almost a thousand years since the first English word, and that word, perhaps significantly, was 'keel', which is to say, ship (the writer was a man called Gildas),[18] and there had been a vernacular literature in English for seven or eight hundred years.

But Tyndale, coming out of the remote Forest of Dean, hard by the Welsh border, somehow or other (and it remains a mystery to me how he did it, but it was an achievement comparable to Martin Luther's, in his German Bible) fashioned, in the pages of his New Testament, the English which we still speak and write; an English employing a vocabulary which if not at first universally understood and assimilated soon was; an English partly derived from the word order and sentence structure of the Greek and especially the Hebrew biblical texts in which Tyndale, a remarkable and precocious classical philologist, was thoroughly proficient.

Tyndale had an intuitive and strong sense of the affinity of English with these ancient tongues, an affinity which he believed was not to be found in the Latin language and in the Latin Bible. 'The manner of speaking is both one. So that thou needed not but to translate it into English, word for word.' So Tyndale gives us the kind of English sentence with which we have become so familiar that we take it for granted: the sentence which rolls along with the assistance of the little copulative 'and'. 'And the King [David] said to Chusi: is the lad safe? And Chusi answered: the enemies of my lord the King and all that rise against thee, to have thee, be as thy lad is. And the king was moved, and went up to a chamber over the gate and wept. And as he went thus he said: my son Absolom, my son, my son, my son Absolom, would to God I had died for thee, Absolom my son.' Tyndale inserted an extra 'my son' for the sake of the rhythm. Otherwise this is a word for word translation. (This is of course from Tyndale's Old Testament translation, on which he was engaged in Antwerp when he was arrested, imprisoned and, after strangulation, burned at the stake in 1536.)

Tyndale's own imperatives, linguistic and religious, can be fully illustrated by these two statements, the one reported long after his death, the other in his own written words. In one of his prefaces, Tyndale wrote: 'For God gave the Children of Israel by the hand of Moses in their mother tongue: and all the psalms were in the mother tongue. The sermons which thou readest in the Acts of the Apostles, and all that the apostles preached, were no doubt in the mother tongue ... Why may we not also?' Back in Gloucestershire, before all this, Tyndale was said to have told a local clergyman of conservative, Catholic views: 'If God spare my life, ere many years, I will cause a boy that driveth the plow, shall know more of the scripture than thou dost.' Note the force of 'I will cause.' The great Erasmus of Rotterdam had written in the Preface to his 1516 New Testament, printed in Greek with a new Latin translation on the facing pages: 'would that' ('*utinam*'), would that the ploughman and even the woman sitting at her spinning should know the scriptures (and that was to borrow an idea from Jerome, writing a thousand years before).[19] The difference between Erasmus's 'would that' and Tyndale's 'I will cause' was crucial.

Yet in spite of his famous 'vaunt', as it has been called, Tyndale was self-effacing. In a secret meeting in as field outside Antwerp with an English government official who was trying to lure him back to England, Tyndale said, in effect, that if the King, Henry VIII, would only make the Bible available in their own language, which had already happened in other countries (England was out of line in this respect), he would be content 'never to write any more', as it were to cease to exist, even never to have existed. And this was what happened, not long after Tyndale's life was tragically cut short, before he had translated the poetic books of the Old Testament, which would have been one of the treasures of English literature. The English Bible was completed by Miles Coverdale, and soon the so-called Great Bible in English was set up, by royal order, in all churches. It was not Henry VIII's intention to release the Bible into the hands of all and sundry. But now the cat was out of the bag and there was no putting it back. Tyndale would now be all but forgotten, his achievement absorbed in versions of the Bible to which no particular names were attached; so far forgotten that when we celebrated the fifth centenary of his birth in 1994 it appeared that beyond a few specialists, no one had ever heard of him. A writer in the *Times* newspaper called Tyndale 'the forgotten ghost in the language'.

And now everyone learned what those specialists had always known: that for those parts of the Bible which Tyndale translated, the whole of the New Testament and much of the Old Testament, more than eighty per cent of the words in what we call the Authorised Version of 1611 are his. Such altogether memorable passages as the account of the Nativity in Matthew ('shepherds abiding in the fields, keeping watch over their flocks by night'), and the story of the Prodigal Son in Luke ('father, I have sinned against Heaven, and in thy sight, and am no more worthy to be called thy son') are wholly his. It was Tyndale who gave us 'the burden and heat of the day', 'filthy lucre', 'God forbid', 'the salt of the earth', 'the powers that be', 'eat, drink and be merry'. The list is endless.

What is extraordinary is that Tyndale's English is actually a more English English, more demotic in its language and tone, than the version of 1611 of three generations later, where a committee has smoothed over many rough edges and produced something more stately, more ecclesiastical, safer. Noah in 1611 'entered into' the Ark. Tyndale's Noah simply 'went' in. The serpent says to Eve in 1611: 'Ye shall not surely die.' In Tyndale he says: 'Tush, ye shall not dye.' (Compare the stumbling words of the modern version known as the Revised English Bible: 'Of course you will not die, said the Serpent', which sounds more like pantomime than Scripture.) The governor of the wedding feast at Cana in Galilee spoke in 1611 of inferior wine being served 'when men be well drunken'; in Tyndale's it is 'when men be drunk'. Translating Luke on Peter's denial, the men of 1611 tell us that 'a certain maid beheld him ... and earnestly looked upon him'. But according to Tyndale 'one of the wenches ... beheld him ... and set good eyesight on him.' That is the difference between Caravaggio (1611) and Brueghel (Tyndale). Only in 1611 does Christ qualify what he says with 'verily, verily', and I am not aware that anyone else in 1611 went around saying 'verily, verily'. So 1611 begins to take the Bible out of the hands of the people and to give it back to the Church, or at least it tries to ensure that when they read the Bible they will be aware that they are doing something 'religious', somewhat detached from the rest of their lives. This is an example of what T. S. Eliot famously called 'the dissociation of sensibility'. 'Scripture', said Tyndale, 'speaketh after the most grossest manner.' The men of 1611 tried to avoid such grossness.

Looking backwards and forwards, we must not exaggerate Tyndale's singularity. Tyndale was not the first Englishman to translate the Bible, although he was the first to print it in the vernacular. As a translator, he was preceded by more than a century by followers of the radically heretical Oxford scholar, John Wyclif, who had his own reasons for wanting Scripture promulgated in English. We used to dismiss these so-called 'Lollard' versions as in every way inferior to Tyndale. But that was to judge them anachronistically, according to the English which Tyndale would teach us to read and to speak. Evidence of the popularity of the Wycliffite, or 'Lollard', Bible is that it exists in more manuscript copies than any other fourteenth-century text, and Professor Janel Mueller insists that it was from no later than the late fourteenth century, the age of Chaucer and Langland, that 'scripturalism' became an important and dynamic principle in the evolution of the language, replacing the 'closed' Latin sentence with the 'openness' we associate with English.[20] The Wycliffite translator Nicholas Purvey declared that his intention was to make 'the sentence as trewe and open in English as it is in latyn', or rather 'more trewe and more open', for to translate the sentence was as much as to translate the sense.[21]

Moreover, to take into account Professor Anne Hudson's recreation of these and many other Wycliffite texts, including the Lollard sermon cycles, the textual evidence of what Hudson has called the 'premature Reformation' of the fourteenth and fifteenth centuries is to put Tyndale into a more credible historical perspective, less of a Carlylean hero or *deus ex machina*.[22] It looks as if Tyndale's importance lay not so much in his resolve to make the Scripture accessible to ploughboys, which was already the ambition of Wycliffite translators, as in his vastly superior Greek and Hebrew philology (Purvey had translated from the Vulgate); and the fact that he commanded the new information technology of print, and brought it into play a full generation or two after it might have been deployed, if it had not been for the public and political fear of heresy which Wyclif and his followers had engendered in England, almost more than anywhere else in Europe.

Tyndale's achievement and the publication strategies of other early Protestant reformers coincided significantly with a revived interest in the by now almost archaic English literature of the late fourteenth century, a kind of English renaissance within the Renaissance: the first printed edition of *Piers Plowman*, preceded in 1532 by a definitive edition of Chaucer, who was seen, with Langland, as a kind of proto-Protestant. And note the patriotism of William Thynne's editorial preface to his Chaucer, which addresses Henry VIII: 'I thought it in maner appurtenant unto my dewtie and that of very honesty and love to my country I ought no lesse to do then to put my helpynge hande to the restauration and bringing agayne to lyghte of the said works'.[23]

To look forwards: Archbishop Thomas Cranmer's 'Book of Common Prayer', designed to be 'understanded of the people', was hardly less formative of the language than Tyndale, equally fluent, but adding weight with its many doublings: 'sins and wickednesses', 'devices and desires', 'goodness and loving kindness', phrases which soon acquired the smoothness of well-worn pebbles. The increasing use of English as the medium for the handling of theological, philosophical and political topics saw the importation on an unprecedented scale of loan words, especially from the Latin, and such 'inkhorn' terms as 'scientific', 'method', 'function', 'impression', 'penetrate', and this led to a self-conscious debate about the true qualities of the English language, and whether those qualities might not be lost through excessive linguistic innovation. George Puttenham, in *The Art of English Poesie* (1586), welcomed the new words as indispensable, advocated the use of what we would call 'received' English, and warned his readers against using the rough English speech heard in the North, while admitting that that was the purest, because the most primitive English.

In a book published 1580, ostensibly a manual for teachers of English in elementary schools, the schoolmaster Richard Mulcaster presented a remarkable sociological theory of the tendency of languages to grow from their primitive state towards perfection, and then to decline into over-sophisticated senescence, declaring that in his own day English was just right, standing where Greek had stood in the days of Demosthenes and Latin in the time of Cicero. Since Mulcaster wrote when William Shakespeare had recently left school, who are we to say that his judgment was wrong? He waxed ecstatic over what he called 'the treasure in our tongue', as bearing the joyful title of liberty and freedom, whereas Latin was a reminder of thralldom and bondage. 'I love *Rome* but *London* better. I favour *Italie* but *England* more. I honour the *Latin* but I worship the *English*. 'Why not all in English?' What, Mulcaster asked, with unconscious irony, what if our English tongue is 'of small reach, spoken in one small island and not even in all parts of that?' 'Tho it go not beyond sea, it will serve on this side ... Our state is no *Empire* to hope to enlarge it by commanding over other countries.'[24] America, and English a universal language: these were things far beyond Mulcaster's imagination. So an Icelander might have defended Iceland's own language and literature in the twenty-first century. Edmund Spenser, one of Mulcaster's students, asked: 'Why a Gods name may we not, as else the Greeks, have the kingdom of our own language?'[25] I am not forgetting that there was serious disagreement about the direction the language should take, especially for any literary purpose, as the new polish of Philip Sidney found Spenser's atavistic rusticity abrasive. But for my purpose, I am more interested in the transcendent vision of Samuel Daniel, who presently conceived what Mulcaster could not imagine:

> And who, in time, knows whither we may vent
> The treasure of our tongue, to what strange shores
> This gaine of our best glory shall be sent,
> T'inrich unknowing Nations with our stores?
> What worlds in th'yet unformed Occident
> May come refin'd with th'accents that are ours?[26]

RELIGION

To come to religion. We have not said all that might have been said about the imperative which drove Tyndale to do what he did. As a follower of Martin Luther,[27] Tyndale was aiming at far more than a simple enabling of his fellow countrymen to understand and articulate their religion in their own words. He was in the business of changing their religion, and language was the instrument of change. He wrote: 'I supposed yt very necessary to put you in remembrance of certain points, which are they ye well understand what these words mean: the old testament, the new testament, the law, the gospel, Moses, Christ.' Professor John Carey writes: 'Tyndale has only one thing to say, and the problem for the critic is how he manages to say it so often ... yet still conduct us forward, alert, through page after page.'[28] This 'one thing' is what Tyndale, following Luther, calls 'the Gospel', the pith of all that pertains to the Christian faith. And the pith is faith itself, defined by Tyndale as 'a living thing, mighty in working, valiant and strong, ever doing, ever fruitful'. The Christian man doesn't ask whether good works are to be done or not, he has done them already, ere mention is made of them, and is for ever doing them, for such is his nature.

To make the Bible a vehicle for this (in a sense) new religion of salvation by faith alone, a religion without priests, or rather, in which every Christian is a priest, Tyndale introduced new, tendentious translations of the traditional terms of religion, and so transformed their religious meanings. The Greek *ecclesia* became not 'church' but 'congregation', *presbyteros* not 'priest' but 'senior' or 'elder', *metanoia* not 'do penance' but to be penitent; charity became love. (The men of 1611 played safe, putting 'charity' back into I Corinthians 13 and restoring 'church', but in this Protestant version we still find 'except ye repent', not 'except ye do penance'.) A conservative complained of what Tyndale had done: 'By this translation we shall lose all these Christian words, penance, charity, confession, grace, priest, church.' Sir Thomas More agreed, and spilt hundreds of thousands of his own polemical words against Tyndale's verbal 'juggling'. Focusing on penance, More protested that it was lawful 'to call any thing in English by what word so ever English men by custom agree upon. And therefore to make a change of the English word, as though that all England should go to school with Tyndale to learn English, is a very frantic folly.'[29]

Perhaps More missed the point that Tyndale had himself gone to school with all England to learn the language of his translation. Janel Mueller observes in More's prolix and tedious literary controversy with Tyndale that as he became ever more authoritarian and dogmatic, he steadily retreated from those 'open' qualities which were the true genius of English into a kind of verbal obfuscation. 'It is hard to avoid the conclusion that More deliberately resigns to Tyndale and the Protestants generally the exercise of native resources for prose composition. He is conceding that the open, vernacular style is a suitable mode for undermining the authority of the Church, not for defending it.'[30] So what has been called 'the triumph of English' becomes hard to separate from the triumph of Protestantism. That is not all that might be said about a matter of continuing complexity, and it rides roughshod over some sensibilities. Catholics and Protestants would dispute for some time to come whether their words clarified, or grossly distorted, the meaning of Scripture.[31]

The title page of Henry VIII's Great Bible, engraved by Holbein, shows the king handing down the Bible to representatives of church and state (or rather, spirituality and temporality), and so on down through the social orders until it reaches the little people in the streets, and even, in the bottom right-hand corner, those in prison. Those who know Latin are responding '*vivat rex*' (in little balloons coming out of their mouths), the women and children with 'God Save the Kynge.' But the people don't have their own bibles in their hands, and they are evidently dependent upon hearing it read and expounded from the pulpit. Later representations will show the people gathered round the pulpit with their bibles open on their laps. Of course we want to know how many people, and what kinds of people, were reached, first by Tyndale's New Testament, then by entire bibles, and how many were able to read for themselves, or to hear the Bible reads by others. We now know more than we did about editions and print runs, and about the modalities of sale and distribution, but such questions can never be answered with any precision. In these circumstances, historians are dependent upon anecdotes, but anecdotes can be very indicative, if they are not made to do more than they are capable of.

So here is one such story, which takes us back to about 1540, told in later life by a man called William Maldon, a native of Chelmsford in Essex. In his youth, Maldon met up with 'dyveres poore men' who had bought a New Testament and on Sundays sat reading it in the lower end of the church, and 'many wolde floke about them to heare them reading'. When Maldon's father prevented him going to these meetings, he joined forces with one of his father's apprentices, and together they saved up enough (it would have been about three shillings, or six weeks' wages) to buy their own copy of the New Testament, which they hid in their beds 'and so exercised it at convenient times'. When the father heard about this he did his best to put the fear of death into his son, much as a modern parent might who found hard drugs in his son's bedroom. In Maldon's words, 'he bestowed his rode on my body'.[32] For the New Testament was a dangerous substance which could lead to a hot and thoroughly unpleasant death.

However, if you prefer statistics to anecdotes, we can say that ten times as many bibles were printed and sold in the 1630s as in the 1570s, to the extent that a kind of saturation may have set in.[33] Anyone who could afford a bible (shall we risk a guess and say, the upper third of the population?) now had one, and then kept it forever (a very different situation from Chelmsford in 1540), so that in the later seventeenth century production actually fell off. My own copy of a bible in the popular version first published in Geneva in 1560, this one dated 1602, has its fly-leaves full of signatures and other marks made by those who owned and read it in the eighteenth century. A nineteenth-century historian famously pronounced that it was in Shakespeare's lifetime that the English people became the people of a book, and that book was the Bible.[34]

Rather more to the point, for my present purpose, is the question, what did people do with their bibles, or rather, what did the Bible do for and to them? The engraved title page of Henry VIII's Bible suggests, as you might expect it to suggest, that it was meant primarily to induce loyal obedience, with the emphasis perhaps on texts like, 'The powers that be are ordained by God.' But one of the official homilies of the newly reformed Church of England, composed in the reign of Henry's son, the homily 'on the Scripture', suggests a more interesting answer to our question. In reading God's word, the homily tells us, the reader who will profit most is the one who is 'turned into it, that is ... in his heart and life altered and changed into that which he readeth.'[35]

What could it mean to be turned, or changed, into what you read? Some of the answers consist of much of the lyric poetry of the early seventeenth century, which, as Barbara Lewalski has demonstrated, can be found in the Bible, with its richly tentacular tropes and metaphors. These include: waters to swim in, waters of almost unplumbable depth; Christ as physician, death and life; sin as darkness or blindness; Christ as light; depictions of the Christian life as warfare, pilgrimage, childlikeness (think of Thomas Traherne); the tropes of sheep and shepherding; the husbandry of seed, plant, vineyard; the metaphors of marriage – the body, the temple, the heart. All are vehicles for uniting the truths of Scripture with the truths of human experience. John Donne wrote: 'There are no such eloquent books in the world as the Scriptures.'[36]

But we are losing sight of the nation. At one rhetorical level, and this was perhaps more than what we call virtual reality, bible stories consolidated and united the Protestant nation in what was seen to be not only a deadly but also an apocalyptic struggle against its popish adversaries, and this, as Linda Colley has told us, would be the function of Protestant ideology for a very long time to come, serving in the eighteenth century to define Britain as a Protestant imperial power.[37] Thus in 1586 John Norden, to be sure a literary hack, published a book called *A Mirror for the Multitude*. Norden's readers were warned against following the multitude along the broad way that leads to destruction. 'From the beginning, the Church of God hath been the least part of the world.' That 'least part', 'the little flock of true Christians', was identified with 'little England', 'the multitude' with 'the mighty monarch of Spain' that 'seemeth to rule'. Norden proceeded to apply to the perilous situation of little England the biblical story of David and Goliath. There was no more equality between naked David with his sling and five stones and the mighty Goliath in his armour than between a mouse and an elephant, but with God on his side, 'with a stone [David] killed this huge and mighty monster.' 'Thus may we, little Israel of England, say, "If the Lord had not been on our side when men rose up against us, they had swallowed us up quick.'"[38] This was two years before the Spanish Armada left port.

But the Bible in the hands of Protestants was not always and necessarily such a consolidating and unifying thing, especially when its expositors turned to the prophetic books of the Old Testament. These books were not read as merely historical documents, for preachers who chose their texts from the prophets were powerfully persuaded (how far they succeeded in persuading their hearers it is harder to tell) by the typology of Israel and Judah of old as applied to their own English nation, which they addressed and apostrophised as if the nation literally stood before them in the pulpit: 'Oh England, England! Oh London!'

What we may call the Israelite paradigm became the commonest of pulpit commonplaces. Here is one preacher, in Bristol: 'Blessed is Israel, because the Lord is their God.' And here is a bishop, who is about to be moved from London to York, preaching his last sermon in London, which he equates with Corinth, which St Paul had been reluctant to leave: 'The city is like, the people are like, my departure from you is like.'[39] Evidently the biblical texts were so many time capsules, or cassettes, to be inserted into the tape-deck of the present. Israel and England 'right parallels'. What these biblical parables tell us, if they tell us nothing else, is that the Bible, and especially the Old Testament, powerfully reinforced the sense of nationhood. For if Christianity, according to a once famous German theologian, is all about God and the soul, the soul and its God, the Old Testament is about God and the nation, the nation and its God. There is nothing in these biblical texts about social, or sectional, or regional differences: just the nation. Empires are without exception evil empires, and most kings, too, are bad news, good and godly ones exceptions to prove the rule. In any case, God and the nation, in their very special relationship, take priority over kings. A preacher stands up before the English Parliament on the eve of the Civil War. 'You that are the representative body of this Nation. You are the Nation representatively ... you stand in the place of the whole Nation; and if you stand for God's cause, the whole Nation doth it in you.' 'As this is a Nationall day, and this Honourable Assembly a National Assembly, so this Text is a Nationall Text, suitable for the occasion about which we are met.' To those modern historians and political scientists who deny the force of national sentiment before the Age of Revolution and Romanticism, I am tempted to say, put that in your pipes and smoke it.

A very superficial reading of this painfully repetitive but rhetorically resourceful pulpit language might suggest that the Israelite paradigm was meant to flatter. 'Ah England', exclaims one preacher, 'God's Signet. God's Jewel, which he hath fostered as tenderly and adorned as graciously as ever he did Judea, the one only Nation, almost, that doth openly and solely profess the true Religion of God!' But the force of the rhetoric is fiercely judgmental, following the lead of the Israelite prophets. Israel was uniquely favoured. But Israel had sinned, a hopeless, chronic, recidivist sinner of a nation, for ever whoring after false gods. So God abandoned Israel, which was led off into captivity. Why suppose that God would deal differently with his modern Israel, England? 'If you forsake him, he will forsake you.' We are at a sermon in London in 1578: God's 'mercies towards us Englishmen, above many other nations, makes his judgements more heavie'. Almost fifty years on, we are in Banbury in 1623: 'We seem to have entered into a contention with the Almightie, whether he shall be more mercifull, or we more sinfull; whether he shall be more constant in doing us good, or we more obstinate in sinning against him.' In 1642, Members of the Parliament, which was about to go to war against its king, heard a preacher declare that to sin in despite of such mercies as God had poured on England was a 'God-provoking', 'land-destroying' sin. 'To sinne with mercy is to make mercy our adversary. And if mercy plead against a Nation, then looke for speedy destruction ... To sinne with the rare and choyce mercies of God (such as the mercies of England are) is a sinne of such transcendent unkindness as that God cannot but destroy such a Person, or such a Nation, that is guilty of it.' The preachers played with their congregations as a cat plays with a mouse. When God said that he would abandon his people, did he really mean it? He told the prophet Jeremiah to stop praying for Israel, since he fully intended to destroy it. Was that for real? Some said that all God's judgments were meant as warnings, never final. It was always five minutes to twelve. Others disagreed. 'God may, and doth sometimes destroy us at once, and give us no warning.'[40]

So disturbing, so divisive, were these judgmental utterances that if their effect was to construct the nation, it was also to construct a divided nation. The prophets had spoken of a godly remnant, who would emerge from the common destruction to renew the nation of Israel. The godly might stand in the gap, warding off God's judgments for a time, and in the end they would at least save their own souls. But the outlook for the multitude, now identified not with an external enemy but with the majority of Englishmen, was bleak. Those serious, prodigious super-Protestants whose unfriendly neighbours called them 'Puritans' readily identified themselves with the godly remnant. The sins for which God was judging England, swearing, drunkenness, fornication, neglect of the Sabbath Day, were not their sins. This was about them, not us. Or, if it was indeed directed at us, we were listening. They were not. Moreover, the kind of preaching we have described became increasingly politicised as the Stuart monarchy pursued what were seen to be ungodly, crypto-Catholic politics both at home and abroad. Prophetic, judgmental preaching was threatening to separate the nation, or a portion on the nation, from its king.

I hope that I have not totally subverted my argument that the English Bible, in the hands of the preachers and the ears of their congregations, forged the English nation as a new kind of nation, a Protestant nation and a biblical people. But it forged a distracted nation which in the 1640s went to war with itself, in part because of all that rhetoric.[41] And then spent the next fifty years in an only partly successful attempt to restore national unity, incorporating Scotland along the way, in the Act of Union of 1707, which is when Great Britain became less but not yet more than an idea.

If you were to look around in the shopping mall of history for an ideology to consolidate a united nation and people, stuck as it was until 1688 with the Stuart monarchy, you would not necessarily choose a biblically based Protestantism. So there are problems which we must not overlook in making English nationality a sub-set of Protestantism. 'It is worth asking,' we find in a collection of essays on *Protestantism and National Identity*, published in 1998, 'whether the reformed faith could ever have been a sound basis for a unifying national identity.'[42] What both the reformed faith and its rejection by English Catholics and an indeterminate number whom we had better call Anglicans proved to be the basis for was the construction of inimical religious identities, Catholic and Protestant, diverging in Puritan and Anglican directions. Puritanism became in itself a many-headed hydra: Presbyterian, Independent, Baptist, Quaker. The future was one of great religious diversity, a functional as well as dysfunctional factor in the making of a pluralistic English politics and society, Voltaire wrote that it was no doubt a good thing for a nation to have only one religion; to have two was a great misfortune, but in England where there were any number of religions, things worked out very well. This was what Max Weber would admire so much about England, contrasting English diversity and individualism with the Prussian authoritarianism, and the Lutheran passivity of his native Germany.

As my long sixteenth century progressed, English Protestants were not only reading and hearing the Bible. They were also absorbing that huge book – two and a half times as long as the Bible – which has ever lived in the popular mind and memory as 'Foxe's Book of Martyrs', and which many seem to have read as systematically – they would have said 'throughly' – as the Bible itself, a chapter or two of each, day by day, week by week, year by year. Foxe was the ultimate historical revisionist. For if Tyndale dictated a new religious lexicography, Foxe rewrote the entire history of the Church from its beginnings to his own day to refute the claims to truth and infallible authority of the Roman Church, and to justify with the lessons of his revisionist history the truth and legitimacy of Protestantism. This was a history controlled by the master principles of persecution and martyrdom, the story of a visible Church ostensibly all-powerful and all-glorious, a persecuting Church which was in truth false and anti-Christian; and of an almost invisible, hidden Church, for ever bleeding victim, but in truth true. To read Foxe 'throughly' was to make a long march through the centuries, but no doubt his readers were most interested in the hundreds of pages devoted to their own English martyrs, the victims of the persecution under Queen Mary of the day before yesterday, the martyrs of the 1550s. These stories of horrifying but heroic deaths and appalling cruelty validated the Protestant faith and damned the so-called Catholics, for had not the prophet Isaiah said of Mount Zion: 'They shall not hurt nor destroy in all my holy mountain?' They read these narratives as Jews would read of the holocaust, or Dutch patriots the documents of the Nazi occupation. The names were familiar, many of the agents still alive. Indeed, 'interested' is altogether too weak a word. As with bible readers, readers of Foxe were turned into what they read. They read about a godly community which had withstood persecution, often to the death, and they identified with and read themselves into that godly community. In a sense they themselves wrote what they read, since Foxe's narratives were supplied by numerous eye-witnesses and other participants who had lived and died the stories now read out, often aloud, from the printed page. And there were stunning and lurid pictures which brought it all back to life, for both the illiterate and the literate.

Foxe's Book of Martyrs was once credited with having invented the idea of England as an Elect Nation. For as long as the author was assumed to have been in command of his book, there were those who pointed out that that was very far from Foxe's intention. His subject was the Church, his expectation that the world was about to end, probably in his lifetime. Nowadays the writers of books such as Foxe's are demoted, especially in such a huge and sprawling work. We are more interested in the readers than the writers. So perhaps Foxe did foster the idea of England as a faithful nation. These reflections of the intentions of our sixteenth-century historians, Foxe and Camden, are pursued later in this volume.[43]

This would be the place to bring into play the constitutional situation of the English nation, especially under Elizabeth: the last of her line, unmarried and unwilling to have her successor so much as mentioned, and the rich climate of Roman history, mingled with the Old Testament, which inspired those close to the centre of power. These are major themes of more than one of the articles which follow in this collection.[44]

HISTORY

Here it is necessary to explore a little further the self-discovery of England, the back cloth to the essays on Camden, Stow, Lambarde and Carew with which these essays conclude. In the sixteenth century, the English people were discovering themselves in their past, or in what they imagined to be their past, and spatially, as they acquired, through maps of an accuracy and sophistication never seen before, and books which complemented the maps with literary observations of the landscape, a sense of where they were, within their own borders and beyond. County historians conducted Elizabethan readers out along the highways, and especially the waterways, of their own country. Hakluyt was a magic carpet which transported them to such exotic locations as Siam, with its sacred white elephants, and the wild and woolly straits of Magellan, a land of fire and penguins.

For the sixteenth century, time and space were linked in an intellectual pursuit which had a name at the time which is now all but forgotten: chorography. Geography is about maps, history is about chaps. Chorography had something in common with both while preserving its own distinct identity. It differed from history in its concern not with people but with places, although it gave an account of places (cities, castles, battle-fields, notable natural features) which was marinated in the past. Chorography differed from what the sixteenth century understood to be Geography in that it was not a science, not cerebral and mathematically based, but an art, a matter of observation, conveyed to those not privileged to be prime observers through rhetorically self-conscious prose. The eyes and ears did the work, not the brain. And the feet. The chorographers travelled. Unlike Prescott, who wrote his great *History of the Conquest of Mexico* without once leaving his native Boston, it was incumbent on the Tudor chorographers to see for themselves what they described. If, like William Harrison, author of a famous 'Description of England' which formed part of Holinshed's *Chronicles*, they had not travelled more than forty miles from their own firesides, that was a source of embarrassment.[45] And if, like the London antiquary John Stow, they were too poor to afford a horse,[46] they walked all the way to see what they had to see. John Leland, in the 1540s, compiled his vast *Itineraries* of all England and Wales, William Lambarde wrote his *Perambulation of Kent* (1579), Stow his *Survey of London* (1597), Richard Carew his *Survey of Cornwall* (1601).

Stow's *London* was a work of parish-by-parish, street-by-street observation. Stow writes as an old man, nostalgically, and less of what he now saw than of what he had seen then, a lifetime ago, in his youth. We encounter in his pages very few living people. It is a book about the dead. Stow remembered, as a small boy, how he had walked every day to the green fields beside the Tower of London to buy a halfpenny-worth of milk, which was three pints in the summer, a quart in winter, 'always hot from the kine, as the same was milked and strained'. Now those fields were all built over. After all, London had trebled in size in this old man's lifetime. What in the sixteenth century activated an interest in the past more than anything else was a sense of rapid and unprecedented dislocative change: above all religious change. Stow's London was punctuated with former religious houses which lay in ruins, or were converted into workshops or rich men's mansions. Stow describes the demolition of one of the great religious houses of the city: 'At that time any man in the city might have had a cart load of hard stone for paving brought to his door for sixpence or sevenpence, with the carriage.' Within a year or two of his own death, Stow told a young man who kept a diary that he had left many new funerary monuments out of his *Survey*. 'Because those men that have been the defacers of that memory whereof they have injuriously robbed others' were 'worthy to be deprived of that memory whereof they have injuriously robbed others.'[47]

And there was also economic change (inflationary prices, something never experienced before), disturbing social change. Stow described openness giving way to enclosure, the privatisation of public spaces, corruption taking over from innocence, warm charity replaced by cold greed. Not everyone shared these regrets. Protestants denounced the Catholic past: good riddance. But old-fangled Catholics and crypto-Catholics like Stow were haunted by a nostalgic sense of the world they had lost, a world which they called 'Merry England', which was always the day before yesterday.[48] So the English people of the sixteenth century remembered what they saw, and much of what they saw, or read as seen, was in the past tense, memory shaping and distorting vision.

But what was the past? John Pocock has written that there were as many pasts as there were social or professional groups with an interest in recalling it. The lawyer's past was not the same thing as the cleric's past, and the herald, whose business was coats of arms and pedigrees, virtually owned his own very special and professional bit of the past. We have seen that Stow's past was an idealised London, caught in a moment of time, 'that declining time of charity'. Pocock then puts the question, can we speak of a national past in the early modern period? 'Nation' is a symbolic entity under which are grouped a diversity of social institutions and activities, many of which possessed pasts of their own, and yet, at the same time, 'nation' attracts to itself myths and symbolic stories suggestive of a common past which may or may not be related to the institutional past. When did a common historical awareness of 'England' begin? Pocock writes: 'I have a fairly strong sense that I do not know, that not many people do know, and that those who ought to know and perhaps do are medievalists.'[49]

To Pocock's vertical and professional divisions – lawyer, cleric, herald – we should add horizontal dividing lines and distinctions of class and wealth, literacy and illiteracy. 'History', for those who had gone through grammar school and perhaps a year or two at a university, meant classical history: Livy closer to home than anything in more immediate touch. There were those who knew every word in the Bible, and that was far more important than anything else. What did the past mean to ordinary, more or less uneducated people, who might be interested as jurymen, to the history of a custom, or of an unwritten law, or to the title deeds of a piece of land? If their memories had to reach back more than forty or fifty years, they would tend to say that things had been like this 'time out of mind'. Was time wholly out of mind for such people? It is hard to say. The evidence of place-names and folklore suggests that the wars against the Danes, a past seven hundred years old, were what still lived in the shared, popular memory.[50] In the seventeenth century, John Aubrey's nurse (who would almost certainly have been illiterate) 'had the history from the Conquest to Charles I' in ballads. It is a good question whether the audiences who flocked to see Shakespeare's history plays in the 1590s learned their history from those plays, or already knew it, and were able to appreciate, with some degree of critical acclaim, what the playwright made of it. For the remainder of this attempt to explore the history of England, we will confine our attention to those who drew and used the new maps, who wrote and read the chorographies, the tiny elite to which the temporal and spatial imagining and discovery of 'England' belonged.

Readers in the sixteenth century who wanted to relate their present to the past read chronicles, a particularly competitive part of the book trade, the fierce competition a good indication of strong public interest.[51] Chronicles are conventionally distinguished from 'history' by those who know and write about these things, or used to be, because they recorded events in an apparently mindless, sequential fashion: this happened and then that, no discrimination in the selection of material, no interest in causation. In a postmodernist age, these somewhat arrogant assumptions are questioned.[52] The chroniclers knew what they were about and they were historians of a kind. Even their one-damn-thing-after another inconsequentiality, and what it is fashionable to call their multivocality, made a kind of sense.

The fact that the late medieval chronicles were adapted to the concerns of particular urban communities as town chronicles, specially chronicles of London, indicates an educated urban readership. In the sixteenth century, authors and syndicates of authors, who included our friend John Stow and his hated rival Richard Grafton, were in competition to produce *the* national chronicle of England. All this culminated in Holinshed's *Chronicles* which appeared in 1577 and, in an enlarged edition, in 1587. Raphael Holinshed headed up a writers' collective, but Holinshed himself was dead before the second edition and definitive edition. Thereafter the history of 'Holinshed' was a little like that of the Mir space station. It was expensive, and nothing quite like it was ever launched again. It remained in orbit for generations. Equally close to the concerns of those living in late Elizabethan and early Stuart England was the collection of human misfortunes gathered from the fourteenth and fifteenth centuries, *A Mirror for Magistrates*, kept in print for two or three generations and apparently read as a kind of daily light for magistrates, like the Northamptonshire Justice of the Peace Sir John Newdigate, whose daily readings were a disciplined study, leading to the collection of maxims and examples which could easily be digested and memorised. What they found, along with their Livy, was a doctrine which no Tudor monarch could willingly have endorsed; that the monarch was no more and no less than a public office, with the monarch, like any other officer, liable to be called to account.[53]

Meanwhile, these same readers would have learned about their national origins, a topic with which all chroniclers began, and one which was hotly contested throughout the sixteenth century. All European nations needed and manufactured their own myths of origins. England was no exception, and it had been given its own very respectable pedigree in the twelfth century by the writer called Geoffrey of Monmouth. Geoffrey, who claimed to be only translating a certain very ancient book, '*vestusissimus liber*', traced the British people and their very name back to Brutus, either the grandson or the great-grandson of Aeneas of Troy, who had settled with his Trojan warriors in Britain, and had founded London as 'New Troy'. Geoffrey also gave King Arthur a singular, salient place in British history, an Arthur around whom swirled Merlinesque legends and prophecies which indicated that ultimately the British (which was to say, the Welsh) would prevail over the Saxons.[54]

The reception, or rejection, of Geoffrey of Monmouth is good example of the complex interaction of sceptical and gullible tendencies in medieval and early modern minds. Those minds were fully capable of operating sceptically and critically, but usually for the kind of reasons which we would call ideological, and they were equally capable of believing ten impossible things before breakfast. Annius of Viterbo forged a book which he attributed to the (for real) Babylonish Berosus, and we call his forgery the Pseudo-Berosus. It filled in several missing centuries of world history, and the sixteenth century, like Nature, abhorred that kind of vacuum. Annius also claimed that his native city of Viterbo was the original centre of Western civilisation, taking precedence over Rome. From the start, some scholars saw right through the Pseudo-Berosus, but those who needed him to plug historical gaps or to fill out a version of history which suited their purposes – and they included Martin Luther and the Scottish humanists – swallowed the whole thing whole. One of the most telling critics of the Pseudo-Berosus, a native of Frisia, went on to prove, to his own satisfaction at least, that the Frisians were the first people, and that Adam and Eve had spoken pure Frisian in Paradise. Anthony Grafton concludes that the best critics made the best forgers, and vice versa.[55]

So it was that Polydore Vergil, an Italian historian engaged by the early Tudors to write a history of England and who, as a foreigner, had no axes to grind, poured scorn on the legends of Geoffrey of Monmouth. Truly, there is nothing more obscure, more uncertain, or more unknown, than the affairs of the Britons from the beginning. In all likelihood Britain had always been inhabited, 'seeing that the island, on a bright day, may easily be seen from the French shore'. As for King Arthur, Vergil observed that according to legend, a magnificent sculpture had been built for Arthur at Glastonbury, 'whereas in the days of Arthur, this abbey was not builded'. Using the same sort of reasoning, Marsilius of Padua had proved that the Donation of Constantine was a forgery. John Rastell, a friend of Thomas More who erected the first purpose-built theatre in England and tried to be the first Englishman to settle in North America, described the British origins myths as 'more marvellous than true', and the story of Brutus 'a feigned fable', which made England the laughing stock of Europe. Rastell reported seeing at Westminster Abbey Arthur's wax seal, bearing the legend 'Arthurus patricius Britanniae Gallie et Dacie imperator'. But this was 'but a thing feigned of late'. Westminster was not founded in Arthur's day. Wax seals were not attached to public documents until the Norman Conquest, and, in any case, wax could never have lasted that long.[56]

That sounds like modern, critical commentary. But John Leland, who had read more books in more languages than Rastell, presently published what he called 'a learned and true' defence of Arthur. Strip away 'old wives tales and superfluous fables', Leland insisted, and you still had a wonderful story. 'Otherwise the History had not hitherto remained in so great reputation.' At this point one wonders whether Leland believed in the truth of Arthur as we believe in the truth of things. Cicero had said it, that history was a branch of rhetoric, a matter of production rather than consumption (research). Invented speeches – what this or that historical character should have said, rather than anything which he might have said – were legitimate, a standard part of the rhetorical repertoire, the *ars historica*. George Nadel has written of these authors as gripped by a strange repetition compulsion: repetition of the same commonplaces about *historia magistra vitae* century after century, generation after generation trying on the same Ciceronian garments.[57]

The battle over the British history rumbled on throughout the sixteenth century, Modern historians, who tend to be on the side of what they take to be progress, have often supposed that the old Galfridian legends were soon discredited and abandoned. The truth is that they were and they weren't. The sixteenth century did not always clearly distinguish between what we should call 'history' and stories (the word 'story' was used for both), and while it was a basic principle, originally laid down by Aristotle and reaffirmed by Cicero, our cracked gramophone record, that the historian should tell the truth, the whole truth, and nothing but the truth, there was a sense that fables might contain a kind of truth even if they were not true in any literal sense. Geoffrey of Monmouth's *Historia* was perhaps intended as a kind of fiction, bearing the same sort of relation to historical truth as Homer's *Odyssey* or the books of Moses. John Rastell said that while he could not precisely affirm Geoffrey's story he would not deny it, since it was full of useful lessons about good princes who wisely and virtuously governed their people and bad princes who daily received their come-uppance from God.[58] Richard Carew in his *Survey of*

Cornwall wrote that while he was not ignorant 'how sorely the whole story of Bru[tus] is shaken by some of our late writers', he had sympathy with those who still wanted to believe it.[59] And even Camden, the greatest antiquary of the age, almost scandalises us when in his *Britannia* he first blows the British history out of the water, but then says, if you like, 'let Brutus be taken for the father and founder of the British nation'; 'I will not be of a contrary mind.'[60]

By then it seems to have been understood that such legends could pass in 'poeticall histories', like Michael Drayton's *Poly-Olbion*, which devoted no less than 236 lines to the British history, The learned John Selden in his pedantic notes printed in the margins of the poem ticked Drayton off for repeating so much rubbish, but this was no more than a friendly flyting between the lawyer and the poet, for whom, as Pocock would tell us, the past had very different characteristics. John Norden wrote: 'The whole matter of that *Brute* is poetical rather than a true history ... But what antiquity had left and we by tradition have received, I ... do not absolutely deny.'[61] In 1590 Theodor de Bry published in four languages Thomas Harriot's *A Briefe and True Report of the New Found Land of Virginia*, and he included his own engravings of Thomas White's drawings of the native inhabitants of the eastern seaboard of North America. To these illustrations were added 'some pictures of the Picts which in the olde tyme did habite one part of the great Bretainne' 'which is now named England'. The point which White and de Bry were trying to make was that these ancient Brits 'have been in times past as savage of those of Virginia'. But the comparison with White's pictures of native Americans seem to make almost the opposite point. The statuesque poses of both Britons and native Virginians, especially those of rank, suggest a certain nobility, noble savages. And I am sure that this idea of primitive nobility was dependent upon the poetical history of Brutus and his Trojans.[62] As for King Arthur, he was only just getting into his stride, waiting in the wings for the role in Henry Purcell's immensely patriotic opera, with its song 'Fairest Isle'.

Long before this, the sixteenth century had begun to acknowledge the Germanic qualities of the English people. There was a small but significant Anglo-Saxon renaissance, which revived the study of the Anglo-Saxon language and grammar, and the Saxon laws. Specially cast type was made to print the Gospels and other religious texts in old English, making the polemical point that the English nation had not depended on Rome for its Christianity and had had the Scriptures in its own tongue centuries before the Protestant Reformation.[63] When, in the early seventeenth century, William Camden published a collection of essays on language, modestly called *Remains*, and dismissed by the author as 'rude rubble and outcast rubbish' left over from his *Britannia*, he made a great deal of England's German ancestors, 'a warlike, victorious, stiff, stout and vigorous nation'. The English tongue had been attracted, like the nation itself, from 'the most glorious of all now extant in

Europe for their moral and martial vigour', the source of English liberty. The Germanic tongue had made an absolute linguistic conquest of a former Roman province, something which had happened nowhere else.[64]

'British' now often meant the same thing as Welsh, and if authors like Drayton still subscribed to the British legend, it was in order to be nice to what he called the 'Cambro-Britons', who remained fiercely defensive of their own past. Sir John Price wrote of his people having 'kept the same country and language this 2690 and odd years, without any commixtion with any other nation.'[65]

Between the ancient Britons and the Anglo-Saxons came the Roman occupation of Britain, and it was thanks to Roman writers like Julius Caesar that 'Britain' as an idea existed, just as Cornelius Tacitus had virtually invented Germany in his *Germania*. (The fact that Caesar and other classical Latin writers knew nothing of the story told by Geoffrey of Monmouth was a knock-down argument for critics of the British history like Polydore Vergil.) Camden's *Britannia*, which made its first appearance as a stubby little book in 1586, and then grew into handsome folios in both Latin and English, was a response to a request of Abraham Ortelius, the great Dutch geographer, that he 'restore antiquity to Britain and Britain to his antiquity', and 'antiquity' meant of course classical antiquity.

Camden began with some route maps of Roman Britain known as the Antonine Itineraries, and his first task was to relate the Itineraries to the landscape, to locate the Roman towns and roads, and the ancient British tribes. Although he was interested in antiquities of all kinds, Camden was especially interested in Roman antiquities, from the massive structure of Trajan's wall running over the far Northumbrian hills, which he visited twice, to coins and inscriptions. The idea was to inform the learned European public about a peripheral offshore island state of which it knew almost nothing, but which had once been a province of the Roman Empire and could now claim to be a not insignificant part of the learned and civilised world.[66]

Camden was also the apotheosis of the enterprise of an English chorography, a word to which we must return in conclusion. Like most producers of Renaissance civilisation, chorography came from Italy, where in the fifteenth century Flavio Biondio (died 1463) had published a pioneering chorographical text, *Italia Illustrata*. In early sixteenth-century Germany, Conrad Celtis and other humanists planned an ambitious *Germania Illustrata* which never saw the light of day, although it led to the publication of a series of regional chorographies.[67]

In England it all began with John Leland, a philologist, humanist, and Latin poet who had studied in both Oxford and Paris, and who, from the late 1530s and through the 1540s, had some sort of royal commission to travel the whole country, taking stock at first of monastic and other libraries (in the years when the dissolution of the monasteries was being planned and carried out), and then of almost anything and everything memorable, Leland and his friend John Bale, a former Carmelite friar who became a Protestant propagandist, playwright and author of the first encyclopedia of English literature, considered it a national disgrace that, as monasteries went under, archives and other monuments were 'as little regarded as the parings of our nails'.[68] By 1546, Leland could proudly inform Henry VIII that 'totally inflamed with a love to see thoroughly all those parts of this your opulent and ample realm', he had 'so travelled in your dominions both by seas-coast and the middle parts', that in six years there was 'almost neither cape, nor bay, haven, creek, or pier, river or confluence of rivers, breeches, washes, lakes, meres, fenny waters, mountains, valleys, moors, woods, cities ... castles' (and so the list goes on and on – but note, no mention of roads) but he had seen them (and note the emphasis on seeing them), 'and noted in so doing a whole world of things very memorable'.[69]

Leland had indeed seen all these things, and the notebooks which contained the observations, thousands of pages, record them all: descriptions of bridges, castles, battle-fields, conversations with locals about strange objects from the past turned up by the plough, memories of the Wars of the Roses. In addition to a whole shelf of books which he intended to write, he promised Henry VIII that he would present him with 'your whole world and empire of England' in what he called 'a quadrate tablet of silver', 'if God send me life to accomplish my beginnings'. It was also his ambition to establish a royal and national library, but that came to very little and would have to wait another two or three centuries to come to fruition. Poor Leland! God was not so kind. Such huge enterprises tend to collapse under their own weight, and soon Leland went mad. People said that he was 'a vainglorious person' who had promised more than he was ever capable of delivering. His friend Bale attributed his insanity to 'a poetical wit, which I much lament', but testified that Leland indeed had all those great works in hand, 'in a forward readiness to have set forth'.[70]

The notes of Leland's itineraries, which were not published in the original state until the nineteenth century,[71] became the more or less common property of the next generation of antiquarians and chorographers. What happened at first was what had happened in Germany: not a description of the whole 'world' and 'empire' of Tudor England, but a number of more limited local and regional histories or 'surveys', mostly of counties. This was the beginning of an enterprise destined to last for four centuries, for its nineteenth- and twentieth-century fulfilment, the *Victoria County Histories*, are still at this day far from complete, and for several counties are still ongoing. And then, Camden began to put it all together in *Britain*. The engraved title page of the English edition of 1610 displays Britain resting on a silver dish, just as Leland had promised Henry VIII. And the dish has handles, so that you can carry Britain into a wider world, Presently, the poet Michael Drayton put Camden into verse in *Poly-Olbion*, one of the longest poems in the language, thirty 'songs', each of 400 lines.[72] I don't suppose that Drayton (unlike Leland) visited more than a tenth of the places his poems described, but you would never know that. You could do worse, in 2011, than tuck *Poly-Olbion* into the glove compartment of your car as you set out on a summer tour of England and Wales.

The English chorographers were friends and colleagues, borrowing each others' materials, paying each other compliments, meeting regularly in the newly invented (but soon to be suppressed) Society of Antiquarians. But they were all themselves, all different. Lambarde wrote with Protestant conviction and even prejudice on his sleeve. Stow was a friend, but he wrote from the other side of the dividing religious fence. And if Stow wrote mostly in the past tense, looking back from a present which he in many ways deplored, Richard Carew's *Cornwall* is a description of his native country in the author's present. Even the rats which infested Cornish houses were having a good time, dancing their 'gallop galliards' in the roof at night. And body lice, which must have been a great nuisance, Carew calls 'slow six-legged walkers'.[73]

How did the chorographers, on foot or horseback, find their ways around? The answer is, by following the course of the rivers, and the sea-coasts, at least in their imaginations, the standard procedure in chorography, where water-ways served as surrogate travellers.[74] Simon Schama in *Landscape and Memory* writes of 'the grammar of hydro-mythology'. 'The new patriotic geography' was 'waterborn'. The convention connects generically with river poems such as John Leland's *Cygnea Cantio* and Spenser's *Epithalamium Thamesis* which are both poems about the sovereign Thames, which in the little world of England assumes the place of the Nile, Danube, de la Plata and Ganges, the four great rivers apotheosised in Bernini's fountain in the Piazza Navona. In Spenser's poem, all the other noble rivers of England are guests at the wedding of the Thames, which rises in springs close to British Wales, runs past royal palaces, and finds the world of commerce in the sea. So Holinshed conducts us down the course of the Thames, that 'noble river', 'beclipping sundry pleasant meadows', passing at length by Oxford, and so arriving in London. Drayton's *Poly-Olbion* is decorated with maps which are dominated by rivers and streams, each of which is assigned to its native genius, or nymph. The great estuary of the Severn becomes the scene for a singing match between the men of Somerset and a rather more varied Welsh choir, competing for possession of the Isle of Lundy, John Norden, a surveyor by trade, was the first to make something of roads rather than rivers, including them on the maps which illustrated his country surveys.

It was in 1579 that the great collection of English maps which we know as Saxton's *Atlas* came off the press, its contents and underlying technology inspired by the *Theatrum Orbis Terrarum* of Ortelius. It would be hard to exaggerate the significance of Saxton. For the first time, it was possible to take in England and Wales at a glance, depicted with a high degree of accuracy, and the right way up; and for the first time to see what A. E. Housman would call the 'coloured counties', each county assigned its own colour, the county maps sold as separates to hang up on your sitting room wall, a source of information and pride. These maps would be in continuous use until the late eighteenth century, when the Ordnance Survey was established. These were the maps which both sides used in the Civil War. Soon it was said that Saxton's maps were 'usual with all the noblemen and gentlemen, and daily perused by them for their better instruction of the estate of this realm touching the quantity, situation, farms and special places of note'.[75] At the centre of power, no one perused the map of England more sedulously than the Prime Minister of the day, Lord Burghley, who could now *see*, as Thomas Cromwell earlier in the century had been unable to see, the whole kingdom, and who lived – and had socio-political clout – where. The relation of the map of all England to the individual county maps perfectly illustrates the dual status of sixteenth-century England as a nation and as a federation of counties.[76]

But far beyond that, with Saxton's *Atlas*, Englishmen, to quote Richard Helgerson, 'for the first time took effective visual and conceptual possession of the physical kingdom in which they lived'. There is a semantics, a symbolism, of maps which extends far beyond their practical utility. It has been said that 'Saxton deserves a place beside Shakespeare as an interpreter of the national consciousness, unity and pride which were the greatest achievements of Elizabethan England.' Maps were both symbols and instruments of power, and Richard Helgerson has asked the legitimate question: who, according to the ideology of the maps, owned the land? According to Saxton's *Atlas*, which has no title page, and where there are no credits for Saxton, nor, for that matter, his patron Thomas Seckford, let alone his staff of surveyors and engravers, it appears that the land is the queen's. In place of a title, she sits enthroned between the Pillars of Hercules and the allegorical figures of Astrology and Geography.[77] The famous Ditchley portrait of 1592 asserts, equally, that England belongs to Elizabeth. To speak biblical language, the southern countries of England are her footstool, the English Channel her washpot. A little before this, a poet had written:

> Elizabeth, great empress of the world,
> Britannia's Atlas, star of England's globe,
> That sways the massy sceptre of her land
> And holds the royal reigns of Albion![78]

But the title page of Camden's *Britannia* is dominated by Britain itself; and of Drayton's *Poly-Olbion*, by the impersonation of England, Albion, a fecund, female figure, draped in Saxton's map, London coinciding more or less with her navel. Helgerson makes much – I think altogether too much – of the fact that England's invasive rulers, Brutus, Julius Caesar, the Saxons Hengist and Horsa, and William the Conqueror, are quite literally marginalised on the title page. It is also too much to say that the Poly-Olbion image is anti-monarchical, and that, by the second decade of James I's reign, 'chorography had become a dangerously political activity'.[79]

But Helgerson is on firmer ground when he suggests that chorographies, county histories, and maps, both flattered and ultimately served the interests of the landed gentry, to whom the future for two or three centuries, the future of the land, would belong. Writing in 1576, and commending William Lambarde's *Perambulation of Kent* to the attention of 'his countrymen', the gentlemen of the County of Kent', one of their number Thomas Wootton wrote: 'The sacred word of Almighty God always excepted, there is nothing either for our instruction more profitable, or to our minds more delectable, nor within the compass profitable, or to our minds more delectable, or within the compass of understanding more easy or facile, than the study of histories: nor that study for none estate more meet than for the estate of Gentlemen: nor for the Gentlemen of England, no History so meet as the History of England ... And this for the purpose I say both unto you my countrymen, the Gentlemen of this County (a portion of the Realm) specially, and to all the Gentlemen of the whole Realm beside generally.'[80]

I end by re-emphasising the eloquent patriotism which has served as the connecting thin red line of this argument. John Bale hoped that his friend John Leland would inspire a successor to take up his work, 'such as is learned and loving to his nation'.[81] Holinshed's *Chronicles* (one and a half million words!) ended with a paean of praise for 'the commonwealth of England, a corner of the world, O Lord, which thou hast singled out for the magnifying of thy majesty'. Camden declared of his *Britannia*: 'the glory of my country encouraged me to undertake it', 'the common love of our common mother and native country, the ancient honour of the British name.' Richard Hakluyt's *Principall Navigations* devoted two million words to the maritime exploits of 'our nation', making what the Victorian historian Froude called a 'national epic'. 'Who ever heard of Englishmen at Goa before now? What English ships did heretofore ever anchor in the mighty river of Plate? Pass and repass the impassable (in former opinion) Straits of Magellan?'

Michael Drayton was the ultimate panegyrist of England as landscape, which *Poly-Olbion* practically deified:

> Of Albions glorious Ile the Wonders whilst I write
> The sundry varying soyles, the pleasures infinite,
> Where heat kills not the colde, nor cold expels the heat
> The calmes too mildly small, nor winds too roughly great,

Drayton appeals to 'the *Genius* of the place' to conduct him 'as with thy hande to showe, which way the Forrests range, which way the Rivers flowe', 'howe thy faire Mountaines stand, and how thy valleys lie'. 'Ye happy Ilands, set within the British Seas.' After 12,000 lines, the epic comes to rest in the wild mountains of Cumberland: 'My England doth conclude, for which I undertook this strange Herculean toyle.' To prevent us ending up in a kind of Edwardian fantasy of the England of Shakespeare's youth, it should perhaps be remembered that Drayton's *Poly-Olbion* was not the most successful poem of the time.[82]

NOTES

1 *Richard II*, II.i., 42, 52, 59; *King John*, V.vii., 121–3, 124–7.

2 J. H. Elliott, 'A world of composite monarchies', *Past and Present*, 133 (1992): 48–71. The agenda of the new but now not so new 'Britishness' is traversed in three collections of essays: *Conquest and Union: Fashioning a British State 1485–1725*, ed. Steven G. Ellis and Sarah Barber (London, 1995); *The British Problem, c. 1534–1707*, ed. Brendan Bradshaw and John Morrill (Basingstoke, 1996); *British Consciousness and Identity: The making of Britain, 1533–1707*, ed. Brendan Bradshaw and Peter Roberts (Cambridge, 1998). John Pocock planted the mustard tree from which this tall tree has grown in 'British history: a plea for a new subject', *Journal of Modern History*, 47 (1975): 601–28.

3 Among a number of dissenters from the 'British' approach, see Keith Brown, 'British history: a sceptical comment', in *Three Nations – A Common History?* ed. R. Asch (Bochum, 1993).

4 Adrian Hastings, 'England as prototype', ch. 2 of his *The Construction of Nationhood: Ethnicity, religion and nationalism* (Cambridge, 1997), and the claim made on p. 4.

5 John W. McKenna, 'How God became an Englishman', in *Tudor Rule and Revolution: Essays for G.R. Elton from his American friends*, ed. DeLloyd J. Goth and John W. McKenna (Cambridge, 1982).

6 See various occurrences of the 'God is English' trope, usually located in the printer's marks in John Aylmer, *An Harborowe for Faithfull and Trewe Subiectes* ('Strasborowe', but properly London, 1559), sig. P4v, in Patrick Collinson, *The Birthpangs of Protestant England: Religious and cultural change in the sixteenth and seventeenth centuries* (Basingstoke, 1988), p. 4.

7 See especially the three presidential addresses to the Royal Historical Society on 'The peoples of Britain and Ireland' by Professor Rees Davies in 1993–97, *Transactions of the Royal Historical Society*, 6th ser., 4–7 (1995–98).

8 John Morrill, 'The British problem, c. 1534–1707', in *British Problem*, p. 8. There is now a rich literature of the sixteenth- and seventeenth-century Gaeldom which linked the Scottish Western Isles and peninsulas with Ireland. See especially the monograph by J. Ohlmeyer, *Civil War and Restoration in Three Stuart Kingdoms: The career of Randall MacDonnell, Marquis of Antrim* (Cambridge, 1993).

9 See the references in n. 2 above.

10 *Proceedings in the Parliaments of Elizabeth I, vol. 1: 1558–1581*, ed. T. E. Hartley (Leicester, 1981), p. 137.

11 Patrick Collinson, 'The shearman's tree and the preacher: the strange death of merry England in Shewsbury and beyond', in *The Reformation in English Towns*, ed. Patrick Collinson and John Craig (Basingstoke, 1998).

12 *The Oxford Dictionary of National Biography*, art. Stanley.

13 Benedict Anderson, *Imagined Communities: Reflections on the origin and spread of nationalism* (rev. edn, London and New York, 1991). Anderson's master idea has inspired an extensive literature, and his book must be a front runner in any citation stakes. See very cognate leads in *The Invention of Tradition*, ed. Eric Hobsbawm and Terence Ranger (Cambridge and New York, 1983).

14 Aylmer, *An Harborowe*.

15 Similar sentiments will be found in Giles Fletcher's account of Muscovy, *Of the Russe Common Wealth* (London, 1591).

16 Conor Cruse O'Brien, *Godland: Reflections on religion and nationalism* (Cambridge, Mass., 1988); Adrian Hastings, *The Construction of Nationhood*, p. 4; Ernest Gellner, 'The sacred and the national', ch. 5 of his *Encounters with Nationalism* (Oxford and Cambridge, Mass., 1994).

17 Production of the 1525 New Testament at Cologne was cut short. The complete New Testament was printed at Worms in 1526. One of the three surviving copies of the New Testament was acquired by the British Library for £1 million in 1994. David Daniell and Yale University Press have published modern-spelling editions of Tyndale's New Testament and Old Testament (1989, 1992). Other writings of Tyndale are cited here from the nineteenth-century edition published by the Parker Society, largely reprinted in *The Work of William Tyndale*, ed. G. E. Duffield (Appleford, 1964). See J. F. Mozley, *William Tyndale* (London, 1937), David Daniell, *William Tyndale: A biography* (New Haven, Conn., and London, 1994). See also Gerald Hammond, *The Making of the English Bible* (Manchester, 1982), and articles published in the journal *Reformation*, 1 (1996).

18 Gildas, *De excidio Britonum* (c. 540); *The Ruin of Britain*, ed. M. Winterbottom (London, 1978).

19 Erasmus, *Paracelsis*, in *Christian Humanism and the Reformation*, ed. J. C. Olin (New York, 1965), p. 97. The Erasmian trope in its original form, as recorded on behalf of St Jerome at his 'little villa of Christ' at Bethlehem, can be translated: 'Apart from the singing of Psalms, there is silence. The ploughman driving his share sings an alleluia ... This is what the shepherds whistle.' The line was established by Lily B. Campbell in her *Divine Poetry and Drama in Sixteenth-Century England* (Cambridge, 1959), pp. 18, 41–3, 49.

20 Janel Mueller, *The Native Tongue and the Word: Developments in English prose style 1380–1580* (Chicago, Ill., and London, 1984), ch. 3, 'Prose in the late fourteenth and fifteenth centuries: the reaches of recursion', on 'open sentences'.

21 *Ibid.*, pp. 111–12.

22 Anne Hudson, *The Premature Reformation: Wycliffite texts and Lollard history* (Oxford, 1988); *Selections from English Wycliffite Writings*, ed. Anne Hudson (Oxford, 1978).

23 *The Works of Geffray Chaucer Newly Printed*, ed. W. Thynne (London, 1532), See John King, *English Reformation Literature: The Tudor origins of the Protestant tradition* (Princeton, N.J., 1982).

24 'Of language', bk 3, ch. 4 of *English Poetics and Rhetoric*, in *English Renaissance Literary Criticism*, ed. Brian Vickers (Oxford, 1999), pp. 225–7; Richard Mulcester, *The First Part of the Elementary* (London, 1582), pp. 61–77, 253–4, 258, 256.

25 Quoted, Richard Helgerson, *Forms of Nationhood: The Elizabethan writing of England* (Chicago, Ill., 1992), p. 1.

26 Samuel Daniel, 'Musophilus, or defence of all learning' (1602–3), *The Complete Works in Verse and Prose of Samuel Daniel*, ed. A. B. Grosart (privately printed, 1885), vol. 1, p. 255.

27 There has been much discussion, not always very sound, of how far Tyndale was dependent theologically upon Luther and remained, in his soteriology, a Lutheran or, on the contrary, diverged radically from Luther. William A. Clebsh, *England's Earliest Protestants 1520–1535* (New Haven, Conn., 1964) and Donald Dean Smeeton, *Lollard Themes in the Reformation Theology of William Tyndale* (Kirksville, Mo., 1986) must be used with extreme caution, and are corrected in Carl R. Trueman, *Luther's Legacy: Salvation and English reformers, 1525–1556* (Oxford and New York, 1994).

28 John Carey in *English Poetry and Prose 1540–1674*, ed. Christopher Ricks (London, 1970), p. 347.

29 *Records of the English Bible*, ed. A.W. Pollard (London, 1911), p. 124; *The Confutacyon of Tyndales Answere*, in *The Complete Works of St. Thomas More*, vol. 8, ed. I. A. Schuster et al. (New Haven, Conn., and London, 1973), pp. 206–7, 212.

30 Mueller, *The Native Tongue and the Word*, pp. 200–20.

31 Thomas Betteridge, *Tudor Histories of the English Reformations, 1530–83* (Aldershot, 1999); Brian Cummings, *The Literary Culture of the Reformation: Grammar and grace* (Oxford, 2002).

32 *Narratives of the Days of the Reformation*, ed. J. G. Nichols (London, 1859), pp. 348–51.

33 I owe these figures to Professor Ian Green of the Queen's University Belfast. See his *The Christians ABC: Catechisms and catechizing in England c. 1530–1740* (Oxford, 1996) and his *Print and Protestantism in Early Modern England* (Oxford, 2000).

34 The pronouncement occurs in J. R. Green's *History of the English People*, many editions. My copy of the 1874 edition has this statement on p. 447.

35 The Homilies, which were in print for three centuries for regular use in Anglican church services, are available in many editions.

36 Barbara Lewalski, *Protestant Poetics and the Seventeenth-Century Religious Lyric* (Princeton, N.J., 1979), *passim*; Donne quoted, p. 84.

37 Linda Colley, *Britain: Forging the nation 1707–1837* (London, 1992).

38 Collinson, *The Birthpangs of Protestant England*, pp. 25–6.

39 Much of the homiletical rhetoric cited here, and more besides, will be found in 'The Protestant nation', ch. 1 of my *Birthpangs of Protestant England*, and in my 'Biblical rhetoric: the English nation and national sentiment in the prophetic mode', see pp. 167–92 below. See, on a more generous canvas, Alexandra Walsham, *Providence in Early Modern England* (Oxford, 1999).

40 Collinson, see pp. 167–92 below.

41 'Wars of Religion', ch. 5 of Collinson, *Birthpangs of Protestant England*; J. S. Morrill, *The Nature of the English Revolution* (London, 1993).

42 Tony Claydon, 'The trials of the chosen peoples: recent interpretations of Protestantism and national identity in Britain and Ireland', in *Protestantism and National Identity: Britain and Ireland, c. 1650–1850*, ed. Tony Claydon and Ian McBride (Cambridge, 1998), pp. 10, 14–15; Peter Lake, 'Presbyterianism, the idea of a national Church and the argument from divine right', in *Protestantism and the National Church in Sixteenth Century England*, ed. Peter Lake and Maria Dowling (London and New York, 1987), pp. 193–224.

43 John Foxe, *Actes and Monuments of matters most speciall and memorable, happening in the Church with an vniversall history of the same, Wherein is set forth at large the whole race and course of the Church, from the primitive age to these latter tymes of ours ... especially in this realme of England and Scotland*. This, the title of the 1583 edition, is included in the variorum edition of 1563, 1570,1576 and 1583 (British Academy and Oxford University Press, 2011), which replaces all earlier versions of Foxe. See among a forest of Foxe studies of the last ten years *John Foxe and the English Reformation*, ed. David Loades (Aldershot, 1997), *John Foxe and his World*, ed. Christopher Highley and John N. King (Aldershot, 2002), John N. King, *Foxe's Book of Martyrs and Early Modern Print Culture* (Oxford, 2006). See pp. 193–215; 245–86 below.

44 See pp. 61–142 below.

45 Harrison's *Description*, originally written for and included in Holinshed, was published separately in the nineteenth century by F. J. Furnivall, and, more recently, by George Edelen (Charlottesville, Va., 1968). See G. J. R. Parry, *A Protestant Vision: William Harrison and the Reformation of Elizabethan England* (Cambridge, 1987) for a Harrison restored to his original intellectual and spiritual integument; and his 'William Harrison and Holinshed's Chronicles', *Historical Journal*, 27 (1984): 789–810.

46 John Stow, *A Survey of London*, ed. C. L. Kingsford (2 vols, Oxford, 1908), vol. 1, pp. xxiv–xxvi.

47 *Ibid.*, vol. 1, pp. 142, 197, 205–8; *The Diary of John Manningham*, ed. R. P. Sorlien (Hanover, N.H., 1976), p. 154. For the effect on the sixteenth-century imagination of the spoliation of the monasteries, see Margaret Aston, 'English ruins and English history: the Dissolution and the sense of the past', in Aston, *Lollards and Reformers: Images and literacy in late Medieval religion* (London, 1984), pp. 323–37.

48 Keith Thomas, *The Perception of the Past in Early Modern England* (London, 1983); Ronald Hutton, *The Rise and Fall of Merry England: The ritual year, 1406–1700* (Oxford, 1994).

49 John Pocock, 'England', in *National Consciousness, History and Political Culture in Early Modern Europe*, ed. Orest A. Ranum (Baltimore, Md., 1975).

50 Thomas, *The Perception of the Past*.

51 F. J. Levy, *Tudor Historical Thought* (San Marino, Calif., 1976).

52 Annabel Patterson, *Reading Holinshed's Chronicles* (Chicago, Ill., 1994). A considerable enterprise relating to Holinshed is now under way in the University of Oxford, headed by Ian Archer, Felicity Heal and Paulina Kewes: a collection of essays may or may not lead to a major revision of Holinshed, comparable to the British Academy work on John Foxe.

53 Scott C. Lucas, *A Mirror for Magistrates and the Politics of the English Reformation* (Amherst, Mass., 2009); *The Monarchical Republic of Early Modern England: Essays in response to Patrick Collinson*, ed. John F. McDiarmid (Aldershot, 2007). Scott Lucas casts

The Mirror in a totally new light from that cast seventy years ago by Lily B. Campbell, *The Mirror for Magistrates* (Cambridge, 1938).

54 *Geoffrey of Monmouth: The History of the Kings of Britain*, tr. Lewis Thorpe (London, 1966). The *Historia Regum Britanniae* was written c. 1136 and first printed in Paris in 1508, but long before that absorbed into the ongoing English chronicles.

55 Anthony Grafton, *Forgers and Critics: Creativity and duplicity in Western scholarship* (Princeton, N.J., 2001); Anthony Grafton, 'Invention of tradition and traditions of invention in Renaissance Europe: the strange case of Annius of Viterbo', in *The Transmission of Culture in Early Modern Europe*, ed. Anthony Grafton and Ann Blair (Princeton, N.J., 1990). Annius of Viterbo (Giovanni Nanni) published his *Commentaria* in 1498. For other mischief which he caused, see John Bale's *Illustrium Majoris Britanniae Scriptorum ... summarium ... per omnes aetates a Japhetho sanctissimi Noah filio* (Ipswich, 1548; Wesel, 1549; Basle, 1557, 1559).

56 *Polydore Vergil's English History*, ed. Sir Henry Ellis, Camden Society (London, 1846), pp. 26–33, 121–2. The geographical argument against the Brutus legend was reinforced by John Twyne, *De Rebus Albionicis atque Anglicis* (c. 1539, published 1590). Twyne believed that the first inhabitants of Britain had walked across an isthmus before England was separated. See Arthur B. Ferguson, 'John Twyne: a Tudor humanist and the problem of England', *Journal of British Studies* 9 (1969): 24–44. John Rastell, *The Pastyme of People: The Cronycles of dyuers realmys and most specyally of Englond* (London, 1529), sigs A-aii, Ciii.

57 *The famous Historie of Chinon of England by Christopher Middleton. To Which Is Added the Assertion of King Arthure Translated by Richard Robinson from Leland's Assetio Inclytissimi Arturii*, ed. W.E. Mead, Early English Text Society, no. 165 (1925); Anthony Grafton, *What Was History? The art of history in early modern Europe* (Cambridge, 2007), pp. 31–2.

58 Rastell. *Pastyme of People*, sig. Aii.

59 Richard Carew, *The Survey of Cornwall*, ed. F. E. Halliday (London and New York, 1953), p. 82. Carew's *Survey of Cornwall* has been published in its entirety, with introductory essays by John Chynoweth, Nicholas Orme and Alexandra Walsham, by the Devon and Cornwall Record Society, new series no. 47 (Exeter, 2004).

60 William Camden, tr. Philemon Holland, *Britain, Or A Chorographicall Description of the Most Flourishing Kingdomes, England, Scotland, and Ireland* (London, 1610), pp. 8, 10, 22. The whole story of the British history in the sixteenth century is traversed in T. D. Kendrick, *British Antiquity* (London, 1950). See also Arthur B. Ferguson, *Utter Antiquity: Perceptions of prehistory in Renaissance England* (1993), and Hugh A. McDougall, *Racial Myth in English History: Trojans, Teutons and Anglo-Saxons* (London, 1982).

61 John Norden, *Speculum Britanniae. The first part an historicall and chorographicall description of Middlesex* (London, 1593); Graham Parry, *The Trophies of Time: English antiquarians of the seventeenth century* (Oxford and New York, 1993).

62 Thomas Harriot, *A Briefe and True Report of the New Found Land of Virginia: The complete 1590 Theodore de Bry edition*, ed. Paul Hutton (New York, 1973).

63 *The Gospels of the Fower Evangelistes. In the olde Saxons tyme out of Latin into the vlgare toung of the Saxons* (London, 1570–1); Aelfric, *A Testimonie of Antiquitie*, ed. M. Parker and J. Josseline (London, 1566?); Robin Flower, 'Laurence Nowell and the discovery of England in Tudor times', *Proceedings of the British Academy*, 21 (1935). This remains

a useful account of the revival of Anglo-Saxon letters, although Flower misidentified Laurence Nowell, the pioneering Anglo-Saxonist, as the dean of Lichfield, whereas he was in fact the dean's nephew. The mistake is rectified in Retha Warnicke, *William Lambarde: Elizabethan Antiquary 1536–1601* (London, 1973). Nowell's literary remains were (somewhat mysteriously) conveyed to Lambarde, author of *The Perambulation of Kent*.

64 William Camden, *Remaines of a Greater Worke, Concerning Britaine, the inhabitants thereof, their languages, names, surnames, empresses, wise speeches, poesies and epitaphes* (editions of 1605, 1614, 1623, 1629, 1636, 1657, 1674). Modern critical editions are the Toronto edition of R. D. Dunn (1984) and the edition by Leslie Dunkling (Wakefield, 1974), pp. 24–5.

65 *Historiae Brytannicae Defensio. Ioanne Priseo Equestris Ordinis Brytanno Authore* (London, 1573).

66 Kendrick, *British Antiquity*, ch. 8, 'Britannia'; Stuart Piggott, 'William Camden and the *Britannia*', *Proceedings of the British Academy*, 37 (1951): 100–217; F. J. Levy, 'The making of Camden's *Britannia*', *Bulletin d'Humanisme et Renaissance*, 26 (1964), 70–97; Hugh Trevor-Roper, 'Queen Elizabeth's first historian: William Camden', in his *Renaissance Essays* (London, 1985). Much of this is now subsumed in Wyman H. Herendeen, *William Camden: A life in context* (Woodbridge, 2007).

67 Gerald Strauss, *Sixteenth-Century Germany – Its Topography and Topographers* (Madison, 1959).

68 John Bale, *The Laboryouse Journey and Serche of Johan Leylande* (London, 1549), Preface. Bale's summary of Leland's talents is worth quoting: 'an excellent orator and poet, moreover a man learned in many sundry languages, as Greek, Latin, French, Italian, Spanish, British, Saxonist, Welsh, English and Scottish'.

69 *The Laborious Journey and Serche of Johan Leylande for Englandes Antiquitees, Geven of hym as a Newe Yeares Gyfte to King* HENRY *the viii. In the xxvii Yeare of his Raygne*, in *The Itinerary of John Leyland* (5 vols), ed. Lucy Toulmin Smith, vol. 1 (London, 1907), xl–xli. The 'New Year's Gift', the original of which is preserved in the Bodleian Library, was given this title by John Bale when he first published the letter in 1549.

70 Bale's Preface to his 1549 edition of *The Laboryouse Journey and Serche*.

71 Leland's *Collectanea*, original manuscripts in the Bodleian Library, where copies were made by John Stow are also preserved, were first printed by Thomas Hearne in 1744. The modern edition is by Lucy Toulmin Smith. More recently a 'user-friendly' abridgement, with an Introduction of some scholarly importance, has been published by John Chandler: *John Leland's Itinerary: Travels in Tudor England* (Stroud, 1994).

72 Michael Drayton, *Poly-Olbion: Or a chorographical description of Great Britain … digested in a poem* (1613–1622). There is a modern, critical, edition by J. W. Hebel, *Poly-Olbion by Michael Drayton* (Oxford, 1933).

73 See pp. 302–5 below.

74 I owe this expression to Professor Andrew McRae of the University of Exeter. See his *God Speed the Plough: The representation of agrarian England, 1500–1660* (Cambridge, 1996).

75 J. B. Harley, 'Meaning and ambiguity in Tudor cartography', in *English Map-Making 1500–1650*, ed. Sarah Tyacke (British Library, 1983), pp. 22–45, p. 27 quoting George Owen, the Pembrokeshire historian and cartographer; S. Tyacke and J. Huddy,

Christopher Saxton and Tudor Map-Making (London, 1980).

76 Burghley's version of Saxton was a wall map composed of twenty sheets, prepared in 1583. The wall map was re-issued in the 1640s as 'useful for all commanders for quartering of soldiers and all sorts of persons, that would be informed, where the armies be'. See Victor Morgan, 'The cartographic image of "the country" in early Modern England', *Transactions of the Royal Historical Society*, 5th ser. 29 (1979): 22–45.

77 Helgerson, *Forms of Nationhood*, p. 107; Harley, 'Meaning and ambiguity in Tudor cartography', pp. 22–45.

78 George Peele, quoted by Roy Strong, *The Cult of Elizabeth: Elizabethan portraiture and pageantry* (London, 1977), p. 154.

79 Helgerson, *Forms of Nationhood*, ch. 3, 'The land speaks'.

80 Lambarde, *A Perambulation of Kent*, pp. vii–x.

81 Bale, *The Laboryouse Journey*, Preface.

82 It may complete this survey to list the most comprehensive accounts of the history of England written, and imagined, within the sixteenth century and somewhat beyond, by Daniel Woolf: *The Idea of History in Early Stuart England: Erudition, ideology, and 'the light of truth' from the accession of James I to the Civil War* (Toronto, 1990); *Reading History in Early Modern England* (Cambridge, 2000); *The Social Circulation of the Past: English historical culture 1500–1730* (Cambridge, 2003).

Chapter 1

The politics of religion and the religion of politics in Elizabethan England

One of the things to be done in haste and repented at leisure is to propose a neat formula by way of a title for an article without thinking through what the formula might mean, and how the subject could be tackled. 'The politics of religion and the religion of politics' sounds fine until you begin to consider how the topics of religion and politics are to be prised apart. To make any sense, my title depends on religion and politics being two distinct substances; and it is not at all clear that that is what they were in Elizabethan England. Are they ever? Not in the Islamic world, to be sure. I wonder how my subject would fare in the context of Barack Obama's United States. Is American religion really religious? And what might we mean by 'really religious'? An old chestnut that, among sociologists of religion. President Eisenhower once said: 'Our government makes no sense unless it is founded on a deeply held religious faith', adding 'and I don't care what it is'.[1] As for Western Europe in the sixteenth century, historians endlessly debate whether its many wars should be called wars of religion, and what was religious and what was political in its violent uprisings and rebellions: some anachronistic dichotomies here, deriving from questions badly put.

In the American and many other modern constitutions there is a formal separation of church and state. My subject is more messily enmeshed, religion and politics tightly entangled with each other. In Elizabethan England the monarch was more than a commander (which is what her prime minister, William Cecil, once called her).[2] She was head of the church, or more properly its supreme governor, which contemporaries said amounted to the same thing.[3] Unlike her father, there is not much evidence that Elizabeth modelled

Revised version of a plenary lecture delivered at the 75th Anglo-American Conference of Historians, Beveridge Hall, University of London, in July 2006, within the theme 'Religions and politics'. Published in *Historical Research*, 82 (2009): 74–89, and reproduced by permission of the Institute of Historical Research and Wiley-Blackwell.

herself on the biblical figure of Melchizedek, who was both priest and king. She was not an ayatollah. Yet, by her authority, and that of the parliament of which she was the principal member, every one of her subjects was legally bound to be present at the liturgical services of the church, twice on every Sunday and holy day, services which were constructed in minute detail in a Book of Common Prayer which, in the eyes of the law, was no more than an appendix to an act of parliament, the Act of Uniformity of 1559. Absence from church, and any deviation from the forms and rubrics of that book, were statutory offences and attracted the secular penalties of fine and imprisonment, penalties sharply increased by a further act of parliament in 1581. Other religious and ecclesiastical misdemeanours invited excommunication. That was a religious matter, but it had political and social implications. So far was religion from being private or voluntary that you could be put to death by incineration for the simple offence of holding beliefs which were contrary to orthodox Christianity. It did not happen very often, but it still happened, so far as we know, to eight persons between 1575 and 1612.[4]

Political interest in religious belief and practice was not, of course, an Elizabethan innovation. Readers of Eamon Duffy's brilliant and hugely influential book *The Stripping of the Altars* might be forgiven for gathering that the politicisation of religion began with Henry VIII.[5] But it was much older than that, and had been ratcheted up by the Lancastrian kings, using the threat of heresy and an act of parliament dealing with heresy to bolster their dubious entitlement to the throne. Henry VIII merely moved the goalposts and changed the rules.

Since parliament had made the religious settlement, it could presumably unmake it, or change it (that had happened several times before, since the 1530s), and many sessions of successive Elizabethan parliaments were dominated by the politics of what Protestant critics of the settlement called 'further reformation'. Parliamentary campaigns to improve the state of the church, by reforming the prayer book, or even changing the very structure of the church, but above all to promote what hot Protestants called a godly preaching ministry, involved some precocious parliamentary politics. The religion of politics and the politics of religion in Elizabethan England in this sense meant a lot of work at the grassroots, gathering evidence and forwarding it to Westminster; petitions claiming to speak for the people of England; procuring the election of the right sort of Members of Parliament; and the lobbying of Members by what we would call pressure groups. The fact that these campaigns all failed (the queen saw to that) does not make them any less significant, for the political as well as the religious history of England. Sir Geoffrey Elton thought that Sir John Neale made too much of all this, but I think that Elton made too little of it.[6]

In principle, all children were baptised, willy-nilly, within days of birth.

The only marriage was marriage in church. Only executed felons and suicides were denied Christian burial. Membership of the church was not so much compulsory as a birthright and a birth obligation, as inescapable as participation in the political body of the commonwealth. Richard Hooker wrote that church and state resembled the sides or the base of the one triangle. There was 'not any man of the Church of England but the same man is also a member of the commonwealth: nor any man member of the commonwealth, which is not also of the Church of England'.[7]

Hooker's pipe dream (for church and commonwealth were not perfectly coterminous) helps us to understand how far it was socially as well as legally difficult to hold beliefs and engage in religious practices which were inconsistent with the social obligations summed up in the concept of neighbourhood. It largely explains why most Elizabethans of a Catholic persuasion were not recusants, or not one hundred per cent recusants; and why, among Protestant dissenters, or Puritans, out-and-out separation was rare, denounced by the majority who have left their opinions on record;[8] and why emigration, to the Low Countries or later America, was often the only option available to those who did separate; and why, even more to the point, the leaders of the many thousands who emigrated to New England in the 1620s and 1630s regarded their transplantation as an acceptable alternative to separation, insisting that that was not what it was. As soon as circumstances at home allowed it, a surprisingly large proportion of the colonists came back to Old England.[9] We may legitimately talk of ecclesiastical patriotism. Hooker also helps us to understand how in the teeming London suburb of Southwark, with perhaps 10,000 inhabitants, virtually everyone who was physically able and of an age to do so, over ninety per cent, took communion in the parish church once a year.[10] Whether that made a religious or a social-cum-political statement is a question which cannot be answered and should probably not be put.

Elizabethan England was a confessional state. If we follow the reasoning of Heinrich Schilling, Wolfgang Reinhard and others, proponents of the currently fashionable notion of 'confessionalisation', the English case was more typical than exceptional. In all parts of Europe, whether confessionally Catholic or Protestant (which further subdivided into Evangelical, or Lutheran, and Reformed, or Calvinist), the growing crystallisation of the religion upheld by the state, setting in concrete the principle of *cuius regio, eius religio*, was one of the building blocks of state formation. In this perspective, religion *was* politics, as indispensable a component as military capacity, or bureaucracy or the power to tax.[11] But, conversely, it was also the case that religion in the form of dissent, which was no less confessional, divided states, in France and Scotland to the extent of civil war. In those conditions religion was dysfunctional for the purposes of state formation.

Contemporaries detected a close affinity, to say no more, between forms of ecclesiastical regiment (as they called it) and political structures. The government of single persons, bishops, was appropriate in a monarchical state. No bishop no king, as James VI and I famously pronounced. The alternative arrangements we know as Presbyterianism, collective government by groups embodying ministerial parity, strenuously advocated by some Elizabethan Protestants as the only church polity allowed by scripture, were thought even by their opponents to be not inappropriate in the few civic republics remaining in sixteenth-century Europe, such as Geneva. But not in a monarchy. The bishops and their spokespersons charged the Presbyterian puritans with being anti-monarchical republicans. They were as much a threat to the monarchical constitution of the state, and indeed, as with the Anabaptists, to the very fabric of society, as they were to the hierarchical structure of the church.[12] It was perhaps significant that the young Thomas Cartwright, who was to become the leading Presbyterian ideologue, took the negative side in a philosophical disputation staged before the queen on her visit to Cambridge in 1564. Debating the proposition that monarchy was the best form of government, he used Aristotle's ideas on mixed government to make the case against it.[13]

Ten years later, in that Herculean engagement with the future Archbishop John Whitgift, the Admonition Controversy, Cartwright wrote: 'And if it were not beside my profession, I could shewe that it agreeth moste with the definition of a cytisen ... that the cytisens should have this intereste off choise off their Maiors and Bailifes.'[14] So Cartwright was a closet republican. What was not beside Cartwright's profession was his insistence that church and state were distinct and separate social constructions, so that ministers of the church ought not to bear civil office, and civil magistrates should not have in their remit ecclesiastical government. Even the chief magistrate and 'head of the commonwealth', although 'a great ornament unto the church', was 'but a member of the same', and amenable to its discipline. So he censured Whitgift for thinking 'that the church must be framed according to the commonwealth'.

But Cartwright, too, did some framing. What was appropriate for the church was the mixed government described by Aristotle: 'For, in respect of Christ the head, it is a monarchy; and in respect of the ancients and pastors that govern in common and with like authority amongst themselves, it is an aristocracy, or the rule of the best men; and in respect that the people are not secluded but have their interest in church-matters, it is a democracy, or a popular estate.' And so with the civil polity of the realm, which 'in respect of the queen her majesty, it is a monarchy, so in respect of the most honourable council, it is an aristocracy, and having regard to the parliament, which is assembled of all estates, it is a democracy'. Whitgift's response was to say that he knew all about the theory of mixed government, but since the buck stopped with the queen, England was without limitation a monarchy.[15]

A Presbyterian of the last generation but one thought that Puritanism 'teemed with political implications': 'A Puritan Aristotelian was from the point of view of absolute monarchists a politically dangerous person.'[16] Peter Lake agrees, writing of 'a coherent presbyterian approach to politics', a politics which had its logical conclusion in the right, or obligation, to resist.[17] The effective extinction of Elizabethan Presbyterianism as a force to be reckoned with was a precondition for another kind of politics, tending towards royal absolutism, which was in the ascendant in the 1590s.[18] The footings of this incipient absolutism were religious. As Ethan Shagan has recently argued, the monarchy was now using religion to generate novel or controversial claims to state power. This was in a religious context, that of a case before the high commission for ecclesiastical causes, a case concerning a puritan minister who had publicly condemned the Book of Common Prayer as 'a vile book', and who, backed by a prominent lawyer, had denied the legitimacy of the commission, which its victims called the English Inquisition. On appeal, the judges in queen's bench upheld the queen's 'imperial' authority as supreme governor to empower that prerogative court; since 'by the ancient laws of this realm this kingdom of England is an absolute empire and monarchy'.[19] In what I have called the nasty nineties, there was a declared war against terror, aimed at puritan extremists who were allegedly prepared to use violence to achieve their ends; a war, to be sure, mostly of words, although there were three barely legal executions.[20]

Let us return to the question of confessionalisation. The concept tends to iron out the differences between Catholic and Protestant Europe. All regimes were involved in similar state-building processes. All religions were equally serviceable for these essentially political purposes. The argument resembles that originally advanced by Jacques Delumeau that, transcending their surface differences, Protestantism and Counter-Reformation Catholicism were engaged in the common enterprise of reforming the manners of ordinary Europeans, turning them into real Christians, and so, incidentally or not, obedient and tractable subjects and citizens.[21] But, paradoxically, the politics of late sixteenth-century Europe depended, even for the consolidation of its regimes, on a perception of the profound and irreconcilable religious differences by which the continent was now divided. The international politics of relations between states were themselves confessional, and had become so as the consequence of the Reformation.

This was new. Traditionally, and historically, diplomacy and war had concerned the interests of ruling families or dynasties, the control of territory and sea lanes, together with bread and butter issues, especially cross-border commerce; a diplomacy engineered by marriage alliances and lubricated with the exchange of gifts.[22] Western Europe had been at one confessionally, and religious differences had entered into international relations only in such exceptional circumstances as the Great Schism at the turn of the fourteenth and fifteenth centuries; and locally, in fifteenth-century Bohemia. True, there were constant clashes of interest between secular monarchies and the papacy, especially over the right to tax and to appoint to church offices. But although ideology, contained in religious texts such as the Bible, was a weapon available to be deployed in these cold wars, this was a matter more of politics than of religion, contests over jurisdiction and competition for resources.

But now western Christendom was divided by a more profound schism, which in the perception of many transcended the mundane matters of state which had been the ordinary stuff of international relations. So far as Protestant England was concerned, mistrust and fear of the Catholic powers, the pope and those rulers deemed to be his agents fuelled the most powerful of political motives and emotions. Anti-Catholicism became the defining ideology, if not of the nation, of dominant forces within the nation.[23] In a parliamentary speech of 1593, Robert Cecil said that 'the occasion of this parliament ... is for the cause of religion and the maintenance thereof amongst us, the preservacion of her Majestie's royall person and the good of this relme, and of our countrie ... The enemie of these be the King of Spaine, together with the Pope, that Antechrist of Roome (for I may well couple them together)'.[24] Politics was now a matter every bit as ideological as it would be in the years of the twentieth-century Cold War, a parallel of which my teacher Sir John Neale, writing in the 1950s, was almost too fond. These sentiments rose to their highest decibels at the time of the Armada, in the rhetoric of the public prints if not on the equivalent of the Clapham omnibus; and in the political theatre of the scaffolds, where more Catholics were executed than in any other year. A pamphlet, hot from the press on 9 October 1588, spoke of 'the Almightie God, who alwayes auengeth the cause of his afflicted people which put their confidence in him, and bringeth downe his enemies that exalt them selues with pride to the heauens'.[25]

My title begins to be less of an artificial contrivance if we put the question: how many Elizabethans, and especially how many in powerful political positions, saw the events on the European stage of their time through these religious spectacles? Most Elizabethan historians have characterised the queen herself as non-ideological. That is not beyond dispute, if only because we know so little about Elizabeth's own religion.[26] Francis Bacon famously said that she was averse to making windows into men's hearts and secret thoughts. But the windows of her own soul are heavily curtained, and there was also, in front of the curtains, a good deal of window-dressing. On repeated occasions this sort of Protestant drew back from marrying a foreign prince of the opposite religious persuasion.[27] Was that only because she knew that such a marriage would be unacceptable to many of her subjects? Elizabeth was reluctant to engage in foreign wars which were at least partly religious in their motivation.

Does that indicate a lack of religious commitment, or simply parsimony?[28] It was against her religion to get into debt.

Unlike many of her counsellors and ministers, the queen was disinclined to prosecute her subjects on grounds of religious belief alone. It appears that she was personally responsible for a critical amendment to a parliamentary bill which would have made it a capital matter to convert to Catholicism, making it instead an offence only to convert with a treasonable intent (we are at the parliament of 1581). Neale called that 'a remarkable story of royal intervention', evidence of Elizabeth's 'hostility to extreme doctrinaire policy', making the resultant anti-Catholic legislation 'political and secular'. So the queen was a *politique* rather than a *dévote*. But Neale was surely at his most anachronistically whiggish when he suggested that at that moment in history 'the English liberal tradition' owed much to his heroine's 'sanity'.[29]

Can we distinguish between the ideologues and the *politiques* in the Elizabethan political class? Increasingly the Elizabethan state was a confessional state. Beyond 1571 no Catholic sat in the House of Commons, or at least none who was identified as such. Government in the counties was more and more taken out of the hands of papists, crypto-papists and 'neuters' and put into the hands of strongly committed Protestants, which happened in a moment in time in East Anglia in 1578.[30] In the 1570s and 1580s the dominant presence and voice in the Privy Council was that of the hotter sort of Protestants, although that body continued to include some of the cooler voices. These politicians believed that there was an international conspiracy to root out the Reformed religion, hatched by French and Spaniards at a meeting at Bayonne. The French massacres of 1572 were the best proof of that. Even some of the most learned and experienced of Elizabethan public figures believed in this scenario: men like Robert Beale, diplomat and civil servant, who knew six languages and had studied and worked for many years at the heart of Europe.[31]

These were the concerns which coloured Sir Philip Sidney's world view. Here are some of the things he heard from his mentor Hubert Languet, a kind of continental equivalent of Beale: Languet to Sidney, November 1573, 'Satan is beginning to gnash the teeth, because he sees that his throne is tottering'; April 1574, 'The Roman Pontiff transforms himself into every shape to prop his falling throne; but God turns his wicked counsels to his ruin.' When Languet told Sidney that he feared that 'these civil wars which are wearing out the strength of the princes of Christendom' would open the way for the Turks to invade Italy, Sidney replied: 'What could be more desirable?' It would put paid to the pope. In May 1574 Languet wrote: 'You English, like foxes, have slunk out of it, with a woman too for your leader, which makes it more disgraceful and discreditable to us.'[32] So, schooled by Languet, Sidney wrote of the continental wars as 'the wounds from which the Church of God is now suffering'. The international Protestant struggle was 'the cause', 'our cause', 'the good cause', 'the true cause'. And he wrote into the poetic code of his *Arcadia* a sense of disgust at the failure of Elizabeth to rise to a challenge which was as much religious as political and military, preferring the politics of a dubious marriage alliance with a French papist.[33]

Those at the heart of government who believed that England's safety depended upon solidarity with 'those abroad who are ... of the same religion that we profess' included the secretary of state (and Beale's brother-in-law) Sir Francis Walsingham, and Elizabeth's special favourite, Robert Dudley, earl of Leicester. Walsingham believed that it was the intention of the Catholic monarchies to 'root out ... the professors of the gospel' everywhere. For him 'the common cause of religion' was the proper basis for English policy.[34] As for Leicester, his military expedition to the Netherlands in 1585–86, which inaugurated open warfare with Spain, in both motivation and composition took on something of the character of a puritan crusade.[35]

But what of the perennial anchorman of Elizabethan politics and government, William Cecil, Lord Burghley? We used to think that Cecil's foreign policy was old-fashioned and secular: particularly the policy of protecting English interests in the Netherlands, limiting the power of Spain but, above all, keeping the French out. Conyers Read posited a factional split in the Privy Council between Cecil and the Walsingham–Leicester axis.[36] But we no longer believe that factional splits were a structural feature of politics before much later in the reign.[37] And now, especially in the work of Stephen Alford, a new Cecil has emerged, more complex, more interesting, but above all more Protestant. Cecil, too, could fear the 'conquest and spoyle of the small flock that are now with all extremity compelled by armes to defend them selves against only the Popes tyrannous bloody and poysoning persequutors'.[38]

It is, of course, possible that the political puritanism of Leicester and Walsingham, or Cecil's robust Protestantism, were expressions of a political rather than a genuinely religious agenda. We are back to what I may call the American question. Cardinal William Allen alleged that Cecil and his pack were 'the politiques of our country, pretending to be Protestants'.[39] In the extraordinary libel published in the Catholic interest against Leicester, *Leicester's Commonwealth*, it was said that the earl, 'being himself of no religion', fed upon 'our differences in religion, to the fatting of himself and ruin of the realm'.[40] Until recently, historians, who replicated the dislike of Leicester expressed by the original Elizabethan historian, William Camden, tended to agree.[41] But that raises questions not only of motivation but also of inner disposition and psychology from which we must, I think, back off, like Elizabeth not presuming to make windows into men's souls. Catholics, using the weapon of the press against the regime, did not back off. For them the entire fabric of Protestant politics, what we nowadays call a Protestant 'monarchical republic', was a Machiavellian ramp.[42]

So much for the 1570s and 1580s, the period dominated by a more or less consensual and emphatically Protestant regime. The religion of politics was to be very different in the final decade, the 1590s. This may appear paradoxical, since this was a decade of patriotic war against Spain; and, in 1591, in expectation of a second Armada, a proclamation establishing special commissions to investigate seminary priests and Jesuits led to an anti-Catholic security operation unprecedented in its scope. And there was some murky politics behind that proclamation.[43] But now there were voices, some close to the centre of power, calling for a measure of accommodation to be extended to the more peaceable Catholics, especially to those prepared to repudiate Spanish patronage; even talk of a common 'Christendom'. The earl of Essex may have been Elisha to his stepfather Leicester's Elijah, but he and his circle, including Francis Bacon's brother Anthony, were part of this new trend.[44] The 1591 proclamation may be paradoxical evidence of this new climate of opinion: the elderly and obsessional Burghley firing a torpedo against this threatening ecumenism. Essex's rival Robert Cecil and the future Archbishop Bancroft were meanwhile engaged in splitting the Catholic ranks by doing business with the party opposed to the Jesuits, the Appellants. This new scenario was coming to its climax and resolution in the contest over the succession. And that was a moment in time from which all parties in the quadrille which was the religion of politics hoped to gain.[45]

When it suited them, Elizabethans were perfectly capable of sorting out religion from politics. The distinction was made by Cecil himself, in his defence of the bloody justice meted out by the state to some Catholics. It is the case that those who suffered the ultimate penalty were not burned as heretics but executed as traitors. Many Elizabethan Protestants regarded 'papists' as heretics and believed that their heresy merited death. The dean of St Paul's said in a sermon preached before parliament that maintainers of false religion ought to die by the sword, and an archbishop of York, preaching on the anniversary of Queen Elizabeth's accession, invoked Old Testament precedents for the killing of 'false prophets': 'Let the blasphemer be stoned.'[46] But the only Catholic to be burned for the heresy of his Catholicism was in the time of Elizabeth's father.[47] Did that mean that the Elizabethan Catholics were not martyrs but traitors? The question has divided Catholic and non-Catholic historians for four centuries.

Cecil insisted that they were traitors in a pamphlet aimed at a European readership, *The Execution of Justice in England*. Those who had suffered the full rigour of the law – and Cecil, writing in 1583, had the Jesuit Edmund Campion in mind – had been dealt with not 'upon questions of religion' but as rebellious traitors, although 'like hypocrites' they had coloured and counterfeited their treasons 'with profession of devotion in religion'. The issue was

simple: the papal bull of deposition of 1570, by which those professing obedience to the pope were released from the obligation of obedience to their lawful
sovereign. Those who had died, including Campion, were executors of this
sentence. So reports that 'a multitude of persons' had been put to torture and
death 'only for profession of the Catholic religion and not for matters of state
against the Queen's Majesty, are false and shameless'.[48] This was not new.
Cecil had written in 1570 that 'there shall be no colour or occasion to shed the
blood of any of her majesty's subjects that shall only profess devotion in their
religion without bending their labours maliciously to disturb the common
quiet of the realm, and therewith to cause sedition and rebellion'. The queen
herself, also in 1570, had said much the same.[49]

So there you have it: religious profession and 'matters of state' clearly separated. Cecil explained that the legal basis for the indictment of Campion and
others was not some new law relating to religion but the fourteenth-century
statute defining treason. The best proof he could offer that his government was
not in the business of persecuting religion *per se* was that numerous prominent Catholics whom he named, both priests and laymen, who lived their
lives quietly and obediently, had been left in peace, even those who held it as a
matter of conscience that the pope was the only supreme head of the church.[50]
He could have added that at many of the executions, the victim had been free
to speak at length from the scaffold about his religious faith, whereas in other
parts of Europe where heresy was punished as such, tongues were cut out or
other means employed to silence the victims. Those who objected, whether
officers or onlookers – and some did – indicated by their protest that in their
perception the victim was indeed being punished for his religion.[51]

Cecil was answered by William Allen in the book called *A True, Sincere, and
Modest Defense*. For Allen it was even more essential to distinguish between
religion and politics. The Catholics for whom he was the apologist would never
have offended the temporal power in defence of the spiritual, 'acknowledging
in divers respects all humble duty to them both'. It followed that the men
for whom he claimed the status of martyrs, 'holy confessors', were unjustly
charged with treason. Not traitors within any reasonable reading of the law of
treason, they had been tormented, arraigned, condemned and executed 'for
mere matters of religion'. It was absurd to suggest that the questions commonly put under torture had nothing to do with religion.[52] One of those not
taken in by Allen's fair words was the most zealous and sadistic persecutor of
Elizabethan Catholics, Richard Topcliffe. Topcliffe's annotated copy of Allen's
Defense survives. His comments include: 'A good science for the king of
Spayddes [should that read "Spayne"?]', and 'here hee fisheth for a Cardenalls
hatt'.[53]

Other Catholic polemicists deployed Allen's rhetoric. Campion's companion Robert Parsons asked the Protestant William Chark: 'Must euerye man

be an enymie to the state, which lyketh not that religion whiche is fauoured bye the State?'[54] Later, in the altered conditions of the early reign of James I, when Catholics were confronted with the Oath of Allegiance, Parsons wrote at great length in justification of the peaceful cohabitation and 'mutuall vnion' of Catholic subjects with Protestants.[55] That had been the ostensible, if somewhat specious, theme, twenty-five years earlier, of *Leicester's Commonwealth*. The frustration of the French marriage had torpedoed the 'probability that some union or little toleration' between Catholics and Protestants would have been one of its consequences.[56] James I now declared that 'we had never any intention in the forme of that Oathe to presse any point of Conscience for matter of Religion, but only to make some discoverie of disloyall affection'. Whether or not that was an honest attempt to condone some limited measure of confessional coexistence is something still vigorously debated.[57]

It has to be said that the distinction between matters of state and matters of religion, on which both Cecil and Allen were equally insistent, was little more than rhetorical and polemical. Cecil knew perfectly well that Catholics were penalised for being Catholics. But the precedent of the Marian persecution of Protestants was one factor inhibiting him from admitting as much; international opinion another. On the other side of the argument. Allen, like Parsons, was up to his neck in the politics of tyrannicide and foreign intervention. The case that individuals, Jesuits and other missionary priests, were sent on a spiritual rather than a political mission was formally correct, in reality specious. There could be no hope for the Catholic faith in England without regime change. With the Armada on its way, the same Allen, in an *Admonition to the Nobility and People of England*, described Elizabeth as 'an incestuous bastard, begotten and born in sin, of an infamous courtesan ... the only poison calamity and destruction of our noble church and country.'[58] Those were extreme words, justifying deposition. Yet, as Michael Questier has argued, the conventional distinction between 'loyal' Catholics, usually alleged to have been in the majority, and 'political' Catholics, machinating against the Elizabethan regime, is unreal. There were many ways of being political.[59] Tyrannicide and plots may have belonged to an extremist minority. But words, especially printed words, were a more acceptable mode of resistance. Even books ostensibly intended to nurture piety may have concealed a political agenda.[60] Perhaps because theirs was the losing side, the politics conducted by Catholics have rarely entered the mainstream historical record.[61]

The polemics of both Cecil and Allen had to pretend that it was possible in Elizabethan England to adhere to and practise a religion different from that of the state, and even opposed to that of the state, without any political consequences. It is time to investigate further the areas of religion in Elizabethan England which were private and voluntary, a prolepsis of a more modern state of religious pluralism; and to consider how far this state of affairs really was apolitical.

Take first the case of the Catholics. Until recently, the history of Elizabethan Catholicism was hagiographical, celebrating the story of the martyrs and other recusants whose blood and guts and prison privations were on record, and who could be identified, numbered and located from the legal record as well as from Catholic sources. That was not bad history, since those things happened, to many hundreds of Elizabethan Catholics. Elizabethan England was a confessional, and a persecuting, state.[62] But the untold and untellable numbers of partially conforming, non-recusant Catholics, pilloried by their own hard-line co-religionists as schismatics and by Protestants as 'church papists', were airbrushed out of the record; just as John Foxe in his Protestant historiography failed to mention the so-called 'Nicodemites' who had conformed under Mary, and even made out the conforming Princess Elizabeth to have been a kind of martyr.[63] There is, at root, a semantic problem here. What might and should we mean by 'Catholics'?[64]

John Bossy presented a sophisticated, less confessional and more sociological account of the English Catholic community.[65] But that very phrase, 'the Catholic community', and Bossy's characterisation of Catholicism as the first of the post-Reformation non-conformities, continued to leave out of account a plurality of Catholic communities of different sorts, and Catholics of no community, except that they were still connected in various ways, through kinship, wealth, local clout, even positions at court, to the majority community.[66]

The conventional historiography conveyed the impression that church papistry was a transient phenomenon of Elizabeth's first decade, terminated by the papal bull of excommunication and deposition of 1570, making a Catholic loyal and obedient to the queen an oxymoron. The character writer John Earle was often cited on the subject of the church papist: 'He loues Poperie wel, but is loth to lose by it.' Earle is quoted as if his account belongs to the 1560s. But he was writing sixty years later, in the reign of Charles I.[67] Now, thanks to Alex Walsham and Michael Questier, the phenomenon of non-recusant, low-profile Catholicism is given the attention it deserves.[68] And Questier has taught us that the simple dichotomy of recusant and church papist is itself too crude. 'Recusant' is problematical. Absence from church was not like parking on a double yellow line. It was not dealt with routinely, by issuing parking tickets, but selectively and for reasons that often deserve to be investigated.[69]

Within extended family networks, there could be relatives of both religions, and even of almost none (thinking of the midland family of the Throckmortons, and, in particular, of Arthur Throckmorton, who, though a Protestant, has left behind an extensive diary, which has more to say about medicine than religion, and who was on good terms with his relations of both religions).[70] Convicted recusants might still attend Protestant wedding services and baptisms, even standing in as godparents.[71] Questier tells us about the Sussex gentry family of Caryll, who in some respects conformed, but were connected to a network of Catholic families in and beyond the county, had friends among the Jesuits and tended to support the Jesuit party against its Catholic opponents: 'The Carylls did not therefore conform to any conventional Catholic occasional conformist stereotype.'[72]

Anthony Browne, first Viscount Montague, was by any reckoning a leading Catholic. He had been the only lay peer to vote against the Act of Supremacy in the parliament of 1559. His connections with Catholic families up and down the country make a kind of gazetteer of what Philip Caraman called the other face of Elizabethan England.[73] Reconstruction of his entourage and affinity makes it clear that we are not mistaken in calling him a Catholic. But Montague himself was a conformist. He continued to be used by the government in diplomatic missions. He took his seat in the House of Lords and in 1571 was even present at a conference between the two houses of parliament to consider a bill to enforce church attendance more strictly and to compel participation in the communion.[74] He enjoyed the warmest of friendships with Sir William More of Loseley, the very model of a godly Protestant magistrate, a sort of relation and a neighbour to some of his lands and interests around Guildford in Surrey.[75] For the most part Montague was left alone in a kind of political no-man's-land, perhaps because he was no friend of Mary Queen of Scots. In August 1591, he entertained the queen, her court and council, at his seat of Cowdray, a great event subject to more than one political interpretation.[76] Not all of Montague's Catholic neighbours in Sussex were so squeaky clean, or so lucky. The Throckmorton Plot of 1584 would have brought a French army of 5,000 ashore in the county – according to John Bossy 'a fairly near thing' – and that gave Philip Howard, earl of Arundel, a one-way ticket to the Tower.[77]

We know, especially from Bossy, what the private, indeed illegal, religion of aristocratic Catholic families consisted of, in the sometimes precarious safety of their own homes and chapels.[78] What we know less about is how non-recusant Catholics ordered their attendance at the parish church: how frequently, and with what kind of disposition. Was their attendance a political and social gesture devoid of any religious significance? Were they aware of what went on in parts of central Europe, where presence at the church of a rival confession was not considered to indicate religious conformity? Anecdotal evidence tells us of people leaving the church or pulling their hats over their faces when the minister began to preach, or reading their Catholic primers so loud as to disturb the service. We learn of a man in Chichester presented in the church court for 'not coming orderly to our parish church who when he comes uses not to stay'.[79] The efforts by the bishops over many years to make it a statutory offence to be absent from the communion suggest that taking the sacrament, as the good people of Southwark did at least once a year, was not something that church papists reckoned to do.[80] But can we be sure about that? Puritan ministers in East Anglia and Essex were in trouble with their bishops for repelling from the communion parishioners whom they believed to be papists; whereas a bishop like John Aylmer of London hoped by gentler means to win such people to general conformity, which no doubt was something which to a considerable extent was achieved.[81] When did a non-recusant Catholic cease in any meaningful sense to be a Catholic? This might be called the Isle of Man question, for on Man there was no Catholic mission, and the old religion withered on the vine as no more than folklorish superstition.

More solid evidence of semi-conformable Catholicism survives in the many grandiloquent tombs of Catholic grandees erected, often in the most demonstrative part of their parish churches, in which they still chose to be buried: such as the tomb of the first Baron Teynham in his parish church of Lynsted near Faversham in Kent, designed by Epiphamius Evesham. It is a monument loudly proclaiming Catholic values, from the crucifix around the neck of the grieving widow, to the pious posture of the sons, kneeling before an altar and ostentatiously turning their backs on hawk and hound, expressive of a kind of Catholic Puritanism.[82]

It has recently been noted that their common experience of estrangement from the established church led Catholics and Puritans to evolve very similar modes of voluntary religious activity.[83] These strategies depended on the legal doctrine that a man's home is his castle;[84] what went on within a household was beyond the remit of the confessional state (not a doctrine which troubled the Richard Topcliffes of the Elizabethan world). Such strategies had been employed long before our period, and would continue, with some consistency, long after it, among various religious tendencies. Before the Reformation, the Wycliffite Lollards, or many of them whom we know about, were not so much occasional as habitual conformists, gathering in their private meetings, or 'schools of heresy', at times not in conflict with Sunday mass. They were neither recusants nor separatists.[85] Theoretical grounds for their way of life were to be found in the ecclesiology of the invisible and visible church. In the Wycliffite tract called *The Lanterne of Lizt* we read that in God's word there were three churches. The first was the 'little flock' of Jesus's followers, 'the chosen number of them that shall be saved'. That was the church invisible. The second church was the material church, 'diverse from this', the 'coming together of good and evil in a place that is hallowed, ... for there sacraments shall be treated and God's law both read and preached'. The religious orders of monks and friars (apparently the third church, 'the fiend's church') are denounced as 'our new feigned sects'; 'People should draw to parish churches and here [sic] their service there, as God's law hath limited, and else they been to blame.'[86]

Margaret Spufford and some of her pupils have demonstrated the continuity of this double way of thinking and living from Lollard times to the period of post-Restoration dissent. The Lollards of early sixteenth-century Buckinghamshire combined their heretical beliefs and the household gatherings in which these things were taught with occupation of the various parish offices appropriate to their station, and performance of the neighbourly things expected of them, such as the witnessing of wills.[87] It was much the same with Baptists and even Quakers in Cambridgeshire and Huntingdonshire in the late seventeenth century.[88] This was a brilliant strategy of having your cake and eating it. The social strength and economic success of these dissenting communities consisted in part in the cultivation of an endogamous social system. Dissenters did business with dissenters, and Quakers, right up to my own family in the last generation, married only Quakers. The extreme example of this endogamous and yet integrated dissent is provided by the small Elizabethan sect of the Family of Love, which enjoyed a presence and some social clout in Cambridgeshire, especially in the village of Balsham. Familists made it not so much a matter of pragmatism as of principle and conscience to conceal their true beliefs, and part of the concealment was to play a normal part in the affairs of their parochial communities, paying their parish rates, even serving as church wardens.[89] This was to take the closing of the windows of the soul to a fine art; so much so that it has been tempting for some to wonder whether Queen Elizabeth herself may have been a Familist. We know that the sect was well represented among her yeomen of the guard.[90] Well Balsham was Balsham, and an unusual place. But only a few miles away was the village of Linton where there were many Catholics, dependants of a notorious recusant, Ferdinando Paris. The plebeian papists of Linton contributed to parish charities, appointed Protestants as the executors of their wills, and even left legacies to the vicar.[91]

I was guilty of disparaging the admirable collection of essays in which the work of the Spuffordians was published, *The World of Rural Dissenters*, as a Polo mint of a book, which is to say, a book with a hole. The hole consisted of much of the history of Protestant dissent between the Lollards and the Restoration.[92] That was because I had spent much of the last fifty years trying to fill that hole, exploring the world of Protestant dissent, which is to say, in crude shorthand, Puritanism. Puritanism had been discussed mainly in terms of its negative reaction to the established church of the Elizabethan Settlement, as non-conformity, and mainly as the non-conformity of Puritan clergy. The subject needed to be dealt with as Bossy and Questier and other historians of Catholicism now deal with their subject: as a shared religious experience and a religious culture.[93] Others have gone farther along this road from where I have begun to leave off: Peter Lake with his heightened sense of the inner and often disruptive dynamics of evangelical Protestantism;[94] Tom Webster with his perception that mutuality and society, the shared search for the ultimate reassurance which is salvation, were what made the godly tick; and what motivated something as drastic as the migration to New England.[95]

There is no room in an article of very general scope to explore the innerness of the Puritan religious experience: sufficient to look briefly, from the outside, at some of the structural features of a Puritan voluntarism lived, without formal separation, within the involuntary confines of a national, established church and a social system intolerant of difference and of what contemporaries called, often with the Puritans in mind, 'singularity'. Some people vigorously denied being religious in the way that these people were religious.

Singularity expressed itself in a withdrawal from much of the social life and culture of local communities, especially on the Sabbath, which Puritans observed with a near Judaic scrupulosity. So no dancing or football, the typical recreations of a Sunday afternoon; no church ales, or May games, no Whitsuntide-cum-Corpus Christi plays and shows.[96] This was more than separation, it was segregation: if indeed that was how it really was. We shall never know. The godly were told to avoid unnecessary company keeping, to have as little to do with the ungodly as possible, since the day was not far off when they would be saying goodbye for all eternity.[97] But did the godly do as they were told? Peter Lake observes that in London they must have gone to the theatre, or the preachers would not have gone blue in the face telling them not to.[98] And was the alehouse really given such a wide berth? Diaries, like that of the young Lancastrian Roger Lowe, suggest not.[99] So here we have negotiations with the majority community every bit as complex and various as those described by Questier for Catholics.

The sermon was, of course, the motor of puritan religious experience. Where the incumbent of the parish was a preacher deemed to be 'godly', who preached acceptable and 'edifying' sermons, his godly hearers were comfortably built into that part of the Anglican establishment. It was the less than godly who might feel themselves to be excluded, and sometimes actually were.[100] Where the ministry in the parish was not acceptable, the godly 'gadded' to sermons elsewhere. In all probability that was an organised, demonstrative thing, consolidating along the way a group already looking and behaving like semi-separatists.[101] But the practice of gadding, where there was no sermon at home, was held by some lawyers not to be illegal and it was not separatist.[102] The preaching rallies known as 'prophesyings', and later 'combination lectures', which had very limited public authorisation, brought together in the market town or some other central location ministers and people from a locality: more voluntary gadding.[103]

A much overlooked part of this religious culture was 'repetition', repetition of the heads of the sermon heard earlier in the day, or even some time before. It seems to have been a nearly universal practice in these religious circles. Repetition could take place in church, in the presence of the minister, but as often as not it happened in people's homes, sermon notes taking the place of the physical presence of the preacher. No doubt there was often prayer offered on these occasions; but not, short of the rubicon of separation, doctrine offered by the lay adherents themselves, on the basis of their own understanding of scripture. When that rubicon was crossed, a separate, gathered church was in the making. But that depended upon circumstances, especially the circumstances of the 1630s and 1640s, and it probably happened rarely in the Elizabethan period.[104]

The question is, how far, and in what respects, according to the law, did these household meetings transgress as 'conventicles'? According to a hardline ecclesiastical judgment, gatherings of more than one household, typically of ten or a dozen persons, were conventicles, and schismatical. They were proscribed, with qualifications, in the ecclesiastical canons of 1604 and, later in the seventeenth century, in the Restoration Conventicle Acts. But the laws relating to lawful and unlawful assembly were sufficiently flexible for so-called conventiclers with any legal know-how to deny that that was what they were. Public duties, which is to say attendance at the services of the parish church, often referred to in puritan sources simply as 'the public', were compatible with private religious meetings. In the later seventeenth century, Richard Baxter insisted that such meetings were not schismatical if held not 'in distaste' of public services, but at a different time and 'in subordination to the publique'. They were 'not a separated Church but a part of the Church more diligent then the rest'. That was how Elizabethan Puritans had understood the status of their private meetings. It is, of course, possible, even likely, that, thinking of the doctrine of the visible and invisible churches, private meetings of the godly came closer to making the little flock of the elect visible than the inclusivity and promiscuity of the whole parish at prayer.[105]

We seem to have drifted away from religion and politics to the rather different discourse of tolerance and intolerance, and to have discovered that Elizabethan England was the scene of a surprising amount of religious latitude. But that very religious diversity was full of political potential. In the factional infighting endemic in many, perhaps most, Elizabethan towns it was often convenient for one party to accuse the other of religious deviance. In Thetford in Norfolk the bottom line of local politics was competition for the various civic offices, the use and alleged abuse of power. But these squabbles were dressed up as a struggle between the 'godly' and the 'popishly inclined'. That was a cunning ploy on the part of the godly, since those allegations led the county magistrates and the Privy Council to intervene on their behalf.[106] The boot was on the other foot in many other towns, where the godly were demonised as 'Puritans' and subjected to defamatory libels and street demonstrations.[107] The cultural bones of contention between the Puritans and the rest – May games and maypoles, dancing, alehouses, stage plays, the whole question of the Sabbath – were matters highly politicised. Ben Jonson's *Bartholomew Fair* was full of that sort of politics, called by a literary scholar 'the politics of mirth'; and the play was itself politically motivated.[108] Parishioners in Balsham in Cambridgeshire did not complain about their neighbours being members of the Family of Love until that became a convenient way to get their own back on a Familist who was getting too big for his boots.[109] In case after case, accusations of popish recusancy were often no more than a weapon with which to pursue a quarrel about something else.[110]

In conclusion, we have arrived at a sort of paradox. Conventional wisdom would have it that ecclesiastical repression provoked organised non-conformity and political agitation for change. And that happened: there is plenty of evidence in the Elizabethan parliaments; and much more when the wind of the 1630s provoked the whirlwind of the 1640s. However, Catholics were not driven by persecution to the politics of resistance, except in such exceptional events as the Gunpowder Plot of 1605. But their semi-tolerated presence, however covert and quiescent, was in itself a politically explosive factor; and so was puritan singularity.

Religion in Elizabethan England was a political matter because the Elizabethan state was unable for lack of resources, or unwilling for lack of conviction and commitment, to enforce the strict religious uniformity which was supposed to obtain. Perhaps it was a mistake even to try, so that this supposedly confessional state finished up with the worst of both worlds. And that, far from making religion apolitical, as it might be in a liberal society, or in a secularised society indifferent to religion, made it the hottest of all political potatoes, capable in the lifetime of many born in Elizabethan England of igniting a civil war from the grassroots up. It was a civil war which grew out of an anxiety about religious pluralism, both Catholic and Protestant.[111] As Richard Baxter would famously remark, the war was begun in our streets before there were any armies on the march.[112]

NOTES

1 E. Ahlstrom, *A Religious History of the American People* (New Haven, Conn., 1972), p. 954.

2 *State Papers and Letters of Sir Ralph Sadler*, ed. A. Clifford (2 vols, Edinburgh, 1809), vol. 2, p. 126.

3 John Parkhurst to Heinrich Bullinger, 21 May 1559 (*Zurich Letters* [Cambridge, 2 vols, 1842–45], vol. 1, no. 12; see C. Cross, *The Royal Supremacy in the Elizabethan Church* [London, 1969], pp. 23, 136–7).

4 J. Coffey, *Persecution and Toleration in Protestant England, 1558–1689* (Harlow, 2000), pp. 99–102, 114–15.

5 E. Duffy, *The Stripping of the Altars: Traditional religion in England c.1400–c.1580* (New Haven, Conn., and London, 1992).

This England

6 P. Collinson, *The Elizabethan Puritan Movement* (London and Berkeley, Calif., 1967; Oxford, 1990); J. E. Neale, *Elizabeth I and her Parliaments, 1559–81* (London, 1953); J. E. Neale, *Elizabeth I and her Parliaments, 1584–1601* (London, 1957); G. R. Elton, *The Parliament of England, 1559–81* (Cambridge, 1986), ch. 8, 9; G. R. Elton, 'Parliament in the 16th century: functions and fortunes', in G. R. Elton, *Studies in Tudor and Stuart Politics and Government*, vol. 3 (Cambridge, 1983), pp. 156–82. See copious prime evidence of these activities in *The Seconde Parte of a Register*, ed. A. Peel (2 vols, Cambridge, 1951) (hereafter *The Seconde Parte of a Register*).

7 Richard Hooker, *Of the Laws of Ecclesiastical Polity: An abridged edition*, ed. A. S. McGrade and B. Vickers (1975), p. 336.

8 P. Collinson, *The Religion of Protestants: The Church in English society, 1559–1625* (Oxford, 1982), pp. 273–8; P. Collinson, 'The English conventicle', in P. Collinson, *From Cranmer to Sancroft* (London, 2006), pp. 164–6.

9 S. Hardman Moore, *Pilgrims: New World settlers and the call of home* (New Haven, Conn., and London, 2007).

10 J. Boulton, 'The limits of formal religion: administration of holy communion in late Elizabethan and early Stuart London', *London Journal*, 10 (1984): 135–54.

11 W. Reinhard, 'Reformation, Counter-Reformation and the early modern state: a reassessment'. *Catholic Historical Review*, 75 (1989): 383–404; H. Schilling, 'Confessional Europe', in *Handbook of European History, 1400–1600*, ed. T. A. Brady, H. A. Oberman and J. D. Tracy (2 vols, Leiden, 1995), vol. 2, pp. 641–75; H. Schilling, 'Confessionalisation in the empire: religious and societal change in Germany between 1555 and 1620', in H. Schilling, *Religion, Political Culture and the Emergence of Early Modern Society: Essays in German and Dutch history* (Leiden, 1992), pp. 205–45.

12 P. Lake, *Anglicans and Puritans? Presbyterianism and English Conformist thought from Whitgift to Hooker* (1988), ch. 1, 'What was the admonition controversy about?'. Many trenchant examples of these allegations against the Presbyterians can be gathered from the polemical works by, or attributed to, the future Archbishop Richard Bancroft (see *Tracts Ascribed to Richard Bancroft*, ed. A. Peel (Cambridge, 1953) and two books of 1593: *Davngerovs Positions and Proceedings* and *A Survay of the Pretended Holy Discipline*).

13 A. F. Scott Pearson, *Thomas Cartwright and Elizabethan Puritanism, 1535–1603* (Cambridge, 1925), pp. 12–17; A. F. Scott Pearson, *Church and State: Political aspects of 16th century puritanism* (Cambridge, 1928), p. 2; P. Collinson, 'Cartwright, Thomas (1534/5–1603)', *Oxford Dictionary of National Biography* (Oxford, 2004) www.oxforddnb.com/view/article/4820 [accessed 16 Oct. 2006].

14 Scott Pearson, *Church and State*, pp. 2–3.

15 Scott Pearson, *Church and State*, pp. 29, 23, 142–3; Lake, *Anglicans and Puritans*, pp. 55–64; *The Works of John Whitgift*, ed. J. Ayre (Parker Soc., 3 vols, Cambridge, 1851), vol. 1, p. 393.

16 Scott Pearson, *Church and State*, pp. 128–9, 146.

17 Lake, *Anglicans and Puritans*, pp. 56–7.

18 J. Guy, 'Introduction – the 1590s: the second reign of Elizabeth I?', in *The Reign of Elizabeth I: Court and culture in the last decade*, ed. J. Guy (Cambridge, 1995), pp. 1–19.

19 E. H. Shagan, 'The English inquisition: constitutional conflict and ecclesiastical law in the 1590s', *Historical Journal*, 47 (2004): 541–63; J. Guy, 'The Elizabethan estab-

lishment and the ecclesiastical polity', in Guy, *Reign of Elizabeth*, pp. 120–49. In the years that followed, the full implications of this reading of the royal supremacy were developed, especially in a 700-page book by the civil lawyer Richard Cosin, *An Apologie of, and for Sundrie Proceedings by Jurisdiction Ecclesiastical* (1591). Richard Hooker took a different view of these matters, less absolutist and more parliamentary, in his *Of the Laws of Ecclesiastical Polity*: but only in bk 8, which was not published until 1648, by which time the theocratic/absolutist ideology had backfired.

20 Bancroft, *A Survay of the Pretended Holy Discipline* and *Davngerous Positions and Proceedings*; Richard Cosin, *Conspiracie, for Pretended Reformation* (1592); P. Collinson, 'Separation in and out of the church: the consistency of Barrow and Greenwood', *Journal of the United Reformed Church History Society*, 5 (1994): 239–58.

21 J. Delumeau, *Le Catholicisme entre Luther et Voltaire* (Paris, 1971) (tr. as *Catholicism Between Luther and Voltaire* [1978]).

22 K. Ploger, 'Foreign policy in the late Middle Ages', *German Historical Institute: London Bulletin*, 28 (2006): 35–46.

23 C. Z. Wiener, 'The beleaguered isle: a study of Elizabethan and early Jacobean anti-Catholicism', *Past and Present*, 51 (1971): 27–62; P. Lake, 'Antipopery: the structure of a prejudice', in *Conflict in Early Stuart England: Studies in religion and politics 1603–42*, ed. R. Cust and A. Hughes (Harlow, 1989), pp. 72–106; J. Miller, *Popery and Politics in England, 1660–88* (Cambridge, 1973).

24 *Proceedings in the Parliaments of Elizabeth I, vol. 3: 1593–1601*, ed. T. E. Hartley (Leicester, 1995), p. 71.

25 'The printer to the reader', an appendix to *The Copie of a Letter Sent ovt of England to Don Bernardin Mendoza* (1588).

26 P. Collinson, 'Windows in a woman's soul: questions about the religion of Queen Elizabeth I', in P. Collinson, *Elizabethans* (London and New York, 2003), pp. 87–117; S. Doran, 'Elizabeth I's religion: the evidence of her letters', *Journal of Ecclesiastical History*, 51 (2000): 699–720.

27 S. Doran, *Monarchy and Matrimony: The courtships of Elizabeth I* (London and New York, 1996).

28 But see the judgment of J. E. Neale: 'Her financial principles were those of sound business: to pay what she owed and spend what she could afford ... They were principles rare among princes in her day and explain that miracle of her age, the solvency of her government' (J. E. Neale, *Essays in Elizabethan History* [London, 1958], pp. 200–1).

29 Neale, *Elizabeth I and her Parliaments, 1559–81*, pp. 386–92.

30 Chapter 4 in this volume; Z. Dovey, *An Elizabethan Progress: the Queen's journey into East Anglia, 1578* (Stroud, 1996); D. MacCulloch, 'Catholic and puritan in Elizabethan Suffolk: a county community polarises', *Archiv für Reformationsgeschichte*, 72 (1981): 232–89; D. MacCulloch, *Suffolk and the Tudors: Polities and religion in an English county, 1500–1600* (Oxford, 1986); A. Hassell Smith, *County and Court: Government and polities in Norfolk 1558–1603* (Oxford, 1974).

31 P. Collinson, *Servants and Citizens: Robert Beale and other Elizabethans* (St Mary's College, Twickenham, 2006), and *Historical Research*, 79 (2006): 488–511.

32 *The Correspondence of Sir Philip Sidney and Hubert Languet*, ed. S. A. Pears (London, 1845), pp. 2, 43, 44, 48, 68.

33 Pears, pp. 478, 75, 91, 146; B. Worden, *The Sound of Virtue: Philip Sidney's Arcadia and Elizabethan politics* (New Haven and London, 1996), p. 56 and *passim*.

34 C. Read, *Mr Secretary Walsingham and the Policy of Queen Elizabeth* (3 vols, Oxford, 1952), vol. 1, pp. 239, 214; Worden, p. 56.

35 S. Adams, 'A godly peer? Leicester and the puritans' and 'A puritan crusade? The composition of the earl of Leicester's expedition to the Netherlands, 1585–6', both in S. Adams, *Leicester and the Court: Essays on Elizabethan politics* (Manchester, 2002); P. Collinson, 'Letters of Thomas Wood, puritan, 1566–77', in P. Collinson, *Godly People: Essays on English Protestantism and Puritanism* (1983), pp. 45–107; E. Rosenberg, *Leicester, Patron of Letters* (New York, 1955).

36 C. Read, 'Walsingham and Burghley in Queen Elizabeth's Privy Council'. *English Historical Review*, 28 (1913): 34–58.

37 S. Adams, 'Faction, clientage and party: English politics, 1550–1603' and 'Favourites and factions at the Elizabethan court', both in Adams, *Leicester and the Court*.

38 S. Alford, *The Early Elizabethan Polity: William Cecil and the British succession crisis, 1558–69* (Cambridge, 1998), pp. 27–8, 53–5. For evidence of Burghley's support for a religiously motivated intervention in the Netherlands, and criticism of the queen for dragging her feet over this, see Chapter 4 in this volume.

39 *The Execution of Justice in England by William Cecil and A True, Sincere and Modest Defense of English Catholics by William Allen*, ed. R. M. Kingdon (Ithaca, N.Y., 1965) (hereafter *The Execution of Justice*), pp. 56, 79.

40 P. Lake, 'From *Leicester his Commonwealth* to *Sejanus his Fall*: Ben Jonson and the politics of Roman [Catholic] virtue', in *Catholics and the 'Protestant Nation': Religion, politics and identity in early modern England*, ed. E. Shagan (Manchester, 2005), pp. 128–61; *Leicester's Commonwealth: The copy of a letter written by a Master of Art of Cambridge (1584) and related documents*, ed. D. C. Peck (Athens, Oh., and London, 1985) (hereafter *Leicester's Commonwealth*); Collinson, *Godly People*, p. 62.

41 See Chapter 10 in this volume.

42 Lake, 'From *Leicester his Commonwealth* to *Sejanus his Fall*'.

43 *Tudor Royal Proclamations, vol. 3: the Later Tudors (1588–1603)*, ed. P. L. Hughes and J. F. Larkin (New Haven, Conn., and London, 1969), pp. 86–93. For what lay behind this proclamation, see forthcoming work by Glyn Parry on John Dee, whose prophecy that the Armada would return in 1592 was exploited by Burghley as a means of out-flanking Archbishop Whitgift and transferring the harassment of the Puritans to the papists. See G. Parry, 'The context of John Shakespeare's "recusancy" re-examined', *Shakespeare Yearbook, vol. 16: the Shakespeare Apocrypha* (Lewiston, N.Y., and Lampeter, 2007).

44 P. E. J. Hammer, *The Polarisation of Elizabethan Politics: The political career of Robert Devereux, 2nd earl of Essex, 1581–97* (Cambridge, 1999); A. Gajda, 'Political culture and the circle of Robert Devereux, 2nd earl of Essex, c.1595–c.1601' (unpublished D.Phil. thesis, University of Oxford, 2005); J. Scott-Warren, *Sir John Harington and the Book as Gift* (Oxford, 2001), pp. 57–98.

45 A. Pritchard, *Catholic Loyalism in Elizabethan England* (1979), pp. 120–201; J. Hurstfield, 'The succession struggle in late Elizabethan England', in *Elizabethan Government and Society: Essays presented to Sir John Neale*, ed. S. T. Bindoff, J. Hurstfield and C. H. Williams (1961), pp. 369–96; *The Struggle for the Succession in Late Elizabethan England:*

Politics, polemics and cultural representations, ed. J.-C. Mayer (Montpellier, 2004).

46 Neale, *Elizabeth I and her Parliaments, 1559–81*, p. 93; *The Sermons of Edwin Sandys*, ed. J. Ayre (Parker Soc., Cambridge, 1841), pp. 72–3. For further evidence of Sandys's bloody-mindedness, see P. Collinson, 'Sandys, Edwin (1519?–1588)', *Oxford Dictionary of National Biography* www.oxforddnb.com/view/article/24649 [accessed 16 Oct. 2006].

47 P. Marshall, 'Papist as heretic: the burning of John Forrest, 1538', *Historical Journal*, 41 (1998): 351–74.

48 *The Execution of Justice*, pp. 7–9, 20. See C. Read, 'William Cecil and Elizabethan public relations', in Bindoff, Hurstfield and Williams, *Elizabethan Government and Society*, pp. 21–55.

49 Shagan, 'The English inquisition', p. 549.

50 *The Execution of Justice*, pp. 9–13.

51 P. Lake and M. Questier, 'Agency, appropriation and rhetoric under the gallows: puritans, Romanists and the state in early modern England', *Past and Present*, 153 (1996): 64–107, at pp. 73–6.

52 *The Execution of Justice*, pp. 58–61, 70–1.

53 Topcliffe's copy of Allen's *Defence* is in San Marino, California, Huntington Library, C373 60060. I owe this reference to Alex Walsham. Cf. Sir John Neale's reference to Topcliffe's copy of *L'Historia Ecclesiastica della Rivoluzion d'Inghilterra*, in which his annotations were still more exuberant, including drawings of the gallows intended for Allen and the author, 'the viper', 'the villain', 'the bastard' (Neale, *Elizabeth I and her Parliaments, 1584–1601*, p. 153).

54 Robert Parsons, *A Brief Censvre vppon two Bookes Written in Answere to M. Edmonde Campions Offer of Disputation* (Douai, 1581), sig. Dviii.

55 Robert Parsons, *A Treatise Tending to Mitigation tovvardes Catholicke Subiectes in England* (St Omer, 1607).

56 *Leicester's Commonwealth*, pp. 78–9, 65.

57 *Stuart Royal Proclamations, vol. 1: Royal Proclamations of King James I 1603–25*, ed. J. F. Larkin and P. L. Hughes (Oxford, 1973), pp. 184–5; A. Walsham, *Charitable Hatred: Tolerance and intolerance in England, 1500–1700* (Manchester, 2006), p. 262.

58 Quoted in M. Questier, 'Elizabeth and the Catholics', in Shagan, *Catholics and the 'Protestant Nation'*, pp. 64–94, at p. 70. See M. L. Carafiello, 'English Catholicism and the Jesuit mission of 1580–1', *Historical Journal*, 37 (1994): 761–74.

59 Questier, 'Elizabeth and the Catholics'.

60 A. Walsham, '"Domme Preachers"? Post-Reformation English Catholicism and the culture of print', *Past and Present*, 168 (2000): 72–123.

61 This is the message throughout the collection of essays in Shagan, *Catholics and the 'Protestant Nation'*.

62 A. Dillon, *The Construction of Martyrdom in the English Catholic Community, 1533–1603* (Aldershot, 2002).

63 A. Pettegree, *Marian Protestantism: Six studies* (Aldershot, 1996), p. 116; T. S. Freeman, 'Providence and prescription: the account of Elizabeth in Foxe's "Book of Martyrs"', in

Doran and Freeman, *The Myth of Elizabeth*, pp. 27–55.

64 Shagan, *Catholics and the 'Protestant Nation'*, pp. 7–8, 14–16; M. Questier, 'Conformity, Catholicism and the law', in *Conformity and Orthodoxy in the English Church, c.1560–1660*, ed. P. Lake and M. Questier (Woodbridge, 2000), pp. 237–61.

65 J. Bossy, *The English Catholic Community, 1570–1850* (London, 1975).

66 M. Questier, *Catholicism and Community in Early Modern England* (Cambridge, 2006).

67 J. Earle, *The Autograph Manuscript of Microcosmographie* (Leeds, 1966), pp. 41–4.

68 A. Walsham, *Church Papists: Catholicism, Conformity and Confessional Polemic in Early Modern England* (Woodbridge, 1993; 2nd edn, 1999); Questier, *Catholicism and Community*.

69 P. Lake and M. Questier, 'Introduction' and Questier, 'Conformity, Catholicism and the law', both in Lake and Questier, *Conformity and Orthodoxy*, pp. xiv, 245.

70 A. L. Rowse, *Ralegh and the Throckmortons* (London, 1962); and *The House of Commons, 1558–1603*, ed. P. W. Hasler (*History of Parliament*, 3 vols, London, 1981), vol. 3, pp. 490–1.

71 Questier, 'Conformity, Catholicism and the law', pp. 254–5.

72 Questier, *Catholicism and Community*, pp. 50–6.

73 *The Other Face: Catholic Life under Elizabeth I*, ed. P. Caraman (New York, 1960).

74 Questier, *Catholicism and Community*, pp. 68–206.

75 Questier, *Catholicism and Community*, p. 84.

76 Questier, *Catholicism and Community*, pp. 169–75.

77 Questier, *Catholicism and Community*, pp. 164–5.

78 Bossy, *The English Catholic Community*.

79 A. Walsham, '"Yielding to the extremity of the time": conformity, orthodoxy and the post-Reformation Catholic community', in Lake and Questier, *Conformity and Orthodoxy*, pp. 211–36, at pp. 231–2; Questier, 'Conformity, Catholicism and the law', p. 242.

80 F. X. Walker, 'The implementation of the Elizabethan statutes against recusants' (unpublished University of London Ph.D. thesis, 1961).

81 *The Seconde Parte of a Register*, vol. 2, pp. 33–4.

82 This account is based on observation. I often took students and visitors to Lynsted when living and teaching in Canterbury. And see the tomb monuments erected for John Caryll at Warnham and Sir John Gage at West Firle, both Sussex examples, and, at Wing, Buckinghamshire, for the Dormers (Questier, *Catholicism and Community*, illustrations 10–13).

83 E. Shagan, 'Introduction: English Catholic history in context', in Shagan, *Catholics and the 'Protestant Nation'*.

84 In the 18th century William Hawkins, following the 17th-century Sir Matthew Hale, pronounced that 'a Man's House is looked upon as his Castle' (Collinson, 'The English conventicle', p. 150).

85 Collinson, 'The English conventicle', p. 156; P. Collinson, 'Night schools, conventicles and churches: continuities and discontinuities in early Protestant ecclesiology', in *The*

Beginnings of English Protestantism, ed. P. Marshall and A. Ryrie (Cambridge, 2002), pp. 209–35, at pp. 221–5.

86 *Selections from English Wycliffite Writings*, ed. A. Hudson (Cambridge, 1978), pp. 115–19.

87 D. Plumb, 'A gathered church? Lollards and their society', in *The World of Rural Dissenters, 1520–1725*, ed. M. Spufford (Cambridge, 1995), pp. 132–63.

88 B. Stevenson, 'The social integration of post-Restoration dissenters, 1660–1725', in Spufford, *World of Rural Dissenters*, pp. 361–87.

89 C.W. Marsh, *The Family of Love in English Society, 1550–1630* (Cambridge, 1994).

90 P. Collinson, 'The religion of Elizabethan England and of its queen', in *Giordano Bruno 1583–5: the English Experience*, ed. M. Cilibertro and N. Mann (Firenze, 1997), pp. 20–1.

91 A. Bida, 'Papists in an Elizabethan parish: Linton, Cambridgeshire *c*.1560–*c*.1600' (unpublished Diploma in Historical Studies dissertation, University of Cambridge, 1992). I was privileged to supervise Mr Bida's work, which should have led to a doctoral thesis but for lack of funding from his native Poland.

92 P. Collinson, 'Critical conclusion', in Spufford, *World of Rural Dissenters*, pp. 388–96.

93 See Collinson, *The Elizabethan Puritan Movement*; Collinson, *The Religion of Protestants*; and many of the essays gathered in Collinson, *Godly People* and Collinson, *From Cranmer to Sancroft*.

94 P. Lake, *The Boxmaker's Revenge: 'Orthodoxy', 'heterodoxy' and the politics of the parish in early Stuart London* (Manchester, 2001); P. Lake with M. Questier, *The Antichrist's Lewd Hat: Protestants, papists and players in Post-Reformation England* (New Haven, Conn., and London, 2002).

95 T. Webster, *Godly Clergy in Early Stuart England: The Caroline puritan movement c.1620–43* (Cambridge, 1997).

96 P. Collinson, 'Elizabethan and Jacobean puritanism as forms of popular religious culture', in *The Culture of English Puritanism, 1560–1700*, ed. C. Durston and J. Eales (Basingstoke, 1996), pp. 32–57; P. Collinson, *The Birthpangs of Protestant England: Religious and cultural change in the 16th and 17th Centuries* (Basingstoke, 1988).

97 P. Lake, '"A charitable Christian hatred": the godly and their enemies in the 1630s', in Durston and Eales, *Culture of English Puritanism*, pp. 145–83.

98 Lake and Questier, *The Antichrist's Lewd Hat*, pp. 425–38, 484–500.

99 Collinson, 'Puritanism as popular religious culture', p. 55.

100 See above, n. 81; and the case of East Hanningfield in Essex, discussed in Collinson, *Elizabethan Puritan Movement*, pp. 349–50.

101 See what was said of those who gadded to hear William Dyke at St Albans: 'Many of this gadding people came from far and went home late, both young men and young women together' (Collinson, *Elizabethan Puritan Movement*, pp. 373–4).

102 In a speech made in the 1628 parliament, Sir Henry Marten, dean of the court of arches, said that if a bishop were to trouble a man for going to another sermon when he had none at home, 'it is against law and I have upon appeals given good costs against the ordinary and I will ever do it' (B. P. Levack, *The Civil Lawyers in England, 1603–42* [Oxford, 1973], p. 191).

103 Collinson, *Elizabethan Puritan Movement*, pp. 168–76; P. Collinson, 'Lectures by com-

bination: structures and characteristics of church life in 17th-century England', in Collinson, *Godly People*, pp. 467–98.

104 Collinson, *Religion of Protestants*, pp. 248–9, 264–7; P. Collinson, 'The English conventicle', pp. 158–61.

105 Collinson, 'The English conventicle'.

106 J. Craig, *Reformation, Politics and Polemics: The growth of Protestantism in East Anglian market towns, 1500–1610* (Aldershot, 2001), pp. 133–51.

107 Collinson, 'Elizabethan and Jacobean puritanism'; 'Introduction' and essays by P. Collinson and A. Fox in *The Reformation in English Towns, 1500–1640*, ed. P. Collinson and J. Craig (Basingstoke, 1998); D. Underdown, *Revel, Riot and Rebellion: Popular politics and culture in England 1603–60* (Oxford, 1985). Copious source material relating to this subject will be found in virtually all volumes of the Toronto series *Records of Early English Drama*.

108 L. Marcus, *The Politics of Mirth* (Chicago, Ill., 1986); P. Collinson, 'Ben Jonson's *Bartholomew Fair*: the theatre constructs puritanism' and L. Marcus, 'Of mire and authorship', both in *The Theatrical City: Culture, theatre and politics in London, 1576–1649*, ed. D. L. Smith, R. Strier and D. Bevington (Cambridge, 1995), pp. 157–81; Lake and Questier, *The Antichrist's Lewd Hat*, pp. 583–608.

109 C. W. Marsh, 'The gravestone of Thomas Lawrence revisited (or the Family of Love and the local community in Balsham, 1560–1630)', in Spufford, *World of Rural Dissenters*, pp. 208–34.

110 Questier, 'Conformity, Catholicism and the law'; Questier, *Catholicism and Community*.

111 Walsham, *Charitable Hatred*, esp. p. 301.

112 Richard Baxter, *A Holy Commonwealth* (1659), pp. 456–7; and see P. Collinson, 'Wars of religion', in *The Birthpangs of Protestant England*, pp. 127–55.

Chapter 2

The Elizabethan exclusion crisis and the Elizabethan polity

I

My title needs to be explained, and perhaps defended. By 'the Elizabethan exclusion crisis' I refer to the sustained concern of much of the 'political nation' in the reign of Elizabeth I to forestall the accession to the English crown of Mary Queen of Scots; and, indeed, to prevent any other remedy for the dangerous vacuum of an uncertain succession which would threaten the Protestant religious and political settlement and all that it stood for. These contingencies included a royal marriage to a foreign Catholic prince, and in particular to the French duke of Anjou, the last to tango with Elizabeth, in the late 1570s. The formulation 'Elizabethan exclusion crisis' is not canonical and may not catch on. It is a question whether a crisis can endure for as many as twenty-seven years, which was the time it took finally to put paid to Mary Stuart's claim in that bloody drawing room at Fotheringhay. (Was the forty-five-year Cold War a 'crisis'?) But historians do speak of an Elizabethan succession problem, often distinguishing between an 'early' (1560s) and 'late' (1590s) succession problem. But in truth this was a problem which lasted the entirety of Elizabeth's reign, exactly the length of the Cold War, only finding a final solution at the moment of her death in 1603. As with the Cold War, the fact that the exclusion crisis ended with less of a bang than a whimper has discouraged the legitimate exercise of counterfactual history. For the might-have-beens of the past have their own lessons to tell about the capacities of former societies.

'Exclusion crisis' is filched from the inflamed politics of a full century later, the period from 1677–83, which Restoration historians have supposed to have

Delivered in Sheffield on 21 April 1993 as the Raleigh Lecture 1993. Published in *Proceedings of the British Academy*, 84 (1994): 51–92, and reproduced by permission of the British Academy.

centred on a campaign to exclude from the succession James, duke of York, the brother of Charles II, who had made public his conversion to Catholicism in 1673.[1] It may seem perverse to invent an Elizabethan exclusion crisis at the very moment when Dr Jonathan Scott invites us to abandon the traditional fixation on a supposed exclusion crisis in the reign of Charles II, 'an historical invention', he tells us. Instead, we should think of the Restoration crisis, an affair concerned more with the politics of the present under the merry but treacherous monarch than with apprehensions about the future, its content and concern summed up in the title of a famous pamphlet by Andrew Marvell, published in 1677: *The Growth of Popery and Arbitrary Government*. Concern about the succession was only a part of these fears, and exclusion of the future James II only one of several possible solutions to the problem. So to speak of an exclusion crisis is to define a greater whole in respect of only one of its parts; in Scott's vivid image to dwell upon the horn of the rhinoceros while ignoring the charging beast itself.[2] According to Scott's critics, this is to underestimate 1673 and the shock to the political system of York's conversion, which, if true, strengthens my hand in talking about an earlier Elizabethan exclusion crisis.

However, there is no conflict between Dr Scott and my intentions in this lecture, even though Scott thinks that Restoration historians would do better to talk about succession rather than exclusion, while I, an Elizabethan historian, substitute 'exclusion' for the more conventional 'succession'. For (Scott suggests) to speak of an exclusion crisis in his period is to look forward to 1688, anticipates a revolution, and connects the political manoeuvres of 1677–83 with the so-called 'long eighteenth century' and its political culture; whereas 'succession', the term actually employed by contemporaries, pulls back towards the earlier Elizabethan problem of the succession, and so recovers 1677–83 for the seventeenth century, indeed for a long seventeenth century which may be said to have had its roots in the late sixteenth century. The Restoration crisis, apart from recapitulating all the elements of the pre-Civil War crisis of 1640–2 (and finding a different outcome only with the benefit of post-1642 hindsight), also tapped within the national memory a repertoire of notions and mantras about an Elizabethan past.

So if I prefer to talk of the Elizabethan exclusion crisis rather than in more neutral terms of certain problems relating to marriage and the succession, it is because of the strength of an essentially Protestant exclusionist sentiment in the context of the long-lasting uncertainties of Elizabethan politics. So far as the marriage question was concerned, it is true that in 1563 the House of Lords petitioned Elizabeth to marry 'where it shall please you, with whom it shall please yow, and assone as it shall please you'.[3] In the 1560s the subject was as full of a certain 'tabloid' fascination as of foreboding.[4] It is also likely that marriage to the Habsburg Archduke Charles would have been widely acceptable, although it was the archduke himself who, in terminating the negotiations, spoke of 'the impediment of religion'.[5] King Eric XIV of Sweden, though a Protestant, was a less plausible candidate, while the consequences of a domestic match with Robert Dudley, earl of Leicester, remain to this day incalculable. But we can be sure about apprehensions at the prospect of a foreign Catholic prince which were never far below the surface, and which in the later 1570s emerged in what appears to have been a political campaign both concerted and orchestrated to frustrate the diplomatically advantageous marriage to Anjou: in effect a mini-exclusion crisis so long as it lasted.[6] The ultimate rejection of a biologically somewhat improbable suit signalled the public unveiling of the Protestant virgin queen. This is the Elizabethan persona most familiar to us, and perhaps always most congenial to her, but one which was fully developed only towards 1580 and back-projected into the earlier years of the reign by William Camden.[7] That was an exclusion crisis successfully surmounted, but at the cost of perpetuating that other exclusion crisis which concerned the succession.

The problem of the succession was always the more ineluctable and pressing, as Elizabeth herself noted caustically in 1566, only placed second to marriage (in the parliamentary petition of that year) 'as for manere sake'. A speech in the same parliament put the common predicament poignantly: 'If God should take her Majestie, the succession being not established, I know not what shall become of my self, my wife, my children, landes, goodes, friendes, or cuntrie ...' 'I tell you, Mr Speaker, that I speake for all England.'[8] Mary Stuart was never without support, and there may have been not a few of the politically aware and active, including perhaps that speaker,[9] whose whole concern was to have the matter settled one way or the other, as it were 'where it shall please you, with whom it shall please you', simply in the interest of stability and damage limitation. Nevertheless, most of the voices we hear were loud with a resolve, often expressed in religious terms and perhaps religiously motivated, to exclude Mary. That concern led in 1584 to the first of those associations and covenants, binding the realm, which were to punctuate the long century to come, the anti-Marian Bond of Association.

It would be absurd to pretend that Elizabethan and Restoration England were not very dissimilar political societies, or to forget the mountain range of the Civil Wars, Commonwealth and Protectorate, which separated two very different landscapes. But in the broad configurations underlying the concept of an Elizabethan exclusion crisis there were striking similarities.

First, the Catholic factor. A dread of popery in the 1560s and 1570s, as in the 1670s, appears to have been already the strongest of all political emotions and imperatives, if not yet as extensive, every bit as intensive. Professor Wallace MacCaffrey calls this 'almost reflexive anti-Popery' 'a permanent low-grade infection in the body politic which could be raised to a fever pitch of fear and suspicion by the prospect of a Catholic consort'.[10] Dr Scott has insisted, for his period, that hostility to popery, although an idiom symbolic of other concerns and interests, should not be reduced to some more secular and rational programme. Nor was it so irrational an ideology as the secular assumptions of historians have traditionally made it.[11] Certainly, if our desire is to understand the mentality of the age, neither reduction nor disdain is helpful.[12] When, in January 1563, the House of Commons petitioned the queen to limit the succession, they spoke in surprisingly vicious terms of a 'faction of heretickes in [her] realme, contentious and malicious papistes', who were lying in wait 'to advauce some title under which they may renue their late unspeakeable cruelty'. Furthermore, they added, 'Their unkindness and cruelty we have tasted.'[13] Although the voice on this occasion may have belonged to the impeccably protestant Thomas Norton, the petition professed to speak for the Commons as a whole and ostensibly had the backing of the Lords to boot. Yet a majority of the lay peers were probably still, at this date, 'papists'.

To have spoken in 1563 of Catholics as heretics is more than merely rhetorically striking. According to Sir Geoffrey Elton, 'heretic' was a term used of Protestants by Catholics but never reciprocated.[14] The strength of such ardent, heart-on-sleeve Protestantism in these early Elizabethan parliaments has never been adequately explained, and indeed has become harder to account for with the current advance of 'revisionism' in both reformation and parliamentary studies.[15] The fact that all members of parliament were supposed to have taken the Oath of Supremacy would not have been sufficient in itself to have given these assemblies such a partisan flavour. Church papists, if not yet so identified, must have been very abundant,[16] and, as the bishops reported in 1564, a majority of the magistrates in most counties were still 'adversaries of true religion', or at best neutral. In Warwickshire, for example, where Shakespeare was born in that same year, only eight out of forty-two Justices of the Peace were identified as 'favourers of true religion'.[17] Even in East Anglia, a region dominated in the 1560s by the crypto-Catholic Howard dynasty, papists and semi-papists would remain prominent in county government until they were somewhat forcibly removed and replaced in 1578.[18]

Yet parliamentary speeches, petitions and votes were already indicative of a kind of Protestant political ascendancy. Religious conservatives and Marian sympathisers like Arthur Hall, the man from Grantham, or Francis Alford, stick out like sore thumbs, rather less typical of Elizabethan parliamentarians than puritan zealots like the Wentworth brothers, Peter and Paul. For Sir John Neale, this was no problem. He wrote that with Elizabeth's succession 'the English Reformation ceased to be a partisan story: it became a national one'. It is no longer easy to believe that.[19] But what will explain the Protestantism of those early parliaments? Perhaps bits and pieces of well-coordinated patronage and electoral machinery of which scant record remains. It may well be that the staunchly Protestant Francis Russell, earl of Bedford, with as many as twenty-five West Country boroughs in his pocket, was part of the explanation. Add Robert Dudley, earl of Leicester, and we may have the makings of an answer.[20]

The second and self-evident point of resemblance between Elizabethan and Restoration political mentalities and configurations was the resolve to exclude from the succession known papists, or from the appropriation of an interest in the crown through marriage of a party likely to advance popery: Mary Queen of Scots and the duke of Anjou in their times, James, duke of York, in his; and, in between, the extreme concern in 1623 to avoid an unpopular, foreign and Catholic marriage for the heir to the throne.[21]

A third factor in common was fear of arbitrary government, fully integrated with anti-Catholicism by the 1670s but already linked with the Protestant cause as early as the 1570s, nationally and internationally. One can detect the linkage in the Elizabethan exclusion crisis since, although publicly and ostensibly the reigning monarch was perceived to be the principal bulwark against popery, she was not fully trusted in that role, particularly given her reluctance to cut Mary Stuart out of the succession, either by legal disablement or by the ultimate excluding agency of the axe, and her apparent willingness to contemplate a marriage of diplomatic convenience with a popish consort. Given the overwhelming evidence of her personal religious conservatism, it appears that much enthusiastic praise of 'the only pyller wheron God's Church in Christendome at this day chefely leaneth'[22] was prescriptive rather than frankly descriptive.[23]

It was feared with some good reason that Elizabeth was deaf to good advice, fatally open to false and flattering counsel. These were certain attributes of tyranny, unless checked, rather than of sound monarchy. Given Elizabeth's childlessness (as, later, Charles II's lack of legitimate offspring), there was a never absent, perceived threat to the Protestant religious settlement and to the state as defined and constructed by that settlement implicit in the principle of hereditary monarchy itself, a threat at the very heart of the constitution, just as there was a threat to the constitution in these particular dynastic and religious circumstances. Extrinsically, it was conceived as a foreign threat, arbitrary government in the form of foreign Catholic powers and consorts: Spain in the 1570s and 1580s, as well as the 1620s, Frenchness if not France itself in 1579. Intrinsically, it was perceived as the threat of an arbitrary dislocation of the ancient constitution and specifically to the political, balanced elements of the constitution, indeed to that elusive quality, liberty, whose name, said Peter Wentworth, was sweet indeed.[24] So in both crises there was a contention not only against a menacing future but with a disturbing and unsatisfactory present; fear of the collusion of the reigning incumbent with popish and arbitrary tendencies. That, under Elizabeth, this was not often said, in as many words, is perfectly understandable.

Fourthly, it follows that the circumstances of the 1570s and 1580s, super-ficially at least like those of the 1670s and early 1680s, tended to separate the interests of the political nation, or of significant portions of it, from those of the reigning sovereign, dramatising the fact that any monarch, and more apparently a monarch without an obvious heir to his or her body, has only a life interest in the crown. This was to open up a certain space between the life and the reversionary interest, which is as much as to say between the king's (or the queen's) two bodies, the natural body and the body politic.[25] It was to emphasise on the one hand the fragility of the natural body and uncertainty as to its future location, the next year, the next week, the next hour; and on the other the near equation of the body politic with the state, which would in any circumstances survive and must therefore look to its own preservation accord-ing to the ancient political principle of self-defence, by means of those who could claim to be its representatives.

Elizabeth was repeatedly urged to limit the succession or to execute justice on the Scottish queen not only for her own safety but for that of her realm and people. And while it was conventional to insist that these two safeties were no more separable than two bodies, or the head from the body, the longer Elizabeth failed to do what was required of her, the more they tended to pull apart. As the bishops insisted in 1572, when the issue was what to do with Mary Stuart:

> In conscience ought she to have a singuler care of her safetie, if not for her selfe sake yet at the leaste for the furtherance of Gode's cause and stay of her countrye, to the maintenance whereof she is bounde before God.[26]

We shall return to that form of the verb to owe which is ought: in conscience *ought* she. These sentiments were echoed in the House of Commons:

> Since the Queene in respect of her owne safety is not to bee induced hereunto, let us make petition shee will doe it in respect of our safety. I have hearde shee delight-eth to be called our mother.[27]

One speaker suggested that the case 'touched the Queene only'. This was the man from Grantham, Arthur Hall, who in the Elizabethan House of Commons was well accustomed to finding himself in a minority of one. He was answered by the obscure John French, evidently a more representative voice for all that he sat for Old Sarum: 'He thinketh it good that he that soe said were caused to declare whie the offence is not as well to the whole state as to her Majestie.'[28] Thus the circumstances of the Elizabethan exclusion crisis activated what may be properly called the Country (although the hidden hand of interests in the Court cannot be excluded), an activation which was the very taproot of Whiggery in the forthcoming English political tradition.

It was with some such considerations in mind that I referred on an earlier occasion to 'the monarchical republic of Elizabeth I',[29] bearing in mind that in the sixteenth century, 'commonwealth' and 'republic' were more or less equivalent and interchangeable terms, the titles in English and Latin respectively of Sir Thomas Smith's treatise on the English state and constitution, *De Republica Anglorum*. There was no perceived incompatibility between 'monarchy' and 'republic'. To speak of a 'monarchical republic' was not, of course, to suggest that this generation sought or so much as dreamed of an acephalous republic with only elected officers. They would have found 1649, cutting off the king's head with the crown on it, nearly inconceivable. But it was precisely because the integrity, security and very being of the state required an uncontested monarch that the Elizabethan protestant political nation was quasi-republican in its thinking and methodology. One might say that monarchy was too important a matter to be left to monarchs. Dr Blair Worden, investigating the roots of seventeenth-century English republicanism, suggests that the form of government mattered less to republicans than its spirit. For John Pocock, civic humanism was 'a language, not a programme'. In the same spirit, Worden suggests that the 'republicanism' of this period was first and foremost a criticism of tyrants rather than a rejection of kings.[30] Professor Quentin Skinner is in agreement. It was characteristic of humanist political thought, the source of classical republicanism, to be concerned less with the fabric of institutions than with 'the spirit and outlook of the men who run them'.[31]

Fifth and finally, there is a link between my exclusion crisis and Jonathan Scott's in the name of Sidney, to which we shall return in search of some of the ideological resonances and refractions of Elizabethan exclusion politics: a link, that is to say, between the Elizabethan Sir Philip Sidney, the posthumously symbolic incarnation of quasi-republican values and virtues, and his grand nephew, Algernon Sidney, victim of the Restoration crisis and martyr of English republicanism. In that proto-Whig manifesto *The Life of the Renowned Sir Philip Sidney*, a work not published until Algernon Sidney's time, Sir Fulke Greville spoke of the Elizabethan danger to which Sidney had opposed himself, of the 'metamorphosing' 'our moderate form of Monarchie into a precipitate absoluteness', a threat especially implicit in the Anjou marriage plan, against which Sidney had spoken boldly and with damaging consequences for his public prospects. For Greville, that excellent prince, Elizabeth, was the best safeguard against tyranny, with the public spiritedness of Sidney acting as a kind of backstop. In his actions and speeches in the politics of this critical episode (and not only in his affecting death at Zutphen), Greville declared that Sidney 'left an authentical president to after ages, that howsoever tyrants allow of no scope, stamp, or standard, but their own will; yet with Princes there is a latitude for subjects to reserve native, and legall freedom, by paying humble tribute in manner, though not in matter, to them'.[32]

With a comparable ambivalence and sense of the difference between true princes and tyrants, Algernon Sidney could write on the same page of his own *Discourses*: 'Nothing is farther from my intention than to speak irreverently of kings'; and 'monarchy can be said to be natural in no other sense, than that our depraved nature is most inclined to that which is worst'.[33] That ironical paradox is as much as to say that, for the line of the Sidneys, the truest republicans were the best monarchists, true monarchists true republicans, which is to say, anti-tyrannicists. This was Penshurst politics. In 1680 a pamphlet was published, its title echoing Greville: 'a pattern or president for princes to rule by and for subjects to obey by': its content Elizabethan and Sidneyian.[34]

II

Nowadays it is unfashionable to find in Elizabethan politics, and especially in Elizabethan parliamentary politics, any premonition of seventeenth-century politics, any prolepsis of civil war and revolution, or even of parliamentary assertiveness. Sir John Neale thought that the tactics of the House of Commons in 1566–67 over the succession represented 'a dawn of a new age', 'harbinger of Stuart conflicts'.[35] Current revisionism laughs him to scorn and declares those perspectives utterly discredited. Parliament existed to legislate, not to play politics: so, very insistently, Sir Geoffrey Elton.[36] Neale may indeed have exaggerated, even invented, the constitutional precocity of the Elizabethan House of Commons in opposing the queen and the regime on such matters. But revisionism goes too far not only in playing down confrontation (for confrontations there most certainly were, if along different lines from those drawn by Neale) but in asserting that in Elizabethan England 'no thread of continuity can be found, no premonition of future tensions'. (Here I quote not from Elton but from Dr Jim Alsop, whose anti-Neale revisionism is even more pronounced.)[37] 'No premonition' is plausible. No historian would be so naïvely Whiggish as to suppose that Elizabethan politicians looked forward in that sense, or considered themselves to be 'harbingers'. But 'no thread of continuity' will not wash. Threads can be picked up at the other end, and they were apparent to the politicians of the Restoration exclusion crisis, who could and did look *back*. Dr Scott speaks of the issue of the succession in the late 1670s carrying 'the unmistakeable echo of its Elizabethan past', of a crisis 'saturated as a whole with Elizabethan nostalgia and imagery'.[38]

A particular backward point of reference was the Elizabethan Bond of Association, a document with a persistent afterlife in the seventeenth century, and one which sheds a distinctive light on our subject. Let us remind ourselves of the circumstances. The year was 1584 – the autumn of that year. Mary Stuart's head was still on her shoulders. But William of Orange was dead, the victim of the assassin's bullet still to be seen, embedded in a staircase, at Delft.

In England, what was intended to look like the entire political nation put its hands and seals to a document, a bond which required its signatories to avenge the violent death of the queen, or even an unsuccessful assassination attempt, by a kind of lynch-law, to be perpetrated on those responsible by all or any of its members. Those subscribing 'joyntly and severally in the bonde of one fyrme and loyall societie' were bound 'to withstande, pursue and suppresse' all manner of persons of what estate soever who should attempt anything that might tend to the harm of her Majesty's royal person 'by force of armes as by all other meanes of revenge'. Moreover, those so committed declared that they would never allow, accept or favour any such 'pretended successor' 'by whom or for whom' such an act should be either committed or attempted, who would be 'unworthy of all government in any Christian realme or [—?] societie': clear notice given of resistance to be offered to a pretender who might in all other respects be the legitimate heir to the throne.[39]

There could be no shadow of doubt that this weapon was directly targeted on the Scottish queen. It was signed and sealed by the Privy Council, the more senior of the clergy (bishops, archdeacons, the heads of Oxbridge colleges), 115 Cornish gentry, more than 200 townsmen of Cardigan and 140 north Yorkshire farmers from around Richmond.[40] This was not precisely a subscription list of English Protestants in 1584. Can Cardigan have contained as many as 200 Protestant householders in any very meaningful sense?[41] Mary herself offered to sign. One can see how it would have been prudent for Catholics and crypto-Catholics to have been bound, cunning for a Protestant regime to have welcomed their signatures, which would have made the papal bull of excommunication against Elizabeth a dead letter for as many as put their names to the Bond. However, such was the strength of sectarian sentiment that in Kent there were those who thought it inappropriate that any known papist should be admitted to 'this loyall societie'.[42] It would be interesting to know (we don't have the evidence) whether the Catholic and semi-Catholic gentlemen of Norfolk and Suffolk who had been removed from local office six years earlier (men of substance like Sir Thomas Cornwallis) subscribed, were prepared to do so, were expected to do so, were allowed to do so. For the Bond of Association defined an essentially Protestant political nation and ascendancy; and a loyalty defined and expressed confessionally.

It was a document which, while it ought to fascinate historians, terrified the Elizabethans. Solemn binding oaths were not trivial things. If Mary Stuart was indeed Elizabeth's true and authentic successor, then this oath was in conflict with a more fundamental oath to obey and serve the queen and her lawful successors, whosoever they might be. Moreover, the Bond constructed a scenario beyond belief, not so much for the Elizabethan conscience as for the Elizabethan imagination. Those subscribing were not distinguished by office or rank. They may indeed have taken the oath in due hierarchical order, which was the case in Lancashire, where the earl of Derby and the Bishop of Chester were the first to be sworn, in a Wigan church.[43] But in the document itself there was no respect of persons. Every man's hand would be against Mary Stuart and the Marians, and, in the ensuing confusion, normality would cease to exist. Thomas Digges, mathematician, engineer and Member of Parliament, wrote:

> Breefly me thought I did behowld a confused company of all partes of the Realme of all degrees and estates then rising in Armes att such a tyme as ther is No Cowncell of Estate in Lyfe, No Lawfull generall, ... no presidents, no Judges, no Sheriffes, no Justices, breefely, noe officers in Lyfe or authoritie to maytayne Justice, preserve peace, or with Lawfull power to commaund obedience, or to guyde and direct such a distracted chaos of armed men confuzedly rising.[44]

Insofar as the signatories were never formally released from their bond, it remained in force, which may have tempted Elizabeth in the winter of 1586–87 to think of summary assassination rather than judicial execution, or at least to use the existence of the Bond as a tactical ploy. Elsewhere[45] I have investigated the efforts of Lord Burghley, with the advice of Digges and no doubt others, to find an acceptable prophylactic against a worst-case scenario within the terms of the Bill 'for Provision to be Made for the Surety of the Queen's Most Royal Person', which the 1584–85 Parliament would enact. Should the Bond itself, which had hitherto proceeded 'mearelie and voluntarilie without coercion of lawe', be built into the statute and legally enforced? Burghley plumped instead for a regularised interregnum, to be provided for in an appendix to the statute.

This was a kite which had briefly flown in the 1560s. In the absence of Elizabeth Tudor, the Privy Council would remain in being and would be augmented to form a Great or Grand Council, acting in the name of the imperial crown of England: 'magnum consilium coronae Angliae', it would be called, a phrase inserted in some drafts of this clause in Burghley's own hand. Parliament would continue to sit, or would be recalled. Within thirty days, it would determine the succession, accepting and receiving 'such a person to the Crown of the Realme as shall to them upon their peaceable deliberations and trials had of them appear to have best right to the same in blood and by the royal lawes of the Realme'.[46]

Right in blood and by the laws of succession preserved, as a kind of outer casing to this scheme, the due form and legality of the constitution. And yet in its inner workings, as envisaged, and in the genuine uncertainties surrounding claims and titles, we are not a thousand miles away from the Polish electoral monarchy. And that the institution of monarchy was in its origins and even in principle elective was a concept as accessible to the devisers of this scheme as it was in the France of the religious wars. Digges feared that it would all prove very messy and reflected on the character of the interregna which accompanied papal conclaves: 'Hell it selfe, every man by force defending his owne, all kind of owtrage, ryot and villanye.'[47] It speaks volumes for the perceived depth of the Elizabethan exclusion crisis that someone who claimed knowledge of that 'hell', had perhaps witnessed it, should nevertheless back the device of a dubiously legal interregnum. England, after all, lacked the benefit of a college of cardinals. Burghley noted what might be called the bottom line: 'The government of the realme shall still contynew in all respectes.'[48] His son, in another critical political context – that of 1610 – which concerned money, would invoke the same principle of *epikeia*: 'The King must not want.'[49] And Oliver Cromwell would continually plead 'necessity'. In Burghley's perception, the kingdom could not continue without 'an Interreyn', and that was the end of the matter. Or rather, it was not. The queen would have none of it and the 'addition' to the Act for the Queen's Safety proved a dead letter. As a footnote to this episode, we may observe that there was another and perhaps more realistic scenario, in the event of a sudden vacuum of power. There might well have been a regency, assumed by the earl of Leicester. But on behalf of whom? And would it have been uncontested?

The Elizabethan Bond of Association was to have a long afterlife, much like some other Elizabethan documents of emblematic significance, such as the so-called 'Golden Speech' delivered to Elizabeth's last parliament. The yellowing bond would be pulled out of the drawer in 1621, in 1641,[50] and in the context of the political crisis of 1677–83, as it would be in 1696.[51] 'What a story you tell of associations in Queen Elizabeth's time!' So, in March 1682, wrote a Tory, or perhaps Lord Halifax, addressing a Whig opponent, probably none other than the earl of Shaftesbury.[52] A new Association to protect the Protestant religion against the threat posed by Charles II's brother and heir had been proposed from time to time in both Houses of the so-called Exclusion parliaments, either as an alternative to exclusion, a form of 'limitation' on the future monarch's powers, or as a means of implementing exclusion itself. A copy of such a document, supposedly discovered in Shaftesbury's closet, was brought in evidence at his trial for treason in November 1681, but it failed to impress the hand-picked Whig jury which duly returned its 'ignoramus' verdict; although legal opinion was later supplied to the king that the Bond (neither signed by Shaftesbury nor in his hand) constituted at least a fineable misdemeanour as a seditious libel, unlawfully given house-room.[53]

How closely did the two Associations, of the 1580s and 1680s, resemble each other, and how parallel were the political circumstances which occasioned them? There can be no doubt that the exclusionist association in the form found in Shaftesbury's study was textually and verbally derived from the Bond of 1584 (as was a later Association of 1696, in William III's time). In both cases, we encounter an apparently spontaneous and extraordinary endeavour on the part of subjects to frustrate the replacement of an ostensibly

Protestant monarch without an immediate heir of his or her own body by a known Catholic with a good hereditary claim to succeed, but who was thought to threaten the Protestant settlement. But Professor J. R. Jones has written of 'deceptively similar circumstances',[54] and whether the circumstances were similar in any way became in itself a debated issue between the emergent and embattled political tendencies of the time. In the perception of the Tories, the circumstances were not at all the same. The 1584 Association had been a loyal undertaking to defend the legitimate sovereign power against pretensions upon a false title, implying on the part of the associators 'indispensible obedience in the subject'. Shaftesbury's Association (if it was his) was no worthy successor to this loyal declaration but a replica of the Solemn League and Covenant of the 1640s, 'the instrument of a treasonable conspiracy against his majesty and the government, under the countenance of a religious association': covert republicanism and pointing to the great crime of January 1649.[55]

By contrast, the Whig perception was of nearly identical circumstances, the main difference being that whereas the Elizabethan Association had been supported by, in a manner of speaking, the entire kingdom, 'courtiers as well as others', 'promoted by the chief ministers of state', in Charles II's time 'many of all orders and ranks', 'calling themselves protestants', had put themselves on the wrong side, a factor which in itself licensed the damaging imputation that what was in truth the national religious cause was merely the obsession of a disaffected faction. 'Do we live in the same clime that our ancestors did?'[56]

Tory polemic made much of the fact that Shaftesbury's Association appeared to exclude from its terms and scope both lords and king. It was composed *rege inconsulto*; whereas the queen had been privy to the Elizabethan Association and had approved of it. Otherwise, in those times, 'no *ignoramus* jury should have rescued the abettors and concealors from the gallows': a recognition of that fact of life which historians would later call Tudor Despotism. Shaftesbury disagreed. Elizabeth had been ignorant of the whole undertaking, which had been mounted on her behalf but without her knowledge. The claim was that on both occasions, true-hearted Protestant subjects had taken their own unprompted and voluntary initiative by erecting a 'loyal societie or association'. The question was: were the first Whigs entitled to find their quasi-republican roots in Elizabethan precedent, and specifically in resistance to the reversionary interest in the English crown of Mary Queen of Scots?

Restoration historians have tended to agree with the Tory version of this story. Dr Scott – even Dr Scott – believes that while the Elizabethan case was a device to protect the crown undertaken, in effect, by the crown, the Restoration revival of the device was a statement made against the regime and ministry. It is understandable that later seventeenth-century historians should have this perception. Not only was Queen Elizabeth glorious and popular, a sun queen, but her after-life, the sunset glow she left behind, was even more benignly mellow. All the Elizabethan points of reference in the later Stuart political crisis referred back to a time of consensuality, when the Protestant settlement was endangered only from the outside, not from within. But an Elizabethan historian, this historian at least, may wish to go even somewhat beyond Shaftesbury's account of Elizabethan political conditions. I am by no means as sure as Professor Jones that the 1584 Bond was 'national in character', and I am more sceptical than Shaftesbury, for whom it represented 'the carriage of the whole kingdom'.[57]

The question whether Elizabeth knew of the Bond, had even herself proposed it, or whether it was in its own time a composition *rege inconsulto*, cannot be answered on surviving evidence. To be sure, copies reached the burghers of Cardigan and the farmers of Richmondshire in the equivalent of today's Official envelope, which arouses so much foreboding when it drops on the doormat. We are not deceived by the words which Sir Francis Walsingham inserted in the circular letter to lords lieutenant, drafted by Burghley, which accompanied the document as it went out into the country:

> Your lordship shall not need to take knowledge that you receyved the coppye from me, but rather from some other frende of yours in thes parts; for that her Majestye would have the matter carried in such sorte as this course helde for her [safety] may seeme to [come more] from the pertyculer care of well affected subiects then to growe from any publycke directyon.[58]

It may be that this postscript conveyed the queen's personal wishes. And even if it did, Walsingham's words have the most interesting political-theoretical implications. But knowledge of Elizabethan politics suggests that 'her Majesty would have the matter carried in such sorte' may have meant: 'we [Walsingham and Burghley, and Leicester, whom Camden named as behind the Bond] would have the matter carried in such sorte'.

For the regime was not the same thing as the queen. The 'and' in the formulation 'the queen and her ministers' was not a simple copulative, fusing monarch and government in one. In Elizabethan conditions, and especially in the 1570s and early 1580s, it was a problematical and even distancing 'and'. Both Burghley and Leicester had occasion to complain of the difficulty they found in fulfilling their obligations, Leicester writing on one occasion: 'Our conference with Her Majesty about affairs is both seldom and slender.'[59] Elizabeth did not like Walsingham. 'God open her Majesty's eyes', was a recurrent refrain. When we say that there was confrontation in successive Elizabethan parliaments, but that the lines need to be redrawn (that is to say, Neale's account of the matter corrected), we mean that in respect of some issues the political components of the regime were so much at odds with the royal that they used the occasion of a parliament to orchestrate these differences and unhappinesses; and not with respect to trifles but in matters concerning the very survival of the state in the perception of its governors. The 1584 Bond of Association professed to be a means to preserve the life of the queen, and likewise the prophylactic legislation with which it was presently replaced. But in truth these were measures to protect the interests of the regime and the state in the event of her untimely death.

III

Moreover, the 'regime' in the relatively open conditions obtaining in the middle Elizabethan years (the 1590s were more repressive) had an extent and a depth which it is hard to square with that notion of 'Tudor Despotism' which the late Professor Joel Hurstfield attempted to revive in the 1960s, asking 'was there a Tudor Despotism after all?', and proposing the concept of 'minority government'.[60] That was more unhelpful than helpful to our understanding of the management of Elizabethan England, unless we mean that its affairs were passing progressively into the hands of a segment of society which may indeed have comprised a statistical minority: Protestants, whose discursive commentary on affairs was 'godly'.

One dimension persistently underestimated in conventional Elizabethan political history, a history organised around the queen and on the devotion paid to her as the mainspring of the whole system, is that of the commonwealth, an idealised and evocative construct and symbol, and the principal vehicle of social and much political comment. 'Commonwealth', a term apparently originating in fifteenth-century conditions[61] and maturing into intense scrutiny in the generation of Thomas More and its immediate sequel, carries many distracting resonances: for one, demotic resonances, so that in the 1530s Sir Thomas Elyot preferred to speak of the 'public weal';[62] for another, socio-economic, as if to be concerned with the common 'wealth' was to be interested only in bread-and-butter matters, which was manifestly not the case. Consequently, historians have confined their interest in commonwealth rhetoric, and even their use of the word, to the middle years of the sixteenth century, a time of alleged 'mid-Tudor crisis', when social moralists, the so-called 'commonwealth men', claimed to have the conscience of the community in their pockets and to speak for the common good over and against private interest, on such social concerns as enclosure, rack-renting, inflation, poverty, and sheep.[63]

When Sir Geoffrey Elton protested that there really were no commonwealth men, at least that there was no commonwealth party, only a gaggle of publicists and preachers who were better at conventional moral diatribes than at economic analysis,[64] he almost denied that Tudor England was a commonwealth, or at least proposed that perception of the commonwealth was weak. In this he agreed with others who had assumed that a publicly aroused concern for the commonwealth was something Utopian, Platonic and transient, an aspect of the Edwardian minority becoming fast redundant under the firm monarchical governance of Elizabeth.[65] A less localised and very traditional argument denies the survival into the second half of the century of the civic humanism of More and Thomas Starkey, leading Professor John Pocock to suggest that while the Elizabethans were theoretically familiar, from their education and their playgoing, with citizenship in the classical Roman sense, they themselves were subjects, not citizens, and knew it.[66] Somewhat outmoded perceptions of the lamentable death of humanist England at the hands of Protestant reformers have led Dr Brendan Bradshaw to characterise Elizabethan political and literary culture as 'a political morality that lacks a social conscience', that conscience having been replaced by the invidious and uncharitable Calvinist division of society into elect and reprobate. The elect could consign the reprobate (equivalent to the socially dependent?) to Hell with a good conscience.[67]

These are false premises. It may be that the positive discrimination in favour of the poor which was a feature of mid-Tudor public discourse was replaced by something like the reverse. But concern for the commonwealth as an interest equivalent to the body politic and committing all of its responsible members was constantly reiterated throughout Elizabeth's reign and beyond.[68] Here, for example, is a treatise on certain problems and conflicts of interest in the cloth trade, composed in the reign of James I by one Walter Morrell:[69]

> For as I am noe principall in the Common Wealth, soe neither am I a meere stranger thereunto, and therefore can noe more safelie exclude my self from carefullnes of the well beinge thereof then one being in a shipp in danger of wreck maie exclude himself from danger, because he is neither master nor pilot.

The motto set out on the title-page of this manuscript treatise is: 'Not borne for our selves but for our countrie.' This was a Ciceronian commonplace, as conventional as the metaphor for the commonwealth of a ship. 'Commonwealth matters' might, it is true, be distinguished from matters of state and regularly were, for example, in the organisation of parliamentary business. But in the context of the Elizabethan exclusion crisis, they embraced a concern for the nation's security and destiny which was politico-religious rather than socio-economic, an even livelier apprehension of shipwreck. Indeed, a good part of the documentation of an active 'commonwealth' sentiment concerned, quite literally, shipping and naval matters, from coastal security to the supply of rigging and cables.[70]

The fact that Morrell's treatise was never printed is indicative of much Elizabethan and post-Elizabethan writing on commonwealth matters and the point is highly significant, for in contrast to the printed pamphlets of the mid-Tudor years, with their propagandist implications, these 'plots' or 'platforms' or 'devices' were often intended 'for your eyes only', the eyes of government.

They were written by those intellectual 'men-of-business'[71] who had the time and the learning to read books for others, or with others, and to make their knowledge available for the public good.[72] In order to understand the gestation and application of ideas in the Tudor state, it is relevant but often difficult to know when such advice was requisitioned, when volunteered. Thomas Norton, the great 'parliament man', claimed that all that he had composed on such matters had been written to order, but that was perhaps merely tactful.[73] On the one hand we have clear evidence that Norton, or the clerk of the Privy Council, Robert Beale, were on occasions asked to spend their leisure time on writing white or green papers on such topics as policy towards catholic recusants and their children, or on matters of constitutional and legal history; in Norton's case, the leisure was secured through a period of enforced residence in the Tower.[74] On the other, Burghley and other members of the government received radical advice papers which they can hardly have commissioned. One example is the memorandum sent to Burghley in perhaps 1572 by the radical Puritan soldier, entrepreneur and Member of Parliament George Carleton.[75] Carleton analysed the state of the realm, distinguishing three religious parties, defined as papists, atheists and Protestants, who in his account sound like Puritans: 'the servants of God and such as do tread the straight path of the Lord to salvation'. Carleton recommended that the first two parties be not only 'misliked' but 'removed', and that faithful Protestants, 'the Queen's own bowels', be either concentrated as a protective militia in the twenty counties nearest London, or permitted to colonise Ireland. Burghley duly endorsed and filed this startling document.

Other cases are more problematical. They include that 'Device for the Alteration of Religion' which has figured so prominently in discussion of the religious settlement of 1559;[76] and that other early Elizabethan advice paper, perhaps a recension of an Edwardian document, 'An order for redresse of the state of the Realme', dated May 1559. This was a well-informed and visionary paper which recommended substantial changes in the relations of the component parts of government and military organisation.[77] But let us by all means assume that normally such contributions to policy formation will have been asked for, by some body or bodies at the centre of power. It nevertheless tells us a world about participation in Elizabethan governmental processes, inspired not merely by obedience but by the acknowledgement of a shared public duty.

And certainly rhetorical patriotism in Elizabethan public texts was extremely widespread. Authors on all kinds of topics, and not least the antiquarians and historians, from Leland to Camden, loudly published that their compelling motive as writers was love of country. Political historians of the reign make a serious mistake if they leave all that sort of thing to the cultural historians, as if such sentiments were part of a disembodied humanist rhetoric which neither sought nor gained any purchase on the world of practical politics. In fact, the adversarial politics of the Elizabethan exclusion crisis were clamorous with claims to have acted in response to patriotic sentiment and duty, even if loyalist and royalist sentiments often came first, as Elizabeth might have cynically remarked, 'for manners' sake'.

Take, for example, the outspoken book written by the lawyer John Stubbs at the climax of the Anjou marriage negotiation: *The Discoverie of a Gaping Gulf Whereinto England is Like to be Swallowed by an other French Mariage, if the Lord forbid not the banes, by Letting her Maiestie See the Sin and Punishment Thereof* (1579).[78] This was a remarkable publishing event, not only for its sequel, the severing of its author's right hand, but for the sophistication both of its intelligent as well as highly polemical representation of international politics, and in its thoroughly digested understanding of Machiavelli. Stubbs was above all a patriot. These are phrases plucked out of Stubbs's text: 'This faithful household of England', 'a region purged from idolatry, a kingdom of light'. 'It is natural to all men to abhor foreign rule as a burden of Egypt, and we of England if to any other nation under the Sun.' Stubbs's professed concern was that 'she and we may lose this English paradise', and he professed to speak for 'every English heart'. But what was said in reply to Stubbs by Lord Henry Howard, the future earl of Northampton, the most neglected of Elizabethan intellectuals, a crypto-papist and supporter of the match? This is Howard's first sentence: 'Dutifull affection to my native country enforceth me at this present to disclose my opinion and conceit in a case now in question and debate of much consequence and importance to the state of this realm.' And here is his last sentence: 'And what herein I have done I humbly refer to the grave and gracious consideration of Her Most Excellent Majesty, my dutiful regard to whom, as also to my country, constrained me to put pen to paper'.[79]

Two hands were struck off by the executioner's axe, with surgeons in attendance, outside Whitehall Palace on 3 November 1579. The other belonged to a certain William Page, long thought to have been a mere publisher or bookseller, since Camden described him as 'the disperser of the copies'. In fact Page was a Member of Parliament – currently the Member for the Bedford borough of Saltash – and secretary and man-of-business to the earl of Bedford, whose interests were in the West Country.[80] Page had in Mary's reign lived in Venice, where he plotted against the Marian regime, at least in his head. So perhaps he too knew his Machiavelli. His offence in 1579 was to have sent fifty copies of Stubbs's book to his friend Sir Richard Grenville. We know from another West Country source what was likely to happen to a sensational and provocative book released into that environment.[81] It would pass from hand to hand and be seen by many more than fifty pairs of eyes. So we understand not only why Page was mutilated but also why the royal proclamation against the *Gaping Gulf*, a lengthy statement, was copied out in full in the register of the Bishop of Exeter.[82] The networks involved in this affair were surely more extensive than we now have means of telling. The printer of the *Gaping Gulf* was the elderly Hugh Singleton, a veteran of militant protestant publication, who seems to have received a last-minute pardon on account of his age. Now Singleton's presses were at that very moment turning out Edmund Spenser's *Shepheardes Calender*, with its thinly concealed critical comments on the Anjou marriage; and Spenser had just become secretary to the earl of Leicester, who was probably orchestrating much of this agitation. Spenser's poem also reflected on the downfall at this time of the Archbishop of Canterbury, Edmund Grindal, another victim of this mini-exclusion crisis.[83]

One may readily cross-reference to the fate of Thomas Norton, who sat in Parliament for the last time in 1581, perhaps alongside Page, whose mutilation will not have made him ineligible to sit in this prorogued assembly. After the dissolution of what was to be his last parliament, Norton was sent to the Tower for reasons which seem to have included known opposition to the Anjou marriage. From prison he darkly hinted that what he had done he had done for public figures more eminent than himself.[84] According to the French ambassador, the queen, at the time of the Stubbs affair, knew perfectly well what was going on. She said that Stubbs and his collaborators were merely the agents, 'les secretaires' of others, 'plus méchans que eulx'. Mauvissière had earlier reported that Stubbs and his abettors would not have done what they did 'sans le consentement de quelques ungs de ce conseil'.[85] For that matter, Sir Philip Sidney would probably not have written what he wrote, directly to the queen, opposing the marriage, without the 'consentement' of 'quelques ungs', primarily his uncle, Leicester.

Such were the 'men-of-business' whom parliamentary studies have brought to the forefront and dressed in new clothing.[86] Neale had called them 'Puritans'. But now we are told that they – and Norton can stand for all – were nothing but good Protestants, working with and for the regime, inside and presumably outside Parliament, in no sense members of a puritanically inspired opposition. This is helpful, but only if we appreciate that the regime itself was sometimes in opposition, and not least in the delicate and dangerous area of exclusion politics, in which fish were fried and chestnuts pulled out of the fire by the likes of the courageous Stubbs, the obscure Page and the famous Norton. The use of Robert Beale and William Davison in bringing Mary Stuart to the block in 1587 is an episode too well known to require more than a passing mention.

The danger, with all this talk of 'men-of-business', has been to make such men mere catspaws and instruments, often in the conduct of more or less routine business. In fact, in a manner typical of the politics of the middle Elizabethan years, they were not courtiers and government stooges. Norton only once and uncharacteristically called himself 'obsequious'. They were their own men, motivated as much by patriotism and protestant conviction as by service obligations to the queen or to their political patrons. Patronage was never a simple top-down relationship in sixteenth- and seventeenth-century politics. And herein, of course, lay their political value, in the conditions of mid-Elizabethan politics. As Walsingham wrote in 1584: you shall not need to say that you heard this from us. You thought of it yourself. And Stubbs, Page and Norton were capable of such thoughts.

These were some of those missiles which remained in their siloes during Elizabeth's long reign, only poking their noses above the surface: missiles in the event never fired, but perhaps ensuring by their presence that they would not be fired. Everyone in this political generation was dead before the queen herself died.

IV

The name of Machiavelli has cropped up in connection with Stubbs and Page. We may ask: were these minor activists in the Elizabethan exclusion crisis harbingers in their intellects of English classical republicanism? Professors Lisa Jardine and Anthony Grafton have shown us with what intensity Livy was read in these middle years of the reign by Gabriel Harvey, for what purposes and with whom he read the Roman historian.[87] Professor John Salmon has explained how a heady mixture of Seneca's stoic philosophy and Tacitus's imperial Roman history (a cocktail which on the Continent was imbibed for the purpose of state-building on a proto-absolutist model) in England became an ideology of critical detachment from the increasingly overbearing late Elizabethan and Jacobean state.[88] This was a tradition running from Leicester through the Sidney circle to the earl of Essex and on into the early years of James I, Prince Henry and his partly disaffected and soon to be disappointed affinity. According to Salmon, the English devotees of Seneca and Tacitus were members of circles 'soured by suspicion and defeat', and their partial alienation was institutionalised in some elements of the Society of Antiquaries, soon suppressed, and in Sir Robert Cotton's semi-public library with its busts of Tacitean emperors, too dangerous a resource to be tolerated by Charles I. This was indeed a very long fuse laid through the reigns of the first Stuarts to the powder keg of civil war.

One of the last Elizabethan neo-stoics, and the first to attempt the writing of modern Tacitean history, was Sir John Hayward, who, with remarkable temerity and from motives far from clear, published a history of the deposition of Richard II and the first year of the usurping Henry IV.[89] This was in the context of the unresolved late Elizabethan succession problem and two years before the Essex rebellion. Hayward dedicated his book to Essex. 'I am Richard the Second, know ye not that?' Elizabeth would ask William Lambarde. Holinshed's 1577 *Chronicle* had included an approving account of Richard

II's deposition, suppressed in the 1587 edition, and Stow's *Chronicle* spoke of the 'election' of Henry IV. All the Elizabethan printed texts of Shakespeare's *Richard II* omit the deposition scene. Hayward's book was said to cunningly insinuate that the like abuses being then in the realm that were in the days of Richard II, the like course might be taken for redress. The attorney-general, Edward Coke, wanted to know, as well he might, why Hayward had published a book limited 'to that story only'. Elizabeth sent Hayward to the Tower (but not immediately, seventeen months after the publication of his history) and wanted to know if he might not be guilty of treason. No, said Sir Francis Bacon, but of felony, yes, 'for he had taken most of the sentences out of Cornelius Tacitus, and translated them into English, and put them into his text.'[90]

But I digress. It is more to the point that Hayward also plagiarised Sir Philip Sidney. In his *Annals of Queen Elizabeth* (a post-Elizabethan text which joins in the canonisation of the woman who would gladly have seen him executed) we find this account of the state of England as Mary Tudor lay dying:

> For every man's mynd was then travayled with a strange confusione of conceits, all things being immoderately eyther dreaded or desired. Every report was greedily both inquired and received, all truths suspected, diverse tales beleeved, many improbable conjectures hatched and nourished. Invasions of strangeres, civill dissentione, the doubtfull dispositione of the succeeding Prince, were cast in every man's conceite as present perills; but noe man did busy his witts in contriving remedyes.[91]

That sounds like the state of the nation at the worst moments of the Elizabethan exclusion crisis; and no wonder, for it comes straight from Sidney's account of the state of Arcadia, betrayed by the negligence of its ruler, the duke Basilius, 'a notable example', Sidney had written

> how great dissipations monarchal governments are subiect unto; for now their princes and guide had left them, they had not experience to rule, and had not whom to obey ... but everything was either vehemently desireful or extremely terrible [compare Hayward's 'immoderately eyther dreaded or desired']. Neighbours' invasions, civil dissension, cruelty of the coming prince, and whatsoever in common sense carries a dreadful show was in all men's heads, but in few how to prevent; hearkening on every rumour, suspecting everything.[92]

In his *Defence of Poetry*, Sidney had compared the roles of history and poetry (fiction), representing them as essentially different. But if Hayward's history borrowed from Sidney's fiction, the fiction was a restatement of Sidney's own role in history, the discourse which he had written to the queen, boldly opposing the Anjou match, in the tradition of honest, plain-speaking counsel. It had done his career no good at all and his Continental mentor and father figure, Hubert Languet, had wrung his hands over such fatal impetuosity.[93] Sidney had then retired to the country, and the sublimation of *Arcadia* was the result. Arcadia's ruler had been warned (in vain) by a faithful counsellor: 'Let them see the benefits of your justice daily more and more; and so must they needs rather like of present sureties than uncertain changes.' These words closely parallel the final peroration of Sidney's discourse to the queen 'touching hir mariage with Monsiur': 'Against contempt at home … lett your excellent vertues of piety Justice and liberality daily, if it be possible more and more shine'.[94]

The rejection of good advice is followed by the inevitable violence of civil war. It is a striking feature of the psyche and imagination of the Elizabethan exclusion crisis that apprehension scenarios of the most bloody kind regularly repeat themselves, in perceptions of the real world and its prospects, and in art. We have heard Thomas Digge's lurid comments on the dangers of the Bond of Association. But very early in the reign there were those fearful prognostications of bloody civil strife which punctuate the succession play *Gorboduc* (part written by Thomas Norton),[95] from which both the *Arcadia* and later *King Lear* seem to have borrowed bits of their plots. Only in the present tense did Elizabethan England experience 'halcyon days'.

V

A suppressed, critical, neo-stoicist republicanism was the product of the last Elizabethan years, an ideology nurtured in reaction to the rather different political climate which, in wartime and old age, had succeeded the politics of the exclusion crisis of the middle years, a climate less consensual, more *dirigiste*, even, in Fulke Greville's words, 'metamorphosing' 'into a precipitate absoluteness', the climate of the 'regnum Cecilianum' (contested by the earl of Essex) which was the 1590s.[96]

The principal intellectual resources of the queen's critics in the exclusion crisis of earlier years were not Seneca or Tacitus, but legal-historical principles from the English past, and the Bible, on which, in the remainder of this chapter, we shall concentrate. It was from Scripture, with explicit reference to Old Testament history, and especially to Old Testament rulers and dynasties, that Elizabeth was incessantly admonished. Dr Margaret Aston wittily imagines her saying: 'I am Hezekiah. Don't tell me *that!*' Hezekiah was the godly king who had declared war on idolatry (2 Kings 18; 2 Chronicles 29). In particular, Hezekiah had broken in pieces the brazen serpent in the Temple, once a symbol of healing but now an idol, a mere 'piece of brass'. Elizabeth was repeatedly admonished to do the same to that modern idol, the cross.[97] 'This is a notable example for all princes, first to establish the pure Religion of God, and to procure that the Lord may be honoured and served aright' (2 Chronicles 29:3, Geneva Bible marginal note).

It was with an utter confidence erected on such scriptural foundations that the Oxford divine Laurence Humphrey in a dedicatory epistle instructed the admittedly young and still untried monarch:

> We advaunce not your might, not your armie, not your wisedome: but wonder at your weakness and infirmitye. We praise not mannes power: but ascribe it to the bountye and mercy of God.[98]

That was at the beginning of the reign, when John Hales, called by a parliamentary sketch writer in 1567 'Hales the hottest',[99] a man who took great risks in the public debates about the succession, told the queen:

> Ye see [God's] power, what he is able to do: he alone can save, and he can destroy; he can pull down, and he can set up. If ye fear him, and seek to do his will, then he will favour you, and preserve you to the end from all enemies, as he did king David. If ye now fall from him, or juggle with him, look for no more favour then Saul had showed to him.

'Thus must your grace do, if ye mind the advancement of God's glory, your own quietness and safety, and the wealth of this your body politic.'[100] A reader of Stubb's *Gaping Gulf* has inscribed on the title-page: 'Per me reges regnant'.[101]

Elizabeth was to be repeatedly reminded that she 'juggled' with God in failing to ensure the perpetuation of secure government by determining the succession. In 1563 the House of Lords, after piling up the biblical examples which ought to guide her conduct (and they were without exception biblical examples, suggesting, as the queen suspected, that this task had been committed to the bishops) concluded: 'Most excellent Princes, the places of the scriptures conteyning the said threatenings be sett furth with much more sharp wordes then be here expressed.'[102] A House of Commons speech four years later resounded with those 'oughts' to which attention was drawn earlier. Her Majesty *ought* to be an upholder and not an overthrower of the people. 'She ought carefully, naturally, and religiously to end all titles and contentions ... She ought not to denie th' establishment of a successor.'[103] In 1572, Elizabeth was warned, again by the bishops (there is no reason to link such sentiments and *démarches* exclusively to something called 'Puritanism'), that she juggled with God in failing to put Mary Queen of Scots to death. 'Because Saule spared Agag although he were a kinge, God took from the same Saule his good sperite and transferred the kingdom of Israell from him and from his heires for evere.'[104]

> By theis and such othere wordes in many places God signefyeth yf his people perishe either in soule or bodie by the slacke or remisse government of them that are appoynted rulers over them and as it weare sheppardes and heardes men to keepe them from daunger, that he will require the blood of his people at their handes.[105]

We may note that in this biblical rhetoric it is not 'your people' but 'his people', God's, which we may regard as transitional to 'the people'.

If Elizabeth thought it improper to shed the blood of kings, she was otherwise instructed by the margin of the Geneva Bible, which commented thus on David's honourable refusal to kill Saul, the Lord's anointed, when he had him at his mercy: he did right, 'to wit in his owne private cause: for Jehu slew two kings at Gods appointment. 2 Kings 9:22' (1 Samuel 26:10). It was this same Jehu who put wicked Queen Jezebel to death without any trial, as the Geneva Bible margin reads 'by the motion of the Spirit of God' (2 Kings 9:33). In the House of Commons in 1572 this was a precedent for killing Mary Stuart ('Jezebel') with no great ceremony: 'Cut of her head and make no more adoe about her.'[106] When Bishop Sandys prepared the book of 1 Samuel for the Bishop's Bible of 1567, he incorporated the Geneva note on 1 Samuel 26:10, which continued to appear in many editions of the Authorised Version of 1611, far into the seventeenth century.[107] Another Geneva note, particularly irksome to James VI and I, Mary Stuart's son, commented on King Asa's failure to kill his wicked mother (or grandmother) Queen Maacah, whom he had justly deposed, thus ignoring clear directives in Deuteronomy 13 to execute idolaters without mercy, whosoever they might be. 'And herein he shewed that he lacked zeale', moved by 'foolish pitie' (2 Chronicles 15:16, Geneva marginal note). The keeper of Mary Stuart in the last months, Sir Amyas Paulet, had that scripture ringing in his ears when he wrote: 'Others shall excuse their foolish pity as they may.' For 'others', read Queen Elizabeth.[108]

The bishops' address of 1572 is the most remarkable single document to have been generated by the Elizabethan exclusion crisis, containing, as it does, a kind of doubly distilled resistance doctrine. In the first place, Mary Stuart had been justly and properly deposed by her own subjects. She was 'the late Queen', called in the accompanying Commons statement 'a queene of late tyme and yet through her own actes now iustely no queene.' Thomas Norton said: 'Why she should be counted a queene he knoweth not.'[109] In the second place, the bishops threatened Elizabeth with the loss of her own throne, at the hands of God by an instrumentality not specified, if she failed to execute justice upon this former queen.

These choice quotations and 'examples' by no means exhaust the relevance of 1 and 2 Kings, 1 and 2 Chronicles, and their Geneva expositors for the institution of monarchy. On this subject both the Old Testament and its commentators display a certain ambiguity. The Geneva comment on 1 Chronicles 29:23 informs the reader that 'the kings of Judah were figures of Christ.' Yet these 'figures', even David, the principal figure, all erred. Godly King Asa erred in consulting the physicians rather than the Lord about his gout (1 Kings 15:23, 2 Chronicles 16:12). And taking account of the rulers of Israel, good Old Testament kings were heavily outnumbered by bad, the institution itself having been a divine concession to human weakness (1 Samuel 8:20). Of the first king in recorded history, Nimrod, the mighty hunter, the Geneva margin declared: 'His tyrannie came into a proverbe as hated both of God and man'

(Genesis 10:9). In the seventeenth century, radical critics of monarchy had no difficulty in finding scriptural support for the view that monarchy and tyranny were synonymous. 'In that they were kings they were tyrants.'[110] On 1 Kings 12:9, the Geneva Bible comments: 'There is nothing harder for them that are in authoritie, then to bridle their affections, and follow good counsell'; on 2 Chronicles 22:4: 'He sheweth that it must needs follow that the rulers are such as their counsellors be, and that there cannot be a good king, that suffereth wicked counsellors.'

Historians of political theory tell us that resistance doctrine, such as the exiles Christopher Goodman, Bishop John Ponet and John Knox constructed in the reign of Mary, was redundant under the wholly acceptable rule of her Protestant sister. The voice of militant Calvinism fell silent, or addressed only matters of ecclesiastical polity, except, of course, in France, the Netherlands and Scotland, where politics were both violent and religiously exacerbated. Apart from failing to take account of some of the evidence which has now been rehearsed, these conventional perspectives ignore the intellectual and active commitment of Elizabethan Protestants to the international scene, and even the hard fact that the leading foreign resistance theorists, Hotman, de Mornay, the Scot Buchanan, were all published in Elizabethan London. And in what year was Buchanan's *De iure regni apud Scotos* printed in London? What year but 1579.[111]

Professor Quentin Skinner has written of 'a few wisps' of resistance theory lingering on in the marginalia of the Geneva Bible, its survival there and almost only there presumably indicative of its literal marginality.[112] They were some wisps! The fact that ideological and political missiles remained in their cold war siloes and were never fired, that the Elizabethans, like Elizabeth herself, for the most part died in their beds, with none of Cassandra's prophecies fulfilled, means not so much that the real history of the reign of Elizabeth has not been written as that, in a manner of speaking, it never happened.

APPENDIX: THE INTERREGNUM SCHEME OF 1584–85

The documents generated in 1584–85 by the plans for a legislated interregnum are, from a constitutional point of view, among the most revealing to have survived from the reign of Elizabeth. Although in the event abortive, and so not much noticed by historians, they shed an unusual light on contemporary perceptions of the role of Parliament in the English polity, and on the political capacities potentially inherent in an acephalous monarchy. If these ideas had been only the brain-child of the mathematician and Member of Parliament Thomas Digges they would be of some interest, since Digges was an exceptionally interesting man. But, as we learn from one of these drafts,[113] the interregnal scheme was backed by the regime, almost as a whole, if that is a correct reading of this statement: 'This was the summe of the things remembered in a conference at the L[ord] Chancellors house these being present.' Those named, in order, were, the lord chancellor (Sir Thomas Bromley), the lord treasurer (Lord Burghley), the earl of Leicester, the lord chamberlain (Lord Hunsdon), the vice-chamberlain (Sir Christopher Hatton), the chancellor of the exchequer (Sir Walter Mildmay) (all these Privy Councillors); together with the three senior judges and the three law officers of the Crown. (The preponderance in this gathering of legal clout, and the absence of such secretarial members of the Privy Council as Sir Francis Walsingham and Sir Ralph Sadler is no doubt significant.) The device of an informal meeting of the Council, out of Court and at the house of the lord chancellor/lord keeper, had been resorted to in 1577 in an attempt to make progress in the critical and legally perilous affair of Archbishop Grindal and the queen.[114]

The documents in question are: NA, S.P. 12/176/11, 22–3, 25–6, 28–30, 32; Huntington Library, MS. EL 1192; Northamptonshire Record Office, MS. F.(M) P.184. They date from the parliamentary recess of 19 December 1584 to 4 February 1585. The paper headed 'The Dangers that may ensue by the Othe of Association' (NA, S.P. 12/176/26; copies in BL, MS. Lansdowne 98, fos 14–18, MS. Add. 38823, fos 14 *et seq.*) rehearses the unsuccessful attempts before the recess to find an acceptable parliamentary substitute for the Bond of Association. 'An exceeding great Committee' which met in the Exchequer Chamber had been not so much divided as fragmented in opinion. The queen had signalled her opposition. One copy of this paper is endorsed by Burghley: 'Mr Digges discourse upon the Association'.[115] The discourse presents the device of an interregnum as a means to resolve the conflict of sworn loyalties and obligations potentially created by the Bond, and to avoid anarchy.

Most of these drafts, some of which are annotated in Burghley's hand, differ in detail while agreeing on the main outlines: an augmented 'Grand' or 'Great' Council with executive powers; all other officers to remain in post and all laws to remain in force; a parliament to be summoned by the Grand Council within thirty days to prosecute and punish those who had plotted or contrived the queen's violent death, 'actor or privie', and to hear claims and determine the title to the Crown: 'in which parliament every competitor shall have libertie to exhibit his title there to receave iudgment'; until such time, an interregnum.

But MS. EL 1192 (annotated by Burghley) envisages that Parliament will be summoned by the Privy Council within ten days of the queen's violent or unnatural death, and will elect the thirty persons who, with the three senior judges, are to form the 'Great Counsell of the Realme'. This draft seems to assume that the principal if not the only task of Great Council and Parliament will be to prosecute and execute the guilty parties. They will exercise their powers if necessary for as much as a year. It is not clear how the interregnum is to be ended, nor whether Parliament will have the power to end it. Perhaps not: 'that the sayd parlyment have power onely to geve justyce and sentence against the offenders ...'. MS. EL 1192 is a statement of what will be done, almost as if the queen were already absent from the scene. Each clause states 'that' various measures 'shall' be taken.

However, the otherwise most substantial and formal of these papers assumes the form of a petition to the queen: 'A breefe discourse against succession knowen, discovering a moste assuered meane for your maiesties safetye'.[116] In the past I (and Professor Lehmberg) have attributed what the writer calls 'these rude notes and collections' to Digges. This must be a mistake, for all the affinity of the discourse to papers more confidently attributable to Digges, including a 'platt' of 21 January 1585, 'De Interregno', which may be profitably read alongside the discourse. The author of the discourse claims to utter not only as a 'faithfull subiect' but as a 'sworne servant', which seems to indicate a Privy Councillor and is consistent with the evidence of the conference at the lord chancellor's house. I am now inclined to attribute the discourse to none other than Lord Burghley: for reasons having to do with his seniority, his known involvement in the scheme, the emphasis placed on 'a meane way', typical of the temper of his mind, and the no less typical dependence on the intellectual originality of someone else, in this case Digges.

The so-called 'breefe discourse' differs from other drafts in substituting for the Grand Council, or at least complementing it with, an executive of '5 or 7 principall persons of this land, as well spirituall as temporall', exercising, 'absolute governemente'. The supporting argument concerns on the one hand the 'commodytes' of such a device, on the other, various 'obiections' and 'daungers'. Among the more arresting of the alleged 'commodities' (especially for the purposes of this essay), it is said that 'that sinister opinion of foreyn Nations, how yowr Maiestie seaketh only yowr owen safetie with owt regardes of the peryll of yowr Realme will be confuted'. (Was it only overseas that this 'sinister opinion' was entertained?) The overwhelming imperative appears to be to substitute a rational process for the blind arbitrament of the sword, it being all but assumed that civil war will otherwise follow the queen's death.

Given that assumption, the writer is not deterred by fears (I think Digges's fears) that experience of a Roman papal election, 'hell it selfe, every man by force defendinge his owen, all kynd of owtragious Ryott and villanye', suggests that any interregnum would be 'monstrous' and 'disordered'; in the English case 'much more horrible', since there would be no accustomed procedure, no College of Cardinals. Moreover, it is predicted that all papists will be united in leaning one way (Mary Queen of Scots is meant), whereas faithful Protestant subjects, 'true Christians', are 'uncertayne and in opinion distracted'.

Further objections, and those of the greatest constitutional interest, condemn the proposed interregnum as an unprecedented innovation.

When the fourteenth-century French estates declared in favour of Philip of Valois, Edward III, sure of his right, very properly paid no attention. As for the English Crown, it was hereditary (according to 'De Interregno', imperial, 'not subject to any but to God alone'), so that Parliament would be exceeding its powers by 'intermeddling' in the disposition of the Crown. England was not Poland, or Denmark. A fine distinction was drawn in responding to this point. Parliament's role would not be 'to create a Prynce against right, but as grave, wise, syncere, honorable Judges to decerne of the rights', the right heir without such judgment exercised being 'not aparant'. The safety of the realm properly concerned 'a supreame government called *Aristocratia*, next *Monarchy* of most perfection; the Polleticke Bodye of the Realme in full Lyfe.' 'I confess Innovations perilouse', unless they were medicinal. But the circumstances were themselves without precedent, calling for the strongest medicine.

And there were in fact many precedents of parliamentary estates playing the kind of role proposed, from English, Scottish, French, and very recent Iberian history. If Philip II had 'patiently' awaited the ruling of the estates in the case of the Portuguese crown, so had Edward III in the case of the French crown, two hundred years earlier. If the English Parliament, a 'presumptious Parliament', had had the power in 1460 to acknowledge the usurping claims of the duke of York, *a fortiori* it could lawfully proceed in this case, empowered, as was proposed, by the reigning monarch and by Act of Parliament. But even if there had been no precedents, 'so much the more Honour' would accrue to the queen for taking an unprecedented step, 'so rare a provision', and this would be a matter of pride and satisfaction to her successors, 'a cause to immortalize your Maiesties fame and renown with all posteritie'. Here, surely, Digges was ventriloquising through Burghley (if it was Burghley); for this was not the kind of argument we tend to associate with the Polonius-like lord treasurer.

Many other difficulties were envisaged. The proposed military force of 40,000,[117] which would have to be deployed forthwith, would be burdensome, would be a threat to civil liberties, and might be recruited by those very contenders for the succession it was meant to deter, so many praetorian guards. The nominated five or seven 'select persons' would be resented by those not selected, those 'left out'. And members of the Grand Council would very probably fall out. The reign of Edward VI was not an encouraging precedent. Members of Parliament forced to declare for one or another 'competitor' would be afraid to speak their minds.

The author of the brief discourse was not unresourceful in argument. The last objection could be met by parliamentary voting Venetian style, by secret ballot, bills and nominations to be deposited in 'a great publicke vesell in the midst of either howse', to be taken out and read by the clerk at random and without naming names, before being burned. If the two houses were to find themselves divided, they should meet as one House, each of the peers to have the votes of three or four Members of Parliament.

But the most substantial objection of all was that, when push came to shove, there could be no guarantee that the rival claimants, and especially their foreign backers (here, again, Mary Stuart was meant), would respect these arrangements, which would depend upon goodwill, fair play and fundamental patriotism, commodities likely to be in short supply. Against this, the proponent of the scheme could only suggest that in such a worst-case scenario, the country would be no worse off than if nothing had been done to prevent it. To ram home the need for emergency legislation, the discourse ends with a spine-chilling account of events across the North Sea: 'The Perills that your Maiestie and Realme standeth in untyll the State be thus setled, by example of the Prynce of Orange.'[118]

Nevertheless, in these documents the ayes do not seem to have had it, even in statements which were ostensibly intended to promote the interregnal strategy. 'So as this kynde of provision ... will hardely serve to avoyde the confusion that is like to followe and setle the realme as is desired.' If the queen, in effect, vetoed these proposals, as it has been thought she did, then this may well have been one of those cases in which her negative voice registered not so much a personal view or idiosyncracy as a perception within the regime itself of insuperable difficulty. It was very characteristic of Burghley to advance discussion of such a difficult and contentious matter by the erection of counterbalancing arguments, and in the course of that process to argue himself into a conservative and inactive position. And perhaps what everybody now decided was that the best and next thing to accomplish was the extinction of Mary Stuart.[119]

NOTES

1 J. R. Jones, *The First Whigs* (London, 1961); K. H. D. Haley, *The First Earl of Shaftesbury* (Oxford, 1968); J. R. Jones, *Country and Court: England 1658–1714* (London, 1978).

2 Jonathan Scott, *Algernon Sidney and the Restoration Crisis, 1677–1683* (Cambridge, 1991), Part One, 'The Restoration crisis'.

3 *Proceedings in the Parliaments of Elizabeth I, vol. 1: 1558–1581*, ed. T. E. Hartley (Leicester, 1981), p. 59 (all further references to Hartley).

4 Norman Jones, *The Birth of the Elizabethan Age: England in the 1560s* (Oxford, 1993), p. 119.

5 Susan Doran, 'Religion and politics at the court of Elizabeth I: the Habsburg marriage negotiations of 1559–1567', *English Historical Review*, 104 (1989): 908–26; Jones, *The Birth of the Elizabethan Age*, p. 150.

6 Wallace T. MacCaffrey, 'The Anjou match and the making of Elizabethan foreign policy', in *The English Commonwealth 1547–1640*, ed. Peter Clark, Alan G. T. Smith and Nicholas Tyacke (Leicester, 1979), pp. 59–75; Wallace T. MacCaffrey, *Queen*

Elizabeth and the Making of Policy 1572–1585 (Princeton, N.J., 1981), *passim*; Wallace T. MacCaffrey, *Elizabeth I* (London, 1993), ch. 16, 'The Anjou match'. The earl of Leicester set the scene for the perception of the courtship in his own country of Warwickshire in a letter to Lord Burghley of 20 October 1578: 'In the meane tyme ther ys no newes here to wryte but [—?] to fynd, for I do assure your lordship, since Q. Marys tyme the papists were never in that jollytye they be at this present in this country' (British Library [hereafter BL], MS. Harleian 6992, no. 56, fo. 112). One may loosely link this with the report of a Warwickshire minister who 'upon rumor of a change of Religion in Mounsiers daies did shave his beard' (*The Seconde Parte of a Register*, ed. Albert Peel [Cambridge, 1915], vol. 2, p. 166). Sir Francis Knollys later wrote of the match as 'the French bondage, agreed uppon by that holy father the poope and plotted owte by the serpentyne subtyltye of Queen mother's head' (The National Archives [hereafter NA], S.P. 12/139/3).

7 The late adoption of the cult of the virgin queen is argued by John N. King in 'Queen Elizabeth I: representations of the virgin queen', *Renaissance Quarterly*, 43 (1990): 30–74. See also his *Tudor Royal Iconography: Literature and art in an age of religious crisis* (Princeton, N.J., 1989), ch. 4, 'The "Godly" queens'. Susan Doran links the relatively new cult to the Anjou courtship and the instruction of the queen by opponents of the match, pointing particularly to the masques and pageants idealising chastity written by Thomas Churchyard and performed at Norwich in August 1578 during the royal East Anglian progress of that summer (Susan M. Doran, 'Juno versus Diana: the treatment of Elizabeth I's marriage in plays and entertainments, 1561–1581', *Historical Journal*, 36 [1995]: 257–74; Thomas Churchyard, *A Discourse of the Queenes Maiesties Entertainment in Suffolk and Norffolk* [1578]). Thomas Bentley's *The Monument of Matrones* (1582) contains a much more copious and still early celebration of the queen's virginity. Bentley is discussed by King in *Tudor Royal Iconography*, pp. 243–56, and by Patrick Collinson in 'Windows in a woman's soul: questions about the religion of Queen Elizabeth I', in *Elizabethan Essays* (London, 1994), pp. 104–8, 116–17. William Camden's account of Elizabeth's speech to her first parliament, 10 February 1559, a reply to the speech that she should marry, differs from the many manuscript versions by committing her more unreservedly to virginity and marriage to her kingdom (William Camden, *The History of the Most Renowned and Victorious Princess Elizabeth Late Queen of England: Selected Chapters*, ed. Wallace T. MacCaffrey [Chicago, Ill., and London, 1970], pp. 28–30; Hartley, pp. 44–5).

8 Hartley, pp. 137–8. The Commons speech of 1566 'on nominating an heir and a bill of succession' (NA, S.P. 46/166, fos 3–11ᵛ) is a document of some notoriety and importance. G. R. Elton attributes it to William Lambarde or 'Lambert' (who he thinks was not one and the same as the noted antiquary), while Dr James Alsop (who is convinced that there was only one William Lambarde) believes that the speaker was John Molyneux (G. R. Elton, *The Parliament of England, 1559–1581* [Cambridge, 1986], pp. 370–2; J. D. Alsop, 'Reinterpreting the Elizabethan Commons: the Parliamentary Session of 1566', *Journal of British Studies*, 29 [1990], 216–40).

9 Molyneux, if not a Catholic, had strong catholic connections. See P. W. Hasler, *The House of Commons 1558–1603* (*The History of Parliament*) (London, 1981), vol. 3, pp. 60–2 (all further references to Hasler).

10 MacCaffrey, *Elizabeth I*, p. 213.

11 Jonathan Scott, 'England's troubles: exhuming the popish plot', in *The Politics of Religion in Restoration England*, ed. Tim Harris, Paul Seaward and Mark Goldie (Oxford, 1990), pp. 107–31.

12 Robin Clifton, 'Fear of popery', in *The Origins of the English Civil War*, ed. Conrad Russell (London, 1973), pp. 144–67; John Kenyon, *The Popish Plot* (London, 1972); Peter Lake, 'Anti-popery: the structure of a prejudice', in *Conflict in Early Stuart England: Studies in religion and politics 1603–1642*, ed. Richard Cust and Ann Hughes (London, 1989), pp. 72–106; John Miller, *Popery and Politics in England 1660–1688* (Cambridge, 1973).

13 Hartley, pp. 91–2.

14 G. R. Elton, 'Persecution and toleration in the English Reformation', in *Persecution and Toleration, Studies in Church History*, vol. 21, ed. W. J. Sheils (Oxford, 1984), pp. 163–87.

15 For reformation revisionism, see J. J. Scarisbrick, *The Reformation and the English People* (Oxford, 1983); Eamon Duffy, *The Stripping of the Altars: Traditional religion in England, 1400–1580* (New Haven, Conn., 1992); Christopher Haigh, *English Reformations: Religion, politics, and society under the Tudors* (Oxford, 1993). For parliamentary revisionism, see Elton, *The Parliament of England*; Michael A. R. Graves, *Elizabethan Parliaments 1559–1601* (London, 1987); *The Parliaments of Elizabethan England*, ed. D. M. Dean and N. L. Jones (Oxford, 1990). See N. L. Jones, 'Parliament and the governance of Elizabethan England: a review', *Albion*, 19 (1987): 327–46.

16 Alexandra Walsham, *Church Papists: Catholicism, conformity and confessional polemic in early modern England* (Woodbridge, 1993).

17 'A collection of original letters from the bishops to the Privy Council, 1564', ed. Mary Bateson, *Camden Miscellany*, p. 9. Camden Society NS 53 (1883), especially pp. 7–8.

18 Diarmaid MacCulloch, *Suffolk Under the Tudors: Politics and religion in an English county 1500–1600* (Oxford, 1986), pp. 195–7.

19 J. E. Neale, *Elizabethan Essays* (London, 1957), p. 24.

20 For the earl of Bedford, see Hasler, vol. 1, pp. 60–3. Hasler is perhaps properly cautious about the extent of Bedford's electoral influence and its politico-religious implications, which I believe Sir John Neale would have made something of if he, as originally intended, had written the 'Introductory survey' to the Elizabethan *History of Parliament* volumes. For Leicester, see Simon L. Adams, 'The Dudley clientele and the House of Commons, 1559–1586', *Parliamentary History*, 8 (1989): 216–39.

21 Thomas Cogswell, 'England and the Spanish match', in *Conflict in Early Stuart England*, pp. 107–33. See also Thomas Cogswell, *The Blessed Revolution: English Politics and the Coming of War 1621–1624* (Cambridge, 1989).

22 Words used by Thomas Digges and Thomas Dannet in the context of the 1572 Parliament. (Hartley, p. 294). In a discourse of 1577 attributed to Sir Humphrey Gilbert it was said: 'It is right well knowne that the Queens Maiestie is the chiefe head of the Church of Christ' (NA, S.P. 12/118/12).

23 See 'Windows in a woman's soul' in Collinson, *Elizabethan Essays*, pp. 87–118, which differs in its assessment of Elizabeth's own religious position from Christopher Haigh, 'The Queen and the Church', in Haigh, *Elizabeth I* (London, 1988), pp. 27–46.

24 Hartley, p. 425. And note the question put in the House of Commons in 1566 by Peter Wentworth's brother Paul: 'Whether hyr Hyghnes' commawndment, forbyddyng the lower house to speake or treate any more of the successyon and of any theyre excuesses in that behalffe, be a breache of the lybertie of the free speache of the Howse or not?' (Hartley, p. 154).

25 Ernst H. Kantorowicz, *The King's Two Bodies: A study in medieval political theology*

(Princeton, N.J., 1957); Marie Axton, *The Queen's Two Bodies. Drama and the Elizabethan Succession* (London, 1977). John Stubbs in his *Gaping Gulf* described the queen's natural body as 'her very self or self self' (p. 68).

26 Hartley, p. 281.

27 Hartley, p. 376. The speaker was Robert Newdigate, a Bedfordshire gentleman returned as 'earnest' in religion by his bishop in 1564 (but as 'indifferent' in Buckinghamshire, where he also had interests). In 1576 he would be a supporter of Arthur Hall (Hasler, vol. 3, pp. 128–9).

28 Hartley, pp. 354, 356.

29 Patrick Collinson, 'The monarchical republic of Queen Elizabeth I', *Bulletin of the John Rylands Library, University of Manchester*, 69 (1987): 394–424; reprinted, Collinson, *Elizabethan Essays*, pp. 31–57. See also '*De Republica Anglorum*: or, history with the politics put back', *ibid.*, pp. 1–29.

30 Blair Worden, 'English republicanism', in *The Cambridge History of Political Thought 1450–1700*, ed. J. H. Burns with the assistance of Mark Goldie (Cambridge, 1991), pp. 443, 446.

31 Quentin Skinner, *Foundations of Modern Political Thought, vol. 1: The Renaissance* (Cambridge, 1978), p. 46.

32 *Sir Fulke Greville's Life of Sir Philip Sidney etc.* First Published 1652, ed. Nowell Smith (Oxford, 1907), pp. 54, 69. Since Sidney was devoted to his uncle Robert Dudley, earl of Leicester ('My cheefest honour is to be a Dudlei'), we may compare Greville's words with Leicester's self-defence when he was in disgrace at the time of the Anjou courtship and of his own marriage. He had served the queen 'so faythfully, carefully and chargeably' 'almost more than a bondman may a yere together, so long as one dropp of comfort was left of any hope' (*scil.*, of marriage), but 'was yet never abased in anye slavyshe manner to be tyed in more than unequall and unreasonable bandes' (Leicester to Burghley, 12 November 1579; BL, MS. Harleian 6992, no. 57, fos 114–15). I have benefited very greatly from discussing Sidney with Dr Blair Worden, and from hearing and reading his papers on the subject. See also Blair Worden, *The Sound of Virtue: Philip Sidney's* Arcadia *and Elizabethan Politics* (New Haven, Conn., and London, 1996).

33 Jonathan Scott, *Algernon Sidney and the English Republic 1623–1677* (Cambridge, 1988), p. v.

34 *Ibid.*, Ch. 3, 'Family background'.

35 J. E. Neale, *Elizabeth I and her Parliaments, 1559–1581* (London, 1953), p. 152.

36 Elton, *The Parliament of England*. See also G. R. Elton, 'Parliament in the sixteenth Century: functions and fortunes', in Elton, *Studies in Tudor and Stuart Politics and Government*, vol. 3 (Cambridge, 1983), pp. 156–82.

37 Alsop, 'Reinterpreting the Elizabethan Commons', See also J. D. Alsop, 'Parliament and taxation', in *The Parliaments of Elizabethan England*, pp. 91–116.

38 Scott, *Algernon Sidney and the Restoration Crisis*, pp. 17–19.

39 Examples of the Bond are in NA, S.P. 12/174; earlier drafts in S.P. 12/173/81–4. For convenience of reference I follow the text printed in *The Egerton Papers*, ed. J. Payne Collier, Camden Society (1840): 108–11. This copy bears the signatures of 95 members of Lincoln's Inn, headed by Sir Thomas Egerton, then Solicitor-General (the original is in the Huntington Library, MS. EL 1193). A letter from Henry Killigrew to William

Davison of 29 December 1580 is suggestive of the background to the Association in the Dutch arena: 'God defend the good Prynce of Orange ... If he were taken from us we might here in Ingland justly feare ...' (NA, S.P. 15/27/65). See David Cressy, 'Binding the nation: the Bonds of Association, 1584–1696', in *Tudor Rule and Revolution: Essays for G. R. Elton from his American Friends*, ed. Delloyd J. Guth and John W. McKenna (Cambridge, 1982), pp. 217–34. See also Alison Heisch, 'Arguments for an execution: Queen Elizabeth's "white paper" and Lord Burghley's "blue pencil"', *Albion*, 24 (1992): 591–604.

40 Examples in NA, S.P. 12/174.

41 Perhaps it did. Lord Burghley wrote in November 1585: 'A grett multitude of people both of gentlemen and Merchants and vulgar people especially in good towns, where they be taught by discreet preachers, very zelous towards God, and thereby earnestly bent to all services for hir Majestie savety' ('The state of the Queene and the realm by Gods provydens'; NA, S.P. 12/184/50).

42 Thomas Scott and Edward Boys to Sir Francis Walsingham, 20 November 1584, NA, S.P. 12/176/9. For Mary Stuart's willingness to sign, see Peter Holmes, *Resistance and Compromise: The Political Thought of the Elizabethan Catholics* (Cambridge, 1982), p. 179.

43 Earl of Derby to Earl of Leicester, 7 November 1584; NA, S.P. 12/175/4.

44 Digges's paper is headed: 'The daungers that may in sue by the oath of Assotiacon hereafter yf yt bee not qualified by a convenient Acte of Parlament'; NA, S.P. 12/176/26; further copies in Folger Shakespeare Library, MS. V.b.303, fos 95–9, BL, MS. Lansdowne 98, fos 14–18, MS. Add. 38823, fos 14ff.

45 Collinson, 'The monarchical republic of Queen Elizabeth I'.

46 NA, S.P. 12/176/11, 22, 23, 25, 28, 30; Huntington Library, MS. EL 1192.

47 NA, S.P. 12/176/26.

48 NA, S.P. 12/176/28.

49 *Proceedings in Parliament 1610*, ed. Elizabeth Read Foster (New Haven, Conn., 1966), vol. 2, p. 301.

50 In the 1621 Parliament, John Pym called for 'somme speedy course against Papists', 'the enemy at home', and proposed 'that every man may take his oath of association or not to be admitted into the Commonwealth'; 'an Oath of Association to be taken and framed for the defence of your Majesty's person, and for the maintenance and execution of the laws made for the establishing of religion' (*Commons Debates 1621*, ed. Wallace Notestein, Frances Helen Relf, Hartley Simpson [New Haven, Conn., 1935], vol. 3, pp. 461–2; Edward Nicholas, *Proceedings and Debates in the House of Commons in 1620 and 1621* [Oxford, 1766], vol. 2, pp. 239–40). In May 1641 in the Long Parliament, the reaction to the army plot led to demands for an oath of association on the Elizabethan model, this leading directly to the Protestation (Conrad Russell, *The Fall of the British Monarchies 1637–1642* [Oxford, 1991], pp. 294–5). I am grateful to Professor Conrad Russell for these references. He informs me that the seal of Pym's uncle John Colles is still attached to the original Somerset Bond in NA, S.P. 12/174.

51 Cressy, 'Binding the nation'.

52 The words occur at p. 336 in the exchanges which follow 'Remarks upon the New Project of Association, in a Letter to a Friend' and 'A modest Vindication of the Earl of

Shaftesbury: In a Letter to a Friend concerning his being elected King of Poland', in *The Somers Collection of Tracts*, vol. 8 (London, 1812), pp. 303–42. Some of this material was 'fixed' on Lord Halifax. The respondent may have been Shaftesbury himself. I am indebted to the Revd Dr Andrew Coleby, who first drew this material to my attention.

53 On the history of the quasi-Elizabethan Association in the exclusion crisis, see Haley, *First Earl of Shaftesbury*, pp. 471, 483, 516, 603, 614–15, 677, 687, 692, 694.

54 Jones, *The First Whigs*, p. 146.

55 *Somers Tracts*, vol. 8, pp. 305–13.

56 *Somers Tracts*, vol. 8, pp. 326–31.

57 Jones, *The First Whigs*, p. 146; *Somers Tracts*, vol. 8, pp. 329–30. Professor J. P. Kenyon described the supposedly 'national' Association of 1696 as 'that bitter faction instrument' (*Robert Spencer Earl of Sunderland 1641–1702* [London, 1958], p. 322).

58 NA, S.P. 12/173/87, 88.

59 Quoted, Penry Williams, *The Tudor Regime* (Oxford, 1979), p. 32. A particularly striking example of mutual wound-licking among Elizabeth's principal servants is the letter of Sir Francis Walsingham to Lord Burghley of 27 May 1580, when the lord treasurer was out of favour. 'I would to God her Majestye were not so easely drawn to be an instrument to execute others passyons ... lettynge her understande howe greatly yt wyll discorage others that succeed you ... I nothing dowbt, but in tyme, her Maiestie whoe of her owne nature is inclyned to deale gratyowsly with every boddye wyll see her error ... And so commyttyng your lordship to the protectyon of him whoe hathe the hartes of prynces in his handes ...' (NA, S.P. 12/138/26).

60 Joel Hurstfield, 'Was there a Tudor despotism after all?', in his *Freedom, Corruption and Government in Elizabethan England* (London, 1973), pp. 23–49.

61 David Starkey, 'Which Age of Reform?', in *Revolution Reassessed: Revisions in the history of Tudor government and administration*, ed. Christopher Coleman and David Starkey (Oxford, 1986), pp. 13–27.

62 Thomas Elyot, *The Boke Named the Governour* (1531), fo. 1.

63 Whitney R. D. Jones, *The Tudor Commonwealth 1529–1559* (London, 1970); see also Whitney R. D. Jones, *The Mid-Tudor Crisis 1539–1563* (London, 1973).

64 G. R. Elton, 'Reform and the "Commonwealth-Men" of Edward VI's reign', in *Studies in Tudor and Stuart Politics and Government*, vol. 3, pp. 234–53.

65 The tradition runs back to Frederic Seebohm, *The Oxford Reformers: John Colet, Erasmus and Thomas More, being a history of their fellow-work* (London, 1869); and can be traced through J. K. McConica, *English Humanists and Reformation Politics Under Henry VIII and Edward VI* (Oxford, 1965).

66 J. G. A. Pocock, *The Machiavellian Moment: Florentine political thought and the Atlantic republican tradition* (Princeton, N.J., 1975). For a more positive but still limited appreciation of the persistence of civic humanist values in later sixteenth-century England, see A. B. Ferguson, *The Articulate Citizen and the English Renaissance* (Durham, N.C., 1965).

67 Brendan Bradshaw, 'The Tudor commonwealth: reform and revision', *Historical Journal*, 22 (1979): 474. See also Brendan Bradshaw, '*Humanitas* and the Christian commonwealth', in *Cambridge History of Political Thought 1450–1700*, pp. 114–31.

68 I share an interest in Elizabethan commonwealth discourse and owe much of my sense of it to Dr William Sherman. See his *John Dee: The Politics of Reading and Writing in the English Renaissance* (Amherst, Mass., 1995), especially ch. 6, '*Brytannicae Reipublicae Synopsis*: a reader's guide to the Elizabethan commonwealth'. I am grateful to Dr Sherman for sharing with me an article which was later published as 'Anatomizing the commonwealth: language, politics and the Elizabethan social order', in Elizabeth Fowler and Roland Greene, eds, *The Project of Prose in Early modern European and New World Writing* (Cambridge, 1997), pp. 104–21.

69 'Morrells Manufacture for the Newe draperie into Three Bookes', Huntington Library, MS. HM 53654. This is a substantial treatise of 100 pages.

70 I owe this point to Bill Sherman. It has particular reference to his work on John Dee.

71 M. A. R. Graves, 'The management of the Elizabethan House of Commons: the Council's "Men-of-Business"', *Parliamentary History*, vol. 2 (1983), pp. 11–38; M. A. R. Graves, 'Thomas Norton the Parliament Man: an Elizabethan M.P. 1559–1581', *Historical Journal*, 23 (1980): 17–35.

72 Lisa Jardine and Anthony Grafton, '"Studied for action": How Gabriel Harvey read his Livy', *Past and Present*, no. 129 (1990): 30–78.

73 These words of Norton deserve quotation in full: 'Among the thinges here advised by aucthoritie in England, which it hath greatly greved me for my contreys sake and for my reverence to the power of her Maiestie and her Counsell to see not followed or not to proceade to the gracious effectes required, I have sometime noted these following and I confesse I have busied my selfe to thinke of some meanes of remedie to be offred secretly to some such personages of her Maiesties counsell as might by power do somewhat toward reformation.' A varied list of topics follows (BL, MS. Add. 48023, fo. 28ᵛ). Norton warned Sir Francis Walsingham that the burdens placed upon him had won him the reputation of a 'busy body' (*Ibid.*, fo. 42ᵛ).

74 Walsingham wrote to the lieutenant of the Tower, apparently without irony: 'Sir for that Mr Norton is presently at leysure by reason of his restraint of his libertie ...' (BL, MS. Add. 48023, fo. 41). Drafts of Norton's 'Devices' sent to Walsingham as they were completed are in BL, MS. Add. 48023, fos 45–8, 49ᵛ–51, 51ᵛ–2ᵛ, 53ᵛ–6ᵛ, 57ʳ; copies of the completed Devices in NA, S.P. 12/177/59, fos 143–70, BL, MS. Lansdowne 155, fos 87ff. For the case of Robert Beale, see Collinson, *Elizabethan Essays*, p. 82.

75 NA, S.P. 15/21/121. See Patrick Collinson, *The Elizabethan Puritan Movement* (London, 1967), pp. 144–5. For Carleton more generally, see Hasler, vol. I, pp. 552–4.

76 J. E. Neale, 'The Elizabethan acts of supremacy and uniformity', *English Historical Review*, 65 (1950): 304–32; Neale, *Elizabeth I and her Parliaments, 1559–1581*, pp. 37–8, 51–3; Norman L. Jones, *Faith by Statute: Parliament and the settlement of religion 1559* (London, 1982), *passim*. The 'Device' is printed (from BL, MS. Cotton Julius F.6, fo. 161) in Henry Gee, *The Elizabethan Prayer-Book & Ornaments: With an Appendix of documents* (London, 1902), pp. 195–202.

77 This memorandum exists in two states among the Egerton manuscripts in the Huntington Library: MS. EL 2580 and MS. EL 2625. The two documents share the same heading and endorsement and early paragraphs are nearly identical. But EL 2625 subsequently diverges into a wider range of topics, monetary, commercial and fiscal.

78 *John Stubbs's Gaping Gulf With Letters and Other Relevant Documents*, ed. Lloyd E. Berry, Folger Documents of Tudor and Stuart Civilization (Charlottesville, 1968). Stubbs's

letters suggest a strong sense of common evangelical commitment within a network of like-minded, semi-public men. See a letter to William Davison of 30 April 1578: 'The Lord knit us faster and faster in our faith, and love and hope of everlasting life, where we shall be forever together with our head, Jesus Christ, whom I beseech to keep you ever his for his mercy' (*John Stubbs's Gaping Gulf*, pp. 106–7).

79 'Lord Henry Howard's answer to *The Gaping Gulf*', in *John Stubbs's Gaping Gulf*, pp. 155–94.

80 Kenneth Barnes, 'John Stubbe, 1579: the French Ambassador's account', *Historical Research*, 64 (1991): 421–6.

81 The reference is to the diary of the Cornishman, William Carnsewe (NA, S.P. 46/16) which records (fos 39ᵛ–40ʳ, 42ʳ) receiving in 1576 'the Admonition of Cartwright for the new order of discipline, and the slipping of the Church of England', reading it, and passing it on to 'Ford the preacher'. Carnsewe presumably referred to *A Second Admonition to the Parliament*, which had been printed four years earlier. From his diary and other sources it is clear that Carnsewe was a strongly committed Protestant, not to say Puritan. He was a Member of the 1559 Parliament and of no other parliament, which tends to confirm a point made earlier in this lecture. He was a neighbour and close friend of the Grenvilles (Hasler, vol. 1, p. 557).

82 The letter from the Privy Council 'for suppressing a certen book intituled the gaping gulf', dated 5 October 1579, was copied into the register of Bishop Woolton of Exeter in full. I owe this reference to Jane Ladley.

83 H. J. Byrom, 'Edmund Spenser's First Printer, Hugh Singleton', *Library*, 4th ser. 14 (1933): 121–56. However, John King doubts whether Singleton is properly described as a specialist 'Puritan' publisher (John N. King, *Spenser's Poetry and the Reformation Tradition* [Princeton, N.J., 1990], Appendix, 'Was Spenser a puritan?', pp. 233–8). See also Anthea Hume, *Edmund Spenser: Protestant Poet* (Cambridge, 1984) and Paul McLane, *Spenser's 'Shepheardes Calender': A Study in Elizabethan Allegory* (Notre Dame, 1961). For the Grindal angle, see Patrick Collinson, 'The downfall of Archbishop Grindal and its place in Elizabethan political and ecclesiastical history', in Collinson, *Godly People: Essays on English Protestantism and Puritanism* (London, 1983), pp. 371–97; Patrick Collinson, *Archbishop Grindal 1519–1583: The struggle for a Reformed Church* (London, 1979).

84 Collinson, 'Puritans, men of business and Elizabethan parliaments', in Collinson, *Elizabethan Essays*, pp. 73–6.

85 Barnes, 'John Stubbe, 1579'.

86 Graves, 'The management of the Elizabethan House of Commons', 'Thomas Norton the Parliament Man'.

87 Jardine and Grafton, 'Studied for action'.

88 J. H. M. Salmon, 'Seneca and Tacitus in Jacobean England', in *The Mental World of the Jacobean Court*, ed. Linda Levy Peck (Cambridge, 1991), pp. 169–88. An earlier version of this essay appeared in *The Journal of the History of Ideas*, 50 (1989): 199–225, under the title 'Stoicism and Roman example: Seneca and Tacitus in Jacobean England'.

89 *The First and Second Parts of John Hayward's The Life and Raigne of King Henrie IIII*, ed. John J. Manning, Camden 4th ser. 62 (1991).

90 *Ibid*. See also Blair Worden, 'Ben Jonson among the historians', in *Culture and Politics in Early Stuart England*, ed. Kevin Sharpe and Peter Lake (Basingstoke, 1994), pp. 67–

89; Lisa Richardson, 'Sir John Hayward and early Stuart historiography', unpublished Ph.D. thesis, University of Cambridge (1999).

91 *Annals of the First Four Years of the Reign of Queen Elizabeth, By Sir John Hayward*, ed. J. Bruce, Camden Society (1840), p. 1.

92 Sir Philip Sidney, *The Countess of Pembroke's Arcadia (The Old Arcadia)*, ed. Katherine Duncan-Jones, World's Classics (Oxford, 1985), p. 277. I am grateful to Blair Worden for drawing this striking parallel to my attention.

93 *The Correspondence of Sir Philip Sidney and Hubert Languet*, tr. Stuart A. Pears (London, 1845). See Richard C. McCoy, *Sir Philip Sidney: Rebellion in Arcadia* (Hassocks, 1979). Sidney's 'Discourse to the Queenes Majesty Touching Hir Mariage with Monsieur' is in *The Prose Works of Sir Philip Sidney*, ed. Albert Feuillerat (London, 1912), vol. 3, pp. 51–60; and forms a set piece in Greville's *Life*.

94 *The Countess of Pembroke's Arcadia*, p. 7; *Prose Works of Sidney*, vol. 3, p. 60.

95 *Gorboduc or Ferrex and Porrex by Thomas Sackville and Thomas Norton*, ed. Irby B. Cauthen (Lincoln, Nebr., 1970); Axton, *The Queen's Two Bodies*.

96 John Guy, 'The 1590s: the second reign of Elizabeth I?', in John Guy, ed., *The Reign of Elizabeth I: Court and culture in the last decade* (Cambridge, 1995), pp. 1–19.

97 Margaret Aston, *The King's Bedpost: Reformation and iconography in a Tudor group portrait* (Cambridge, 1994), 'Elizabeth as Hezekiah', pp. 113–27, and *passim*.

98 Laurence Humphrey, *The Nobles, or of Nobilitye* (1563), Epistle.

99 Hasler, vol. 2, pp. 238–9. The character of 'the hottest' refers to his intemperate intervention in the politics of the succession, which led to imprisonment in the Fleet and the Tower and 'ruined him'.

100 *The Acts and Monuments of John Foxe*, ed. S. R. Cattley, vol. 8 (London, 1839), pp. 677–8.

101 Cambridge University Library, class mark SSS.18.19.

102 Hartley, pp. 58–62.

103 *Ibid.*, p. 134. This is the speech variously ascribed to Lambarde and Molyneux (see n. 8 above).

104 Hartley, p. 275. The biblical reference is to 1 Samuel 15:11.

105 *Ibid.*, p. 278.

106 The speaker was Richard Gallys, a townsman and innkeeper of Windsor (Hasler, vol. 2, p. 163). This version of his words was recorded by an anonymous diarist. Thomas Cromwell's version would have it that Gallys said: 'She may have her head cutt of and noe more harme done to her' (Hartley, pp. 324, 349).

107 Gerald Bowler, 'English Protestants and resistance theory, 1553–1603', unpublished Ph.D. thesis, London 1981, pp. 291 *et seq.*

108 Patrick Collinson, *The English Captivity of Mary Queen of Scots* (Sheffield, 1987), pp. 4–5.

109 Hartley, pp. 274–82, 283, 408.

110 Christopher Hill, *The English Bible and the Seventeenth-Century Revolution* (London, 1993), p. 218. And see much more to the same effect in Hill's chapter 'The Bible and radical politics', pp. 196–250. On the politics of the Geneva Bible marginalia, see also Richard L. Greaves, 'Traditionalism and the seeds of revolution in the social principles

of the Geneva Bible', *Sixteenth-Century Journal*, 7 (1976): 94–109, Richard L. Greaves, 'The nature and intellectual milieu of the political principles in the Geneva Marginalia', *Journal of Church and State*, 22 (1980): 233–49.

111 This paragraph owes much to Dr Bowler's thesis, 'English Protestants and resistance writings. And see his article, '"An Axe or an Acte": the Parliament of 1572 and resistance theory in early Elizabethan England', *Canadian Journal of History*, 19 (1984): 349–59.

112 Skinner, *Foundations of Modern Political Thought*, vol. 2, pp. 221–2.

113 'xxim. Jan. 1584 [/5] De Interregno'. This 'platt' (as it describes itself) survives among Sir Walter Mildmay's papers, Northamptonshire Record Office, MS. F.(M) P.184. I am grateful to the Trustees of the Late Earl Fitzwilliam for permission to cite the Fitzwilliam of Milton papers.

114 Collinson, *Archbishop Grindal*, pp. 259–61. Curiously enough, the evidence for this meeting also survives, uniquely, among Mildmay's papers.

115 J. E. Neale, *Elizabeth I and her Parliaments 1584–1601* (London, 1957), pp. 44–5; Hasler, vol. 2, p. 38. Neale also attributes to Digges a related paper recommending the raising of an emergency military force of 40,000 (BL, MS. Lansdowne 119, fos 123–32).

116 Copies in NA, S.P. 12/176/32; and Northamptonshire Record Office, MSS. F.(M) P.96, F.(M) P.4. Stanford Lehmberg (*Sir Walter Mildmay and Tudor Government* [Austin, Tex., 1964], pp. 248–9), who attributes the brief discourse to Digges, identifies MS. F.(M) P.4 as the discourse converted into a speech which Mildmay may have intended to make.

117 There is a cross-reference at this point to 'a particular Breef discourse of that matter'; i.e. BL, MS. Lansdowne 199, fos 123–32. This strengthens the case for attributing 'De Interregno' to Digges.

118 This is followed in the copy in Mildmay's papers (MS. F. [M] P. 96) by 'A conference of your majesties sacred estates Royall with this Patterne of the Prince of Orange'.

119 I have benefited from discussing these points with Professor Wallace T. MacCaffrey.

Chapter 3

Servants and citizens: Robert Beale and other Elizabethans

It was a great honour, and a provocation to many a nostalgic wander down memory lane, to have been invited to deliver the original version of this chapter as a paper at the Tudor and Stuart seminar to honour the memory of Joan Henderson. When I first arrived at the Institute of Historical Research in October 1952, Joan was already there. I did not presume to guess for how long she had been there, but as the years went by it was as if she had been part of the furniture of the place for ever. She was one of a number of extraordinarily diligent women whom Professor Sir John Neale – her supervisor and mine – had recruited to share his lifelong addiction to the subject of Elizabethan parliaments, approached through what he called the biographical method, an idea borrowed from another century, and from Sir Lewis Namier. In 1950, at an Anglo-American Conference, Neale announced: 'I am gradually having the parliaments of Elizabeth's reign ... studied in this way.'[1] Who did the studying? Well there was Helen Miller, who received a generous and just tribute in the preface to the first volume of *Elizabeth I and her Parliaments* ('I owe a special debt to Miss Helen Miller'). There was a rather less generous reference to the sterling work of Norah Fuidge ('these figures are taken from a London M.A. thesis on the personnel of this Parliament [the Parliament of 1563] by a student of mine, Miss Norah Fuidge. I have revised them').[2]

One looks in vain in the second volume for any reference to Joan Henderson's work on the Members of Parliament of 1589. But perhaps she would not have minded all that much. A more generous and self-effacing scholar one could never hope to meet. If she was always there, it was never to advance herself but to pursue a lifelong and selfless devotion to the discipline of history, and

Revised version of a paper given at the Tudor and Stuart Seminar at the Institute of Historical Research on 8 November 2004. Published in *Historical Research*, 79 (2006): 488–511, and reproduced by permission of the Institute of Historical Research and Wiley-Blackwell.

to help, whenever she could, a great many younger, apprentice historians, who included myself. And she did as much for generations of pupils at the secondary level of their education, at least two of them destined to become illustrious household names: Lord Tebbit and Sir Roy Strong, who sat in the same class.

As was said of Sir Christopher Wren, *si monumentum requiris, circumspice*. In the case of Joan Henderson, your circumspection should be directed to the three volumes and 1,892 pages of the Elizabethan section of the *History of Parliament*, in itself a monument to Sir John Neale's biographical method, resembling those grandiose baroque tombs of his beloved Elizabethans. No, I sell it short; this was an entire Elizabethan mausoleum.[3] Joan Henderson's initials appear below no fewer than sixty of the biographies of Members of Parliament of which these three volumes largely consist. All of Joan's subjects had been members of the 1589 parliament, twenty-four of them of that parliament only.

'Other Elizabethans'! To scan these biographical articles is to be reminded how little we know about most of those Elizabethans, sufficiently important to themselves and to their families, their friends and their enemies, important enough to be returned to Westminster: inhabitants of little worlds we have lost, in spite of our best endeavours. 'Little is known of him', 'very little is known', 'little has been ascertained': these are phrases which make a litany (as they constituted the agenda for many a seminar on Monday evenings in the England Room of the Institute of Historical Research, back in those same 1950s).[4] But, of course, these little pieces of agnosticism conceal a great many painstaking but often unprofitable hours spent in the archives.

However, among Joan Henderson's sixty Members of Parliament are some whom A. L. Rowse would have called 'eminent Elizabethans', as well as others who, if not exactly eminent, were – well – interesting. They include Anthony Ashley, Member for Tavistock in 1589 and for Old Sarum in 1593, who at the age of seventy-one, 'in his dotage', according to John Chamberlain, married the daughter of a leading courtier, 'by whom he hath promise or expectation to become some great man'. Ashley himself was never a great man, but by his first marriage he had a grandson who was: Anthony Ashley Cooper, earl of Shaftesbury.[5] And then there was Thomas Atkins, Member for Gloucester in six parliaments, including 1589, a quarrelsome man, who in the 1572 parliament described Mary Queen of Scots as 'the burthen of the earth', but who was himself burdensome to his enemies in the Welsh marches, who called him 'corrupt and partial' and complained of his 'unjust and indirect dealings'.[6] George Beeston, Member for Cheshire in 1589, his only parliament, was recovering at the time from fighting against the Spanish Armada, it was said at the age of eighty-nine, although he seems to have been no more than sixty-eight. But it is undeniable that in 1588 he had commanded four 'great ships', including the *Dreadnought*, and had been knighted on board the *Ark Royal*.[7]

His son, Hugh Beeston, was a sturdy parliamentarian. In 1601 he complained that those in the lower end of the House of Commons could not hear what the Speaker was saying. He was there to represent the town of Bodmin, but he belonged to Denbighshire, and, he declared, 'if I should not speak somewhat for my country, I dare not go thither again'.[8]

William Cecil (Stamford, 1589) was the ne'er-do-well grandson of Lord Burghley who in his youth sowed wild oats in Italy, fell into debt in his maturity and illegally married a thirteen-year-old who died in childbirth, but in due course inherited the earldom of Exeter and became a Privy Councillor.[9] Oliver Cromwell (Huntingdonshire in 1589 and in seven more parliaments) had a more famous nephew, who inherited his name.[10] Peter Eure (Lincoln, 1589) was another parliamentarian to marry a young wife in old age. According to Chamberlain he had been 'hammering about her all last term'.[11] Sir Francis Godolphin (Cornwall, 1569) was a great man in that county, and in the Scilly Isles, the chief organiser of beacons and fortifications at the time of the Armada.[12]

Edward Hoby, who sat in nine parliaments and was Member for Berkshire in 1589, was the son of a famous father, Sir Thomas Hoby, and of a no less illustrious mother, the learned Elizabeth Cooke, the sister-in-law of Burghley, who from her second marriage was known as Lady Elizabeth Russell. Lady Russell was a formidable character and the younger Hoby was an awkward customer. In 1589 he complained that the business of the House was being leaked to outsiders, who included – guess who – his uncle, Lord Burghley, 'being no member of this House'. In 1601, he picked up words spoken by Burghley's son, his cousin Sir Robert Cecil, that 'Mr Speaker shall attend my lord keeper'. 'Attend? It is well known that the Speaker of the House is the mouth of the whole realm, and that the whole state of the commonalty of a kingdom should attend one person I see no reason ... Our Speaker is to be commanded by none, neither to attend any, but the Queen only.'[13]

George More sat in twelve parliaments between 1584 and 1626, always for Surrey or the county town of Guildford, the very model of an Elizabethan godly magistrate. In 1601 he joined the campaign against monopolies ('this eating and filthy disease of monopolies I have ever detested with my heart'), even while he opposed making use of the issue to put pressure on a queen who 'in her clemency and care to us hath taken the matter into her own hands': sturdiness controlled by judicious self-censorship.[14] Sir Henry Saville, a great scholar, was Member for Bossinney in 1589, his career neatly compassed by Joan Henderson in 292 words.[15]

Such were some of Joan's Elizabethans. Among this motley crew of Members of Parliament there are names which justify my title of 'servants and citizens'. Thomas Atkins, Hugh Beeston, Edward Hoby, George More, all from time to time spoke and conducted themselves as if they belonged to a republic, to what Sir Thomas Smith called *Republica Anglorum*, not only servants and subjects of a monarch but patriots and citizens of a national common-wealth. Even Saville was significant for more than disinterested scholarship. His translation of Tacitus appeared at a critical juncture in political history, and had important political implications and repercussions.[16] But the most important biography which Joan Henderson contributed to the Elizabethan volumes of *The History of Parliament* was undoubtedly that of Robert Beale. And Beale for Joan was not a line of duty chore but the study of a lifetime. We shall return to Citizen Beale.

Elizabethan politics and public life, whether inside or outside parliament, brought into dynamic interaction, sometimes collision, two forces which were almost contradictory but each typical of the tendencies of the age. These were monarchy with aspirations to be authoritative, even in some sense absolute; and a public ethic of civic humanism which emphasised the duty to the body politic, the commonwealth, shared, according to rank, degree and responsibil-ity, by all of its members, who may be defined as adult males and household-ers. Sir Thomas Smith, in that book *De Republica Anglorum*, defined the com-monwealth as 'a society or common doing of a multitude of free men collected together and united by common accord and covenants among themselves for the conservation of themselves as well in peace as in war', which sounds like an account of what we should call a republic, consisting of consenting, co-operating citizens.[17] In nine successive editions in translation, Smith's book bore the title *The common-wealth of England, and the maner of gouernment thereof.* A Venetian ambassador observed that England was 'quasi come repub-lica' (almost like a republic).[18]

There was no reason, in contemporary perception, why commonwealths, even republics, should not also be monarchies. Most were. As Algernon Sidney wrote, later in the seventeenth century: 'All monarchies in the world which are not purely barbarous and tyrannical have ever been commonwealths.'[19] So, in the same book, Smith said that the kingdom of England was 'absolute'. The prince was 'the life, the head, and the authority of all things that be done in the realm of England'.[20]

There was a way to reconcile these apparently irreconcilable principles, which was to define England as a mixed monarchy, 'not a mere monar-chy ... nor a mere oligarchy nor democracy but a rule mixed of all these'. But that is someone else speaking, the future bishop John Aylmer in 1559, and Smith never used the expression 'mixed monarchy'. Rather, it has been said, his account of the English constitution was a muddle. We are told that he says 'a great many things, some of them contradictory, many of them simply divergent and unreconciled'. But since Smith claimed to be describing not a 'feigned commonwealth', like More's *Utopia*, but the way things actually were, if there was a muddle it was not in Smith's head but in the constitution of

England as he accurately observed and described it.[21]

Sentiments of a kind of patriotic republicanism, nourished by a neo-classical education, were certainly far more prevalent in Elizabethan public discourse than has been acknowledged in the past.[22] The English renaissance in that sense had not terminated with Henry VIII's execution of Sir Thomas More and other acts which even judicious historians are tempted to call barbarous and tyrannical. So far as the reign of his younger daughter was concerned, it is as if eyes have been blinded to the contours of the political landscape by the dazzling sunlike glare of the Gloriana queen. Bridging the worlds of More and the Elizabethans, Cathy Shrank in her important book *Writing the Nation in Reformation England* has shown how deeply implicit was a civic national consciousness in the explorations of the English language for a variety of purposes by such mid-Tudor figures as Andrew Borde, John Leland, William Thomas, Thomas Smith and Thomas Wilson. There are similar insights in Tom Betteridge's still more recent *Literature and Politics in the English Reformation*.[23]

The Elizabethans might have pretended to have been blinded, but in truth they were not, and the best of them, in this well-established tradition of Protestant humanism, were equally devoted to their *patria*, their native country. There was a cracked gramophone record which a certain kind of Elizabethan, patriot and citizen as much as subject, never tired of playing, and the tune had been composed by Marcus Tullius Cicero in his *De officiis*.

> Mr Speaker, the heathen man Tully said that man is not born for himself only, but partly for his parents, partly for his children, and partly for his country. And surely Mr Speaker, I do condemn him as very unnatural that regardeth neither parents [nor] children, and him most unnatural and unworthy to live in any commonwealth that regardeth not his country.[24]

The speaker was a member of the 1567 parliament. And here is Sir Thomas Smith, writing his dialogue about the social ills of the commonwealth against the background of the political crisis of the summer of 1549:

> Albeit I am not of the King's Council ... yet, knowing myself to be a member of the same Commonweal and called to be one of the Common House, where such things ought to be treated of, I cannot reckon myself a mere stranger to this matter no more than a man that were in a ship might say that, because he is not percase the master or pilot of the same, the danger thereof did pertain nothing to him.[25]

The image of a ship in danger was another of those Ciceronian cracked records.

The circumstances of Elizabethan politics, more especially in the central decades of the reign, the 1570s and 1580s, tended to place in opposition the monarchical and republican elements in the constitution. Not that anyone at any time expressed what we should call republican, in the sense of anti-monarchical, sentiments. One could say that in the mindset of Elizabethan citizens monarchy was much too important a matter to be left to monarchs. That is the political message of Sir Philip Sidney's romantic fiction *Arcadia*.[26] The particular circumstances were the queen's singularity, as the last of her direct line, her sex, her disinclination to marry and produce an heir, and her repeated refusal to name a successor; and also her sustained disinclination to engage actively in the geopolitical struggle developing between Catholic and Protestant Europe. The unresolved succession issue provoked, in the parliament of 1567, outbursts like these: 'Her Majesty ought to be an upholder, and not an overthrower of her people.' The threatening word 'ought' was repeated five times in the sentences which immediately followed. 'Since the Queen in respect of her own safety is not to be induced hereunto, let us make petition she will do it in respect of our safety.'[27]

The question, by the time we get to the parliament of 1572, was the exclusion from the succession of Mary Queen of Scots, whether by execution or by an act disabling her from succeeding to the crown of England. In the event, Elizabeth allowed neither remedy, neither an axe nor an act.[28] It was the bishops who took her to task in almost menacing terms for her failure to provide not only for her personal safety but for the safety and future of the commonwealth: 'In conscience ought she to have a singular care of her safety, if not for her self sake yet at the least for the furtherance of God's cause and stay of her country, to the maintenance whereof she is bound before God.' The bishops defined the monarch as 'the minister of God and a public person', which was close to the reasoning of near-republicans like the Scottish intellectual George Buchanan that the office of monarch was no different from any other public office – publicly accountable. It was also an office from which he, or more properly she, could be displaced. The bishops in their memorandum of 1572 referred several times to Mary Stuart as 'the late Queen of Scots', evidently sharing the view of lay parliamentarians that she was 'a queen of late time and yet through her own acts now justly no queen', which was fully to endorse the politics of Buchanan.[29] And in all this rhetoric there was an implicit suggestion that Elizabeth was acting more like a tyrant than a true monarch, since Thomas Smith had defined a tyrant as one who 'regardeth not the wealth of his people'.[30] Two Members of Parliament were bold enough to assert that if the queen continued to be 'unmindful' of their safety, 'her true and faithful subjects, despairing of safety by her means, shall be forced to seek protection elsewhere'.[31] What kept Elizabeth secure on her throne was not so much the unthinking devotion with which historians like Neale credited her subjects as that in practice they had nowhere else to look.

It was in the Privy Council that the shoe pinched and that the dilemma of early modern monarchy was most acutely felt.[32] In 1586, when the question of what was to be done about Mary Stuart still hung in the balance, Elizabeth's secretary of state, Sir Francis Walsingham, wrote: 'I would to God her Majesty would be content to refer these things to them that can best judge of them, as other princes do.'[33] At the crux of the Anjou marriage negotiations in 1578, with Dutch affairs also high on the agenda, Burghley wrote, despairingly: 'A strange thing it is to see God's goodness, so abundantly offered for her Majesty's surety, to be so daintily hearkened unto.'[34]

The problem of counsel, classically stated by Sir Thomas More in *Utopia*, was ultimately insoluble, in both political practice and conscience. This was how none other than Lord Burghley attempted to square the circle towards the end of a forty-year career as a councillor:

> I do hold and will always this course in such matters as I differ in opinion from her Majesty as long as I may be allowed to give advice. I will not change my opinion by affirming the contrary, for that were to offend God, to whom I am sworn first. But as a servant I will obey her Majesty's commandments and no wise contrary the same, presuming that she, being God's chief minister here, it shall be God's will to have her commandments obeyed, after that I have performed my duty as a counsellor.[35]

Twenty-five years earlier, he had written: 'Our parts is to counsel, and also to obey the commander.'[36] A lesser functionary, William Davison, was advised by his superiors not to allow his private opinions to colour the advice he gave as an ambassador: 'You are to be commanded, and bound to follow the bounds of your charge by just limitation. And although things be sometimes ordered much against your mind, yet you must submit yourself to the same.'[37]

It was not only in the highest counsels of state that the dilemma was faced. The essence of religious non-conformity had been stated by St Peter in the Acts of the Apostles. Often, perhaps normally, to obey God was to obey God's agents, earthly rulers. So St Paul in Romans. But in the last resort it was necessary to obey God rather than man. So religious persons were even more aware than politicians of where their higher duties lay. In his famous and fatal letter to the queen of 1576, Archbishop Edmund Grindal requested that she should 'not use to pronounce so resolutely and peremptorily, *quasi ex auctoritate*, as ye may do in civil and extern matters'.[38] The consequence of his letter, and of his conscientious refusal to obey an explicit royal order, was suspension, threatened deprivation, and the end of a career: whereas at equally critical moments none of Elizabeth's Privy Councillors was ever actually sacked, not even Walsingham, for all that Elizabeth detested him and his all too intrusive advice. The most overt confrontation of the two great political principles in contention in Elizabethan England was between Presbyterianism and an essentially monarchical hierarchical principle. No bishop, no king. Not, of course, that Grindal was a Presbyterian. Rather, he foreshadowed those bishops and other senior clerics who in the years to come would draw their own lines in the sand beyond which the power of the prince and magistrate ought not to trespass.[39]

From here on I deal not with Lord Burghley, nor with Archbishop Grindal, nor with Presbyterians and neo-Episcopalians, but with those Elizabethans, public men but below the rank of Privy Councillor, whom we are entitled to acknowledge as citizens of Elizabethan England, not merely subjects. They were not Privy Councillors; and yet they seem to have adhered to a concept of counsel which was much wider than the limited numbers of those admitted and sworn to the Privy Council. Usually implicit rather than explicit in expression, these Elizabethan citizens had a view of their political world in which counsel was a duty more widely imposed than any narrow definition, and a kind of right; a right as well as a duty of any responsible member of the English commonwealth, and, for many, a God-given right, or rather obligation. This comes through from a good deal of oratory in the Elizabethan House of Commons, the assertion that any Member of Parliament was by that title a counsellor; even that he, as a representative of electors and constituents, stood for many others who were equally what Tony Blair might call stakeholders, not only in their own local communities but in the commonwealth of England. These were not political theorists but the men who were actually doing the hands-on work of government, whether in local administration, financial management or foreign diplomacy. William Davison, ambassador in the Netherlands and answerable to the secretariat of state, in effect to the foreign office, was told not to allow his own opinions to colour the reports he sent over. But Davison was on the spot. He wrote of himself: 'I living here where I see and observe how things pass.'[40]

When Peter Wentworth was examined about his scandalous speech in parliament in 1576, the speech which was halted in its tracks when he uttered those unforgivable words, 'none is without fault, no, not our noble Queen', he told a committee of parliament gathered in the star chamber which probably consisted mainly of Privy Councillors:

> I am now no private person; I am a public and a counsellor to the whole state in that place ... And therefore, if you ask me as counsellors to her Majesty, you shall pardon me; I will make no answer. But if you ask me as committees from the House, I will then willingly make you the best answer I can.[41]

The distinction between 'counsellors to her Majesty' and counsellors 'to the whole state' is highly significant. Sir John Neale may have made too much of Peter Wentworth, but Sir Geoffrey Elton made too little of him.[42] We have seen that Sir Thomas Smith claimed that it was his membership of the House of Commons which entitled and obliged him to comment on the issues of the day.

Those who played the kind of role to which Wentworth aspired, and deployed that sort of rhetoric, were called by Elton, and by Professor Michael Graves who dreamed up the term, not 'citizens', not 'public persons', but 'men of business'.[43] For all that 'man of business' has been imported from a later century (you will find it in the novels of Anthony Trollope), the term has its uses. These were in a real and important sense men of business, for the most part ceaselessly busy lawyers. But there are two problems with the way the term has been deployed by Graves and Elton. For one thing, it implies a special client–patron relationship with leading Elizabethan politicians which detracted from the role of active, responsible citizenship which I believe these men were conscious, and capable, of exercising. Graves writes of 'conciliar men of business'. Patron–client relations were the very fabric of early modern society, but they were not exclusive, and they were not the same thing as the relation of master to servant. Our men of business were servants of a broadly conceived English commonwealth, not merely of their patrons in council and court. And for another, 'man of business' was restricted by Graves to men without offices of profit under the crown, as if such offices would in themselves restrict their independence as, let us say again, citizens. It is undeniable that the status of non-office-holders as 'private men' gave them a perhaps deceptively independent and indifferent voice in parliamentary debate, which paradoxically enhanced their political usefulness. The council, or a particular councillor, was often, so to speak, behind the arras. But it is still an unnecessary and limiting restriction. We shall spend most of the rest of this chapter in exploring the career and political outlook of Robert Beale, who held office as clerk to both the Privy Council and the council in the north, stood in from time to time as secretary of state, and performed many other public functions.

Let us focus briefly on the quintessential 'man of business', the 'great parliament man' (as his son described him), 'honest, poor, plain Norton' in Beale's description, Thomas Norton, whose biography Graves has written.[44] Norton was the indispensable link-man between the government and the city of London. Although he was not on the government's pay-roll, Graves is fully entitled to call him an 'establishment man', with friends in high places. As a parliament man, he had drafted more bills than most of his fellow Members of Parliament had had hot dinners. He was frequently called upon by the government to produce white or green papers on this or that, what at the time were called 'Devices'. But in 1582 his outspokenness on public issues, including the state of the church and whether the queen should make an unpopular French marriage, landed him in the Tower, where he had been more accustomed to interview Catholic prisoners on the rack, most recently Edmund Campion. There, in the Bloody Tower, he languished while, in the world outside, his wife lost her reason.[45]

Norton knew that he had been used by men greater than he was, who had then thrown him to the wolves. He told William Fleetwood, the recorder of London and a close colleague: 'You know I took a course in policy, but not plainly, to advance that which the queen's most noble counsellors advised.' He wrote to Burghley, reminding him of the burdens he had borne in the recent parliament, at great risk to himself, since he was well known to have 'too busy a wit'.[46] But it was because of his wit and the fact that Norton was his own man that he had been used to bear those burdens. Prison is often a place to bring out the most profound self-examination. Norton wrote: 'Lord, how I wonder at my self that I should offend my Queen Elizabeth! and therefore no marvel though all the world wonder at me, that wonder at my self.' Yet when Norton told his son 'I have no dealing with the queen but as with the image of God', he did not mean that he made the queen his God but that his higher obedience to God defined and even limited his obedience to the queen. He wrote: 'And surely the only true subjects are whom conscience hath fast tied unto her.'[47]

There is no reason why we should distinguish absolutely between public Beale and private Norton, or between Beale, Norton and William Davison, ambassador and later secretary of state, who in 1587 bore the ultimate burden of the Elizabethan man of business, which was to carry the can for the execution of Mary Queen of Scots. He carried the can for those greater men, Burghley first and foremost, who wanted Mary dead. But that is not to say that Davison was any less determined to secure her execution. Nor is there any reason to put in different categories Norton and James Morice, who was a salaried member of the government as attorney of the court of wards. The earl of Essex wanted him to be made attorney-general, while the formidable Lady Russell thought he ought to become master of the rolls. She wrote to Sir Robert Cecil: 'Poor man ... O good nephew, the gravity, wisdom, care of maintaining the law of the land, learning and piety of the man!' She wrote '*In publicum bonum*', and lamented that God would not allow England to have 'such a public magistrate' as Morice.[48] But Morice, like Norton and, as we shall see, like Beale, suffered from an outspokenness which came from conscience and a heightened civic-mindedness.[49] These were all men of business, but also good and conscientious citizens of the Elizabethan commonwealth, more or less regardless of their formal links with the regime, or lack of such links.

It is time to turn away from these other Elizabethans and to concentrate our attention on Joan Henderson's longstanding friend, Robert Beale. But before I proceed I should acknowledge not only the exemplary inspiration of Joan but the indispensable contribution made to our knowledge of Beale by Dr Mark Taviner in his St Andrews University doctoral thesis of 2000, 'Robert Beale and the Elizabethan polity'. And I should also declare a personal interest. At about the time that I began my own researches into Elizabethan Puritanism, a subject for which Beale was an indispensable source (that was in the early 1950s), the British Museum acquired that extraordinary archival treasure trove, the Beale papers, known from an earlier provenance as the Yelverton manuscripts: eighty-five of the surviving ninety-five Beale volumes. You have to go to Aberdeen and Salt Lake City to see them all. At that time they were not catalogued, nor would be for decades to come. Sometimes almost falling out of their original vellum bindings, some of them still wrapped in pieces of late medieval liturgical parchment, you had to read them as specially reserved manuscripts, on one of those puffy dark green cushions. The British Library catalogue of 1994, forty years after their acquisition, came none too soon.

Thus it was that I came to know the mind of the man who left behind all those papers, his extensive learning and experience in civil law, diplomacy and what we would call medieval constitutional history, his supreme bureaucratic competence as a kind of Elizabethan Sir Humphrey;[50] and even more the character of the man, expressed in a vigorous, scarcely legible hand, a thick pen scrawled across the tops and margins of the documents which he filed, or surviving in a daunting holograph. This was the Beale of whom Archbishop Whitgift complained to Burghley in 1584: '[I was] never abused more by any man at any time in my life than I have been by him ... It seemeth that he is someway discontented and would work his anger on me'. Beale for his part told Burghley that he had never heard such speeches as he had received from Whitgift, although he had spoken with many 'at home and abroad ... far greater personages than his lordship is'.[51] Those 'personages' included Mary Queen of Scots, with whom he had been talking only a few days before. Beale had diplomatic dealings with Mary on four several occasions, and he would read her execution warrant from the scaffold at Fotheringhay two years later.

Others with whom Beale, the seasoned diplomat, had had significant and indeed protracted dealings included the prince of Orange, and his opposite numbers in most of the chanceries of Europe. Taviner tells us that Beale was involved 'in virtually every diplomatic project of the later Elizabethan years', 'a diplomatic jack-of-all-trades'.[52] His routine responsibilities entailed writing to the king of Morocco in Spanish (1580), and to the signoria of Venice in Italian (1585).[53] In the 1590s he became increasingly expert and active in both French and Danish affairs. Taviner suggests that what is missing from the famous painting of the peace conference between England and Spain at Somerset House in 1604, an event celebrated in 2004 in a grand art-historical jamboree, is the necessary presence of functionaries such as Beale (although Beale was dead by 1604), hovering over the shoulders of the principal participants. That was how it would have been at Nonsuch in 1585, when the decision to intervene militarily in the Netherlands was taken.[54]

I would not claim Robert Beale as a friend. For one thing, we know so little about him at a personal level. All that Taviner found out on that score after four years in the Yelverton manuscripts was that Beale suffered from toothache in 1576 and that in 1587 he sent his wife a present of two lanterns and four pairs of bellows.[55] But the survival of a vast amount of public material for an Elizabethan political figure of the second rank is unique. It is why Beale is a subject where, say, Sir Henry Killigrew, is not. But it also explains why we have a biography of Killigrew, and of William Davison, and of Thomas Norton, while no-one has dared to write a biography of Beale.[56] To do that you would not only have to have a thorough knowledge of the Yelverton manuscripts and of the subjects they document. You would need to trawl the archives of most European states. I stand in some awe of Beale, and have done for fifty years. Since Beale wrote nothing which even by today's generous criteria can be called literature, he is not likely to attract the attention of the literary scholars, young Turks like Cathy Shrank and Tom Betteridge, who seem to me to be making the running on Tudor politics, as well as letters. So I'm not sure who can be looked to to do the serious work on Beale which deserves doing. Mark Taviner may not be entirely lost to scholarship, but he makes his living elsewhere.

If one were to attempt anything like a biography it would explore the formation of this fiercely Protestant politician in mid-Tudor Coventry, already a little English Geneva, and the place, according to Beale, 'where it pleased god to give me the beginning of my understanding'.[57] This was under the influence of two considerable mid-Tudor public figures, his uncle (or grandfather) Sir Richard Morison and Morison's friend and colleague Sir John Hales, who became, in effect, his surrogate father; and then a taste of the Marian Protestant exile in Morison's house in Strasbourg and in Zurich as part of the household of the future bishop and sometime tutor to Lady Jane Grey, John Aylmer. According to Roger Ascham, Aylmer taught Jane Grey 'so gently, so pleasantly, with such fair allurements to learning'; but Beale came to detest his schoolmaster, and the feeling was reciprocated. (It has to be said that Lady Jane Grey, through Ascham, is almost the only person I know to have had a good word to say for Bishop Aylmer. Those who do not have a good word – not one good word – include Brett Usher, his biographer in the *Oxford Dictionary of National Biography*.)

Beale remained overseas, at the heart of Europe, for much of the following decade, acquiring six foreign languages and studying, among other subjects, a good deal of civil law, at Wittenberg, perhaps at Padua, and certainly at Paris. It was a formation which reminds one of Sir Philip Sidney's mentor, the diplomat Hubert Languet, whom Beale met at Wittenberg, and with whom he had regular dealings, twenty-one of Languet's 1,000 surviving letters being addressed to Beale.[58] It is the beginning of wisdom to understand that Beale was anything but a little Englander. His fierce anti-Catholic views were not, as they might have been half a century later, those of an Anglocentric, but part of the Calvinist international. Beale cut his political and juristic teeth in these years in touring continental universities in the interest of proving the validity of the clandestine marriage of the claimant to the succession, Lady Catherine Grey, and the earl of Hertford, a cause championed by Hales and the eye of the storm of Protestant politics in the mid fifteen-sixties. Beale wrote a tract, 'A large discourse concerning the marriage between the earl of Hertford and the Lady Katherine Grey'. He later repudiated his own argument.[59] But this meant that Beale was on the queen's black list, and this was a cloud which continued to overshadow his English career when he became Clerk of the Privy Council in 1572. Archbishop Whitgift was not wrong in detecting some chips on Beale's shoulder. But how did he overcome these black marks? Only, it seems, through his extraordinary talents, which no-one could deny.

The mature Beale was a political intellectual of remarkable erudition and sophistication, but underlying that sophistication was what may seem to us a simplistic, black and white view of the world as locked in a kind of Huntingtonian war of civilisations, with the king of Spain cast as 'the only author and continuer of all this mischief'. But this cold war mentality was widely, perhaps universally, shared among the sort of Elizabethans we are discussing, and by none more so than Hubert Languet's *protégé* Philip Sidney.[60] The search for an effective pan-European Protestant alliance, which Beale actively shared with Languet, is described by Dr. Taviner as the *leitmotif* of his diplomatic life.

In 1566, Beale married a woman who made him brother-in-law to Sir Francis Walsingham. Whether the marriage was the fruit of the connection or the beginning of it is not known, Walsingham's early career being even more shadowy than Beale's; only that Walsingham and Beale soon had a ball and socket, tongue and groove relationship, very close and altogether like-minded colleagues. In 1571 Walsingham became resident ambassador in Paris, with Beale as one of his personal secretaries. It has been an understandable assumption on the part of historians, perpetuated in the *Oxford Dictionary of National Biography*, that Beale, together with Walsingham and Sidney, was an eye-witness to the St Bartholomew's Day massacres in August 1572, consolidating their shared view of the world, like 9/11 for many modern Americans. But in fact Beale had returned to London a few months earlier, and was sworn Clerk of the Privy Council in July 1572.[61] Not that he was unaffected by the massacre, which confirmed rather than changed his outlook on the world. He did not need to be an eyewitness to believe that Catholicism was an atrocious religion and a threatening political system. 'By these late horrible accidents in France', Beale assured Burghley, 'the conjuration of the Council of Trent to root out all such as contrary to the pope's traditions make profession of Christ's Gospel ... so manifestly now appeareth as I think it cannot be denied of any persons.' Such was the perceived state of the world in 1572. It was in character that Beale turned the events in France against 'our lazy prelates', who were too 'choken up with worldly riches and pride' to be moved by 'these tragedies'.[62]

As clerk of the council, Beale had direct and constant access to the queen, bringing to her perhaps every other day piles of papers to sign, and there is no reason to suppose that on such occasions he stood mute in the royal presence, unable to answer royal questions. On one recorded occasion, he insisted that Elizabeth sign the papers he placed before her, even though her 'head ached'.[63] 'I could not have any access unto her Majesty until noon.' Beale distilled years of experience in this function in his 'Treatise of the Office of a Councellor and Principall Secretarie to her Ma[jes]tie',[64] to which before we are finished we shall return.

But always Beale had to struggle to conceal his own opinions on the great issues of the day, which were very different from those of his mistress. On one occasion, when on an embassy to the Netherlands, he wrote a letter which earned some frank advice from the earl of Leicester. His dispatch had contained a bitter attack on the bishops. The context was the very same which had sent Thomas Norton to the Tower: the politico-religious climate exacerbated both by the later stages of the unpopular Anjou marriage negotiation, and by episcopal intransigence in the face of a concerted demand from the House of Commons for church reform. Leicester instructed Beale: 'Pray you when you have cause to write at large of your affairs there, to eschew as much as you can to enter into any cause that concerns this matter of ours at home, I mean touching our bishops or state of religion, in sort to mislike them.' By all means share such thoughts with him, but not in letters intended for the queen. 'For that I do use to show your discourses to her Majesty, who liketh very well of them, and the last I durst not, for this respect.'[65]

It was on the matter of religion, and of the politics entwined with religion, that Elizabethan citizens like Beale had particular difficulty in conducting themselves as obedient servants of the state and its head. Beale, like Norton, had been driven to the edge by what he had witnessed in the parliament of 1581. A programme of religious reform which had high-level backing, and which the queen, as a tactical manoeuvre, had kicked into the long grass, referring it to the bishops, had been thrown back in the teeth of its sponsors by John Whitgift, still only bishop of Worcester, but already marked out to succeed the disgraced Archbishop Grindal. It was eight years later that Beale wrote to the lord chancellor, Sir Christopher Hatton: 'Your lordship can I think remember what angry words the then bishop of Worcester used to your lordship and Sir Walter Mildmay. I have not forgotten what that honourable counsellor then reported.' 'In all the histories and records of times past never any prince or subject gave such an insufficient or opprobious answer.'[66] Addressing Whitgift directly, Beale accused him of having charged the House of Commons with 'malapertness', 'as though it became them not to deal with their betters'.[67]

When Whitgift arrived at Lambeth, in November 1583, Beale hoped, briefly, that he could be persuaded to pursue a more reasonable and moderate course.[68]

But once the new archbishop had disclosed his intention to secure absolute conformity to the Elizabethan religious settlement in its entirety by imposing subscription to the three articles, which is what he had been appointed by the queen to do, Beale made himself Captain Ahab to the archbishop's Moby Dick. When delegations of non-subscribing ministers appeared before the Privy Council, Beale was standing in for the absent Walsingham as a full member of that body, and later he had to apologise to Burghley for having been 'overbold in speaking in Council', casting out 'some words in matters concerning papists, God's and her Majesty's mortal enemies'. Overbold or not, Beale was appointed to refer petitions from the suspended ministers in Kent and Suffolk to Whitgift and to 'require' his presence before the council. When Whitgift appeared he dismissed the non-conformists as young, ignorant and over-enthusiastic ('beardless boys, princocks'), and he resented the humiliating position he found himself in. (Later, he wrote, 'it is not for me to sit in this place, if any curate in my diocese or province may be permitted so to use me'.) But this brought from Beale the stinging rejoinder that the archbishop was confronting weighty matters of learning and divinity.[69] The climax of his lawyerly resistance to the subscription campaign of 1584 took the form of a 'book to the archbishop', one of those dossiers we have learned to call 'dodgy', but certainly the weightiest if most casuistical of all challenges to the legality and expediency of Whitgift's programme.[70]

Later Beale called at Lambeth, ostensibly to recover his 'book'. The result was a series of furious exchanges. 'He fell into very great passion with me', Whitgift complained to Burghley, 'which I think was the end of his coming'. 'Bearing with him doth puff him up.' Beale had bawled at Whitgift in the hearing of everyone: 'His speeches were intolerable'; 'He forgot himself.'[71] Well, that's our man, only slightly distorted in the prism of the archbishop's jaundiced opinion. Beale then set off on one of his missions to Mary Queen of Scots in Sheffield, but the controversy continued. On his return he defended his conduct in 'The answer of Robert Beale concerning such things as have passed between the lord archbishop of Canterbury and him'.[72]

Beale was not so far out on a limb as you might think. In 1584 Whitgift, who would have to wait another three years to become a Privy Councillor, was in an exposed and uncomfortable position. Lord Burghley was definitely not his friend. In a letter which has often been quoted, Burghley complained to Whitgift that 'by chance' he had come across a set of twenty-four articles 'formed in a Romish style', on the basis of which the archbishop proposed to examine the ministers resisting subscription. The thing was 'so curiously penned, so full of branches and circumstances, as I think the inquisitors of Spain use not so many questions to comprehend and trap their preys'. Now where had Burghley got that idea? By chance? No. For once this is a question we can answer. He had just been told by Beale that Whitgift's articles were devised with a 'cunning which savoureth more of a Spanish inquisition than Christian charity'.[73]

Some of the ministers whom Beale resolutely defended in the 1580s, and in the major star chamber action against some of them in 1591, were Presbyterians: which is to say that they were both intellectually and actively opposed to the episcopal hierarchy of the church, and also hostile to the Book of Common Prayer, opponents of the Elizabethan settlement in something like its entirety.[74] Where did Beale stand on these issues? In his answer to Whitgift, he declared: 'I am none of them that would have archbishops or bishops pulled down, or the form of the Church altered.' He continued to make this disclaimer. In 1593, he told Burghley: 'If any man can prove that I ever assented to any new plot of reformation or consented to have the present estate altered, I desire no further favour than to be hanged at the court gates.'[75]

I am not sure whether to believe Beale or not. Yelverton MS. 70 (BL, Add. MS. 48064) is a fat dossier of papers relating to the cause of further, radical reformation, a collection which parallels the 'Seconde Parte of a Register' manuscripts in Dr Williams's Library, and one of the main sources for my researches into the Elizabethan Presbyterian movement. It was a dossier not casually assembled but intended to provide ammunition for a determined onslaught on particular bishops, especially Aylmer of London and Thomas Cooper of Winchester. Beale wrote a speech which he intended to make in the parliament of 1584, alleging that the bishops were acting contrary to the Henrician Act for the Submission of the Clergy, and even against Magna Carta. It amounts to 40,000 words and if delivered would have run for four or five hours. (There is no evidence that it was. Parliamentary rhetoric was not the way that Beale operated.[76]) When he defended the puritan ministers in the trials of 1590 and 1591, Beale's position was that there was nothing illegal about their conferences 'to think upon some plot of reformation'; whereas if such meetings had taken upon themselves an executive authority, 'this is offensive to law and being proved will touch them indeed', the essence of the defence being that there had been no such usurpation of the authority legally vested in the bishops. But this was a defence attorney's argument, as it happens an effective one since Beale was able to demonstrate that where this prosecution was concerned, the mountains had laboured and had given birth to a ridiculous mouse. 'There would be no lawful and sufficient proof found of such unlawful and heinous matters as were pretended.' Note 'lawful' and 'sufficient'.[77]

Beale was somewhat differently aligned with the regime in the winter of 1586–87, when the fate of Mary Queen of Scots was coming to its final and bloody denouement. For all his frequent diplomatic encounters with the lady, Beale was committed to her extinction and had been for many years before he helped to bring that event about. Nothing personal. Personally, Beale and

Mary got on well, better than Beale and Whitgift, and Mary gave Beale a gold chain worth £65.[78] But in 1573 he had advised Burghley, who hardly needed to be persuaded, that Mary was 'the principal cause of the ruin of the two realms of France and Scotland' and had 'prettily played the like part here'. All Europe was amazed at Elizabeth's 'overmild' leniency in 'nourishing in her own bosom so pestiferous a viper'.[79] Four years later, Beale brought back from Germany a manuscript text of Buchanan's seminal anti-Marian political treatise, *De jure regni apud Scotos*, two years ahead of the first print edition of the work.[80] Beale was the acknowledged expert within the Elizabethan regime on all matters concerning Mary Stuart.

After Mary's decapitation that expertise became a liability, for Beale, who had dispatched the warrant for the execution to Fotheringhay, no less than for William Davison, who had secured the queen's signature to the warrant. Of this the Yelverton manuscripts contain ample evidence, together with the copy of the warrant acquired by Lambeth Palace Library in 1996, in which Beale has added his own version of the queen's signature to those consenting to the deed, commenting elsewhere 'her Majesty's hand was also in the copy', an odd thing for a good lawyer to do. It was Beale to whom Burghley himself had entrusted the fatal warrant, and Beale who took the necessary letters to his brother-in-law Walsingham, who was laid up with some illness; Beale, too, whose servant carried the warrant to Fotheringhay.[81]

The reason why Beale kept such a detailed record of the whole affair was that once Mary was dead the firm alliance of most members of the regime in promoting the execution began to unravel. Just as the queen had made it clear that she would have preferred an extra-judicial act of assassination, so her principal ministers and advisers, Lord Burghley above all, finding themselves in the direct firing line, shifted the blame for the judicial act onto the shoulders of Davison and, less directly, of Beale. Beale, not himself under threat, appears in the documents as an observer and commentator, collecting and collating no less than five versions of Davison's star chamber trial.

This was when men of business became catspaws or scapegoats. But in no other major event in Elizabethan history is it so clear that the likes of Beale and Davison were no mere functionaries but had acted in their own right and out of conviction, a conviction in Beale's case born of almost twenty years of studied attention to the problem posed by Mary Queen of Scots: the Elizabethan citizen as willing assassin, but only by due process of law. Beale's treatise on the office of a principal secretary contains this advice to his successors:

> When there shall be any unpleasant matter to be imparted to her Majesty from the Council, or other matters to be done of great importance, let not the burden be laid on you alone but let the rest join with you. Excuse yourself by your years and for lack of experience; do not overthrow yourself for any of their pleasures or other respect as Mr Davison did.[82]

After 1587 Beale's diplomatic career had another fourteen very busy years to run. But nothing was ever the same again. In 1593 he told Burghley that he was 'so much maligned at home and abroad for the carrying down of the commission for the execution of the late Scottish Queen', since which he had had neither credit nor countenance.[83] That was written at a time when Beale's enemies had finally caught up with him, and when his situation was not unlike that of Thomas Norton in 1581: in the aftermath of a parliament excluded from both the court and the House of Commons and under house arrest. Not until 1597 was he reinstated as Clerk of the Privy Council. Beale had worked with James Morice in a carefully planned attack on procedures in the ecclesiastical courts, the issue of the *ex officio* oath which, in effect, ruled out anything like the Fifth Amendment of the United States constitution as a means of legal defence. Archbishop Whitgift later wrote that 'in the Lower House of that Parliament he openly spoke of matters concerning ecclesiastical jurisdiction, etc., contrary to her Majesty's express pleasure ... For the which he was also at that Parliament time committed'. But no such speech survives, and there was more to this affair than that. Beale had been framed (it looks like that) by a position he had taken on taxation, the double subsidy being debated in that wartime parliament. The matter was formal and technical. This was only the second occasion on record when Beale apologised for anything – 'He acknowledged that he mistook the question propounded' – but it gave his enemies the opportunity they needed. Beale knew that the true cause of his disgrace was that he was alleged to be 'a plotter of a new ecclesiastical government'.[84] We are now in what I have called 'the nasty nineties'.[85] The political climate was very different from that in the 1570s and 1580s, when leading politicians like Walsingham and Leicester and Mildmay were still in charge, a climate which had favoured a second-rank figure of the stature of Beale. There were many signs of an incipient absolutism, not good times for semi-republican citizens. If anyone deserved the accolade of Her Majesty's Loyal Opposition it was Beale. But by the 1590s the title was almost redundant.

However, Beale was too valuable not to be used. Two years after a disgrace which was evidently only temporary, Burghley wrote to him in his own hand as 'your assured loving friend', asking him to help with a whole shopping list of historical and political questions. When did the pope begin to encroach upon the sovereignty of the crown of England? How far was the pope's jurisdiction restricted in France and in Spain? Which queens before Mary Tudor and Mary Stuart and Elizabeth had governed as hereditary monarchs, 'solely without marriage'? 'Mr Beale I am bold because I know that you can satisfy in sundry things'; 'I think I shall weary you with so many questions, for I am weary in scribbling of them.' And then, when Beale had had time to respond: 'Mr Beale I heartily thank you for your tardy answers to my questions, persuading with myself that few or none others could so amply answer the same.'

Thomas Norton had been used in exactly the same way when in the Tower in 1581.[86]

So Robert Beale remained a valued servant of the Elizabethan regime and was no doubt content to be so regarded; which in no way diminished his autonomy within himself and within the system as a highly informed, deeply concerned and committed member of the commonwealth. This amphibious role is best illustrated by Beale's political testament, 'A Treatise of the Office of a Councellor and Principall Secretarie to her Ma[jes]tie', which he seems to have composed for the benefit of Sir Edward Wotton, who was expecting to become just that thing. It was 1592, a little before Beale's troubles of the following year. Here Beale is playing the role of a political Polonius. Conyers Read discovered the treatise and in 1925 included it as an appendix in the first volume of his *Walsingham*. But it is to be found – guess where – among the Yelverton manuscripts.

Beale's treatise descends into much detail, particularly concerning the office of principal secretary in relation to the Privy Council, and the connections between the council and other judicial and semi-judicial bodies, such as the court of requests; and about the vast amount of information with which the secretary should be furnished, from matters relating to Catholic recusants to the forts along the south coast, to stocks of weapons, powder and munitions, and the state of the navy; as well as a knowledge of the affairs of other European states, not to speak of 'the Muscovite, the Turk, the king of Barbary, and all others with whom this state hath had any doings', which looks like exceeding the resources of the present United States state department and the Pentagon put together.

In these concluding remarks I am concerned only with the dealings of the secretary with the sovereign, 'things to be done with her Majesty'; for here we see the problem of counsel in action, and the role of a servant of the Elizabethan state who was also his own man. But so far as Privy Council matters were concerned, I am not sure that Beale's advice is wholly irrelevant today: 'Have a care that the time be not spent in matters of small moment'; 'Favour not secret or cabinet councils which do cause jealousy and envy'. But here is the secretary, or clerk, before the queen: 'Learn before your access her Majesty's disposition by some in the privy chamber with whom you must keep credit, for that will stand you in much stead'; 'When her highness is angry or not well disposed, trouble her not with any matter which you desire to have done, unless extreme necessity urge it'; 'When her highness signeth, it shall be good to entertain her with some relation or speech whereat she may take some pleasure'; 'Be not dismayed with the controlments and amendments of such things which you shall have done, for you shall have to do with a princess of great wisdom, learning and experience ... The princes themselves know best their own meaning and there must be time and experience to acquaint them with their humours before a man can do any acceptable service'; 'Give no occasion that either her Majesty or any other do think that you do it as though you esteemed your own wit better than theirs, but only of conscience and duty'; 'Take heed you do not addict yourself to any faction that you may find among the councillors. You shall find that they will only use you for their own turns, and that done set little by you afterwards'.

After reading and reflecting on these Machiavellian maxims, I can only agree with the wisdom of the Renaissance historians, that only those who had themselves been deeply immersed in affairs were fit to write the histories of their own times.[87] Robert Beale, who better, could have written the history of Elizabethan England which we, mere professional historians, four centuries on, merely aspire to write. He knew the way it was, in Ranke's famous phrase, *wie es eigentlich gewesen*. And the Right Honourable Tony Blair could well have learned from the last of Beale's maxims: 'By the reading of histories you may observe the examples of times past, judging of their success.'[88]

NOTES

1 J. E. Neale, *Essays in Elizabethan History* (1958), p. 229.

2 J. E. Neale, *Elizabeth I and her Parliaments, 1559–81* (1953), pp. 12, 90 n. 1.

3 *The House of Commons 1558–1603*, ed. P. W. Hasler (3 vols, 1981). That this mausoleum was designed and constructed by Sir John Neale was a matter almost disguised in its unveiling. P. W. Hasler's 'Introductory survey' replaced an introduction which had been drafted by Neale, and Edward Miller, chairman of the editorial board of the History of Parliament, suggested that Neale, unlike the editors of earlier volumes in the series, had not been hands-on in his oversight of the project. That occasioned wry amusement among Neale's quondam research students (myself included), who had endured scores of seminars which were little more than editorial meetings of the 'History of Parliament' team. One should be careful not to die before the completion of such an undertaking. The sad fact is that if Neale had not devoted his declining years to the History of Parliament, he might have written a notable biography of the earl of Essex.

4 Hasler, *The House of Commons 1558–1603*, vol. 1, pp. 360, 400, 429, 512, 551 and so on (we are still in the 'C's). (All further references to Hasler.)

5 Hasler, vol. 1, pp. 354–5.

6 *Ibid.*, pp. 361–2.

7 *Ibid.*, pp. 419.

8 *Ibid.*, pp. 419–20.

9 *Ibid.*, pp. 581–2.

10 *Ibid.*, pp. 681–2.

11 Hasler, vol. 2, pp. 91–2.

12 *Ibid.*, pp. 198.

13 *Ibid.*, pp. 320–3.

14 Hasler, vol. 3, pp. 80–3.

15 *Ibid.*, pp. 350.

16 J. H. M. Salmon, 'Seneca and Tacitus in Jacobean England', in *The Mental World of the Jacobean Court*, ed. L. Levy Peck (Cambridge, 1991), pp. 169–88; M. Smuts, 'Court-centred politics and the uses of Roman historians, c.1590–1630', in *Culture and Politics in Early Stuart England*, ed. K. Sharpe and P. Lake (Basingstoke, 1994), pp. 21–43.

17 *De Republica Anglorum by Sir Thomas Smith*, ed. M. Dewar (Cambridge, 1982) (hereafter *De Republica Anglorum*), p. 57.

18 *A Short-Title Catalogue of Books Printed 1475–1640* (rev. edn, 1976–86), nos 22,857–68; the Venetian observer is quoted in C. Shrank, *Writing the Nation in Reformation England 1530–80* (Oxford, 2004), p. 5.

19 Quoted in P. Collinson, 'The state as monarchical commonwealth: "Tudor" England', *Journal of Historical Sociology*, 15 (2002): 89–95, at p. 93.

20 *De Republica Anglorum*, p. 88.

21 M. Mendle, *Dangerous Positions: Mixed government, the estates of the realm, and the making of the 'Answer to the XIX propositions'* (Tuscaloosa, Ala., 1985), pp. 52–6.

22 See, among recent contributions to a debate on these matters, P. Collinson, '*De Republica Anglorum*, or, history with the politics put back' and 'The monarchical republic of Queen Elizabeth I', both in P. Collinson, *Elizabethans* (London and New York, 2003), pp. 1–57; Chapter 2 in this volume; M. Peltonen, *Classical Humanism and Republicanism in English Political Thought, 1570–1640* (Cambridge, 1995); A. M. McLaren, *Political Culture in the Reign of Elizabeth I: Queen and commonwealth 1558–85* (Cambridge, 1999); Shrank, *Writing the Nation in Reformation England*.

23 Shrank, *Writing the Nation in Reformation England*; T. Betteridge, *Literature and Politics in the English Reformation* (Manchester and New York, 2004).

24 *Proceedings in the Parliaments of Elizabeth I, vol. 1: 1558–1581*, ed. T. E. Hartley (Leicester, 1981), p. 129 (all further references to Hartley).

25 *A Discourse of the Commonweal of this Realm of England Attributed to Sir Thomas Smith*, ed. M. Dewar (Charlottesville, Va., 1969), Preface.

26 B. Worden, *The Sound of Virtue: Sidney's Arcadia and Elizabethan politics* (New Haven, Conn., 1996).

27 Hartley, pp. 134, 376. The second quotation belongs to the parliament of 1572, and to the debates about the fate of Mary Queen of Scots.

28 G. Bowler, '"An Axe or An Acte": the parliament of 1572 and resistance theory in early Elizabethan England', *Canadian Journal of History*, 19 (1984): 349–59.

29 Hartley, pp. 274–82.

30 *De Republica Anglorum*, p. 53.

31 Hartley, p. 298.

32 J. A. Guy, 'Monarchy and counsel: models of the state', in *The 16th Century*, ed. P. Collinson (The Short History of the British Isles, Oxford, 2002), pp. 113–42.

33 J. E. Neale, *Queen Elizabeth* (1934), p. 274.

34 Burghley to Lord Cobham and Sir Francis Walsingham, 19 July 1578; *Relations politiques des Pays-Bas et de l'Angleterre sous le règne de Philippe II*, ed. K. de Lettenhove (11 vols, Brussels, 1882–1900), vol. 10, pp. 659–61.

35 Cambridge University Library, MS. Ee.3.56, no. 85.

36 *State Papers and Letters of Sir Ralph Sadler*, ed. A. Clifford (2 vols, Edinburgh, 1809), vol. 2, p. 129.

37 Lettenhove, *Relations politiques des Pays-Bas et de l'Angleterre*, vol. 10, pp. 449–50.

38 P. Collinson, *Archbishop Grindal, 1519–83: The struggle for a Reformed Church* (1979), pp. 233–52.

39 Collinson, *Archbishop Grindal, passim*.

40 Davison to Sir Francis Walsingham, 11 May 1578; Lettenhove, *Relations politiques des Pays-Bas et de l'Angleterre*, vol. 10, p. 461. I have tended to regard the claim that the House of Commons represented an extended council, all Members of Parliament being councillors, as a posture of resistance to the Elizabethan establishment, as articulated, for example, by Peter Wentworth. But Dr Glyn Parry has taught me to see that it could be in the interest of the Privy Council, especially when divided on matters of policy, to acknowledge that the Commons was such a body, if only to refer outwards and downwards what could not otherwise be resolved (see G. Parry, 'Foreign policy in the parliament of 1576', forthcoming, in *Parliamentary History*, special issue). In 1586, following the Babington Plot, Burghley told Walsingham: 'We stick upon Parliament, which her Majesty mislikes to have, but we all persist, to make the burden better borne and the world abroad better satisfied' (quoted in Guy, 'Monarchy and counsel', p. 134).

41 Hartley, p. 435.

42 J. E. Neale, 'Peter Wentworth', *English Historical Review*, 39 (1924): 36–54 and 175–205, reprinted in *Historical Studies of the English Parliament*, ed. E. B. Fryde and E. Miller (2 vols, Cambridge, 1970), vol. 2, pp. 246–95; G. R. Elton, 'Parliament in the 16th century: functions and fortunes', in G. R. Elton, *Studies in Tudor and Stuart Politics and Government* (4 vols, Cambridge, 1974–92), vol. 3, pp. 156–82, at pp. 159–61; G. R. Elton, *England under the Tudors* (2nd edn, London, 1974), pp. 314–19; P. Collinson, 'The religious factor', in *The Struggle for the Succession in Late Elizabethan England: Politics, polemics and cultural representations*, ed. J.-C. Mayer (Montpellier, 2004), pp. 254–62.

43 M. A. R. Graves, 'The management of the Elizabethan house of commons: the council's "men-of-business"', *Parliamentary History*, 2 (1983): 11–38; M. A. R. Graves, 'Thomas Norton the parliament man: an Elizabethan M.P., 1559–81', *Historical Journal*, 23 (1980): 17–35; G. R. Elton, *The Parliament of England, 1559–81* (Cambridge, 1986); P. Collinson, 'Puritans, men of business and Elizabethan parliaments', in Collinson, *Elizabethans*, pp. 59–86.

44 M. A. R. Graves, *Thomas Norton: The Parliament man* (Oxford, 1994).

45 Collinson, *Elizabethans*, pp. 72–7.

46 Collinson, *Elizabethans*, pp. 75–6.

47 Collinson, *Elizabethans*, p. 75.

48 Hasler, vol. 3, pp. 98–100.

49 Collinson, *Elizabethans*, pp. 67–9.

50 The character of Sir Humphrey in the BBC comedy *Yes Minister* epitomised the wily civil servant.

51 BL, MS. Lansdowne 396 fos 30–2, Archbishop Whitgift to Lord Burghley 'touching Beale'; BL, Add. MS. 48039 fo. 53r, 'The aunswere of Robert Beale', P. Collinson, *The Elizabethan Puritan Movement* (1967), pp. 255–8.

52 M. Taviner, 'Robert Beale and the Elizabethan polity' (unpublished Ph.D. thesis, University of St Andrews, 2000), pp. 169, 177. I am most grateful to Dr Taviner for permission to refer to his dissertation, which contains the most authoritative account of any aspect of Robert Beale's career.

53 *Ibid.*, pp. 169–70.

54 *Ibid.*, p. 175.

55 *Ibid.*, p. 18.

56 A. C. Miller, *Sir Henry Killigrew: Elizabethan soldier and diplomat* (Leicester, 1963); N. H. Nicolas, *Life of William Davison, Secretary of State and Privy Counsellor to Queen Elizabeth* (1823); Graves, *Thomas Norton*.

57 Taviner, 'Robert Beale and the Elizabethan polity', p. 47.

58 Taviner, 'Robert Beale and the Elizabethan polity', p. 645; Worden, *The Sound of Virtue*, p. 51. On 8 Jan. 1578, Languet wrote to Sidney about 'the excellent Master Beale', 'his character, his genius and manifold experience' (*The Correspondence of Sir Philip Sidney and Hubert Languet*, ed. S. A. Pears [1845], pp. 132, 136).

59 Taviner, 'Robert Beale and the Elizabethan polity', pp. 180–1.

60 Worden, *The Sound of Virtue*.

61 Taviner, 'Robert Beale and the Elizabethan polity', pp. 104–5.

62 *Ibid.*, p. 194; BL, Cotton MS. Titus F III fo. 306.

63 Taviner, 'Robert Beale and the Elizabethan polity', p. 152.

64 'A Treatise of the Office of a Councellor and Principall Secretarie to her Ma[jes]tie' (1592), printed in C. Read, *Mr Secretary Walsingham and the Policy of Queen Elizabeth* (3 vols, Oxford, 1925), vol. 1, 423–43 (from Yelverton MS. 162 [BL, Add. MS. 48151]).

65 BL, MS. Egerton 1693 fos 9–10, Leicester to Beale, 7 July (1581).

66 Collinson, *Elizabethan Puritan Movement*, pp. 205–7.

67 BL, Add. MS. 48039 fo. 42, Beale to Whitgift, 7 May 1584.

68 Collinson, *Elizabethan Puritan Movement*, pp. 243–4.

69 *Ibid.*, pp. 255–6.

70 BL, Add. MS. 48039 fos 1–49. For a detailed discussion of the circumstances which provoked and accompanied Beale's 'book', see P. Collinson, 'The puritan classical movement in the reign of Elizabeth I' (unpublished Ph.D. thesis, University of London, 1957), pp. 425–7, 441–3. The phrase 'dodgy dossier' was coined by the media to describe the labour government's 2003 briefing document used to justify the war with Iraq.

71 Collinson, *Elizabethan Puritan Movement*, p. 258; Collinson, *Elizabethans*, pp. 77–8.

72 BL, Add. MS. 48039 fos 48–56r.

73 *Ibid.*, pp. 270–1.

74 *Ibid., passim.*

75 *Ibid.*, p. 190; Collinson, 'Puritan classical movement', pp. 280–1; Hasler, vol. 1, p. 413; Collinson, *Elizabethans*, pp. 81–2.

76 BL, Add. MS. 48116 fos 154 *et seq.*; Collinson, *Elizabethans*, p. 81; J. E. Neale, *Elizabeth I and her Parliaments, 1584–1601* (1957), pp. 66–8. Neale described the 'speech' as a treatise, 'much too long to have been delivered as written'. Beale's first recorded parliamentary speech was made in 1593, although in 1589 Gilbert Talbot reported that 'Mr Beale hath made a very sharp speech which is nothing well liked by the bishops' (Hasler, vol. 1, p. 412).

77 Collinson, *Elizabethan Puritan Movement*, pp. 421–2; Collinson, 'Puritan classical movement', pp. 1113–14, digesting papers in BL, Add. MS. 48064.

78 G. M. Bell, 'Beale, Robert (1541–1601)', *Oxford Dictionary of National Biography* (Oxford, 2004) www.oxforddnb.com/view/article/1804 [accessed 3 May 2006].

79 Taviner, 'Robert Beale and the Elizabethan polity', p. 196.

80 *Ibid.*, p. 201. See Roger Mason's and Martin Smith's edition of the *De jure regni apud Scotos* (R. A. Mason and M. S. Smith, *A Dialogue on the Law of Kingship among the Scots: a critical edition and translation of George Buchanan's De jure regni apud Scotos Dialogus* [Aldershot, 2004]).

81 Taviner, 'Robert Beale and the Elizabethan polity', pp. 221–2. Beale's papers relating to the execution are in BL, Add. MS. 48027. See Chapter 10 in this volume.

82 Read, *Mr Secretary Walsingham and the Policy of Queen Elizabeth*, vol. 1, p. 425.

83 Taviner, 'Robert Beale and the Elizabethan polity', p. 154; 'Robert Beale's apology relating to proceedings in parliament' (versions in BL, MS. Lansdowne 73 fos 4–13; Add. MS. 48064 fos 106–15).

84 Hasler, vol. 1, pp. 413–14; 'Robert Beale's apology'.

85 P. Collinson, 'Ecclesiastical vitriol: religious satire in the 1590s and the invention of puritanism', in *The Reign of Elizabeth I: Court and culture in the last decade*, ed. J. Guy (Cambridge, 1995), pp. 150–70. And see, in the same collection, J. A. Guy, 'Introduction. The 1590s: the second reign of Elizabeth I?', pp. 1–19.

86 BL, Add. MS. 48101 fos 303, 328. See Collinson, *Elizabethans*, pp. 72–82.

87 Chapter 9 in this volume.

88 Read, *Mr Secretary Walsingham and the Policy of Queen Elizabeth*, vol. 1, p. 443.

Chapter 4

◆

Pulling the strings:
religion and politics in
the progress of 1578

I

In July and August 1578, Elizabeth I and her court went on progress deep into East Anglia, the only extensive royal tour of that region. From 16 to 22 August the great travelling show reached the second city of the kingdom, Norwich, referred to by the Spanish Ambassador as 'the North'.[1] There are a number of episodes in the course of the 1578 progress which have made it into many accounts of Elizabethan history and culture, some of them literary. There was the encounter at Audley End with the University of Cambridge, when Gabriel Harvey, in Thomas Nashe's hostile account 'ruffling it out huffty tuffty in his suit of velvet', made a favourable impression on the queen, who said that he looked 'something like an Italian', which Harvey was not sure was entirely a compliment, but to which he responded with a published volume of verses, *Gratulationum Valdinensium libri quatuor* (1578).[2] Then came a strange little iconoclastic drama played out at Euston, near Newmarket, which seems to have signalled a sea change in the politics of East Anglia. The climax was reached in elaborate celebrations at Norwich, stage-managed and choreographed by Thomas Churchyard, a native of the city, which may have had a serious and substantial political purpose. The twin panegyric accounts of the queen in Norwich composed by Churchyard and Bernard Garter,[3] rushed to the press immediately after the events they celebrated, make this one of the

Revised version of an essay published in *Progress, Pageants and Entertainments of Queen Elizabeth I*, edited by Jayne Archer, Elizabeth Goldring and Sarah Knight (Oxford University Press, 2007). Reproduced by permission of Oxford University Press. I am grateful to Dr Simon Adams for his comments and suggestions on this chapter.

best recorded of all Elizabethan progresses. It is the only one to have been the subject of a monograph: *An Elizabethan Progress*, in which Zillah Dovey provides an account of the people and places visited in this progress.[4] In this chapter I will address the polities – and, in particular, the religious factor in the politics – of the 1578 progress.

Elizabethan history is in the course of being rewritten – not, of course, for the first time.[5] The essence of this new approach, reflected, very variously, in the work of Simon Adams, Stephen Alford, Susan Doran, John Guy, Anne MacLaren, and to a modest extent in some of my own writings, is to be less queen-fixated.[6] Much of this new Elizabethan history explores the major fault-line in the polity, a line often dividing the queen from her councillors and other policy-makers. It was out of the East Anglian progress of 1578, from Bury St Edmunds, that the earl of Leicester wrote: 'Our conference with Her Majesty about affairs is both seldom and slender.'[7] But that must mean, because a great deal was going on, internationally, in the summer of 1578, that the conference of Privy Councillors like Leicester, without the benefit of the queen's presence and participation, must have been far from seldom and slender. Never before or after, in their correspondence among themselves, did the governors of Elizabethan England do less to disguise the fact that they had the greatest difficulty in inclining the queen to their way of thinking. The conundrum of counsel, which was the greatest political problem of an age which brought into uncomfortable partnership nearly absolute monarchy and a civic-minded humanism, was never more nakedly exposed. East Anglia in 1578 is where historical geology is best able to uncover the fundamental fault-line in Elizabethan politics.

Given the marked policy differences between the queen and many of her councillors and courtiers, it sometimes looks as if there were two governments, not one, in mid-Elizabethan England. The issues included policy towards the Netherlands (where it could be said that events were coming to a moment of crisis in the months of the 1578 progress, if that were not the normal state of Dutch affairs), and also towards Scotland; the problem of both recusant and non-recusant Catholicism; religious affairs more generally (overshadowed in 1578 by the continued suspension and disgrace of Archbishop Edmund Grindal); what to do with and about Mary Queen of Scots; and the perennial operatic question of a royal marriage, now building up to the last act, the affair of 'Monsieur', as the duc d'Alençon and Anjou was known. On all these momentous matters it was a question of proposing and disposing; often the council proposing and the queen disposing – although in the case of the Anjou match the reverse would be true. The overture to that last act was performed at Norwich.

II

The route and destination of the 1578 progress, as of all the summer progresses undertaken by Elizabeth, was in itself a matter which was not merely personal to the queen, nor solely the concern of the Lord Chamberlain, who was formally responsible for what were called the queen's 'gests'. There were negotiations and decisions within the courtly as well as conciliar machinery of government which are mostly concealed from us. For 1578, the question is: did the queen take her court and council to East Anglia or did they take her? If the latter scenario is the more likely, why? Who decided on the exact itinerary, and again, why?

To know when, and by whom, the final decisions about a summer progress were taken, we should need to be privy to the processes of decision-making. In July 1576, Gilbert Talbot told his father, the earl of Shrewsbury, that there was 'no certainty' about the itinerary for that summer: 'For these two or three days it hath changed every five hours.'[8] On how far the East Anglian tour of July to September 1578 was known, how early, and to whom of the interested parties (thinking especially of the involuntary hosts in the country), the evidence is not consistent. Already in May of that year Talbot reported to his father: 'It is thought her Majesty will go in progress to Norfolk this year, but there is no certain determination thereof as yet.'[9] On 18 June, the earl of Leicester was concerned that his friend Lord North had no time 'to furnish his house according to his duty and honourable good will'.[10] In the event, North came over from his house to pay his respects at Audley End, and it was only on the return leg of the progress, five weeks later, that he played host at Kirtling, having in the meantime built new kitchens and refurbished other rooms.[11] Thomas Churchyard, who arrived in Norwich on 25 July to oversee the pageants which would greet the queen, thought that Norfolk and Suffolk had 'but small warning' of the event.[12] In fact, Norwich had received due warning in mid-June.[13] But in mid-July Sir Nicholas Bacon, the Lord Keeper, was uncertain whether the queen would progress as far as Suffolk, while as late as 20 July the Norfolk gentleman Sir Christopher Heydon hinted in a letter to Bacon's son Nathaniel of Stiffkey that the queen might not be coming as far as Norwich after all, 'if the bird sing truly that I heard this day'.[14] The next day, the earl of Northumberland was asking Burghley for news of 'the certainty of Her Majesty's progress'.[15] Whether these conflicting reports reflect a simple muddle or something more significant and political, we cannot say. But given almost everything that happened in the course of the progress, we are entitled to suspect that the decision to head for Norwich, through Suffolk, was taken by the dominant group in the Privy Council, and perhaps more personally by Robert Dudley, earl of Leicester, whose interests, in several dimensions, were most affected; although we cannot discount disagreements within the council itself over the route to be followed.[16]

III

In taking the heart of government, court and council, into East Anglia, those whose business was government must have known that they were entering a region of delicate instability, still trying to adjust to the spectacular fall of its greatest magnate, Thomas Howard, duke of Norfolk, executed only six years earlier. Behind the Howards remained what was left of the affinity of Mary Tudor, whose 1553 *coup d'état* had been mounted from Suffolk. Howard had left behind a political detritus in patterns and networks of office-holding, patronage, and social prestige. This was a region whose very soul was at stake, as progressive, Protestantising, elements compered for the upper hand with conservative, Catholic, or crypto-Catholic forces.[17] The queen was lodged, it might have seemed indiscriminately, in the houses of Protestants, Catholics, and crypto-Catholics. But that did not mean that her government intended to be religiously neutral: quite the opposite.

The diocese of Norwich, consisting of Norfolk and Suffolk, was described by Gabriel Harvey's enemy Andrew Perne, Master of Peterhouse, one of the heads of Cambridge houses who would have kissed the queen's hand at Audley End on 27 July 1578 and himself a Norfolk man, as 'that great disordered diocess'.[18] One of the issues defining the fault-line between queen and council was how to address that disorder. The instinct of the Privy Council, or at least of the Leicesterians within it, which was also the agenda for the 1578 progress – and there is no reason to suppose that Lord Burghley had a different agenda – was to complete the local revolution which Norfolk's downfall entailed by placing the government of the region in reliable Protestant hands. The queen, on the other hand, like her late Archbishop of Canterbury, Matthew Parker (another Norfolk man), will have laid the blame for the disordered state of the diocese upon her first bishop of Norwich, John Parkhurst. Parkhurst was a learned and dedicated Protestant evangelist, but he was a naive and incompetent administrator, too indulgent to radical Puritan tendencies but also weak in his dealings with Catholic elements which were more strongly entrenched in Norfolk than anywhere else in southern England, with the possible exception of Sussex.[19] With neither faction effectively disciplined, the result was polarisation. Someone in Norfolk said that 'the state could not long stand thus, it would either to papistry or puritanism'.[20]

The queen, determined that no such thing should happen, favoured the third way, which we may call, at the risk of perpetrating an anachronism, Anglicanism: strict conformity to the terms of the ecclesiastical settlement, Catholic and Puritan dissidence to be handled with equal severity. The improbable instrument she chose (or had chosen for her) was Edmund Freke, who was appointed bishop of Norwich in 1575. Why improbable? Freke had a history of fellow travelling with Puritans, He was known to have opposed the imposition of vestments, and he had favoured the preaching conferences known as prophesyings, the defence of which had spelt nemesis for Archbishop Grindal. He seems to have owed his advancement from the bishopric of Rochester to Norwich in part to Leicester, and both Leicester and Burghley probably congratulated themselves on having avoided the appointment of one or other of the stern advocates of conformity (including John Whitgift) whom the late Archbishop Parker had put on his own short-list.[21] But once at Norwich he changed his mind. This was perhaps thanks to the pressure placed upon him by two women: the queen, whose almoner he was, which meant that he was regularly attendant upon her at court; and his wife, who had the bishop firmly in her control. The result has been called by the latest historian of the Elizabethan episcopate 'the most calculated volte-face in the history of the Elizabethan church, a ruthless career-move'.[22]

It didn't do Freke much good. In his first year, he suspended most of the leading non-conformist preachers in his diocese, reportedly 'putting down' as many as twenty exercises of preaching in Norwich alone. The most famous preacher of all, John More, the legendary 'apostle of Norwich', was among those silenced.[23] The leading Protestant gentry of the county were naturally alienated, and compromised by what was said about them at court. Reports reached the queen that 'divers gentlemen' of Norfolk were 'anabaptists'; Nathaniel Bacon and his friend William Heydon were incensed and told Leicester so.[24] Bishop Freke, who could not survive without political allies and friends, was obliged to look for support on the other side of the fence. Norfolk was soon buzzing with rumours. Known Catholics were infiltrating the bishop's household. Freke was careful when he dealt with recusancy, on one occasion calling a notorious recusant back into custody only because he had been put under pressure to do so, 'very sharp reprehension from my lords of the council for my lenity extended towards you and the rest in question for religion in these parts'.[25] A dinner party at the bishop's country house was attended by known recusants and church papists, among them Sir Thomas Cornwallis, sometime comptroller of Mary Tudor's household and the principal agent to the duke of Norfolk, now living quietly in political retirement, a moderate and reasonable recusant, popular with the queen, and with friends across the politico-religious spectrum.[26] When Freke, who was short of money, confessed that he sought translation to a quieter diocese, Cornwallis was reported to have said: 'Nay that shall you not my lord', offering to subscribe to a fund to keep him at Norwich. Thus encouraged, the bishop was said to have uttered 'in some rage': 'Nay, they say the puritans have removed me hence, but before God I will tarry here in despite of them all, to plague the whole generation of them, striking the board with his fist very angrily.'

Meanwhile, Freke had fallen out with his diocesan chancellor, John Becon, a *protégé* of Bishop Parkhurst and a client of Leicester. This was far from a sideshow. As Freke struggled to get rid of Becon and as Becon, fiercely litigious, entrenched, it became a *cause célèbre*.[27] Becon was a near-Presbyterian, well known as a leader of the Puritans in Cambridge in the early 1570s.[28] Cornwallis, who was accused of constant interference in the conduct of ecclesiastical justice, broadly in the Catholic interest, was working closely with Freke to replace Becon with William Masters, another suspected papist, whom Freke's predecessor, Bishop Parkhurst, had unwisely appointed to the office under pressure from Cornwallis.[29]

Both the cause of the Norwich preachers and the Becon affair had been brought to the attention of Leicester, Burghley, and other councillors before the royal progress reached Norwich in August 1578. In May, Dr Becon had discussed More's case with Leicester. He told Nathaniel Bacon that he would have to be content to be called a favourer of Puritans 'when generally all the good men in the country are calumniated that way'. But who was it, he asked, who for the last eighteen months had been spreading slanderous rumours about Puritanism as far as the court itself?[30] Radical Puritanism was not a paper tiger. In 1583, fewer than 175 citizens, 'with infinite more in this shire of Norfolk', were to petition the queen in favour of a non-episcopal, Presbyterian church settlement.[31] But the preferred policy of the Privy Council was to favour the middle ground, defusing a potentially dangerous situation with moderation, persuading the preachers to be somewhat conformable. This was where Leicester stood, and it was what the whole Council, Burghley in the forefront, tried to achieve when they reached Norwich in August 1578; whereas the queen favoured a hard line, with a series of interventions in religious matters which the latest historian of the Elizabethan Church, Brett Usher, has censured: 'Her actions were more likely than not to exacerbate the tensions between her unnecessarily narrow conception of "Ecclesia Anglicana" and the moderate, evangelical tradition of Protestant churchmanship upon which her settlement principally relied for its survival and advancement.' Her interventions, Usher concludes, were 'invariably disastrous'.[32]

We need to join the progress at an earlier staging post along the road to Norwich: Euston Hall near Newmarket, the home of a wealthy young Catholic, Edward Rokewood, whose family was closely allied to the Cornwallises.[33] And then we should backtrack to Bury St Edmunds, which the progress had left for Euston on 9 August. At Euston there was a sample of what was now to happen throughout East Anglia, a curious piece of carnivalesque theatre. For what took place as the queen was saying her goodbyes and thankyous and preparing to leave Rokewood's house we are dependent, for better or worse, on a far from dispassionate account supplied to the earl of Shrewsbury by Richard Topcliffe, the notorious papist-finder-general of Elizabethan England, whose evidence has to be evaluated with scepticism.[34] According to Topcliffe, a search for a piece of missing plate led to the discovery, in a hay-house, of an image of the Virgin Mary. Then, 'after a sort of country dances ended, in Her

Majesty's sight the idol was set behind the people, who avoided'. The queen commanded that the image be burned, 'which in her sight by the country folks was quickly done, to her content, and unspeakable joy of every one but some one or two who had sucked of the idol's poisoned milk'.

This curious piece of near-fiction raises more questions than we can hope to answer. How fortuitous was the discovery of the image? Had it perhaps been planted? What was the role of the country people? Would their dancing have happened, image or no image? What does 'who avoided' mean? Above all, what role was the queen playing? Was it as active and as approving as Topcliffe suggests? Or was this not rather something arranged for her benefit? Is this evidence of conciliar manipulation, even of a plot hatched before the progress ever left Greenwich? Why had Euston been chosen as a staging post? The house was small and there were many more convenient places to stay in the vicinity. We can confirm what Topcliffe otherwise reports: Rokewood was later summoned to appear before the Privy Council at Norwich and committed to prison, the beginning of a long ordeal for the Rokewoods which would culminate in the involvement of another member of the family in the Gunpowder Plot of 1605. But whether at Euston there was a face-to-face encounter between Rokewood and Lord Chamberlain Sussex, who asked him how, as someone excommunicated for papistry, 'he durst presume to attempt' the queen's royal presence, we cannot say. However, that something out of the ordinary happened at Euston may be confirmed by an even more garbled account from the Spanish Ambassador, who reported that at one of the houses which had received the queen 'her people found an altar with all the ornaments thereupon ready for the celebration of Mass', and that the family had received the queen 'with crucifixes round their necks'.[35]

The progress had come to Euston from Bury St Edmunds. This was another religious problem area, and was to become more so in the years immediately following the progress of 1578.[36] In that summer, the events known to history as 'the Bury stirs' were only just beginning. Jurisdictionally, the stirs were problematic. Bishop Freke was trying to impose his ecclesiastical authority over the town through his commissary, which was opposed by the local archdeacon, the future Bishop John Still, a fellow traveller with the Suffolk Puritans, and by some of the local Protestant/Puritan gentry. At a later stage, the bishop would be supported by the assize judges, his opponents by the Privy Council. At issue in 1578 was the religious ascendancy of two preachers, who were both non-conformists and associated with the exercise of prophesying which Bishop Parkhurst had authorised. Bury was beginning to polarise between two leading townsmen, Thomas Badby, a Puritan, who had turned the ruins of the abbey into a stately home, and the religiously conservative Thomas Andrews. In the years to come, the Privy Council would normally support the Puritan faction in its feud with Bishop Freke and his supporters.

But in August 1578 there was perhaps an attempt at even-handedness. While the queen was lodged with Badby in the abbey, Burghley and Leicester stayed with Andrews.[37] From a petition sent to Burghley a few days after the royal party had left Bury, it appears that one of the preachers, John Handson, had been examined by Burghley and others upon complaints of his non-conformity. But it also appears that the result was that for the time being Handson was left undisturbed.[38] And Robert Jermyn of Rushbrooke, Badby's nephew, the leader of the up-and-coming Puritan gentry of West Suffolk, was among the Suffolk gentry now knighted.[39]

And so to Norwich. Much more happened in Norwich in August 1578 than what a Victorian author unkindly called 'absurd speeches' and 'grotesque pageants'.[40] The Privy Council addressed the struggle between Bishop Freke and the Norwich preachers, imposing a settlement which was better news for the preachers than for Freke. Freke was forced to accept a promise of limited conformity from the non-conformists, led by the 'apostle' John More; although others more radical and unreconciled soon headed out of Norwich in a southerly direction, to establish on the borders of Suffolk and Essex what history knows as the Dedham *classis*.[41] Two years later, when Freke tried to extricate himself, he was given a sharp reminder from the Privy Council that he ought to handle the preachers 'as charitably as becometh a man of his profession'.[42] The Council also threw its weight behind Dr Becon in his struggle with Freke. Burghley filed away Becon's plan for a church constitution (supplied to him by Freke's enemies), which would combine the best elements of episcopacy and Presbyterianism, 'a form of government' which, the Lord Treasurer was led to believe, was evidence of 'his desire of good proceedings'.[43] Thanks to the patronage of Leicester and Walsingham, Becon was rapidly advanced to the chancellorships of, in succession, Chichester and Coventry and Lichfield, where further trouble ensued.[44] A commission composed of Protestant/ Puritan loyalists appointed to look into the affair after the court had left Norwich produced a copious if suspect dossier on Freke's dealings with a number of papists and crypto-papists, headed by Cornwallis. It was said in Norfolk that Becon owed his position to the Council, Masters, his rival for the post, to the queen.[45] This was just one of the many little cracks that ran out from the fault-line in the Elizabethan polity.

Meanwhile, it was a time of judgment for the religious conservatives among the governors of Elizabethan Norfolk and Suffolk. Edward Rokewood was only one of twenty-three recusants and suspected recusants, all ranking gentlemen, who were summoned to appear before the Privy Council in Norwich. One list of culprits, and what was done with them, is in Burghley's own hand.[46] Rokewood and Robert Downes, the man who had boasted that he had the bishop on his side, faced a lifetime of intermittent imprisonment. Others were bailed and put under house arrest. The elderly and immensely wealthy Sir Henry Bedingfield, once a Privy Councillor to Queen Mary, failed to appear, but was seen two days later at the next stopover on the progress, and bound over.[47] From Hengrave, at the end of the month, the Council wrote to the bishop 'touching such order as is to be taken by him with the papists in Suffolk'.[48] Although the Privy Council knew better than to lay hands on the queen's friend Sir Thomas Cornwallis, it was a clear victory for the evangelical cause. While the papists were discountenanced, several gentlemen of proven Protestant credentials had been countenanced, indeed knighted.[49] By early September, Leicester was able to tell Sir Nicholas Bacon that his sons Nicholas and Nathaniel were back in good favour with the queen. Sir Thomas Heneage, not known as a Puritan, wrote to Walsingham: 'My lords, with the rest of the council, have most considerately straightened divers obstinate and arch Papists, that would not come to church; and by some good means Her Majesty has been brought to believe well of divers loyal and zealous gentlemen of Suffolk and Norfolk, whom the foolish bishop had maliciously complained of to her as hinderers of her proceedings, and favourers of Presbyterians and Puritans.'[50] We can guess what those 'good means' were. Nathaniel Bacon now wrote to Leicester: 'The especial prayer of us all is that God will with his spirit guide your lordship both in this and all other your actions.'[51] Here were the origins of a potent legend: that when Elizabeth had crossed into Suffolk, to be met by the gentlemen of the county, all accompanied by their preachers, she had declared: 'Now I have learned why my County of Suffolk is so well governed, it is because the Magistrates and Ministers go together.'[52] I am sure that she said no such thing, but East Anglia now looked forward to a century of government by those heavenly twins, godly magistracy and ministry.[53] To coin a phrase, the purpose of the 1578 progress appears to have been regime change.

IV

Thus far, I have discussed what went on in Suffolk and Norfolk in the course of the 1578 progress, publicly and politically, as if it had to do only with religion. But 'only with religion' is, for the sixteenth century, an oxymoron. The religious issues were the political issues, and vice versa. I have explored, on an earlier occasion, the considerable political implications of the sequestration and threatened deprivation of the Archbishop of Canterbury, Edmund Grindal, which was interpreted at the time as symbolic of a general reaction in policy.[54] In January 1578, Sir Francis Knollys, a councillor privileged by his blood relationship to the queen, had written a letter in which religious and political motives were inextricably linked: 'The avoiding of her Majesty's danger doth consist in the preventing of the conquest of the Low Countries betimes; secondly, in preventing of the revolt of Scotland from her Majesty's devotion unto the French and the Queen of Scots; and thirdly, in the timely preventing of the contemptuous growing of the disobedient papists here in England.' He added: 'But if the bishop of Canterbury shall be deprived, then up starts the pride and the practice of the papists. And then King Richard the Second's men [i.e. flatterers and false counsellors] will flock into Court apace and will show themselves in their colours.'[55]

The politics of the perilous situation in the Low Countries, a conflict suffused with religion, was what mainly preoccupied Elizabeth's ministers as they trailed around behind and before her. When Leicester complained, from Bury St Edmunds, that conference with the queen was but seldom and slender, it was that politics to which he referred. If what happened in the summer of 1578 in East Anglia, the most prosperous of all English regions, would determine its politics for the next century, what was at stake in the Netherlands, the most advanced economy of the world of its time, was the future of Europe itself for the next three hundred years.[56] In the immediate aftermath of the disastrous defeat of Gembloux, before which a united and embryonic Netherlands state had seemed a realistic possibility, the Privy Council was as nearly united as it could ever be on the need to come to the aid of the Dutch, and to prop up the shaky fortunes of William of Orange. Even Sir Nicholas Bacon, hardly a Puritan hothead, wrote: 'I see no way so sure for your Majesty as to keep the Prince of Orange in heart and life.'[57] The immediate need was for money, and it was money, or the lack of it, which dominated the diplomatic correspondence of that summer. But the decision to intervene had already been taken, certainly by Leicester and his friends. The queen was of another persuasion, and military intervention would be delayed for another seven years. As early as 1577, rumour had it that Leicester was about to cross the North Sea with an expeditionary force: 'This is his full determination, but yet unknown unto her Highness, neither shall she be acquainted with it until she be fully resolved to send.'[58] Elizabeth, of course, was not so resolved, and the result has been called a set of 'strange diplomatic quadrilles'.[59]

The interventionist majority on the Privy Council stood between what might be called the militant tendency on the left and, on the right, the conservatism, religious and otherwise, of, amongst others, the queen, just as it did in addressing the religious differences in Norfolk and Suffolk. William Davison was Ambassador in the Netherlands, and very much part of the militant tendency. In his dispatches to the queen he allowed his own ideological commitment to colour his advice. When he cooperated with the Puritan divine Walter Travers in establishing a Presbyterian form of worship in the church of the English merchants in Antwerp, Sir Francis Walsingham warned him: 'If you knew with what difficulty we retain what we have, and that the seeking of more might hazard (according to man's understanding) that, you would then, Mr Davison, deal warily in this time, when policy carries more sway than zeal.'[60] A few days earlier, Walsingham had had occasion to write to Davison: 'You shall do well hereafter to forbear to set down your private opinion in the public letters you send us the Secretaries, for that some give out that you are more curious in setting down your own discourses (a matter not incident to your charge) than in searching out the bottom of the proceedings there and advertising such particularities as were fit for Her Majesty's knowledge.'[61] Secretary Wilson wrote: 'You are to be commanded, and bound to follow the bounds of your charge by just limitation. And, although things be sometimes ordered much against your mind, yet you must submit yourself to the same.'[62] Davison, 'I living here where I see and observe how things pass',[63] thought that he knew what had to be done: keep out the French, drive out the Spaniards, and secure the cause of religion and liberty. But, he added, 'I do live here utterly ignorant of the success of things in our Court.'[64]

Throughout the months of the progress, Walsingham, with Lord Cobham, a finely balanced duo of Protestant and near-Catholic, was himself in the Netherlands, engaged in a critical diplomatic mission ostensibly aimed at pacifying and neutralising this region, but with more than one agenda, a mission which was so frustrating – as the queen continually and repeatedly reneged on what many on that side of the North Sea were expecting of her – that by September he was on the verge of resignation, resolved to give up diplomacy as a bad job: 'God send me well to return and I will hereafter take my leave of foreign service.'[65] He whimsically suggested that he and Cobham would be hanged on their return, he hoped after due trial, where the gravest charge would be that they had had more regard for the queen's honour and safety than for her finances. 'There is a difference between serving with a cheerful and languishing mind.'[66] Those travelling with the queen shared his deep frustration, so that the letters passing between Walsingham in Antwerp and the court in East Anglia are some of the best evidence we have of the deep division between the queen and her Privy Council on the most salient issue in foreign policy. Never before or after were the inmost thoughts of Privy Councillors committed to paper as they were in the summer of 1578, unless it was at the time of the trial of Mary Queen of Scots eight years later, when Walsingham was moved to write: 'I would to God her Majesty would be content to refer these things to them that can best judge of them, as other princes do.'[67] Normally the Ambassador, Davison, would have been in regular communication with the Secretaries of State, Walsingham and Sir Thomas Wilson. But with the principal Secretary of State thrust into the unwelcome role of ambassador, it was Walsingham himself who was corresponding with Burghley, Leicester, Sussex, and the up-and-coming star, Christopher Hatton.

When Leicester came down from Buxton to join the progress in late July, he told Walsingham that the queen's mind had recently changed, and that he had gone almost beyond the limits of the protocols of counsel in trying to persuade her where her best interests lay, Walsingham hoping that his 'wonted manner of plainness in causes that so deeply touch Her Majesty' would have the desired effect.[68] Burghley wrote in similar terms from Audley End on 29 July: 'All this and much more alleged with all manner of earnestness and importunity, to her displeasure ... A strange thing it is to see God's goodness, so abundantly offered for Her Majesty's surety, to be so daintily hearkened unto.'[69] On 6 August, the earl of Sussex wrote from Bury: 'It resteth in God to dispose her heart as shall please him.' Sussex thought that by trying to please the queen there was a risk of dividing 'the good of her from the good of the realm, and so the ill of her from the ill of the realm', which in the end would deceive both her and the realm.[70] Plain speaking from someone on the far right of our politico-religious spectrum! The next day Leicester wrote to Walsingham of the queen: 'It is no small alteration I find in Her Majesty's disposition ... How loth she is to come to any manner of dealing that way, specially to be at any charges, it is very strange.'[71] On 9 August, Secretary Wilson wrote from Thetford: 'Temporising hath been thought heretofore good policy. There was never so dangerous a time as this is, and temporising will no longer serve.'[72]

On the same day, Burghley wrote to the ambassadors: 'It is at this present determined here that, if, upon your answer, necessity shall induce Her Majesty to send forces, my Lord of Leicester will come over without delay and the army shall follow. Nevertheless, though this be for the present earnestly meant, I can assure nothing, but this only that I am here uncertain of much.'[73] Leicester told Davison that at Norwich they were almost close enough to hear 'the voice of that people'. 'Well', he commented, 'God help them and us too, fearing our need will be more than theirs.'[74] On 29 August, Leicester wrote to Walsingham: 'It were needless to discourse at large to you what dealings here hath been on all sides to further this good cause, because there followeth so small fruit thereof.'[75] Two days later, Burghley told Walsingham that 'we of her council are forced greatly to offend [the queen] in these and Scotland matters'.[76] By early September, Walsingham was warning Burghley that by whatever advice the queen had been directed to deal so hardly with the Dutch, 'depending as they do chiefly upon her favour in their necessity', the result would prove so perilous to herself and to the reputation of her realm 'that she will curse them that were authors of the advice when she perceives that they had more regard to some private profit ... than to her safety'.[77] I think that this was aimed at Sussex, or at Hatton, who was finding that to be an echo to the queen's thoughts and fears was a safe road to advancement.

V

Thus far I have not mentioned the role of François, duc d'Alençon and Anjou, 'Monsieur'. Yet Anjou, in his absence, was central to the politics of the progress, as he was to the diplomacy of the English ambassadors, which was aimed at preventing him from filling the dangerous vacuum in the Netherlands by coming to terms with the Estates.[78] His representatives were part of the progress, witnesses to all that went on. What did Anjou signify? Would he keep the French out of the Netherlands, or would he draw them in? Did policy demand that the queen marry Anjou, or would his role in the Netherlands be an alternative to marriage? Was Anjou serious in his marriage overtures, or was he double-dealing? Was the queen engaging in sincere courtship behind the backs of her ministers? The letters passing to and fro in July, August and September 1578 make it clear that no one at the heart of government had any idea how to answer those questions. Sometimes Anjou was seen as part of the problem, sometimes as the solution. When Walsingham wrote to Burghley on 28 August, it is clear that he was thoroughly confused: 'I find that Venus is presently ascendant in your climate. But when I consider the retrograde aspects that the present cause in hand is subject unto, I can hope after no great good. I pray God there ensue no harm thereof.'[79] William Davison made it clear, in all his dispatches, that he regarded Anjou as bad news. For the Dutch, Davison reported, it was 'a question in policy very hard to discuss whether [it] were better to accept or reject him ... The question is then what shall be done with him.'[80] Walsingham believed that Monsieur was deceiving the queen.[81] Leicester's advice was that Walsingham should seem neither to favour nor to oppose the marriage, since the queen's own intentions were obscure.[82] Sussex was no less sceptical.[83] But in mid-August, Walsingham told Leicester that 'the match were not to be misliked, seeing the necessity Her Majesty and the realm hath of the same'.[84] Yet he would be loath 'to lay any great wager on the matter'.[85] But in writing to Walsingham in late August, Leicester expressed regret that the queen had done nothing to satisfy Monsieur's expectation 'in the matter of marriage', which might have given her some security. Beyond that he had no advice to offer.[86] Just before she left Norwich, Elizabeth received advice from Sussex about the benefits which might grow 'by this marriage at this time', and about the perils which would follow 'if she married not at all'.[87]

VI

To marry not at all? It was in the cultural context of the 1578 progress, and in Thomas Churchyard's Norwich, that Elizabeth I was first publicly celebrated as the Virgin Queen. The allegorical symbolism was transparent in the entertainment staged by Churchyard on the fourth day of the visit, 'Tuesday's Device'. Churchyard claimed that this playlet was almost improvised, taking the opportunity of the queen passing on a certain route to her dinner, and perhaps seizing the advantage of one of the few fine days in a sodden week, when most events were rained off. Churchyard, disregarding the 'many doubts' expressed, 'many men persuaded to tarry a better time', 'hastily prepared my boys and men, with all their furnitures'. But there must have been more to it than that. The plot concerned a series of encounters between Venus and her son Cupid, both 'thrust out of Heaven', a grey-headed Philosopher, and Dame Chastity, accompanied by her maids, Modesty, Temperance, Good Exercise, and Shamefastness. Elizabeth was thoroughly involved in the action. Chastity, claiming that the queen had chosen the best life – that is, one of celibacy – handed her Cupid's bow to shoot with as she pleased, since 'none could wound her highness's heart'. 'Then sith (o Queen) chaste life is thus thy choice, | And that thy heart is free from bondage yoke, | Thou shalt (good Queen) by my consent and voice, | Have half the spoil, take either bow or cloak.' 'The song sung by Chastity's 'maids' reiterated in line after line 'chaste life', contrasted with 'lewd life'. 'Chaste life a precious pearl, | doth shin as bright as Sun.' In Bernard Garter's account of the Saturday pageant, in which Cupid's golden arrow was again handed to the queen, Diana, presenting her with a bow and silver-tipped arrows, used the phrase 'Virgin Queen', which we do not find in Churchyard: 'Who ever found on Earth a constant friend, | That may compare with this my Virgin Queen?' 'The Virgin's state DIANA still did praise.' Garret's account of the Monday proceedings contains a further reference to the queen as 'a Virgin pure, which is, and ever was'.[88]

Churchyard claimed that, following his Tuesday show, 'I had gracious words of the Queen openly and often pronounced by her Highness.' Before reading on, he wrote, 'you must thoroughly note what my discourse thereof hath been'.[89] Whose 'discourse' was it? Who had put Churchyard up to it? It is easy to conclude, as Susan Doran has done, that the Norwich shows were devised by opponents of the Anjou match, perhaps in particular by Leicester, whose opposition to the match would become rather more clear in 1579 and 1580; perhaps even that the whole libretto of the progress, Leicester's libretto, had this anti-Anjou purpose.[90] But as we have seen, in August 1578 everyone, including Leicester, was in at least two minds about Anjou. As was the queen, which may explain why she congratulated Churchyard on his drama of Venus, Cupid and Chastity. We can assume that a marriage between Elizabeth and Leicester was no longer likely, and had not been, at least since 1575 and Kenilworth. That was not the message of Philip Sidney's masque 'The Lady of May', performed in the queen's presence at Wanstead earlier in the summer of 1578; although the contested politics of intervention in the Netherlands probably was.[91] That Leicester was about to marry the widowed Countess of Essex was a secret already leaking in several directions, although not apparently in the direction of Gabriel Harvey, for all that he was Leicester's man.[92]

Book II of his *Gratulationum Valdinensium libri quatuor*, presented to the queen in manuscript at Audley End and in print at Hadham on 15 September, was one of the last literary attempts to promote a marriage between Elizabeth and Leicester.[93] What was going on in Norwich during those rainy August days was an expression of widely shared doubts and fears about the Anjou match. Opinions ranged from an open-minded scepticism (which the queen certainly shared) to the downright hostility of those who thought like Davison, and his close friend John Stubbs, whose *The discoverie of a gaping gulf wherinto England is like to be swallowed by an other French mariage* would be published exactly a year later.[94] Stubbs had written to Davison on 30 April 1578: 'The Lord knit us faster and faster in our faith and love and hope of our everlasting life', wishing him 'happy success' in his 'godly endeavors': the authentic voice of political Puritanism, which was one of the most insistent voices of that summer of 1578.[95]

VII

I end with a coda. Among his other qualities, the earl of Leicester was given to writing revealing letters, self-promoting, self-protecting, self-righteous, full of injured pride. On 27 September 1578, Leicester wrote such a letter to his colleague and, I think we can say, friend, Lord Burghley. The letter had to do with matters concerning the Mint, on which Leicester had not been properly consulted, perhaps because in July he had been out of touch, at Buxton. Hatton wrote to Burghley on 28 September saying that he had heard that he was in trouble with Leicester, 'his taking offence towards you in that he was not made privy to this last warrant for the coining of money', and that in Hatton's opinion it was much ado about nothing, which does indeed seem to have been the case.[96] Nevertheless, Leicester believed that he had been shabbily treated, something he could neither understand nor accept. He and Burghley had been together for weeks, so why had nothing been said? 'For we began our service with our sovereign together, and have long continued hitherto together, and touching your fortune I am sure your self cannot have a thought that ever I was enemy to it.' 'Your lordship hath been acquainted with me now almost thirty years, and these twenty years in service together. What opinions you have in deed of me, I may for these considerations alleged somewhat doubt, though I promise you I know no cause in the world in my self that I have given you other than good.' No one had ever deserved so well at Burghley's hands as Leicester. So why this opposition? 'Well, my Lord, you may suppose this to be a strange humour in me to write thus and in this sort to you, having never done the like before.'[97] The notion of Conyers Read that Burghley and Leicester represented polar opposites in the Elizabethan polity, forever repelling each other, fails to convince. But this letter is evidence that it was always an uneasy relationship.

Yet it is altogether understandable that Leicester should have been agitated on 27 September. Four days earlier, he had entertained the queen to lunch at his great house at Wanstead, the final event in that marathon of a progress, which had started out ten weeks earlier. Three days before that, he had been quietly married, in that same house, to Lettice, Countess of Essex. The queen was not supposed to know and she may not have known. Everyone must have been feeling the strain of those long July, August and September days: the strains of travelling and of hectic and mostly abortive diplomacy. As Gabriel Harvey's enemy Thomas Nashe might have put it, Leicester's odd letter was that summer's last will and testament. In that entertainment, Nashe's Summer declares that he would have already died, but that 'Eliza' had bidden him to 'live and linger' until 'her joyful progress was expired'.[98]

NOTES

1   *Calendar of Letters and State Papers ... in the Archives of Simanacs, 1568–79*, ed. Martin A. S. Hume, 4 vols (London: HMSO, 1892–9), vol. 2 (1894), pp. 606–7, 613. Dr Adams has suggested to me that one reason why Elizabeth never penetrated into the true 'North' was that for many years that would have entailed a meeting with Mary Queen of Scots, something which, for contrary diplomatic reasons, she could neither undertake nor be seen, if in the vicinity, not to undertake.

2   Cambridge University Library, University Archives, Letters B9, B13 a–c; *The Progresses and Public Processions of Queen Elizabeth*, ed. John Nichols, 2nd edn, 3 vols (London: John Nichols, 1823), vol. 3, pp. 109–15; Virginia F. Stern, *Gabriel Harvey: His life, marginalia and library* (Oxford: Clarendon Press, 1980), pp. 39–46.

3   Bernard Garter, *The Ioyfvll Receyuing of the Queenes Most Excellent Maiestie into hir Highnesse Citie of Norwich* (London: Henrie Bynneman, 30 Aug. 1578); Thomas Churchyard, *A Discovrse of the Queenes Maiesties Entertainment in Suffolk and Norffolk* (London: Henrie Bynneman, 20 Sept. 1578). Both texts are available in *Records of Early English Drama: Norwich 1540–1642*, ed. David Galloway (Toronto: University of Toronto Press, 1984), pp. 243–330.

4   Zillah Dovey, *An Elizabethan Progress: The Queen's journey into East Anglia, 1578* (Stroud: Alan Sutton, 1996). But see, more generally, Mary Hill Cole, *The Portable Queen: Elizabeth I and the politics of ceremony* (Amherst, Mass.: University of Massachusetts Press, 1999), pp. 141–4.

5   Chapter 5 in this volume.

6   Simon Adams, *Leicester and the Court: Essays on Elizabethan politics* (Manchester: Manchester University Press, 2002); Stephen Alford, *The Early Elizabethan Polity: William Cecil and the British succession crisis, 1558–1569* (Cambridge: Cambridge University Press, 1998); Susan Doran, *Monarchy and Matrimony: The courtships of Elizabeth I* (London: Routledge, 1996); Susan Doran and Thomas S. Freeman (eds), *The Myth of Elizabeth I* (Basingstoke: Palgrave Macmillan, 2003); John Guy (ed.), *The Tudor Monarchy* (London: Arnold, 1997); John Guy (ed.), *The Reign of Elizabeth I: Court and culture in the last decade* (Cambridge: Cambridge University Press, 1995); A. N.

McLaren, *Political Culture in the Reign of Elizabeth I: Queen and commonwealth 1558–1585* (Cambridge: Cambridge University Press, 1999); Patrick Collinson, 'The monarchical republic of Queen Elizabeth I', in Guy (ed.), *The Tudor Monarchy*, pp. 110–34; Chapter 2 in this volume; Julia Walker (ed.), *Dissing Elizabeth: Negative representations of Gloriana* (Durham, N.C.: Duke University Press, 1998).

7 Leicester to Sir Francis Walsingham, 1 Aug. 1578, 'in much haste, her Majesty ready to horseback, at Bury': *Relations politiques des Pays-Bas et de l'Angleterre sous le règne de Philippe II*, ed. Kervyn de Lettenhove, 11 vols (Brussels: n.p., 1882–1900), vol. 10, pp. 678–80.

8 Edmund Lodge, *Illustrations of British History*, 3 vols (London: G. Nicol, 1791), vol. 2, p. 150.

9 *Ibid.*, p. 171.

10 Sir Christopher Hatton to Leicester, 18 June 1578; Longleat House, MS. Dudley II, fo. 178. I owe this reference to Simon Adams.

11 Dovey, *An Elizabethan Progress*, pp. 114–18; *Progresses*, ed. Nichols, 2nd edn, vo. 2, pp. 236–46.

12 *Records of Early English Drama: Norwich*, p. 295.

13 Dovey, *An Elizabethan Progress*, pp. 17–18.

14 *The Papers of Nathaniel Bacon of Stiffkey*, ed. A. Hassell Smith and Gillian M. Baker, 4 vols (Norwich: Centre of East Anglian Studies, University of Norwich, 1983), vol. 2, p. 19.

15 *Calendar of the Manuscripts of the Most Hon. the Marquis of Salisbury ... Preserved at Hatfield House, Hertfordshire*, 14 vols (London: HMSO, 1883–1923), vol. 2 (1888), pp. 189–90.

16 A footnote on p. 196 of Diarmaid MacCulloch, *Suffolk and the Tudors: Politics and religion in an English county, 1500–1600* (Oxford: Clarendon Press, 1986), reporting a communication from Simon Adams, has been hardened up into an over-confident assertion that Leicester was 'involved in the planning of the progress' (Susan Doran, 'Juno vs Diana: the treatment of Elizabeth's marriage plans in plays and entertainments, 1561–1581', *Historical Journal*, 36 (1995), pp. 257–74 at p. 271; Doran, *Monarchy and Matrimony*, p. 150). He may well have been. But Dr Adams knows of no surviving evidence that Leicester's role was central or decisive.

17 For the background, and much of the content, of what follows, see Diarmaid MacCulloch, 'Catholic and Puritan in Elizabethan Suffolk: a county community polarises', *Archiv für Reformationsgeschichte*, 72 (1981): 232–89; MacCulloch, *Suffolk and the Tudors*; A. Hassell Smith, *County and Court: Government and politics in Norfolk 1558–1603* (Oxford: Clarendon Press, 1974).

18 Quoted (from Inner Temple Library, MS. Petyt 538/47, fo. 494) in Patrick Collinson, 'Perne the Turncoat: an Elizabethan reputation', in Collinson, *Elizabethan Essays* (London: Hambledon, 1994), pp. 179–218 at p. 181 n. 6.

19 Smith, *County and Court*, pp. 201–2. For the case of Sussex, which the Privy Council treated very differently, in effect deposing the Bishop of Chichester (Richard Curteys) for being too high-handed in his handling of the Catholic gentry, see Roger B. Manning, *Religion and Society in Elizabethan Sussex: A study of the enforcement of the religious settlement, 1558–1603* (Leicester: Leicester University Press, 1969).

20 NA, S.P. 15/25/119, fo. 280ᵛ. SP 15/25/119 contains a fat little dossier (fos 268–86) headed: 'The principal solicitors and instruments of the bishop of Norwich his un-advised dealings, detected by oath of discreet and faithful deponents, and by other apparent likelihoods plainly discovered.' This rather suspect dossier is the source for some of the circumstantial detail that follows.

21 *Conferences and Combination Lectures in the Elizabethan Church: Dedham and Bury St Edmund's, 1582–1590*, ed. Patrick Collinson, John Craig, and Brett Usher (Woodbridge: Boydell [and] Church of England Record Society, 2003), pp. xlii–l.

22 Brett Usher, *William Cecil and Episcopacy, 1559–1577* (Aldershot: Ashgate, 2003), pp. 118–19, 120–2.

23 Patrick Collinson, *The Elizabethan Puritan Movement* (Oxford: Clarendon Press, 1990), 202–4; Smith, *County and Court*, 208–25; *Conferences and Combination Lectures*, ed. Collinson, Craig, and Usher, pp. xlvii–xlviii.

24 Draft letter from Bacon to 'a noble lord', almost certainly Leicester, 24 Jan. [1578?]; Folger Shakespeare Library, Washington, DC, Case 1472, Bacon Folder 11. I owe this reference to Hassell Smith.

25 Bishop Freke to Ferdinando Paris of Pudding Norton, 13 Mar. 1582; Pembroke College, Cambridge, MS. Letter Book relating to the Paris family, fo. 46.

26 MacCulloch, 'Catholic and Puritan', 235.

27 Smith, *County and Court*, pp. 210–23.

28 Victor Morgan, *A History of the University of Cambridge*, 4 vols (Cambridge: Cambridge University Press, 2004), vol 2, pp. 71, 73.

29 Smith, *County and Court*, pp. 210, 216.

30 John Becon to Nathaniel Bacon, 23 May 1578, *The Papers of Nathaniel Bacon*, vol 2, pp. 8–9; Patrick Collinson, 'The Puritan Classical Movement in the reign of Elizabeth I' (unpublished doctoral thesis, University of London, 1957), pp. 312–19, 882–5; Smith, *County and Court*, pp. 210–11.

31 *The Seconde Parte of a Register*, ed. Albert Peel, 2 vols (Cambridge: n.p., 1915), vol 1, pp. 157–60.

32 Usher, *William Cecil and Episcopacy*, pp. 182–3.

33 MacCulloch, *Suffolk and the Tudors*, pp. 85, 187–8.

34 Richard Topcliffe to Shrewsbury, 30 Aug. 1578: Lodge, *Illustrations*, vol. 2, pp. 187–8.

35 *CSP… Simanacs, 1568–79*, ed. Hume, vol. 2 (1894), p. 613.

36 The latest and best account of the 'Bury stirs' is in John Craig, *Reformation, Politics and Polemics: The growth of Protestantism in East Anglian market towns, 1500–1610* (Aldershot: Ashgate, 2001).

37 Dovey, *An Elizabethan Progress*, pp. 47–8.

38 Craig, *Reformation, Politics and Polemics*, pp. 90–1.

39 MacCulloch, *Suffolk and the Tudors*, p. 196; Collinson, 'The Puritan Classical Movement', pp. 866–930.

40 Augustus Jessopp, *One Generation of a Norfolk House: A contribution to Elizabethan history*, 3rd edn (London: Fisher Unwin, 1913), p. 95.

41 *Conferences and Combination Lectures*, ed. Collinson, Craig, and Usher, pp. xlvii–xlviii.

42 Collinson, *The Elizabethan Puritan Movement*, p. 203.

43 *HMC … Salisbury*, vol. 2 (1888), pp. 195–8; Collinson, 'The Puritan classical movement', pp. 236–9, 883–5.

44 Manning, *Religion and Society in Elizabethan Sussex*, pp. 118–19; Collinson, *The Elizabethan Puritan Movement*, pp. 183–7.

45 NA, S.P. 12/126/3, 6, 19, 23, 41, 41I; SP 15/25/119, 120.

46 Reproduced from a Hatfield House manuscript as a facsimile in Dovey, *An Elizabethan Progress*, p. 90.

47 *Acts of the Privy Council of England*, ed. John R. Dasent, 25 vols (London: HMSO, 1890–1964), vol. 10 (1895), pp. 310–16.

48 *Ibid.*, p. 317.

49 MacCulloch, *Suffolk and the Tudors*, pp. 196–7.

50 *The Papers of Nathaniel Bacon*, vol. 2, p. 20; *Calendar of State Papers, Domestic Series, Addenda, 1566–1579*, ed. Mary Anne Everett Green (London: HMSO, 1871), p. 548.

51 A draft letter from Bacon to Leicester (Folger Shakespeare Library, Bacon Papers). I owe this reference to Hassell Smith.

52 William Gurnall, *The Magistrates Pourtraiture* (London: printed for Ralph Smith, 1656), p. 38.

53 Patrick Collinson, *The Religion of Protestants: The Church in English society, 1559–1625* (Oxford: Clarendon Press, 1982); Patrick Collinson, 'Magistracy and ministry: a Suffolk miniature', in Collinson, *Godly People: Essays on English Protestantism and Puritanism* (London: Hambledon Press, 1983), pp. 445–66.

54 Patrick Collinson, 'The downfall of Archbishop Grindal and its place in Elizabethan political and ecclesiastical history', in Collinson, *Godly People*, pp. 371–97.

55 Knollys to Secretary Wilson, 9 Jan. 1578; BL, Harleian MS. 6992, no. 44, fo. 89.

56 Charles Wilson, *Queen Elizabeth and the Revolt of the Netherlands* (London: Macmillan, 1970), p. 43.

57 NA, S.P. 12/115/24. See Robert Tittler, *Nicholas Bacon: The making of a Tudor statesman* (London: Cape, 1976), pp. 168–86.

58 NA, S.P. 15/25/35.

59 Wilson, *Queen Elizabeth and the Revolt of the Netherlands*, p. 59.

60 Conyers Read, *Mr Secretary Walsingham and the Policy of Queen Elizabeth*, 3 vols (Oxford, Clarendon Press, 1925), vol. 2, p. 265.

61 Walsingham to Davison, 2 May 1578 (*Relations politiques*, ed. de Lettenhove, vol 10, pp. 438–9).

62 Wilson to Davison, 6 May 1578 (*ibid.*, pp. 449–50).

63 Davison to Walsingham, 11 May 1578 (*ibid.*, p. 461).

64 Davison to Walsingham and Wilson, 8 May 1578 (*ibid.*, pp. 453–5).

65 *Ibid.*, pp. 813–19. Walsingham to Heneage, 2 Sept. 1578 (Read, *Mr Secretary Walsingham*, vol. 1, p. 422).

66 Walsingham to Hatton, Walsingham to Thomas Randolph, both 29 July 1578; *Relations politiques*, ed. de Lettenhove, vol. 10, pp. 664–5; quoted in Read, *Mr Secretary Walsingham*, vol. 1, pp. 393–4.

67 J. E. Neale, *Queen Elizabeth* (London: Jonathan Cape, 1934), p. 274.

68 Leicester to Walsingham, 20 July 1578, Walsingham to Leicester, 23 July 1578 (*Relations politiques*, ed. de Lettenhove, vol. 10, pp. 613–15, 630).

69 Burghley to Cobham and Walsingham, 29 July 1578 (*ibid.*, pp. 659–61).

70 Sussex to Walsingham, 6 Aug. 1578 (*ibid.*, pp. 696–7).

71 Leicester to Walsingham (*ibid.*, pp. 678–80). This letter is dated 1 Aug. in de Lettenhove.

72 Wilson to Walsingham, 9 Aug. 1578 (*ibid.*, pp. 710–11).

73 Burghley to Cobham and Walsingham, 9 Aug. 1578 (*ibid.*, p. 710).

74 Leicester to Davison, 18 Aug. 1578 (*ibid.*, p. 741).

75 Leicester to Walsingham, 29 Aug. 1578 (*ibid.*, pp. 772–3).

76 Burghley to Walsingham, 31 Aug. 1578 (*ibid.*, p. 783).

77 Walsingham to Burghley, 2 Sept. 1578, quoted in Read, *Mr Secretary Walsingham*, vol. 1, pp. 416–18.

78 Read, *Mr Secretary Walsingham*, vol. 1, pp. 373–422.

79 Walsingham to Burghley, 28 Aug. 1578 (*Relations politiques*, ed. de Lettenhove, vol. 10, pp. 766–7).

80 Davison to Leicester, 18 July 1578 (*ibid.*, p. 606).

81 Walsingham to Leicester, 29 July 1578 (*ibid.*, pp. 662–3).

82 Leicester to Walsingham, 1 Aug. 1578 (*ibid.*, pp. 679–80); quoted in Read, *Mr Secretary Walsingham*, vol. 1, p. 402 n. 3.

83 Sussex to Walsingham, 6 Aug. 1578 (*Relations politiques*, ed. de Lettenhove, vol. 10, pp. 696–7).

84 Walsingham to Leicester, 18 Aug. 1578 (*ibid.*, p. 744); quoted in Read, *Mr Secretary Walsingham*, vol. 1, pp. 402–3.

85 Walsingham to Leicester, 28 Aug. 1578 (*Relations politiques*, ed. de Lettenhove, vol. 10, p. 765).

86 Leicester to Walsingham, 29 Aug. 1578 (*ibid.*, pp. 772–3).

87 Sussex to Walsingham, 29 Aug. 1578 (*ibid.*, pp. 774–5).

88 *Records of Early English Drama: Norwich*, pp. 304–14, 261, 275, 287.

89 *Ibid.*, pp. 305–6.

90 Doran, 'Juno vs Diana', pp. 270–2; Doran, *Monarchy and Matrimony*, pp. 150–2.

91 Doran, 'Juno vs Diana', pp. 269–70.

92 On 22 Aug. 1578, William Fulke, master of Pembroke Hall, wrote to the Fellows from Norwich, instructing them to renew Harvey's fellowship for another year, at 'the ernest request' of Leicester. *Letter-Book of Gabriel Harvey*, A.D. *1573–1580*, ed. E. J. L. Scott (London: Camden Society, 1884), p. 88.

93 Stern, *Gabriel Harvey*, pp. 40–6.

94 *John Stubbs's 'Gaping Gulf' with Letters and Other Relevant Documents*, ed. Lloyd E. Berry (Charlottesville: University of Virginia Press, 1968).

95 *Ibid.*, pp. 106–7.

96 Hatton to Burghley, 28 Sept. 1578; *HMC ... Salisbury*, vol. 2 (1888), p. 208.

97 Leicester to Burghley, 27 Sept. 1578 (NA, S.P. 12/125/73).

98 Charles Nicholl, *A Cup of News: The life of Thomas Nashe* (London: Routledge & Kegan Paul, 1984), pp. 135–6.

Chapter 5

Elizabeth I and the verdicts of history

O ne of the things that I remember about Mandell Creighton, biographer
of Elizabeth, great historian and notable bishop, bearing a marked physical resemblance to the current Archbishop of Canterbury, is that when controversy raged over Darwin's *Origin of Species*, he wrote to his fiancée suggesting that Darwin's theory was very dubious and that he would be happy
for her to sort it all out for him. 'I have not time for it, and would rather
read some Italian history.'[1] That story attracted my attention, since by instinct
and thwarted ambition I am a thoroughly Darwinian biologist and I only
accidentally stumbled into becoming some sort of historian. I had my formation at the Institute of Historical Research, which I still regard as my spiritual home. I remember that fifty years ago, I suppose to the day, the Monday
evening seminar at the Institute was suspended so that we could all attend the
Creighton Lecture, given in 1952 by Sir Lewis Namier. There have been some
hard acts to follow!

In the last year of his life, Matthew Parker, who was Queen Elizabeth's
first archbishop of Canterbury, found it difficult to look on the bright side.
Drafting a letter to Lord Burghley, which he never signed, he complained of
'this [Machiavellian] government' (which was not very tactful – Burghley after
all was in charge of it), and he expressed regret that he had ever agreed to
become one of its servants. He had only consented to serve out of loyalty to
Elizabeth's mother, Anne Boleyn, whose chaplain he had once been. He went
on: 'I fear her Highness shall be strangely chronicled.'[2] Parker wrote better
than he knew, although we might want to add to 'strangely' 'variously': 'I fear
her Highness shall be strangely and very variously chronicled.'

Revised version of a paper delivered as the Creighton Lecture in the Beveridge Hall,
University of London, on 11 November 2002. Published in *Historical Research*, 76 (2003):
469–91, and reproduced by permission of the Institute of Historical Research and Wiley-
Blackwell.

The pluralisation of 'verdicts' in my title is very intentional. Where do we start with the many verdicts of history on such a monarch, such a woman, and where do we end? We should not confine our attention to the verdicts of professional historians. Many Victorian and post-Victorian readers learned their Elizabethan history not from James Anthony Froude nor, dare I say it on this occasion, Mandell Creighton, but from that dark Gothic novel by Walter Scott, *Kenilworth*; just as their great grandchildren have absorbed it from the postmodernist film *Elizabeth*, which (I am told) had more to do with the late Princess Diana and Indian mythology than with the real Elizabeth Tudor; and which managed to be even more contemptuous of historical truth than Scott, rather as if the known facts, together with a good many facts hitherto unknown, were shaken up like pieces of a jigsaw and scattered on the table at random.[3] However, it may be no less dangerous to sit in front of David Starkey's series on television and to suppose that one is seeing it all exactly the way it happened Even twentieth-century newsreels can be very deceptive, and in 1560 there was no Pathé or Movietone, let alone CNN and Sky News. The good people of Los Angeles are even more at risk. Each year in May they attend in their tens of thousands the Renaissance Fayre, held in the Ventura Hills where all those Hopalong Cassidy films were made. And there they gawp at Queen Elizabeth I as virtual reality, more virtual than real, riding around the fairground on a white horse with her great red wig, just as she appeared at Tilbury in 1588, and to my eyes in 1984 looking very like Glenda Jackson, while her courtiers toiled behind in their heavy furs. The temperature was 110 degrees Fahrenheit.

I don't want to suggest that earlier generations were so ignorant of Elizabethan history as to be at the mercy of romantic fiction. That precursor to *1066 And All That*, *The Comic History of England*, published in 1847 by Gilbert Abbott A'Beckett, with illustrations by John Leech, who was one of the original building blocks of *Punch*, presumed on the part of its readers a sophisticated knowledge of the subject. Witness this account of how the news of the execution of Mary Queen of Scots was conveyed to her son:

> The ambassador let him have his cry completely out, and then drawing himself up with an air of some dignity, observed: 'When you have left off roaring, and can hear me speak, I will tell you the rights of it.' 'Nobody has any right to murder my mamma' was the reply of the boy ... The messenger, nevertheless, persisted that the Queen of England meant nothing by signing the death-warrant; that, in fact, she had been only 'in fun'; and as he wound up with the offer of an increased pension to James, the heartless brat dried his eyes, with the observation, that 'What's done can't be undone'.

As for William Davison, the fallguy for the ensuing political storm in England, he went about exclaiming, 'I! Well that is the coolest! – 'Pon my word! What next?' But he soon found out what was next, for he was committed to prison and fined £10,000.[4] The humour depended on both the author and the reader knowing the facts of the matter, from which indeed *The Comic History* did not stray all that far. You could not do it now.

I want to draw attention at the outset to Archbishop Parker's use of that word 'chronicled'. Although the historical chronicle was a literary genre which saw a good deal of cutthroat competition in Tudor England (Stow versus Grafton, and then the take-over bid by the consortium called Holinshed), there was a notion that there ought to be only one more or less official and reliably authentic account of the recoverable past, something not so far from the Chinese model of historiography, where (I understand) the rice-paper archives were routinely shredded after being subsumed into the one, officially approved, imperial history. If the bottom line for the historian was to tell the truth (as Cicero had insisted), and there was only one truth, then it had to be so. Readers of Holinshed were told that chronicles were 'books of credit',[5] hence the efforts of the nervous authorities to censor that vast tome.[6] But the fact that there never was a uniform English history, nothing to place alongside the Book of Common Prayer, tells us a great deal about the devolved polity of Tudor England, which was not at all like imperial China.

It was further thought that recording the history of great affairs, high politics, was a task which should only be undertaken by those who had had firsthand acquaintance with them. A failed Elizabethan politician and diplomat, Francis Alford, who was angling for a research grant which would enable him to tackle a history of Elizabeth's reign, remarked: 'To write a [hi]storie there apertaineth more then a schollers knowledge.'[7] Ideally Elizabeth should have been her own historian, and indeed Sir Henry Saville, the translator of Tacitus, expressed the flattering wish that she might prove to be her own Tacitus.[8] Or Lord Burghley perhaps should have been the man. But Elizabethan politicians were not allowed to resign or retire, and none of them wrote his memoirs (or, so far as I know, kept diaries – no Elizabethan Chips Channons or Edwina Curries).

Instead, Burghley made the state papers accessible to William Camden. It was, Camden explained, Burghley who 'imparted to me, first his own, and then the Queen's Rolls, Memorials and Records, willing me to compile from thence an Historical Account of the first Beginnings of the Reign of Queen Elizabeth'. When Camden boasted of his heroic engagement with 'great Piles and Heaps of Papers and Writings of all sorts', he was not only laying claim to the credentials of an industrious researcher. (But, credit where credit is due, his archival commitment was very great, and unusual. Francis Bacon, who got research assistants to do the hard work for his book on Henry VII, thought such labours beneath the dignity of a historian; rather like those professors of anatomy who left the handling of human organs to their assistants.) Camden was also telling us that all those rolls, memorials and records had admitted him to the highest counsels of state, almost as if he had been himself an agent.[9] When Machiavelli, in political disgrace and exile, sat down to write some of that Italian history which interested Creighton so much, he took off his workaday dress, the clothes he wore to go down to the pub, and put on the silken robes of a courtier.[10] Similarly, Camden distinguished between himself as a mere workaday antiquarian, the author of *Britannia*, and as a historian, an occupation requiring diplomatic experience and command of the higher reaches of eloquence.[11] But we should not sneer at the protocols of Renaissance historiography. Who better to tell us about the Cuban Missile Crisis than Robert MacNamara?

Camden was not only the first but, for one hundred years and more, the only historian of Elizabeth's reign of whom any account was taken. Although composed in the form of Tacitean 'Annals', his book was as much chronicle as history, and so it was by Camden that Elizabeth was 'chronicled', and, yes, strangely chronicled. It is worth a glance in passing at those who started work on the project only to give up: not only Alford, but Francis Bacon, who wrote no more than two or three paragraphs (which contain his memorable verdict on the Tudors – 'those barren princes').[12] Sir John Hayward managed to cover the first three years of the reign, ending with perhaps the most deflationary final paragraph of any history ever written: 'Thus, while great matters were acted abroad, nothing of any moment either happened or was observed at home.'[13] (Hayward was only interested in the beginnings of reigns: witness his notorious book on the deposition of Richard II and the usurpation of Henry IV, and another book on the Norman Conquest.[14]) And then there was John Clapham, whose 'Certain Observations Concerning the Life and Reign of Queen Elizabeth' was written very soon after her death but intended only for his children and never published (and nor, for that matter did Hayward's book make it into print); and which was little more than a eulogy for Clapham's master, who was the same Lord Burghley.[15]

So Camden had no rival. When, in the mid-eighteenth century, Thomas Birch published his *Memoirs of the Reign of Queen Elizabeth From the Year 1581 till her Death*, mostly a digest of Anthony Bacon's manuscripts in Lambeth Palace Library, he had some critical things to say about Camden but suggested that the last thing that anyone needed was a new history of Queen Elizabeth: 'To relate over again the same series of transactions diversified only in the method and style, and with the addition of a few particular incidents, would be no very agreeable undertaking to the historian, and certainly of little use to the reader.'[16] The year was 1754! Birch could not know that well over one hundred books professing to be biographical accounts of Elizabeth and her reign would be published between 1890 and the present day, not to mention whole shelves of aspectual and monographical historical works, together with all that fiction, in print, celluloid, electronics and impersonation. And in 2003, when we commemorated the fourth centenary of Elizabeth's death, there would be a new avalanche. That anniversary was even the excuse for this lecture. Birch would have been appalled. I hope that I am more interesting (if less industrious) than Birch. People still quote what Samuel Johnson said about him: 'Tom Birch is as brisk as a bee in conversation, but no sooner does he take a pen in his hand than it becomes a torpedo to him and numbs all his faculties.'[17] But I am so far in agreement with Tom Birch that the other day I returned a cheque for £1,000 to Blackwell's, asking to be released from a contract to write yet another of those many books; and I am glad to say that they helpfully complied. So my 36,000 words for *The Oxford Dictionary of National Biography*, and this chapter, will be all that I myself have to offer by way of a verdict on Elizabeth I. The fourth centenary will, of course, generate perhaps more than one book which will tell us things we did not previously know. Simon Adams, in his biography for Yale University Press, is going to do what I had thought to be impossible: tell a story in many ways different from all earlier accounts of Elizabeth's adolescent years; and perhaps David Loades will also add to our knowledge.

Back to William Camden, and, as a young researcher in Elizabethan history, I was told: 'It's all in Camden, and what's not in Camden won't hurt.' For someone born in 1929 and reared on historians like J. E. Neale, Leslie Rowse and S. T. Bindoff, who all reached for their dictionary of superlatives when they wrote about Elizabeth (Bindoff called her 'the matchless flower'[18]), it was a bit of a shock to find that Camden was very far from contributing to the canonisation of the lady, that indeed he could be read as a kind of devil's advocate in the canonising process; and, farther, to learn that Camden was by no means unique among her early historians and biographers in avoiding the role of hagiographer royal. Deflationary, revisionist books are now all the rage (there are two useful collections of revisionist essays, *Dissing Elizabeth: Negative representations of Gloriana* [1998] and *The Myth of Elizabeth* [2003]).[19] But for a pupil of Sir John Neale this has involved an intellectual and even emotional U-turn. It once seemed only right and proper that Rowse should dedicate his *The England of Elizabeth* 'To the glorious memory of Elizabeth queen of England', dating his preface 'Empire Day, 1950'. It was in that same year that Neale delivered his own Creighton Lecture, a celebration of 'The Elizabethan age'.[20]

That was not Camden's style. Here was no misty-eyed nostalgia for an 'age', which Neale, adapting Churchill, called 'their finest hour'.[21] Camden dedicated his *Annals* not to Elizabeth's memory but to his country and to posterity, 'at the altar of truth'. The preface, an essay in the rhetorical form *ars historica*, makes it less a book about Elizabeth than a book about history, Camden's major venture into that field, and his references to 'that Renowned Queen' and 'that Incomparable Princess' are almost perfunctory. At the end there is the obligatory obituary notice, but it is no more than seventy words long, which would hardly suffice for a church monument, and twenty-five of those words have to do with the consolation offered to a grieving kingdom by the advent of Elizabeth's virtuous successor, James I.[22] It is not Elizabeth but Mary Queen of Scots, denounced by Holinshed in the year of her execution as 'malitiouse and murtherous',[23] who is eulogised, especially in Camden's obit: 'A woman most constant in her religion, of singular piety towards *God*, inuincible magnanimitie of minde, wisedome aboue her sex, and passing beauty [I think that the translator meant "surpassing beauty", in Camden's Latin "formaque venustissima"].'[24] Compare the description of the same woman recorded by Richard Fletcher, dean of Peterborough and later bishop of London, who saw her head cut off: 'somewhat rounde shouldered, her face broade and fatte, duble chinned ...'[25]

Commentators on Camden's *Annals* have often assumed that the book was a celebration of a great monarch, if only, it seems, because that must have been what the author intended. Wallace MacCaffrey tells us that Camden's history was 'conceived as a monument to the achievement of Queen Elizabeth and her government', but that that purpose was attained by the rhetorical device of holding back on the praise and, 'more obliquely, more delicately', letting the historical record speak for itself'.[26]

Well, perhaps, but there are other reasons why Camden and his collaborator, Sir Robert Cotton, were rather cooler than cucumbers in their handling of Elizabeth. There was a political reason, explored by Hugh Trevor-Roper in his Neale Lecture of 1971, *Queen Elizabeth's First Historian*.[27] The Elizabeth project, which had lapsed after Burghley's death, revived only when James I needed ammunition to use in defence of his late mother against the greatest historian of the age, the French scholar Jacques-Auguste de Thou, who for his account of Scottish affairs had been over-dependent, *faute de mieux*, upon James's anti-monarchist tutor, George Buchanan. An early eighteenth-century critic complained that Camden had been induced 'rather to vindicate the Honour and Integrity of the king's Mother ... than to do right for a Mistresse' who had turned a mere schoolmaster into something rather better, a herald of arms. The justice of that observation was challenged at the time, by Camden's admirable editor, Thomas Hearne.[28] But even though Camden protested in his preface that he had not feared 'present Power', and while Trevor-Roper called the book 'magnificently uncourtly', there is something in the charge. Camden was worried about how James would take his positive portrayal of Mary's dedicated enemy, Sir Francis Walsingham, 'a true Roman spirit'; he agonised over his account of how Elizabeth reacted to and dealt with the news of Mary's execution; and he issued instructions that the second half of his book was not to be published in his lifetime. He even suggested (to return briefly to a point already made) that James I might like to publish it over his own name.[29] Camden's biographer, William Smith, would later report that it was 'the censures he met with in the business of *Mary* Queen Scots [*sic*]' which deterred him from proceeding any greater distance along such a troublesome road. Camden had told de Thou: 'inchoatia invida, continuatio labor, finis odium' (history is in the beginning envy, in the continuation labour and in the end hatred).[30]

For the strange and paradoxical fact is that Camden's history of the reign, for all that it was the first, was already an alternative, revisionist history, not the history that I learned at my supervisor's knee. The *Annals* are suffused with the conservatism of the Westminster circle, of which Camden was a leading light, and where Anglicanism seems to have been invented.[31] Lurking behind the text is that shadowy but important figure, Henry Howard, earl of Northampton under James I, who may stand for a strand or tendency of anti-Protestant-ascendancy conservatism.[32] Howard was a patron of Cotton, and Camden's character for his brother, the duke of Norfolk, executed in his presence in 1572, could hardly have been more favourable.[33] By contrast, Camden dipped his pen into vitriol whenever he wrote about Robert Dudley, earl of Leicester. Trevor-Roper thought that Camden's hatred of Leicester was a unique aberration in a work otherwise marked by strict historical impartiality. It was not. The denunciation of Leicester and of all Leicesterians was a governing, structural principle of the whole conception. And 'Leicesterians' meant Puritans, whom Camden called 'Protestantes effervescentes', 'Zeloti'. He was particularly critical of the 'declamationes et exclamationes' uttered against Mary Queen of Scots by what he calls the 'vehement', ecclesiastical sort of persons.[34]

A similar dispassionate, but far from neutrally dispassionate, attitude towards the dominant politico-religious tendency in Elizabethan England marks in one way or another other early attempts to write the history of the reign. John Clapham says very little about religion, but what he does say is vociferously anti-Puritan. Hayward's 'Annals', unlike Camden's, were a panegyric ('Excellent Queene! what doe my words but wrong thy worth? what doe I but guild gold?'),[35] but it was not a Protestant panegyric. In writing a history of the reign of Edward VI, Hayward forgot to mention that something happened at that time called the Reformation.[36] That there was a Reformation, indeed an iconoclastic holocaust in the first year of Elizabeth's reign, Hayward could not deny, but he made clear his own negative feelings on the matter: 'the extreemes in religion are superstytione and prophan[itie] ... betweene which extreames it is extremely hard to hold the meane.'[37] In his *Britannia*, Camden found it necessary to apologise for writing favourably about the dissolved monasteries.[38]

It may be that in each case these writers were swayed by their own moderate, even anti-hot-Protestant bias. But it is also relevant that they wrote 'civil' history, and (generally speaking) in a Tacitean mode. Tacitus wrote about bad times, when it became rather more safe to do so, and half-hoped for better times under Vespasian; just as that early English Tacitean, Sir Thomas More, hoped, but was not confident, that Henry VII and Henry VIII would prove less tyrannical than Richard III. Ideally, we should read Camden only in the Latin in which he wrote, which is terse, using one word where three or four are required in English, urbane and implicitly critical of both politicians and extremities, including the extremities of religious effervescence. These civil historians were very conscious that they were not writing ecclesiastical history, a subject which Camden would later exclude from the specifications for the history chair which he founded at Oxford.[39] So Camden, as Elizabeth's historian, distanced himself from 'the Writer of the Ecclesiastical History' and dealt with such matters 'with a light and chary Hand'.[40]

You might think that 'the Writer of the Ecclesiastical History' – who, to give him his name, was John Foxe, whose 'Book of Martyrs' was where effervescent Protestants for generations to come would learn their history – would have supplied the verdict on Elizabeth which this historian, in his knee-pants, gathered from Rowse and Neale. Not so. Recent fine-tooth-combing work on the account in Foxe of Elizabeth's troubles in the reign of her sister, and of how it changed in successive editions, reveals that the intention of this almost fictional story was not adulatory but prescriptive and admonitory, reminding Elizabeth that only God had preserved her and advanced her to her throne, and that if she dallied with this Protestant God she could only expect the worst.[41] In an 'oration' addressed to the queen by that militant Protestant John Hales, 'at her first Entrance to her Reign', and included by Foxe in *Actes and Monuments* only in the third edition of 1576 (and why then?), Elizabeth was told: 'If ye fear [God], and seek to do his will, then he will favour you, and preserve you to the end from all enemies, as he did king David. If ye now fall from him, or juggle with him, look for no more favour than Saul had showed to him.'[42] It is hardly too much to say that in these ultra-Protestant critical perceptions, Elizabeth was a puppet queen. The puppet master was God, whose ways and will were well known to those Protestant men who played the prophet Nathan to Elizabeth's David.

So these early verdicts made Elizabeth the victim of what modern politicians call a double whammy. The delicate balancing act which she conducted, tolerating both Leicester's Puritanism and obedient Catholics like Henry Howard, executing Mary Queen of Scots, but only after fifteen years of refusing to do so, carried that risk. In the words of the Book of Revelation, quoted against her in Bury St Edmunds in 1581, she was a Jezebel who had caused her servants to commit fornication.[43] Some thought her, in the words of the same scripture, 'neither hot nor cold', and early verdicts on her reign were critical, from both the hot and the cold standpoints. Yes, she was strangely chronicled.

I suppose there can be such a thing as a triple whammy. Catholic extremists purveyed their own strange chronicle, a mirror image of Mary Stuart as demonised by Protestants, Elizabeth as Jezebel, the daughter of both adultery and incest. In an imaginative account of Elizabeth's last days, recorded by her maid of honour Elizabeth Southwell, who turned Catholic, made a bigamous marriage to Sir Robert Dudley and took up residence in Florence, the juiciest part was that Mary Stuart had a sort of posthumous revenge when Elizabeth's body, lying in state at Whitehall and surrounded by 'severall Ladies', Southwell included, suddenly exploded. 'Her bodie and head brake with such a crack' that it split the wood and the lead of the coffin. This black little memoir was grist to the mill of the Jesuit Robert Parsons, who used it in his *The Judgment of a Catholicke English-man* (1608).[44]

Regard that as a diversion. Back to the mainstream. Where did Elizabeth the Protestant paragon and national heroine come from? Posthumously, from Camden's English translators, but also from popularising writers like Thomas Heywood, who turned Foxe's narrative of the near-martyr Elizabeth into the play *If you know not me, ye know no bodie* (many editions from 1605 onwards), as well as the prose work *England's Elizabeth: her Life and Troubles, during her minoritie, from the Cradle to the Crowne* (1631), which Heywood offered as a necessary supplement to Camden's account 'from the Scepter to the Sepulchre'.[45] It was thanks to Heywood that Samuel Pepys could write: 'I have sucked in so much of the sad story of Elizabeth from my cradle.'[46]

Of Camden's translators, two out of three were not very competent. One even knew no Latin, but worked from a French edition. This man, Abraham Darcie, blew a rousing fanfare in his brave title page, where Camden's text becomes *The true and royall historie of the famous Empresse Elizabeth ... of ... happy memory*, adorned with images of Sir Francis Drake's ships off the coast of Peru, and the defeat of the Armada: 'Albions comfort Iberias terror'. Elizabeth was 'this Heroicke Empresse', 'Albions best Queen', 'the most Religious, learned and prudent Empresse that ever lived on earth'. Darcie was soon outdone by Robert Norton, son of the Elizabethan 'parliament man' Thomas Norton and himself an artillery man, whose version of Camden in successive editions is the one we all use and quote, although as a translation it is not up to much (Edmund Bohun in his *The Character of Queen Elizabeth* (1693) called it 'intolerably bad').[47] Norton celebrated the 'Halcyon Dayes' of 'our late glorious Soveraigne of renowned Memory', 'this Queene of Queenes', 'an admiration to all the Princes of her time, and a Patterne to all that should come after her'.

Norton noticed that Camden had not pulled out all the stops he might have done, and so he added, out of 'worthy Authors', new material and some added flavour, radically altering the kind of book that the *Annals* is. So this is where we find what Neale turned to account in his biography, especially in the chapter called 'The affability of their prince': a golden legend of spontaneous outpourings of love and devotion; the people 'running, flying, flocking to be blessed with the sight of her Gracious Countenance as oft as euer she came forth in Publicke'; a monarch 'thinking it her greatest strength to be fortified with their loue, and her greatest happinesse to make them happy', 'borne to possesse the hearts of her Subiect'. No doubt this kind of stuff consolidated rather than invented the character of a monarch whose style really was affable. Richard Niccols, in his *Funeral Oration* for Elizabeth, called her 'greater than Alexander ... for the world which he subdued by force, she conquered by love'.[48] Writing in the same year, Thomas Dekker wrote of 'a nation that was almost begotten and born under her; that had never shouted any other *Ave* than for her name'.[49] Well they would say that, wouldn't they, in 1603. Yet we have to admit that this affable queen was more than an imaginative piece of spin-doctoring.

But why the seventeenth-century consolidation and amplification of the legend? Why did Camden's translators peddle a version of Elizabeth so much at variance with the intention of the original Latin text? The answer lies at the door of her Stuart successors. There had been another side to Dekker's and Richard Niccols's paeans of sentimental praise. Several late Elizabethan commentators reported that England could not wait to be rid of an elderly woman as their monarch, and to replace her with a real rather than substitute man. *King Lear* reflects this mood: 'an idle and fond bondage in the oppression of aged tyranny'; 'We have seen the best of our time. Machinations, hollowness, treachery'. Lear's kingdom had been ruined by the rule of women. Although rarely articulated as such, Elizabeth's gender had always been the problem. The stuff of Elizabethan politics for most of those forty-five years had been how to find an acceptable path back to normality in the shape of a male successor, virile and virtuous in the Protestant sense. A female ruler was almost a contradiction in terms, an aged female ruler even more so, and the adulation industry was a paradoxical reaction to that fact, making the best of a bad job. Behind all that adulation men – especially Robert Dudley, earl of Leicester; and Burghley and the Privy Council as a body – had provided that essential masculine element which counterbalanced Elizabeth's sex and alone made her rule tolerable: the essence of what I have called 'the Elizabethan monarchical republic'.[50]

But the point of *King Lear* is that everybody gets everything wrong. It soon turned out that Elizabeth had been Cordelia all along. After a few years of James I and his son, England could not wait to get her back. James had begun the task of teaching the English nation what masculinity was about. He told parliament: 'Precedents in the times of minors, of tyrants, or women or simple kings [are] not to be credited.'[51] No more monarchical republics. But there was a public reaction to the new monarchy, which took the form of a revived commemoration and celebration of Elizabeth's accession day, 17 November, oddly called 'crownation day', with bell-ringing and school holidays, which lasted at Westminster into the early nineteenth century.[52]

Sometimes, both James I and Charles I were bracketed as Protestant and nationalist militants along with Elizabeth, as in Darcie's and Norton's title pages and prefaces. John Speed's *History of Great Britaine* (1611) (which incidentally was as anti-Leicester, anti-Puritan and pro-Mary Stuart as Camden), found the solution to an awkward historiographical problem in making Elizabeth 'the last monarch to reign over the southern half of the Isle of Britain', 'the greatest in fame that ever ruled before her, as if all their vertues had made a confluence in her'.[53] This monarchy found not so much an end as a period with the succession of James, 'inlarger and uniter of the British empire; restorer of the British name'. But that was persuasive rhetoric, an invitation to Elizabeth's successors to emulate their glorious precursor. Camden's translator Robert Norton had been in charge of the guns at La Rochelle, and no-one could have known better the sad difference between Elizabethan and Stuart foreign policy.[54]

It is significant that Elizabeth's speech to her last parliament, the so-called 'Golden Speech', was reprinted at the most critical moments in the seventeenth century: in 1628, 1642, 1679, 1688, and always just the bare text of the speech, without comment but for the queen's engraved portrait. In 1679, the circumstances of 1601 which prompted the speech (the fiscal crisis over monopolies) were distorted. The speech was now said to have been occasioned by 'her delivery from the Popish Plots'; and in 1688 the text bore no resemblance to the speech as originally given.[55] With the politics of the exclusion crisis of 1679–81, the wraps were well and truly off. Surrounded by pope-burning ceremonies, a huge statue of Elizabeth was erected on Temple Bar, and whig poetical hacks supplied their own libretto:

> Your Popish Plot and Smithfield threat
> We do not fear at all,
> For lo, beneath Queen Bess's feet
> You fall, you fall, you fall.
> A Tudor! A Tudor! We've had Stuarts enough,
> None ever reign'd like old Bess in her ruff.[56]

Dryden wrote with disgust about 'the Queen whose feast the factious rabble keep'.[57] When William of Orange landed in England, it was thought prudent he should delay his entry into London until after 17 November, even though he was supposed to be the latest thing in Protestant heroics, an Elizabeth redivivus.[58] This was another piece of very strange chronicling. Certainly Elizabeth herself would have found it strange.

And so it was that tory and whig versions and verdicts on the subject of Elizabeth were to compete through the politicised history of the next century. Whiggishness on the whole prevailed, even with a tory like David Hume, whose *History of England* (the Tudor volumes appeared in 1759), definitive for its age, credited Elizabeth with vigour, constancy, magnanimity, penetration, vigilance and prudence – in Seller and Yeatman terms a thoroughly Good Thing.[59] No writer of consequence wrote, as some modern debunkers have done, of a 'do nothing queen',[60] who merely went on going on, and who owed her fame to an immune system which worked and to a great deal of luck. Such whiggishness came to its full flowering with Henry Hallam's *The Constitutional History of England* (1827), and in Thomas Babington Macaulay, for whom the secret of Elizabeth's greatness lay in her identification with the nation and its manifest destiny. Her apparently absolute power (inviting comparisons with 'the Great Turk') actually depended upon the love of her subjects. 'Her memory is still dear to the hearts of a free people.'[61] As Shakespeare put it, 'not Amurath an Amurath succeeds, but Harry Harry'.[62] This was already the verdict which my generation would later find in A. F. Pollard, and in his pupil, J. E. Neale.

By now, the tumult and the shouting had died down. Neale noticed that the first leader in *The Times* on 17 November 1858 was on the subject of manure.[63] Elizabeth was one of the more prominent and permanent ornaments on the national mantelpiece, and the only question remaining was how often it should be dusted. Tennyson wrote, consensually, as befitted a laureate, of 'the spacious times of Great Elizabeth'. But now it was time for the queen to be reclaimed by the historians, who were about to become a learned profession; and in what is left of this chapter I must perform a kind of Research Assessment Exercise on their very various scholarly verdicts and achievements.

Do not worry, there will be no weary trudge through 200 or 300 verdicts, many of them inevitably repetitive. I am afraid that a former regius professor at Oxford (who has ever heard of the Reverend Dr Edward Nares?) was not the last historian of the period of whom Macaulay might have written: 'Compared with the labour of reading through these volumes, all other labour, of thieves on the treadmill, of children in factories, of negroes on sugar-plantations, is an agreeable recreation.'[64] (Nares on Lord Burghley [1828–31] consists of three fat volumes, almost 2,000 utterly unreadable pages,[65] a dreadful warning to dry-as-dust historians.) Let us concentrate rather on the high spots, a hop, skip and a jump from Lingard, to Froude, to Creighton (nodding on the way to Agnes Strickland), and so on to Neale and the post-Nealeians, in whose number I count myself.

The Catholic priest John Lingard, who narrowly missed becoming a cardinal, and whose *History of England* appeared in eight volumes between 1819 and 1830, was a remarkable case, almost the first Englishman to lay claim to the distinctive separateness of the historical discipline. For his fidelity to the documentary record he has been called 'the English Ranke'. He wrote in 1806 'my object is truth', and this was evidently not some kind of Catholic truth (Lingard would never have joined the Catholic Truth Society), but the objective truth to which the archives testify and to which we should all subscribe.[66] He reprimanded what he called 'speculative and philosophic historians' for perverting historic truth (an implicit attack on Hume). In his great *History*, Lingard devoted particular attention to the reign of Elizabeth, and this is what he said about the Babington Plot, which brought Mary Stuart to the block: 'I do not think that the charge against the Scottish queen carries with it any great appearance of improbability. It is very possible that a woman who had suffered an unjust imprisonment for twenty years ... might conceive it lawful to preserve her own life and recover her liberty by the death of her oppressor.'[67] Compare the conspiracy, *agent provocateur* theories of later, Jesuit historians. Edwin Jones's recent and admirable study of Lingard observes: 'The state of modern scholarship on this matter is not further advanced than Lingard took it.'[68] Neale read Lingard,[69] but remained unrepentant in his conviction that the only good Catholic historian was a dead one. And, of course, Lingard was dead, but not I think thereby good. (You will have to take that on trust, trust in my memory: no footnote reference.)

But, as postmodernists, amongst others, tell us, there is often a hidden reason behind archival positivism. Not every historian tells the truth which everyone and all ages will accept simply because it is the truth. And in Lingard's case the motive was the subtle realisation that only by beating Protestant historians at their own game could he convince the world that his own religion was the right one. These were the years in which Catholic emancipation headed the political agenda. Lingard wrote: 'In my account of the Reformation I must say much to shock Protestant prejudices: and my only chance of being generally read by them depends upon my having the reputation of a temperate writer. The good to be done is by writing a book which protestants will read.'[70] And Lingard was read, not only by Catholics.

But more of those who wanted to know about Tudor history would soon consult the wonderfully readable James Anthony Froude, an ex-Tractarian who was emphatically not a Catholic, and whose Tudor history was a vehicle for the kind of anti-Catholicism which Lingard, over-optimisitic, had hoped to extinguish; and who became even more at home in the archives than Lingard, even the Spanish archives of Simancas. A. F. Pollard remarked in the old *Dictionary of National Biography*: 'No previous history has incorporated so much unpublished material.' Perhaps unconsciously echoing Camden, Froude wrote of these exertions: 'I have been turned into rooms piled to the window-sill with bundles of dust-covered despatches and told to make the best of it. Often I have found the sand glistening on the ink where it had been sprinkled when a page was turned.'[71] We have all experienced that thrill: the only thing which keeps us going as historians, even in the postmodernist wilderness which, like desertification in west Africa, moves inexorably towards us. Our oasis, the Institute of Historical Research.

But for Froude there would not be a lot to talk about, historiographically, before we reach the second half, almost the last quarter, of the twentieth century. For Froude raised the questions about Elizabeth which have been renewed in our own time. He began with conventional admiration, but long before the end he had fallen out with a woman who he found was full of tortuousness and artifice, without substance. He came to share what he believed to be the privately held opinion of her ministers that 'she had no ability at all worth calling by the name'. And this was his famous verdict on the reign, his bit of strange chronicling:

> Vain as she was of her own sagacity, she never modified a course recommended to her by Burghley without injury to the realm and to herself. She never chose an opposite course without plunging into embarrassments, from which his skill and Walsingham's were able to extricate her. The great results of her reign were the fruits of a policy which was not her own, and which she starved and mutilated when energy and completeness were most needed.[72]

A. L. Rowse commented: 'This is not the less wrong for having been often quoted.'[73] I am tempted to say, it may not be the less right for having been confuted by Rowse. But it has to be significant that Froude's history of the Tudors on a heroic scale was not carried beyond 1588 and the defeat of the Armada. (And Camden, too, had been more than half inclined to stop there.) Perhaps, as Rowse suggests, Froude was by then tired of the subject. But to write Elizabethan history in terms of the positive electrical charges coming from Burghley and Walsingham, and the negativity of Elizabeth, becomes more difficult in the 1590s. I am not sure that any historian has yet mastered the difficulty presented by the 1590s, least of all in the dry-as-dust two-volume appendix to Froude written in the early twentieth century by Edward P. Cheney, *A History of England From the Defeat of the Armada to the Death of Elizabeth*.

Froude cast a long shadow. In his now forgotten *The Great Lord Burghley* of 1898, Martin Hume wrote that Burghley 'did more than any other man to guide the nation into the groove of future greatness'; that it was he to whom Elizabeth looked to 'save her against herself', and who kept the queen 'upon the straight path up which she led England from weakness, distraction, and dependence, to unity and strength'.[74] Mandell Creighton's *Elizabeth* had appeared two years earlier, and for all his episcopal tut-tutting about Elizabeth's dubious morals, private and public, Creighton redressed the balance of Froude and prepared the way for the adulation which would follow in most twentieth-century treatments of the subject. Once Creighton had written: 'As for the Tudors, they are awful; I really do not think that anyone ought to read the history of the sixteenth century.'[75] But now he restored the image of a queen whose 'imperishable claim to greatness' lay in 'her instinctive sympathy with her people ... There are many things in Elizabeth which we could have wished otherwise [there you go]; but she saw what England might become, and nursed it into the knowledge of its power'.[76]

What about the alarmingly prolific Agnes Strickland, author, with her sister Elizabeth, of the best-selling and multi-volume *Lives of the Queens of England* (in its fourth edition by 1854) and later caricatured by Trollope as Lady Carbury in *The Way We Live Now*? Carbury wrote to her publisher: 'I almost think you will like my "Criminal Queens". The sketch of Semiramis is at any rate spirited ... Cleopatra, of course, I have taken from Shakespeare. What a wench she was!'[77] The fact that Strickland worked in archives as far afield as St Petersburg did not make her a critical historian. So far as Elizabeth is concerned, she was a distraction, a 790-page distraction, and a damaging distraction at that, since she was uncritically dependent on the late seventeenth-century Italian Gregorio Leti. It was perhaps unfortunate that Strickland had learned Italian and translated Petrarch, for Leti was the source of numerous unhistorical myths, his history of Elizabeth in Neale's definitive judgment 'utterly worthless ... adorned with letters of his own fabrication'.[78] There is more merit in the devout Tractarian Charlotte Yonge's translation (1879) of a French work, *La jeunesse d'Elisabeth d'Angleterre*, by Louis Wiesener.[79]

In the first three quarters of the twentieth century, history was at its apogee as an academic subject, Tudor history especially; and above all in London University, the university of Pollard and Neale, and, whether he liked it or not, of Elton. In 1952 I was inclined to research African history, but was advised that if I came to J. E. Neale's London seminar I would learn what history was all about, and could then take it to Africa if I so chose. On several counts, no comment. I think that what happened to Elizabeth in this seventy-five years was that the Land-of-Hope-and-Glory trappings and trimmings were progressively jettisoned, even while the woman herself was hoisted to ever higher pedestals. Neale, marinated like Froude in the archives (but never so far as I know those of Simancas), came out of them with convictions quite unlike Froude's. His two volumes on the Elizabethan parliaments, for all that they were intended, like all Neale's books, for that mythical beast, the Intelligent General Reader, included all Elizabeth's parliamentary speeches, in full. To quote: 'I have treated the Queen's own speeches as sacrosanct.'[80]

What has happened since Neale? Not, I think, a biography as good as his. But in all the serious work of the last thirty or forty years, the subject has been not so much celebrated as critically interrogated. Frances Yates and Roy Strong are only the best-known names in an art-historical industry devoted to the legend of Elizabeth, but they wrote in full knowledge that it was a legend, and that legends have to be fabricated.[81] Post Yates and Strong, the legend itself has been brought down to size by being put into its proper context, for example by Helen Hackett in her *Virgin Mother, Maiden Queen* (1995). The idea that Elizabeth filled a niche in the national psyche left vacant by a deposed Virgin Mary is shown to be fanciful. Many of the images deployed and the allegories applied to Elizabeth were conventional when representing queens, whether regnant or consort.[82] Virginal chastity and fruitfulness were praised in equal measure, in the case of Elizabeth's mother, for example, and of her half-sister, at a time when the Virgin Mary herself was still available for popular veneration. In work like Hackett's the very notion of a 'cult' of Elizabeth, which, as perpetuated by twentieth-century historians, she attributes to nostalgia, is subjected to critical scrutiny of a kind which is applied to all the Tudor monarchs in Sydney Anglo's *Images of Tudor Kingship* (1992). Anglo writes:

> It has ... become a commonplace to write about the 'projection' of the image of royalty as though Renaissance potentates employed advertising agencies and public relations teams; about 'propaganda' as though these monarchs were each served by their own equivalent of Joseph Goebbels; and about 'princely patronage' as if early modern states had arts councils and cultural policies.[83]

Meanwhile attention has shifted towards what Wallace MacCaffrey in 1968 taught us to call the Elizabethan regime.[84] Neale himself began this trend with his Raleigh Lecture of 1948, 'The Elizabethan political scene', which explored the almost biological complexity of that tentacular organism, the Elizabethan court.[85] But this was in many ways a false dawn, partly because of an article published by Joel Hurstfield in 1967, the title of which was, I think, one of those *questions mal posées*, 'Was there a Tudor despotism after all?'; and which introduced the unhelpful concept of Tudor government as 'minority rule', an expression which I believe to have been borrowed from the transient politics of what, in the late 1960s, was still Rhodesia.[86] This was part of an ongoing discussion with Sir Geoffrey Elton about the place of parliament in the Tudor constitution, which was at worst anachronistic and at best only part of the story.

But to a greater extent the dawning realisation of the true nature of Elizabethan politics was impeded by the pathological emphasis which Neale applied to his otherwise helpful concept of a political scene. His was a vision of a squalid, materialistic competition for place and profit, downward and degenerative as the competition for a limited supply of goodies grew ever fiercer. This was a Namierite perception, the philosophy of which would lure Neale into the *History of Parliament*. MacCaffrey redressed some of the balance in his essay on 'Place and patronage in Elizabethan politics', published in the Neale

Festschrift of 1961, reinterpreting Neale's 'scene' as benignly functional in cementing loyalty to the regime.[87] But there was still insufficient sense of the politics of the Elizabethan political scene in a non-Namierite sense, a politics transcending King Lear's 'court news ... /Who loses, and who wins; who's in, who's out'. Simon Adams has done most to change our thinking by advising us to think less in terms of 'faction', at least until we get to the later years of the reign, and more of conciliar consensuality. That piece of revisionism includes a rehabilitation of the political reputation of the Earl of Leicester, by some 400 years none too soon.[88]

I hope that it will not be thought arrogant on my part to claim that what we may call the new Elizabethan political history, a post-Eltonian even more than a post-Nealeian history, is encapsulated in the phrase 'the Elizabethan monarchical republic' which I invented in the mid-eighties with a little bit of help from Quentin Skinner; and further elaborated a few years on in my Raleigh Lecture of 1993, 'The Elizabethan exclusion crisis'.[89] Otherwise my part in these revisions has been minor, as compared with that of younger historians such as Stephen Alford, Susan Doran and Anne McLaren and, at the level of political ideas, Markku Peltonen.[90] The backcloth to this reconstruction of Elizabethan high politics has been the contribution of what we may call the socio-political historians who have mapped the active participation in public affairs and at many layers of society and of locality of pretty well everybody, meaning by 'everybody' those adult males who in Tony Blair's phrase were considered to be 'stakeholders' in their communities, 'the better sort' in all those deserted Sweet Auburns of the many worlds we have lost. Here was the formula once beloved by medievalists, 'self-government at the king's command', given new and enhanced meanings; something very far removed from Hurstfield's 'minority government'.[91]

At the level of national politics, the 'monarchical republic' idea insists that Elizabethan subjects were also, in their own estimation and in frequent utterances, citizens. They lived out the Ciceronian commonplace that their country, which they called the commonwealth, and which for Sir Thomas Smith was *Republica Anglorum*, had a claim on their active virtue, and that while not necessarily captains or pilots of the ship of state, they shared the responsibility of ensuring that it did not run onto the rocks. It was no doubt presumption on the part of the Member of Parliament who, in a speech in 1567, said: 'For I tell you, Mr Speaker, that I speake for all England',[92] but it is a presumption which we cannot afford to ignore.

There was civic humanism in such utterances, and often militant Protestantism too. There was also a sense of crisis, even of acute danger. The argument is not a whiggish argument which sees what lay beyond the later seventeenth century as already anticipated in the later sixteenth. The monarchical republic was the result of a highly unusual circumstance: a female monarch who was the last of her direct line, who failed to do what was necessary to produce an heir, and who steadfastly refused to determine an indeterminate succession. This would have been dangerous at the best of times, but these were the worst of times, especially for as long as Elizabeth's most likely successor, Mary Stuart, foreign, Catholic and conspiratorial, kept her head on her shoulders. This was the nub of the exclusion crisis, the single issue on which the monarchical republic most forcefully expressed itself. As one Member of Parliament put it in 1572, 'Since the Queene in respect of her own safety is not to bee induced hereunto [executing Mary], let us make petition shee will doe it in respect of our safety. I have heard shee delighteth to be called our mother.'[93] (Our sources, which are silent as to tones of voice, cannot tell us whether that was said respectfully, or ironically, even sardonically, and of course the sardonics could have been concealed in the respect.) And so it was that the political nation, with Lord Burghley at its head, deliberated and, so far as it could, acted as if it were the government, planned for a kind of interregnum in the event of the queen's death, and eventually managed to cut off Mary Stuart's head while the queen pretended to be looking the other way.[94] Cavour famously said that Italy must look after itself. The Elizabethan political nation knew that that was equally true in the case of the commonwealth of England. They were for the queen, of course, but so far as was feasible also against the queen, since they might at any moment find themselves without the queen.

There remains a great deal still to talk about. Elizabethan history is not yet tied up with pink ribbon and put away in a drawer for safe keeping, and I hope never will be. Neale used to say 'there are no pundits in history', although Hurstfield suspected that he made an exception of himself. The 1590s were very different. John Guy has called them the second reign of Elizabeth, anticipating in many ways the early Stuart monarchy.[95] We need to go on discussing why that should have been so. The history of gender is now unavoidable, although it may be noticed that I have so far tried my level best to steer around it. There have been three or four books in the recent past on the implications of John Knox's argument that female government (the 'regiment' of women) was unnatural government, and of the various responses to Knox.[96] We shall not necessarily agree on how important it was that Elizabeth was a woman, whether in all the circumstances there would have been a crisis, not so much of authority as of the directions to be taken by authority, even if she had been a gay man equally disinclined to marry, and to breed. Watch this space.

How far does all this add up to an adverse verdict on Elizabeth I and her supposedly glorious rule? You may think that it must. Or, alternatively, you may conclude that for Elizabeth to have held her corner in these circumstances, to have become anything but a monarchical cipher, adds to our sense of her greatness; and that she was quite right, on all sorts of grounds, to have resisted the pressure to embrace more adventurous, expensive and risky policies. Biographers like Paul Johnson have praised her above all for her courageous conservatism, have made that their main theme.[97] But it is happenstance rather than policy which determines the course and outcome of a history like hers. Elizabeth gambled on the unlikely chance of living to the age that she did, outliving the problems which loomed so large in the 1570s and 1580s. The odds were long, and the stake was the very survival of England as a Protestant nation. As I have remarked elsewhere, it is not so much the case that the true history of Elizabethan England has not yet been written as that in a sense it never happened; not the history fearfully imaged by those who prophesied that Elizabeth would be strangely chronicled. We do not need to be told that things can very often work out quite differently from our apprehensions.

NOTES

1 L. Creighton, *The Life and Letters of Mandell Creighton* (2 vols, London, 1904), vol. 1, p. 93.

2 The letter in which these observations occur is not signed, dated or addressed, but is in Parker's hand and is to be found among Lord Burghley's papers (BL, Lansdowne MS. 15, no. 34, fo. 66).

3 T. Betteridge, 'A queen for all seasons: Elizabeth I on film', in *The Myth of Elizabeth*, ed. S. Doran and T. S. Freeman (Basingstoke, 2003), pp. 254–8. For a startling revelation of the vast extent and variety of more or less unhistorical sources available for acquiring some 'knowledge' of Elizabeth, literary, dramatic, pictorial, cinematographic, not forgetting waxworks, see M. Dobson and N. J. Watson, *England's Elizabeth: An afterlife in fame and fantasy* (Oxford, 2002).

4 Gilbert Abbott A'Beckett, *The Comic History of England* (London, 1848), vol 2, p. 116.

5 Raphael Holinshed, *The Firste Volume of the Chronicles of England, Scotlande, and Irelande* (London, 1577), p. 766.

6 A. M. Patterson, *Reading Holinshed's Chronicles* (Chicago, Ill., and London, 1994), pp. 2344–63.

7 London, Inner Temple Library, Petyt MS. 538.10 fo. 11v.

8 Publius Cornelius Tacitus, *The Ende of Nero and Beginning of Galba*, tr. Sir Henry Savile (1591), epistle.

9 Chapter 9 in this volume. For Bacon's 'dignity' and dependence on research assistants, see Francis Bacon, 'The dignity and advancement of learning' (translation of his *De Augmentis*), in *The Works of Francis Bacon, 1561–1626*, ed. J. Spedding and others (14 vols, 1857–74), vol. 4.

10 I owe my knowledge of Machiavelli's visits to the pub, where he played *hosteria* and *trich-trach* 'with the miller and the baker', to P. Burke, *Popular Culture in Early Modern Europe* (Aldershot, 1978), pp. 110–11. Niccolò Machiavelli, *The Prince*, tr. G. Bull (London, 1995), p. 19.

11 Chapter 9 in this volume; P. Collinson, 'History', in *A Companion to English Renaissance Literature and Culture*, ed. M. Hattaway (Oxford, 2000), pp. 59–60; D. R. Woolf, 'Erudition and the idea of history in Renaissance England', *Renaissance*

Quarterly, 40 (1987): 11–48; D. R. Woolf, *Reading History in Early Modern England* (Cambridge, 2000), p. 23.

12 *The Letters and Life of Francis Bacon*, ed. J. Spedding (7 vols, 1861–72), vol 3, p. 250.

13 *Annals of the First Four Years of the Reign of Queen Elizabeth by Sir John Hayward*, ed. J. Bruce (Camden Soc., vol 7, 1840), p. 107.

14 L. Richardson, 'Sir John Hayward and early Stuart historiography' (unpublished Ph.D. thesis, University of Cambridge, 1999).

15 *Elizabeth of England: Certain observations concerning the life and reign of Queen Elizabeth by John Clapham*, ed. E. P. Read and C. Read (Philadephia, Pa., 1951).

16 Thomas Birch, *Memoirs of the Reign of Queen Elizabeth, From the Year 1581 Till her Death, from the Original Papers of Anthony Bacon* (London, 1754), vol. I.

17 *Dictionary of National Biography*.

18 S. T. Bindoff, *Tudor England* (Harmondsworth, 1950), pp. 306–7.

19 *Dissing Elizabeth: Negative representations of Gloriana*, ed. J. M. Walker (Durham, N.C., 1998); Doran and Freeman.

20 J. E. Neale, 'The Elizabethan age', The Creighton Lecture, 1950 (1951); repr. in his *Essays in Elizabethan History* (London, 1958), pp. 21–44.

21 Neale, 'The Elizabethan age', p. 21.

22 William Camden, *Tomus alter et idem; Or the historie of the life and reigne of Elizabeth*, tr. Thomas Browne (1629), bk 4, p. 384. For a somewhat fuller referencing of what immediately follows, see Chapter 10 in this volume.

23 Raphael Holinshed, *Holinshed's Chronicles of England, Scotland and Ireland* (6 vols, London, 1807–8), vol 4, p. 897.

24 William Camden, *The Historie of the Most Renowned and Victorious Princesse Elizabeth*, tr. Robert Norton (London, 1630), bk 3, p. 112; William Camden, *Gulielmi Camdeni Annales Rervm Anglicarvm et Hibernicarvm*, ed. Thomas Hearne (3 vols, Oxford, 1717), vol. 2, p. 537.

25 BL, Add. MS. 48027 fo. 690v. Cf. P. E. McCullough, '"Out of Egypt": Richard Fletcher's sermon before Elizabeth I after the execution of Mary Queen of Scots', in Walker, pp. 118–49.

26 William Camden, *The History of the Most Renowned and Victorious Princess Elizabeth, Late Queen of England: Selected chapters*, ed. W.T. MacCaffrey (4th edn, Chicago, Ill., and London, 1970), p. xxxi.

27 H. Trevor-Roper, *Queen Elizabeth's First Historian: William Camden and the beginnings of English 'civil history'* (1971); repr. in his *Renaissance Essays* (Chicago, Ill, 1985), pp. 121–48.

28 *Camdeni Annales*, vol. I, sig. a2.

29 Chapter 10 in this volume.

30 *Ibid.*

31 P. Croft, 'The religion of Robert Cecil', *Historical Journal*, 34 (1991): 773–96; B. Worden, 'Ben Jonson among the historians', in *Culture and Politics in Early Stuart England*, ed. K. Sharpe and P. Lake (Basingstoke, 1994), pp. 67–89; J. Merritt, 'Religion, government and society in early modern Westminster, 1525–1625' (unpublished Ph.D. thesis,

University of London, 1992). A key figure in giving Westminster this religious character, apart from the status of a royal peculiar, seems to have been Gabriel Goodman,
dean of Westminster from 1561 to 1601.

32 L. Levy Peck, *Northampton: Patronage and politics at the court of James I* (London, 1982);
L. Levy Peck, 'The mentality of a Jacobean grandee', in *The Mental World of the Jacobean
Court*, ed. L. Levy Peck (Cambridge, 1991), pp. 148–68. John Bossy has work in progress
on the neglected and important subject of what Henry Howard was up to in the reign
of Elizabeth (see references to Howard in J. Bossy, *Under the Molehill: an Elizabethan
spy story* (New Haven, Conn., and London, 2001).

33 Chapter 10 in this volume.

34 *Ibid.*

35 Read and Read, pp. 63–5; Bruce, p. 8.

36 Sir John Hayward, *The Life, and Raigne of King Edward the Sixt* (London, 1630). See
Richardson.

37 Bruce, pp. 28–9.

38 William Camden, *Britannia*, tr. Philemon Holland (London, 1610), Preface.

39 H. Stuart Jones, 'The foundation and history of the Camden chair', *Oxoniensia*, 8–9
(1943–4): 169–92, at p. 175.

40 *The History of the Most Renowned and Victorious Princess Elizabeth* (MacCaffrey edn),
p. 6.

41 T. S. Freeman, 'Providence and prescription: the account of Elizabeth in Foxe's "Book
of Martyrs"', in Doran and Freeman, pp. 27–55.

42 Freeman, pp. 42–3.

43 J. Craig, *Reformation, Politics and Polemics: The growth of Protestantism in East Anglian
market towns, 1500–1610* (Aldershot, 2001), p. 104.

44 C. Loomis, 'Elizabeth Southwell's manuscript account of the death of Queen Elizabeth
[with text]', *English Literary Renaissance*, 26 (1996): 482–509.

45 Thomas Heywood, *England's Elizabeth: Her Life and Troubles, during her minoritie, from
the Cradle to the Crowne* (1631), epistle. See T. Grant, 'Drama queen: staging Elizabeth
in *If You Know Not Me, You Know Nobody*', in Doran and Freeman, pp. 120–42.

46 *The Diary of Samuel Pepys*, ed. R. Latham and W. Matthews (11 vols, London, 1970–83),
vol. 8, pp. 388–9.

47 Edmund Bohun, *The Character of Queen Elizabeth ... Her Virtues and Defects* (London,
1693), Preface.

48 Richard Niccols, *Expicedium. A funeral oration, upon the death of the late deceased princesse of famous memorye, Elizabeth* (London, 1603), sig. A3v.

49 E. Calhoun Wilson, *England's Eliza* (1st edn, Cambridge, Mass., 1939; 1966), pp. 392–3.

50 A. N. McLaren, *Political Culture in the Reign of Elizabeth I: Queen and commonwealth,
1558–85* (Cambridge, 1999); A. McLaren, 'The quest for a king: gender, marriage, and
succession in Elizabethan England', *Journal of British Studies*, 41 (2002): 259–90; J. M.
Richards, 'The English accession of James VI: "national" identity, gender and the personal monarchy of England', *English Historical Review*, 117 (2002): 513–35; P. Collinson,
'The monarchical republic of Queen Elizabeth I', *Bulletin of the John Rylands Library*,

69 (1987): 394–424 (repr. in P. Collinson, *Elizabethan Essays* [London and Rio Grande, 1994], P. Collinson, *Elizabethans* [2003], pp. 31–57, and in *The Tudor Monarchy*, ed. J. Guy [London and New York, 1997], pp. 110–34).

51 Quoted in McLaren 'Quest for a King', p. 290.

52 J. E. Neale, 'November 17th', in J. E. Neale, *Essays in Elizabethan History*, pp. 9–20.

53 John Speed, *The Historie of Great Britaine* (London, 1623), p. 1237, dedicatory epistle, addressed to James I.

54 *Dictionary of National Biography.*

55 For three versions of the speech as delivered on 30 November 1601 in the council chamber at Whitehall, see *Proceedings in the Parliaments of Elizabeth I*, ed. T. E. Hartley (3 vols, Leicester, 1981–95), vol. 3, pp. 289–97. The third version was the basis for a number of MSS. and printed texts which appeared in the course of the 17th and 18th centuries. See also an account of the complex history of the speech in J. E. Neale, *Elizabeth I and her Parliaments, 1584–1601* (London, 1957), pp. 388–93. For the points made here, see *Queene Elizabeths Speech to her Last Parliament* (1628? and 1642 edns); *The Last Speech and Thanks of Queen Elizabeth of Ever Blessed Memory to her Last Parliament, after her delivery from the popish plots etc.* (1679); *A Second Spech of Queen Elizabeth (of Famous Memory) 1601, in the 44th year of her reign* (1688). Part of the legend was to present the 'Golden Speech' as Elizabeth's 'last speech' to parliament. The real last speech was delivered in the house of lords on 19 December, and is preserved in a unique copy once in the possession of Henry Howard, later earl of Northampton (and Sir Robert Cotton's patron) (BL, MS. Cotton Titus C VI fos 410–11). I will not forget the day in 1955 when, as Sir John Neale's research assistant, I was sent to the British Museum to confirm the existence of this speech from a note he had made in the 1920s; and to transcribe it.

56 J. Miller, *Popery and Politics in England, 1660–88* (Cambridge, 1973), p. 74; Dobson and Watson, pp. 70–1.

57 Neale, *Essays*, p. 22.

58 *Ibid.*, p. 16.

59 A. L. Rowse, 'Elizabeth and the historians', *History Today*, 3 (1953): 632.

60 M. A. R. Graves, *Thomas Norton the Parliament Man* (Oxford, 1994), p. 409.

61 Rowse, 'Elizabeth and the historians', p. 636.

62 *King Henry IV, Part II*, V.2.48.

63 Neale, *Essays*, p. 19.

64 Thomas Babington Macaulay, *Essays Critical and Historical*, ed. A. J. Grieve (1834), vol. 1, p. 77; J. Hurstfield, 'William Cecil, 1520–98: minister to Elizabeth I', *History Today*, 6 (1956): 791–2.

65 Edward Nares, *Memoirs of the Life and Administration of William Cecil, Lord Burghley* (3 vols, 1828–31).

66 E. Jones, *John Lingard and the Pursuit of Historical Truth* (Brighton, 2001), p. ii.

67 Jones, *John Lingard*, p. 154.

68 *Ibid.*, p. 155. See also 'John Lingard and the birth of modern historiography in England', in E. Jones, *The English Nation: the Great Myth* (Stroud, 1998), ch. 6.

69 Neale, *Essays*, p. 110.

70 Jones, *English Nation*, p. 175.

71 A. L. Rowse, *Froude the Historian: Victorian man of letters* (Gloucester, 1987), p. 73.

72 Rowse, 'Elizabeth and the historians', p. 638; J. A. Froude, *History of England From the Fall of Wolsey to the Defeat of the Spanish Armada* (12 vols, London, 1872), vol 12, pp. 502–11.

73 Rowse, *Froude*, p. 70.

74 M. A. S. Hume, *The Great Lord Burghley: A study in Elizabethan statecraft* (London, 1898), pp. xi, 498.

75 Creighton, *Life and Letters of Creighton*, vol. 1, p. 289.

76 Mandell Creighton, *Queen Elizabeth* (London, 1896), pp. 198–9.

77 Anthony Trollope, *The Way We Live Now* (Oxford, 1982), p. 1.

78 Neale, *Essays*, p. 87.

79 L. Wiesener, *La jeunesse d'Elisabeth d'Angleterre, 1535–58* (Paris, 1878), tr. C. M. Yonge (2 vols, 1879).

80 J. E. Neale, *Elizabeth I and her Parliaments, 1559–81* (London, 1953), p. 11.

81 F. A. Yates, *Astraea: The imperial theme in the 16th century* (London and Boston, 1975); R. C. Strong, *Portraits of Queen Elizabeth I* (Oxford, 1963); R. C. Strong, *The Cult of Elizabeth: Elizabethan portraiture and pageantry* (London, 1977); R. C. Strong, *Gloriana: The portraits of Queen Elizabeth I* (London, 1987).

82 H. Hackett, *Virgin Mother, Maiden Queen: Elizabeth I and the cult of the Virgin Mary* (Basingstoke, 1995). See also J. N. King, *Tudor Royal Iconography* (Princeton, N.J., 1989).

83 S. Anglo, *Images of Tudor Kingship* (London, 1992), p. 3. But for several valuable explorations of the representational and symbolical aspects of Tudor politics, almost of politics as gesture, see *Tudor Political Culture*, ed. D. Hoak (Cambridge, 1995).

84 W. T. MacCaffrey, *The Shaping of the Elizabethan Regime* (Princeton, N.J., 1968).

85 Neale, *Essays*, pp. 59–84.

86 J. Hurstfield, 'Was there a Tudor despotism after all?', in his *Freedom, Corruption and Government in Elizabethan England* (London, 1973), pp. 23–49.

87 W. T. MacCaffrey, 'Place and patronage in Elizabethan politics', in *Elizabethan Government and Society: Essays presented to Sir John Neale*, ed. S. T. Bindoff, J. Hurstfield and C. H. Williams (London, 1961), pp. 95–126.

88 S. Adams, *Leicester and the Court: Essays on Elizabethan politics* (Manchester, 2002).

89 Collinson, 'The monarchical republic'; Chapter 2 in this volume.

90 S. Alford, *The Early Elizabethan Polity: William Cecil and the British succession crisis, 1558–69* (Cambridge, 1998); S. Doran, *Monarchy and Matrimony: the courtships of Elizabeth I* (1996); McLaren, *Political Culture*; M. Peltonen, *Classical Humanism and Republicanism in English Political Thought, 1570–1640* (Cambridge, 1995).

91 M. J. Braddick, *State Formation in Early Modern England, c.1550–1700* (Cambridge, 2000); S. Hindle, *The State and Social Change in Early Modern England, c. 1550–1640* (Basingstoke, 2000). For a succinct attempt to synthesise some of these insights and

approaches, see P. Collinson, '"The state as monarchical commonwealth": "Tudor" England', *Journal of Historical Sociology*, 15 (2002): 89–95.

92 *Proceedings in the Parliaments of Elizabeth*, vol. I, p. 137.

93 *Ibid.*, p. 376.

94 Chapter 10 in this volume.

95 J. A. Guy, 'The 1590s: the second reign of Elizabeth I?', in *The Reign of Elizabeth I: Court and culture in the last decade*, ed. J. A. Guy (Cambridge, 1995), pp. 1–19.

96 See, e.g., C. Levin, *'The Heart and Stomach of a King': Elizabeth I and the politics of sex and power* (Philadelphia, Pa., 1994) and A. Shephard, *Gender and Authority in 16th Century England: the Knox debate* (Keele, 1994). See also McLaren, *Political Culture.*

97 P. Johnson, *Elizabeth I: A study in power and intellect* (London, 1974).

Chapter 6

Biblical rhetoric:
the English nation and national sentiment
in the prophetic mode

When members of the Elizabethan parliaments demanded of their queen that she marry or otherwise determine the succession to the crown, they sometimes spoke with feeling of England, the nation which they claimed to represent and for which they offered to speak. 'For I tell you, Mr Speaker, that I speake for all England, yea, and for the noble English nation, who in times past (with noe small honour) have daunted and made the proudest nations agast.'[1] According to political science, such rhetorical flights are not to be mistaken for expressions of 'nationalism', which, like steam-power, was a substance not invented until the eighteenth century was preparing to give way to the nineteenth.[2] Early modernists hope that they may at least be permitted to write of 'patriotism'. Granted that there were many 'patrias', from the homestead and parish pump upwards and outwards, this chapter will focus on that species of patriotism which was national sentiment. Where did national patriotic sentiment come from, or, a more modest and manageable question, where and how did it find a voice?

In *Forms of Nationhood*,[3] Professor Richard Helgerson has found various 'forms' articulated in those Elizabethan and immediately post-Elizabethan books which, with Shakespeare (and especially in this connection, the history plays), make up the greatest cultural monument to the span of Shakespeare's life, the 1560s to the 1620s, books which began as ambitious undertakings and grew in substance and stature from their first editions: Christopher Saxton's *Atlas* (1579–), William Camden's *Britannia* (1586–), Richard Hakluyt's *Principall Navigations (Navigations, voiages, traffiques and discoveries of the English nation)* (1589–), John Foxe's *Acts and Monuments* (1563–), written

Originally published in *Religion and Culture in Renaissance England*, edited by C. McEachern and D. Shuger (Cambridge, 1997). Reproduced by permission of Cambridge University Press.

for the instruction of what Foxe called 'this my-country Church of England',[4] Michael Drayton's prodigious geographical and hydrographical poem *Poly-Olbion* (1612–), which called upon 'Thou *Genius* of the Place', 'my England', to guide the poet in his exploration of 'Albion's glorious Ile'.[5] Camden declared of his *Britannia*: 'the glory of my country encouraged me to undertake it'.[6] The one-and-a-half million words of Holinshed's *Chronicles* (1577–) ended the annals of England with an encomium for 'the commonwealth of England, a corner of the worlde, O Lord, which thou hast singled out for the magnifyieng of thy maiestie'.[7] As early as 1532, William Thynne's *editio princeps* of Chaucer was motivated by 'love to my country'.[8]

All these hugely ambitious publishing enterprises were so many alternative means of discovering and constructing the English nation in both space and time, in an age when 'the fascination with time … permeated European culture', and with it 'the meticulous study of time past', that 'hermeneutics of the past' which was chronology.[9] There was also self-discovery and disclosure in language, especially at what has been called the 'pivotal' moment of William Tyndale's realisation of the New Testament in a highly vernacular English, defended by Tyndale's ringing affirmation of the right to the Bible 'in the mother tongue';[10] and in Richard Mulcaster's passionate outburst of a generation later: 'I honour the Latin, but I worship the *English*'.[11] For all these constructions, the greatest resource was the past. Chaucer's English, for example, was a treasure retrieved from the past, his editor wondering that a tongue so rude and imperfect should have been framed 'to suche a sweete ornatenesse and composycion'.[12]

But which past? Professor John Pocock has told us that there are many pasts, which different professions and interest groups recall and recreate for their several purposes. England was a society in which 'a cleric, a lawyer, and a herald might remember very different historical pasts and remember them for different reasons'. But 'nation', no less a mental construct, in Benedict Anderson's phrase an 'imagined community', 'attracts to itself myths and symbolic stories suggestive of a common past which may or may not be related to the institutional pasts'.[13]

Our Elizabethan Member of Parliament seems to suggest that the nationhood for which he claimed to be the mouthpiece came out of that past which consisted of almost unrelenting warfare with France and Scotland ('making the proudest nations agast'). He might alternatively have appealed, as his early Stuart parliamentary successors would, to the laws of England as constituting its usable past and embodying the spirit of its nationhood.[14] Another resource was a more remote Roman past, reverberant with citizenship, republican values, nationhood, or, in the literature of the principate and Empire, instructive of political conduct in a monarchy, a past recovered for a public purpose by humanism and sustaining a sense of the nation as a commonwealth.[15] We may quote our same Member of Parliament, in his speech of 1567: 'Mr Speaker, the heathen man Tully said that man is not borne for himself only, but partlie for his parentes, partlie for his children, and partlie for his cuntrie';[16] an oft-repeated Ciceronian commonplace.

But there is yet another source of nationhood, the religious imagination, which is the conscience, informed and excited by the Bible. For the Bible was both past and landscape, a landscape almost as familiar as England itself and more accessible to the Elizabethan mind than America or those other exotic regions described by Hakluyt: since for every reader of Hakluyt there were a hundred Bible readers or (in church) Bible hearers. The Bible, according to one preacher, was nothing less than 'Englands Looking-Glasse'.[17] The Bible, especially in the Geneva version first published in 1560 and distributed in England with great frequency from 1576, was as much a part of Helgerson's 'Elizabethan writing of England' as any of the books with which he deals. For, as J. R. Green perceived long ago, it was precisely in Shakespeare's lifetime, or in the years separating the middle of Elizabeth's reign from the meeting of the Long Parliament in 1640, that the English became people of that book in particular.[18] That the Bible 'wrote' Elizabethan and seventeenth-century England is no more than we should expect. Professor Debora Shuger has written that religion was 'the master-code of pre-capitalist society'; 'the cultural matrix for explorations of virtually every topic'; 'the discourse through which it interpreted its own existence'.[19]

It was as Bible readers that the bishops, in the context of another Elizabethan parliament (it was 1572 and they were demanding the head of Mary Queen of Scots on a platter), spoke of the nation not as *the* people (the resonances that that has for us are entirely anachronistic), nor *as your* people (which, in addressing the queen we might have expected), but as *his* people, which is to say, God's people.[20] For this was to think of the English people and nation in the personalised and possessive terms characteristic of the Old Testament. Christopher Hill has suggested that the close relationship of the nation to its God, which that 'his' implies, was a median point in the historical progression from feudal fealty to the prince to citizenship in the modern and impersonal abstraction of the state, in effect a journey from 'your people' *via* 'his people' to 'the people'.[21] 'His people' threatened to detach the nation from the monarch, to insist that ultimately it was not hers but his, just as the queen herself was nothing but God's officer and servant. 'Per me Reges regnant', wrote an Elizabethan reader on the title-page of a political pamphlet which carried criticism of the queen to the point of sedition.[22] This man was a Bible reader too, familiar with the voice of God and not afraid to express it.

Richard Helgerson looked for the most telling religious expressions of nationhood in the apocalyptic of Foxe's *Acts and Monuments*, and also in the polemical apologetic of Richard Hooker's *Laws of Ecclesiastical Polity*

(1593), without doubt another of the great Elizabethan books. But it is not to detract from Foxe or Hooker to acknowledge the Bible as the supremely important source of the religious apprehension of English identity; which, as Christopher Hill has demonstrated in *The English Bible and the Seventeenth-Century Revolution*, provided not only justification but rhetorical and meta-phorical articulation for much of what happened to the English nation in the seventeenth century, the idiom in which it conversed with itself.[23] While that looks self-evidently true, not all seventeenth-century historians will agree with Dr Hill that biblical rhetoric was an idiom and no more, a means of packaging and addressing concerns which were in reality secular. The preacher Thomas Case was not speaking in an elaborate idiomatic code when, Bible in hand, he asked the Long Parliament:

> And what is the Quarell all this while, Is it not *Religion* and the *Truth* of God? The truth of the *Doctrine*, the truth of *Discipline*, the truth of *Worship*? ... Surely had not the *Gospel*, and the *Government* of Jesus Christ been precious in their eyes they might have compounded for their civill Liberties upon infinitely cheaper terms then it hath cost them already, and yet the Lord knows what it may cost them more![24]

The Bible is not so much one book as a whole library of books, a very mixed collection of periods, genres and styles, for all that Protestants insisted upon its essential unity and coherence of meaning. So we may ask: which portions of Scripture were most formative of national self-consciousness? The New Testament addresses the question, what must I do to be saved? – and not simply individualistically but with reference to the nation reconstructed as the Church, a building compacted of lively stones, or a body with Christ as its head. The poetical books of the Old Testament (the Psalms and Canticles) nourished and inspired the imagination, providing for the protestant imagination a spiritual commentary on salvation according to the New Testament paradigm. Those parts furnished Donne, Herbert and Milton with metaphorical and poetical invention and repertoire.[25]

But as for the experience of the nation, an experience as much religious and moral as historical and political, that was both mirrored and constructed by the Old Testament as history and prophecy. History and prophecy, and especially the so-called Minor Prophets, had more meaningful and urgent things to say to the English nation in the generation of Shakespeare and his children than that fourth biblical strand, the Apocalyptic, which has received an almost disproportionate attention from cultural and intellectual historians:[26] and for reasons which may have more to do with the arcane fascination of the mille-narian dreams of Daniel and Saint John the Divine, and their implications for chronology, than with the evidence of their impact (inevitably quite scarce) on the general Elizabethan and post-Elizabethan consciousness. The Apocalyptic mode fed into speculative patternings of history, the mysterious number-crunching of Daniel and Revelation, whereas in the historical and prophetic mode there was little sense of development over time or of an anachronism between the worlds of the Old Testament and of the present. England was taken back into the Old Testament, the Old Testament forward into the sixteenth century, 'Israel and England ... right Parallels' in the words of one preacher, England's sins 'too parallel to those of Ephraim' according to another.[27] The synchronised impact was immediate, and immediately challenging.

It goes without saying that this by no means exhausts the available biblical modes. The strong appeal of the Old Testament for this society has impressed many observers; when he had finished his book on the Bible, Christopher Hill found that he might as well have called it *The Old Testament and the Seventeenth-Century Revolution*.[28] But within many strands and dimensions of the Old Testament, it may be that the proverbial, sententious 'wisdom' mode, in a word 'Solomon', was the most accessible, fitting easily into the instinctively aphoristic as well as moralistic early modern mind.

Nevertheless, the portions of Scripture which counted for our purpose were history and prophecy. What did they perform for English national consciousness? They were not the ultimate source of that consciousness, and by no means the taproot of that national patriotism which was expressed in hyperbolic claims to pre-eminence and peculiarity as an elect nation, even *the* elect nation. The role of biblical history and prophecy as it was deployed in the pulpit (and especially from the national pulpit of Paul's Cross in London), and in the published sermon literature, seems to have been to intensify such sentiments but also to contort them and to drive them inwards as it contributed a more searching and sombre religious and moral dimension to questions concerning the nation's present standing and likely destiny. All this was implicit in what has been called the 'Israelite paradigm' of nationhood.[29]

But before engaging with the nation and, as we shall see, castigating it, the preachers in the prophetic mode had to construct it as their own kind of 'imagined community'. By addressing the English nation as the Minor Prophets had addressed Israel, the prophetic preachers, first at Paul's Cross and later, with an intensified sense of national occasion, before the Long Parliament, attributed to it a fictional, or at least contrived identity, implicit not only in the detailed development of their discourse but in the decision to address the nation in the often repeated apostrophe, O England! In that the preachers called for a united, national response, their preaching offered to unite the nation in the renewal of its national, covenanted relation with God. So a united nation and church was not merely the political programme of the official Henrician, Edwardian, and Elizabethan reformations. It was part of the original thrust of the Reformation as evangelism and prophecy which carried through into the Paul's Cross sermons of the Jacobean age, renewing itself in the 'Fast Sermons' preached before Parliament in that second reformation which immediately preceded the Civil War. However, the preachers seem to have known (for it was built into their biblical-prophetical sources) that they would *not* evoke a national response, that God's covenant would be honoured not by the whole nation but only by a remnant, a remnant which might for a time redeem and preserve the nation, but which would also survive the temporal ruin of the nation. For this was the experience in the Bible of Israel and Judah.

Therefore such preaching was of necessity divisive, and conventionally and loosely associated with 'Puritan' tendencies in Elizabethan and early Stuart England. It was religiously but also socially divisive insofar as its pathological rhetoric of moral outrage and alarm discriminated between supposedly godly and allegedly ungodly elements in society. And it was politically divisive, to the extent that the policies and actions of the royal government diverged from the preachers' prophetic imperatives, not only in specific content but in the absence of religious commitment, the lukewarm-ness and compromise attacked in the early 1620s in the sermons and clandestine publications of the likes of Thomas Scott, incensing James I and provoking him to restrain, at Paul's Cross and generally, such rampant 'abuses and extravagances' in preaching. For that matter, conformist preachers in this mode could and did castigate Puritanism itself as a form of national apostasy.[30] This politicisation of the prophetic mode, which was already a feature of the 1620s in response to the diplomacy of the Spanish and French matches, came to full fruition in the 1640s. It was equivalent to the divergence of the nation, as a religious idea and construct, from the monarchy and the state. This was a divergence not tolerable or sustainable in the prevalent ideology of seventeenth-century England. Hence, we might say, arose the Civil War and its confused aftermath, to the (considerable) extent that it was a war of religion.

These developments may be interpreted as a more or less rational response of these divines to what they observed to be happening in society, in the auditories sitting in front of them, and in politics: a perceived declension in the religious and moral rectitude of the protestant nation which they sincerely believed was becoming ever more profound and scandalous as the Reformation passed from memory into history. But historians of third-generation New England have taught us to be on our guard against the rhetoric of declension. Declension was written into the prophetic scenario, where an unregenerate and incorrigible people with corrupt and idolatrous priests and rulers had their indispensable roles to play. Hence the common name for such sermons in the New England case, Jeremiads. Whether prophetic preaching rested on a true assessment of the case was of secondary importance.[31]

We now know that the famous marginal comment in John Aylmer's 1559 text *An Harborowe for Faithfull and Trewe Subiects*, 'God is English', was not

Protestant hype but an old trope. It was in the fourteenth century, not in the sixteenth, that God became an Englishman, and in 1559 Aylmer was sounding a late echo of Hundred Years War bellicosity. His book was in the press even as what we may call the two hundred years of intermittent warfare between England and France were ending, and his belated apology to the French and the Scots, inserted in some copies of the *Harborowe* after the conclusion of peace at Câteau-Cambrésis,[32] makes it even clearer than the jingoistic text itself that this was not yet the voice of a new and distinctively Protestant patriotism. He wrote, Aylmer explains, in wartime. 'They delte wyth us roughly: and could we speake or thinke of them frendly?' 'But now the times being altred, and they become of enemies frendes: we muste and ought to thinke wel of them, so longe as they deale not ill with us.' According to this Christian spokesman, a future bishop, we are to love our friends but hate our enemies.

Nothing in the account of preaching in the prophetical vein which follows is intended to deny the continuing force and appeal of what we may call simple, two-dimensional, rhetorical patriotism, defining itself in comparison with other, inferior nations. Aylmer had advised his readers, as if they were Muslims, to fall flat on their faces before God seven times a day, thanking him that they had been born Englishmen, not French peasants, nor Italians, nor Germans (not to speak of what Aylmer called the 'piddling' Scots). With the Elizabethan age, these Gilbert-and-Sullivanesque sentiments stretched their horizon to take in the whole globe. In *The Glory of England* (1615), Thomas Gainsford compared his native land with China, India and Turkey, to the utter detriment of all three. 'My ioy exceedeth for not being a native amongest them.' 'Oh happy England! O happy people! O happy London!'[33]

Wartime, from Crécy to Alamein and Normandy, invariably brought the Church's vocal artillery into action in a patriotic barrage which asked few awkward questions. There was nothing out of the ordinary about Aylmer, except for his odd little ceasefire apology to the quondam enemy. So it was that Stephen Gosson, an actor and playwright turned preacher, invoked 'the God of S. Stephen, the God of S. George, the God of her Maiestie, the God of us all' and assured a war-weary late Elizabethan London: 'This hath beene the practice of the Church of *England* by the testimonie of our owne Chronicles, when the honour of our nation, the chivalrie of England, hath beene in the fielde.' Why was the enemy so regularly beaten? 'If you will knowe the reason, the praiers of the Church of *England* have prevailed more than the gold of Spaine.' Thirty years on, after another chapter of far from glorious military operations, Richard Bernard contrived this rousing call to arms: 'In *going forth, consider* what you be, against whom you fight, and for what. Remember that Great Britaine is inferiour to no Nation: and that by the prowesse and valour of *English* and *Scots* [now no longer Aylmer's "piddling" Scots!], glorious victories have been obtained.' There followed a litany of names: 'Generall *Norrice* in the Low Countries', 'Lord *Grey* in Ireland', 'the never-dying Names of *Drake, Furbisher* and *Hawkins*'. 'Be couragious still, and cease not to upholde the renowne of this our Name and Nation.' These things were said in a book called *Bible-Battells*, which found in the Old Testament not prophetic judgment but an exemplary military manual. 'Greater armies I never read nor heard of in any Historie ... The storie is rare, in respect of the incredible slaughters': Gideon's little force had slain of the enemy 120,000; Jeroboam lost 500,000 chosen men in his war against Abijah. How this Somerset country parson would have relished the Somme, from a safe distance! *Dulce bellum inexpertis.*[34]

But for many Protestant publicists, such robust, religiously fortified patriotism was complicated. The mid-Tudor writer Thomas Becon, who aimed for a wide audience, was a voice both of the past and of the future, albeit he wrote for the present. His wartime bellicosity was tempered by a lingering Christian humanism of the Erasmian kind. And it was directed by a prophetic conscience which, like so many pulpit utterances of the next two or three generations on national themes, was more critical than it was altogether encouraging. Becon chose the moment of Henry VIII's last French war, 1542–43, to publish a book first christened *The new pollecye of war*, but then promptly renamed *The true defence of peace, called before the pollecy of warre*. Sympathy was expressed for 'the Christian public weal', by which Becon meant not his own country but the whole of Christendom, 'other kingdoms with whom we be knit together in one faith'. He believed that his own country would prevail in any just war, but only if it turned to God in repentence. And then came the prophetic wail, to be heard so often from the pulpit for a full century to come. 'O England, England, mine owne native country!'[35]

In that century, the trope that God is English, or that England was a special object of God's favour and concern, would be endlessly repeated, if only rarely with the full and robust exclusiveness of Milton, for whom God was '*Brittain's God*', who 'hath yet ever had this Iland under the speciall indulgent eye of his providence'.[36] And this is the moment to observe that *an* elect nation, rather than *the* elect nation, seems to have been the most consistent message, even in the excessive prose of Milton, for whom England's peculiarly elect role was a blessing intended for all Christian nations: especially if we discount the purely rhetorical element in many of these figures and flourishes, which were never intended to be understood as simple statements of the facts of the matter.[37] In his parliamentary Fast Sermon 'Englands Looking-Glasse' (22 December 1641), Edmund Calamy told his hearers: 'This Text may fitly be called a Looking glasse for *England* and *Ireland*, or for any other Kingdom whatsoever; wherein God Almighty declares what he can do with Nations and Kingdoms, and what he will do.'[38] So Christopher Hill may commit an error of judgment when he writes: 'We need not get involved in squabbles about whether England was thought to be "the" or "a" chosen nation.'[39] There is nothing in the least futile about a question which concerns the balance of ethnocentricity and ecumenism in English Protestant consciousness. Its imperfect resolution would affect things as non-trivial as the history of the British Empire and the notion of American exceptionalism and of the 'redeemer nation'. After all, many Jews and all Ethiopian Christians have had no truck with the indefinite article, and English Protestant Christians, on the whole, were different in this respect, eschewing grossly ethnocentric exclusivism. They were not, to borrow the name of a more recent sect, British Israelites.

In the prophetic mode, which was the more authentic voice of Protestant nationhood, the notion of God's special relationship with England as paradigmatically Israel was invested with a new and enhanced meaning. For the prophetic mode was judgmental, inward-searching, and self-critical, not at all triumphalist, or only on the terms that all success and prosperity were to be ascribed to God alone. Far from promising future greatness, the preachers predicted only imminent ruin, unless ... In concern and tone, their sermons may have differed in this respect from much fourteenth-century Hundred Years War preaching (about which we know very little), as they certainly did from some of the preaching which has accompanied more recent wars.[40] The message of these prophets was that while God had chosen Israel and favoured it above all other nations, Israel had so far forgotten God that he would visit it with corrective judgments and might even, as in the prophecy of Hosea chapter 1, repudiate and divorce his people as no longer his people: 'and I will not be your God'. For in the fourth chapter of Hosea we find that God had a controversy with Israel, understood by sixteenth- and seventeenth-century commentators to be in all reality a legal prosecution. Israel – and for Israel read England – must answer for 'capital crimes' contained in several 'bills of indictment'. An acquittal was neither deserved nor likely.[41] 'Because thou hast rejected knowledge, I will also reject thee ... For ye are not my people and I will not be your God.'

Of all these 'crimes' – which typically included swearing, drunkenness, abuse of the Sabbath – 'idolatry' was the most capital and most central to the prophetic complaint. Christopher Hill has remarked: 'It is impossible to over-emphasize the importance given in the Old Testament to rejection of idolatry.'[42] For idolatry was not one of a shopping list of sins but contained within itself all sin and apostasy: the false religion of 'popery', to be sure, but also the sinful presumption and materialism which was perceived to be the bitter fruit of Protantism.

So these texts were bound to direct preachers in the prophetic mode to the utterance of an equally drastic verdict against Protestant England. However, the fact is that the preachers, especially when confronted with an audience in principle national, as at Paul's Cross, chose these texts and were free to have chosen others; and that they were evidently deeply impressed, in a manner typical of the fascination for the Renaissance mind of 'correspondences', by the exact symmetry of ancient Israel and modern England, 'right parallels', London to all intents and purposes Jerusalem. Jeremiah and Hosea were so many cassettes, to be inserted into the tape-deck of the present. The prophet's historical points of reference had their exact equivalents for the preacher. For example, the miracle of the crossing of the Red Sea was replicated in its 'counterpane', the wonderful deliverance of 1588.[43]

All this, whatever else its effect, was likely to reinforce a sense of national identity, nation-state and capital city, over and above more local and provincial identifications of 'my country', such as county, since although the preachers occasionally identified the English counties with the tribes of Israel,[44] the prophetic mode of necessity encouraged an understanding of community which was national rather than localised or, for that matter, universal. Not that it excluded other senses of community, the strength of 'country' rhetoric consisting in its elasticity. In 1618, Robert Reyce referred to his native county of Suffolk as 'this continent', defined by those mighty rivers, the Waveney and the Stour.[45]

Prophetic preaching equally reinforced a sense of the imagined community of the nation as something other than the monarchical state and state-church. So, although Debora Shuger is entitled to say that the space vacated by the collapse of the universal Church of the Middle Ages was filled institutionally by a state-church under royal headship (and is particularly entitled to say so in a book devoted to the great Anglican apologists),[46] it was not the only construct which filled that space. As Christopher Hill reminds us, in the Old Testament paradigm neither the nation nor God himself was ever on good terms with the institution of monarchy for very long. The lesson to be learned from the two books of Samuel and of Kings was that in desiring a king, Israel desired, sinfully, to be like other, idolatrous nations, electing to be no longer a pure theocracy. This was a weakness which God indulged, but at great cost. For most of Israel's kings and some of Judah's proved to be moral failures and religious apostates, and even the good and godly ones had their falls – not least David, for all that English Bible readers were told that he was a type of Christ, and, of course, wise Solomon. Good King Asa, in old age, was even censured for relying on the physicians rather than God to cure his gout. But the prevalent sin amongst these three unsatisfactory rulers was idolatry, or the complacent toleration of idolatry in tyrants worse than themselves. Their examples, either as idolaters or as worthy iconoclasts, were continually pushed under the noses of the rulers of reformation England. Dr Margaret Aston suggests that Queen Elizabeth I must have become heartily sick of the model of good King Hezekiah, whose destruction of the idol of Moses's brazen serpent ought to encourage her to abandon that equally idolatrous symbol of the cross, to which her own piety seems to have been warmly attached.[47]

Finally, the invocation and construction of the nation in the prophetic mode ignored in the generality of much of its rhetoric all social and political distinctions, investing an entire and undifferentiated people – England – with a shared moral and religious responsibility. In that nation was equivalent to people, there were at least potentially demotic resonances. How did a theology of the nation relate and reconcile itself to that theology of the individual confronting God which we often assume to have been the central preoccupation of Protestant Christianity? Here our little bark strikes a large rock, too large and of too technical a nature to be subjected in an essay such as this to geological investigation. Rather we shall jettison some ballast and hope to float free. The rock was first located on the charts of Puritan theology by Perry Miller. Did preachers in the prophetic mode suppose that God had a covenant with the nation distinct from his gracious covenant with elect individuals and with his invisible and elect Church, a covenant of works rather than of grace, subject to the terms of the old law rather than the new, a national covenant? Miller thought so, and has been followed by Dr Michael McGiffert in a close study of the English Hoseads.[48] But Dr Theodore Bozeman thinks otherwise, and appears to be right.[49] Just as 'country' could be made to mean a number of things in early Stuart public rhetoric, so these preachers moved imperceptibly between their address to the individual, to the Church, to the nation, and to covenanted groups and remnants within both Church and nation. In principle, the entire baptised nation (and other Christian nations) stood covenanted in the same way, by the same gracious bond, as the individual was bound. Both were bound to a legal and moral performance of its terms, what Bozeman calls 'the blunt and fearful *quid pro quo* of the Israelite paradigm'. Both, if they erred, could expect temporal, corrective judgments. Bozeman calls this 'an excellent coherence of themes'.

It might otherwise be called a confusion of themes,[50] but probably there was no confusion, rather 'a greatly satisfying harmonization'. If there was confusion (for who, in Hosea and in the derivative Hoseads, was 'Israel', who 'Judah', who were 'my people', 'them', 'us'?), the preachers were in control of the confused categories and applications of their own rhetorical agenda, turning them to their own instrumental as well as rhetorical advantage. The essential point is the strong, organic connection between self and society.

It is perhaps understandable that while this material, which we may call Paul's Cross prophecy, has attracted the attention of a few learned articles, it has not grabbed the headlines in the manner of the Apocalyptic mode, and has not interested many ranking historians of the period. Christopher Hill's book, *The English Bible and the Seventeenth-Century Revolution*, refers to almost every seventeenth-century printed text which could conceivably relate to his subject, but not to these sermons, following Lord Dacre (Hugh Trevor-Roper) in discussing the Long Parliament Fast Sermons as if they were an innovation of the 1640s rather than the climax of a full century of English Hoseads and Jeremiads.[51] Not to be outdone, New England historians discuss the late seventeenth-century Jeremiad as an American invention. The neglect is understandable, since the burden of these sermon texts is theologically limited, intellectually impoverished, and almost unbearably repetitious. The sermons depend for any interest they are capable of arousing on rhetorical variation and invention, a hundred new ways to say old things. The message is always the same: most favoured, most obligated, most negligent. We are at Paul's Gross in 1578: God's 'great mercies towardes us Englishmen, above manye other nations, make his judgements more heavie'. And now we are at Banbury in 1623: 'We seem to have entered into a contention with the Almightie, whether he shall be more mercifull, or we more sinfull; whether he shall be more constant in doing us good, or we more obstinate in sinning against him.' Aging members of the Long Parliament heard from Edmund Calamy in 1642 what they had been hearing all their lives. To sin in despite of so much mercy was a 'God-provoking', 'Land-destroying' sin.

> To sinne with mercy is to make mercy our adversary. And if mercy plead against a Nation, then looke for speedy destruction ... To sinne with the rare and choyce mercies of God (such as the mercies of England are) is a sinne of such transcendent unkindnesse, as that God cannot but destroy such a Person, or such a Nation, that is guilty of it.[52]

Not only Puritans and not only preachers kept up this refrain. According to the poet George Wither in *Britains Remembrancer* (1628),

> The Jewish commonwealth was never deigned
> More great deliverance than thou hast gained.

Quoted in isolation, these two lines out of 26,000 (!) may give a false impression, for Wither was no Gainsford. His monstrous poem was all about judgment for sin, specifically the plague, which struck London with such devastating effect in 1625. It was 'a Declaration of the MISCHIEFES present', and 'a Prediction of IUDGMENTS to come', 'if Repentance prevent not'. Christopher Hill has called Wither's plague epic 'the major literary achievement' of the genre of God's threatened abandonment of England.[53]

We should by no means disregard all the Ohs and Ahs in this discourse, those unconsidered particles of speech, indicative of what Hazlitt would later call 'emphatical language', to which Dr J. H. Prynne has recently devoted an entire lecture. *A Christian Dictionarie* of 1612 lists no less than five varieties of biblical 'Oh', including 'the voice of one chiding and speaking to another, in way of reprehension', and 'the voice of one exhorting and encouraging to dutie'.[54] To appreciate the full force of the preacher's emphatical Ohs and Ahs (doubtless orchestrated with appropriate gestures) we may quote at large from a sermon of William Whateley, known to some as 'the roaring boy of Banbury', his *Charitable teares* (1623):

Oh the oathes and blasphemie in our Nation! O, the contempt of Gods Word and Gospell in our Nation! O, the pride and idlenesse in our Nation! O, the drunkennesse whoredome and filthinesse in our Nation! If Rome or Constantinople abounded with swearing and cursing, who could looke for better there? If France and Italy were full of whoredome, who could expect other in those corners of Popish Darknesse? But England, Ah England! Gods Signet, Gods Iewell, which he hath fostered as tenderly, and adorned as graciously, as ever he did Iudea, England, the one onely Nation, almost, that doth openly and solely professe the true Religion of God: I say, England aboundeth in all these sinnes. What shall we say or doe? Whither shall we turne our selves? And how shall we comfort our selves for this, when even England is full of all wickednesse? What? Swearing in England? Cursing in England? Lascivious dancing, dallying, and wantonnesse on the Lord's Day in England? Contempt of Gods Word, drunkenesse, pride, idlenesse in England? Even in England, where there is so much preaching and so much hearing?

And so the roaring boy continues, with hardly a pause for breath, 'O, breake our hearts within us, and let our eyes drop downe teares to think of it!'[55] Preaching at Paul's Cross soon after the strong earthquake of 1580, James Bisse made liberal use of the apostrophe 'Oh England!' If Christ were present, he would weep over England as he had wept over Jerusalsm, saying: 'O England, England, if thou hadst even known at the least in this thy day those thinges which belong unto thy peace.'[56]

The historian naturally wants to know, and it may be all or most of what he wants to know, what the effect of this relentless message, at once rhetorically over-charged and conventional, may have been for those exposed to it. We cannot safely extrapolate from the few recorded reactions which have survived, although we may be tempted to do so. We can refer, for example, to the detailed notes which a Kentish clothier, Robert Saxby, made of the sermons which he heard on his regular business trips to London in the reign of James I and (after 1629) when he took up permanent residence in the capital.[57] Many of these sermons were in the prophetical mode. After hearing (as he often did) the famous divine William Gouge at the Blackfriars (we are told that godly visitors to London 'thought not their business fully ended' until they had heard Gouge), Saxby noted: 'It fareth with us as it did with the Israelites.' Another preacher reminded his auditory, which included Saxby, of the English nation and land, how it had been so mercifully called upon and was yet so slack in the performance of true religion and virtue, 'that we may justly looke for the sharp wrath and punishment of the Lord to be powred downe upon us for our greate neglecte of torning unto the Lord by spedy Repentance'.

The second chapter of Lamentations, from which this sermon was preached, Saxby thought 'very Remarkabell'. Indeed, many of the sermons Saxby heard were 'remarkable', at least all those that he literally remarked – that is, wrote down. But what did Saxby do about it? These sermon notes suggest that hearers like Saxby may have been connoisseurs of the preacher's strong, judgmental rhetoric, considered that rhetoric to be of the essence of a good, 'edifying' sermon, and reacted accordingly, for as long as they sat in church, perhaps with a certain amount of hawking and spitting, to indicate an appropriate emotional response before going about their business.[58]

But, to be sure, this was not an alien discourse in early seventeenth-century England. The pulpits were echoed, however crudely, by the cheap pamphlet literature of the day which drew very much the same moral from sensational events, be they fact or fiction.[59] Floods, fires, monstrous births, and above all such unique and generally arresting 'providences' as the 1580 earthquake, all inspired an ephemeral literature on the theme of 'speedy repentance' which, in spite of a certain obvious literary contrivance, smelling of Grub Street, nevertheless seems to reflect the common popular reaction to such events and phenomena. The surviving evidence of these literary and sub-literary genres suggests that historians of post-Reformation religion of the revisionist school[60] should not assume as a matter of course that the pulpit went against the grain of popular and consensual culture and moral values, purveying bitter and unwelcome medicines to congregations which refused to admit that they were sick.

If the pamphleteers supplied a market and satisfied a demand, the preachers were, quite literally, paid to say what they said; were paid even to complain that their words were unwelcome and rejected by the hearers, for such was the fate and function of the prophet/preacher and in itself a familiar commonplace. The rhetorical power of their utterance was no doubt valued not at all for its intellectual originality but as we appreciate a virtuoso performance of a familiar piece of music. It must also be the case that if these preachers had succeeded beyond their wildest expectations and had achieved the 'speedy repentance' of which Saxby made careful notes, and on a universal scale, they would have been out of a job. Their continued usefulness depended paradoxically upon repeated failure, or the allegation of failure.

Viewing the prophetic mode as a professional skill, and its deployment as a means of professional self-advancement, it is clear that the calling of the Long Parliament and the institution of the parliamentary Fast Sermons, which, as I have argued, were only in a very limited sense an innovation, further enhanced the role of the preacher and the plausibility of his claim to be a national voice, or the voice of God to the nation. If, according to the early twentieth-century liberal Protestant Adolf Harnack, the essence of Christianity was God and the soul, the soul and its God,[61] the religion of the Fast Sermons was about God and nation, the nation and its God. This made the career of Stephen Marshall, hitherto by no means the most famous of the godly preachers of Jacobean and Caroline Essex;[62] and of his preaching partner-in-tandem, Edmund Calamy, who, in the sermon of 1641 called 'Englands Looking-Glasse', simultaneously flattered and elevated the nation, Parliament, and himself, the preacher, while ostensibly setting about the nation's castigation: 'You that are the representative Body of this Nation ... You are the Nation representatively ... you stand in the place of the whole Nation; and if you stand for Gods cause, the whole Nation doth it in you.' 'As this is a *National day*, and this Honourable Assembly a *National Assembly*, so this Text is a *National Text*, suitable for the occasion about which we are met.' 'National Repentance will divert National judgments and procure National blessings.'[63] All those repetitions of 'national' were artful, not inadvertent. Is anyone still prepared to deny the potency of a kind of national consciousness in early modern England? Such were the expectations of 1641. Did the preacher altogether trust his own rhetoric? He knew that the prophetic record itself, together with all recent historical experience since the Reformation, made national repentance very unlikely. The diversion of national judgments and the procurement of national blessings (the halcyon days of Queen Elizabeth; the great deliverances, from the Armada in 1588, the Gunpowder Plot in 1605, the Spanish Match in 1623) had been in despite of the neglect of national repentance, not a reward for it. Although some preachers professed to believe that all of God's judgments were conditional, never final, that it was always the eleventh hour, others threatened that the next time, if not this time, God would actually mean it. That was the lesson of Hosea; and even more of Jeremiah, for Jeremiah had been explicitly instructed not to pray for this people, 'for I will not hear thee!' (Jeremiah 7:16). Thomas Jackson, preaching on that text in Canterbury Cathedral, warned: 'The Lord grows to be resolute.' His sermon was called *Judah Must into Captivitie*.[64] But perhaps Jackson's chilling message was no more than conventional, fit for the occasion. He preached every day of the week, had an immense repertoire, especially of funeral sermons, and lived in great wealth and comfort, even after the outbreak of the Civil War.[65]

We return to Calamy who, like Stephen Marshall, had a rather good Civil War. In that same sermon, 'Englands Looking-Glasse', he included this notable warning, one of the more arresting sentences achieved in the entire corpus of judgmental preaching: 'If you will not learn righteousnesse by our History, God will make you the next History.' His text, Jeremiah 18:7–10, spoke of God plucking up, pulling down, destroying nations; and of God, repenting of the evil he had 'thought' to do, building and planting repentant nations.[66] Deuteronomy 28 indicated the method which God the plucker up and puller down would employ. 'The Lord shall bring a nation against thee from afar', a nation of 'fierce countenance'. In 1629, William Hampton had preached a Paul's Cross sermon on this scripture which was published as *A proclamation of warre from the Lord of Hosts. Or, England's warning by Israels ruine: shewing the miseries like to ensue upon us by reason of sinne and security.* Would God himself declare war upon his peculiars, his favorite? Yes, he would, if they continued to reject him. 'If you forsake him, he will forsake you.' 'O sinfull England! O wretched England!'[67]

These preachers were past masters of the art of suspense, on which their success and reputation no doubt in part depended. In a sermon called *Reformation and desolation*, Stephen Marshall said that no man could possibly determine the precise time of this or that nation's total ruin. 'Politicians, and some divines will tell you of the fatall period of Kingdoms', perhaps 500, perhaps 600 years. He and his hearers were 575 years away from the Conquest.[68] Calamy said that sometimes God gives warning of a great judgment to come by delivering small judgments (as a major earthquake in Southern California might be preceded by warning tremors?). But by no means always. 'God may, and doth sometimes destroy us at once and give no warning.' Marshall asked: 'What shall we do then? First beleeve it, *not that England shall be ruined*, I say not so; but beleeve that great is the wrath of God which is kindled against us, that we stand upon ill terms before him.'[69] Another preacher described his text as 'a Prophecy so strangely enterwoven with threats and promises, that it appears as so much Checker-work of Judgements and mercies'.[70]

On 23 February 1642, Calamy preached on 'Gods free mercy to England', and he professed some optimism about still more undeserved blessings yet to come. 'God doth sometimes shew Mercy to a Nation when it least *deserves* it, and least *expects* it.' 'God hath freed us from *Civill* Warres, which of all warres are most *uncivill*, from intestine warres, warres that would have eaten out our own bowels; from wars of *Protestant* with *Protestant*, which of all warres are most cruell.' The churches of England were indeed set in a warlike posture, but they were to fight 'with *prayers and tears* (which are the Churches weapons)'.[71] Did Calamy really expect peace? What motivated this cruelly false promise, apart from the good mood he found himself in? ('I am all for mercy this day.') On the afternoon of the same day, Marshall preached a more famous sermon, 'Meroz cursed', which if not actually intended as a call to arms in a civil war (it is not capable of such a patent meaning, and on the face of it this was one of the least political of the Fast Sermons), was heard to be such a call, has been so read by all historians, and was probably meant as a warmongering sermon on the many occasions when Marshall repeated it.[72] Two years later, with war engaged and becoming a habit, the well-named Jeremiah Whitaker would preach on Haggai 2:7: 'And I will shake all Nations.' 'God is dashing *England* against *England* ... Christian against Christian ... The English against the English.'[73]

So the prophetic mode, which constructed and ostensibly united the nation in its shared religious relationship with God and moral responsibility before God, was almost designed to split, fragment, and, what was worse, dichotomise it, just as the Protestant Reformation itself belied in its divisiveness its uniting affirmations and aspirations. The binary distinction between the better part and the worse part was instinctive to Protestantism, together with the conventional wisdom that the worse part would always constitute the greater part, the better the smaller.[74] (New England, where these relations were said to be reversed, was a wonder.) 'Be of good comfort little flock'; 'where two or three are gathered together in my name'; 'straight is the gate and narrow the way and few there be that find it'. The separatist enterprise to form gathered churches of the visibly worthy, 'be they never so few', was mistaken in its applied ecclesiology, but not in its understanding that the worthy would never be numerous.[75] It was not some sectarian but Bishop Jewel who wrote: 'We shall not go in routs; for we shall be but few', adding that the few would be 'enough to condemn the ungodliness of the wicked'.[76]

Protagonists of Protestant England like Jewel, looking out over the battlements of the beleaguered isle,[77] identified that small rout, the few, with little England, the multitude with Rome and Spain. John Norden in *A Mirror for the Multitude* (a proleptic text, printed two years before the Armada sailed) puts this boast into the mouth of 'hautie *Pharaoh* of Rome': 'What is God that can deliver little Englande out of my handes?' The king of Spain had vowed that he would 'winne little Englande to subiection'. And indeed, 'we little Israell of Englande' could say, 'if the Lorde had not beene on our side when men rose up against us, they had swallowed us up quicke'. Yet the Lord was on their side, as he was with little David when he slew Goliath.

> Whereby wee shall have due proofe, that it is not the multitude that imbrace his trueth, nor that can resist, suppresse, or prevayle against the same, although from the beginning the church of God hath bin farre the least part of the worlde, the least part of everie countrey and kingdome; the least part of everie Citie, yea the least part of everie congregation. Yet such hath beene the care, and loving affection of God towardes his fewe and small number that he hath not suffered them at anie time to take the foyle at the handes of his adversaries beeing, never so manie and mightie.[78]

That, on the face of it, was uniting, an expression of John Foxe's vision of the English people and church united in one ship,[79] or the many fabled little ships which in 1588 confronted the Spanish fleet.

But note 'the least part of everie congregation'. Even Norden, a jingoistic hack, presented an England divided against itself. 'But alas too many are the dissembling christians of these daies.' The English would prevail against the Romish Babylonians only 'if we shew our selves true christians in deede, and not key cold or newters'. 'A great volume might be replenished with such like manifest testimonies of colde Christianitie in England.'[80] Decades of denunciation of 'land-destroying sins' were corrosive and divisive: corrosive, because these might be the very sins committed by those seated in front of the preacher; divisive for the opposite reason, since the preacher often represented himself as in collusion with a captive audience of the converted, 'us', who shared in the preacher's detestation of the sins committed by 'them'. Those who flocked and gadded to the sermons of the roaring boy of Banbury were not drunkards and whoremongers, or were not thought to be so, except in the satirical polemic of the anti-Puritan drama.[81] Their fault, the fault of respectable household-ers and magistrates, was the secondary, but in contemporary perception more heinous, fault of allowing such abuses to flourish unchecked. To condone the swearing of little boys in the street would bring down the wrath of God no less surely than to utter curses oneself.

The other side of this coin was the homiletical commonplace that the presence of the godly in the church and nation might stave off, if only for a time, God's heavy judgments. According to Banbury's roaring boy, 'seldome doth God breake in upon a people, till there be none, or in a manner none left to stand in the gap'.[82] We have, claimed a parliamentary preacher in June 1642, 'many of the true servants of God among us, for whose sake we have cause to hope that the Lord will spare the Nation'.[83] But the same audience had already heard this grim warning from Stephen Marshall: 'God never prom-ised that the sincere Reformation of a few should prevent the judgment of a multitude.'[84] In the 1590s, the great William Perkins, preaching on the same text, Zephaniah 2:1–2 ('O nation not desired'), called upon a congregation of merchants gathered in Cambridge at the Stourbridge Fair to be so many Noahs, Daniels and Jobs in their generation. 'If we do thus, when judgments come we shall either turn them away from our nation or at the least we shall deliver our own souls.'[85] Thirty years later, in Canterbury Cathedral, one of Perkins's pupils, the well endowed Thomas Jackson, administered the same very conditional comfort, promising for the righteous, a poor lookout for the unrighteous: 'How ever things go, it shall be well with the just ... Pray, pray, pray, you shall at the least deliver your own souls.'[86] That was as much as to say that the prophetic mode of preaching would not in the end affirm the nation in the paradigm of Israel, but would rather write it off, as beyond preservation or redemption, save for the godly remnant: which was the eschatology of the Old Testament prophets themselves.

Christopher Hill has observed that the phrase a 'peculiar people' ceased, progressively, to be equivalent to 'chosen people' in the sense of the elect and chosen people of England, and acquired a more sectarian resonance, the self-description of a little rump of saints in some backstreet Bethel.[87] It is a percep-tion which one might expect from a historian, like Hill (and like the present writer), reared in the traditions of English non-conformity (Methodist in his case, Quaker and Baptist in mine). The realised Puritan Commonwealth and even more the Protectorate of the mid-seventeenth century incorporated, according to Professor William Lamont, not that 'godly rule' for which all that we have surveyed in this chapter was merely a preparation, but something like its denial and reverse: godless rule.[88] As Dr Christopher Haigh has written, by

1600 England was a Protestant nation; but not a nation of Protestants. Turning that around, by the late 1650s it appeared that England was a nation of some godly people but not yet, or no longer, a godly nation.[89] In New England, as Professor Edmund Morgan tells us, the Puritans eventually settled for their own salvation and that of their children, a tribalism which somewhat dimmed the original vision of a city set on a hill.[90] If Utopia is nowhere, the Millennium is never, and prophecy's success is a self-fulfilling self-defeat, dependent upon repeated and compounded disappointments and failures.

NOTES

1   T. E. Hartley (ed.), *Proceedings in the Parliaments of Elizabeth I, vol. 1: 1558–1581* (Leicester, 1981), p. 137 (all further references to Hartley). This notable speech from the 1567 Parliament, 'on nominating an heir and a bill of succession', has been variously attributed to William Lambarde (whether the antiquarian or not is itself a matter in dispute) and John Molyneux, the more plausible candidate. See G. R. Elton, *The Parliament of England, 1559–1581* (Cambridge, 1986), pp. 310–12; J. D. Alsop, 'Reinterpreting the Elizabethan commons: the parliamentary session of 1566', *Journal of British Studies*, 39 (1990), 216–40.

2   Ernest Gellner, *Nations and Nationalism* (Oxford, 1983), p. 138. See also Elie Kedourie, *Nationalism* (rev. edn, London, 1961). For a different view, see Anthony D. Smith, *The Ethnic Origins of Nations* (Oxford, 1986), ch. 1. In ch. 4 of John Barnie, *War in Medieval Society: Social values and the Hundred Years War* (London, 1974), nationalism is defined as a people's awareness and articulation of its collective identity, based on common racial, linguistic and geographic factors. Barnie thinks it vain to look for this in the fourteenth century, where there is evidence only of 'a crude form of patriotism'. Instead, 'nationalism in its fullest sense was the product of the fifteenth century' (p. 97). See also the book referred to in the next note, and the essays collected in Vincent Newey and Ann Thompson (eds), *Literature and Nationalism* (Liverpool, 1991).

3   Richard Helgerson, *Forms of Nationhood: The Elizabethan writing of England* (Chicago, Ill., 1992).

4   John Foxe, *The Acts and Monuments of John Foxe*, ed. S. R. Cattley, (London, 1841), vol. 1, p. 514.

5   Michael Drayton, *The Poly-Olbion: A chorographical description of Great Britain*, 2 vols (Manchester, 1889), vol. 1, *The First Song*.

6   William Camden, *Britain, Or a chorographicall description of the most flourishing kingdome, England, Scotland and Ireland* (London, 1637), Epistle.

7   Holinshed, *Holinshed's Chronicles*, 6 vols (London, 1808), vol. 6, p. 952.

8   *The Workes of Geffray Chaucer, newly printed* (London, 1532), Scolar Press facsimile (Menston, 1969). The preface to 'the Kynges Hyghnesse' states that the editor is 'William Thynne, chefe clerke of your kechyn', but the copy from which the facsimile has been taken bears this evocative note: 'This preface I sir Bryan Tuke knight wrot at the request of Mr Clark of the Kechyn then being tarrying for the tyd at Grenewiche.' Tuke was a royal secretary. There could be no better example of the convergence of a kind of humanism and the interests of the state/commonwealth.

9 Anthony Grafton, *Joseph Scaliger: A study in the history of classical scholarship*, 2 vols (Oxford, 1993), vol. 2, *Historical Chronology*, pp. 2–10.

10 William Tyndale, *The Work of William Tyndale*, ed. G. E. Duffield, The Courtenay Library of Reformation Classics, no. 1 (Appleford, 1964), pp. 324–6. See Janel M. Mueller, *The Native Tongue and the Word: Developments in English prose style 1380–1580* (Chicago, Ill., 1984); A. B. Cottle, *The Triumph of English, 1350–1400* (London, 1969). Mueller differs from R. F. Jones, *The Triumph of the English Language* (Stanford and London, 1953), both in her stress on 'scripturalism' and in placing the 'triumph' in a much earlier period. Jones made four passing references to Tyndale and none to the late fourteenth-century Wycliffite Bible translators.

11 Richard Mulcaster, *Mulcaster's Elementarie*, ed. E. T. Campagnas (Oxford, 1925), p. 269.

12 [Sir Bryan Tuke], Preface to *The Workes of Geffray Chaucer*.

13 J. G. A. Pocock, 'England', in Orest Ranum (ed.), *National Consciousness, History, and Political Culture in Early-Modern Europe* (Baltimore, Md., and London, 1975), p. 99. See Benedict Anderson, *Imagined Communities: Reflections on the origins and spread of nationalism* (London, 1983).

14 J. G. A. Pocock, *The Ancient Constitution and the Feudal Law: A study of English historical thought in the seventeenth century* (Cambridge, 1957). The question of the origins of English national self-consciousness is ultimately one for the very early medievalist, the Anglo-Saxonist, since they evidently lay in confrontation with that 'other' which was Celtic.

15 J. G. A. Pocock, *The Machiavellian Moment: Florentine political thought and the Atlantic republican tradition* (Princeton, N.J., 1975); Lisa Jardine and A. L. Grafton, '"Studied for action": how Gabriel Harvey read his Livy', *Past and Present*, 129 (1990): 30–78; also Malcolm Smuts, 'Court-centered politics and the use of Roman historians, *c.* 1590–1630', David Norbrook, 'Lucan, Thomas May and the creation of a republican literary culture', and Blair Worden, 'Ben Jonson Among the Historians', all in Kevin Sharpe and Peter Lake (eds), *Culture and Politics in Early Stuart England* (London, 1994); J. H. M. Salmon, 'Seneca and Tacitus in Jacobean England', in Linda Levy Peck (ed.), *The Mental World of the Jacobean Court* (Cambridge, 1991), pp. 169–88; and now, especially, Markku Peltonen, *Classical Humanism and Republicanism in English Political Thought 1570–1640* (Cambridge, 1995).

16 Hartley, p. 129.

17 Edmund Calamy, 'Englands Looking-Glasse' (preached 22 Dec. 1641, published London, 1642), in Robin Jeffs (ed.), *Fast Sermons to Parliament*, part 1 of Jeffs (ed.), *The English Revolution*, 44 vols (London, 1970), vol. 3, pp. 11–80.

18 J. R. Green, *A Short History of the English People* (London, 1874), p. 447.

19 Debora Shuger, *Habits of Thought in the English Renaissance: Religion, politics, and the dominant culture* (Berkeley, 1990), pp. 5–6, 9.

20 Hartley, p. 278.

21 Christopher Hill, 'The Protestant Nation', in Hill, *Collected Essays, vol. 3: Religion and Politics in 17th Century England* (Brighton, 1986), pp. 28–9.

22 Entered on the title-page of a copy in the Cambridge University Library (shelf-mark SSS.18.19) of John Stubbs, *The Discoverie of a Gaping Gulf whereinto England is Like to be Swallowed by another French Marriage, if the Lord Forbid not the Banes* (London, 1579).

23 Christopher Hill, *The English Bible and the Seventeenth-Century Revolution* (London, 1993).

24 Thomas Case, 'Gods rising, his enemies scattering' (preached 26 Oct. 1642; published London, 1644), *Fast Sermons*, vol. 4 (London, 1970), p. 210. For contrasting views of the Fast Sermons' agenda, whether political stratagem or orchestrated by religious imperative, see Hugh Trevor-Roper, 'The Fast Sermons of the Long Parliament', in Hugh Trevor-Roper, *Religion, the Reformation and Social Change and Other Essays* (London, 1967), pp. 294–344; John F. Wilson, *Pulpit in Parliament: Puritanism during the English Civil Wars, 1640–1648* (Princeton, 1969).

25 Barbara Lewalski, *Protestant Poetics and the Seventeenth-Century Religious Lyric* (Princeton, 1979); Lily B. Campbell, *Divine Poetry and Drama in Sixteenth-Century England* (Cambridge, 1959).

26 Richard Bauckham, *Tudor Apocalypse*, The Courtenay Library of Reformation Classics, no. 6 (Appleford, n.d.); Paul Christianson, *Reformers and Babylon: English apocalyptic visions from the Reformation to the eve of the Civil War* (Toronto, 1978); Katharine R. Firth, *The Apocalyptic Tradition in Reformation Britain 1530–1645* (Oxford, 1979); G. J. R. Parry, *A Protestant Vision: William Harrison and the Reformation of Elizabethan England* (Cambridge, 1987).

27 Thomas Adams, 'Englands sickness', in *Works* (London, 1629), pp. 302–48; Edward Reynolds, 'Israels petition in time of trouble' (preached 27 July 1642, published London, 1642), *Fast Sermons*, vol. 3 (London, 1970), p. 242.

28 Hill, *The English Bible*, p. 440.

29 Michael McGiffert, 'God's Controversy with Jacobean England', *American Historical Review*, 88 (1983): 1151–76.

30 Thomas Cogswell, *The Blessed Revolution: English politics and the coming of war 1621–1624* (Cambridge, 1989); Thomas Cogswell, 'England and the Spanish match', in R. Cust and A. Hughes (eds), *Conflict in Early Stuart England* (Harlow, 1989), pp. 107–33; Peter G. Lake, 'Constitutional consensus and puritan opposition in the 1620s: Thomas Scott and the Spanish match', *Historical Journal*, 25 (1982): 805–25; Kenneth Fincham and Peter Lake, 'The ecclesiastical policies of James I and Charles I', in Kenneth Fincham (ed.), *The Early Stuart Church, 1603–1642* (London, 1993); Alexandra Walsham, 'Aspects of providentialism in early modern England', unpublished Ph.D. thesis (Cambridge University, 1995), pp. 251–2.

31 Perry Miller, *The New England Mind: From colony to province* (Cambridge, Mass., 1953); Robert Middlekauff, *The Mathers: Three generations of puritan intellectuals 1596–1728* (New York, 1981); Michael McGiffert, 'American puritan studies in the 1960s', *William and Mary Quarterly*, 3rd ser., 27 (1970): 36–67.

32 John Aylmer, *An Harborowe for Faithfull and Trewe Subiects* (London, 1559). Some copies of the *Harborowe* (e.g. Cambridge University Library, shelf-mark Bb*.11.37¹) contain an additional Epistle 'to the faithful and Christian Reader', together with some *errata*. For the likely origins of the 'God is English' trope, see John McKenna, 'How God became an Englishman', in DeLloyd Guth and John McKenna (eds), *Tudor Rule and Revolution: Essays for G. R. Elton from his American friends* (Cambridge, 1982), pp. 25–43; Joseph Strayer, 'France: the Holy Land, the Chosen People, and the Most Christian King', in T. K. Rabb and J. E. Seigel (eds), *Action and Conviction in Early Modern Europe: Essays in memory of E. H. Harbison* (Princeton, N.J., 1969), pp. 3–16.

33 Aylmer, *Harborowe*, sig. P4r; Thomas Gainsford, *The Glory of England, Or, a true description of many excellent prerogatives and remarkable blessings, wherby she triumpheth over all the nations of the world* (London, 1618). For Gainsford as a Protestant and patriotic journalist, see Michael Frearson, 'The English Corantos of the 1620s', Ph.D. thesis (Cambridge University, 1994). On the rhetorical theme of civic greatness in Jacobean England (Britain), see ch. 4 of Peltonen, *Classical Humanism*, 'Francis Bacon, Thomas Hedley and the true greatness of Britain'.

34 Stephen Gosson, *The Trumpet of Warre. A sermon preached at Paules Crosse the seventh of Maie 1598* (London, 1598), sigs. B4, E4; Richard Bernard, *The Bible-battells. Or, the sacred and the military. For the rightly wageing of warre according to Holy Writ* (London, 1629), Preface, pp. 3–5. There are many examples of Christian militancy in the sermons preached to the Artillery Company of London. See, for example, Thomas Adams, *The Souldiers Honour* (London, 1617); John Everard, *The Arrieban: A sermon preached to the company of the military yarde* (London, 1618); Thomas Sutton, *The Good Fight of Faith* (London, 1624); William Gouge, 'The dignitie of chivalry' (preached 1626, printed 1631 in part 3 of *Gods Three Arrowes: Plague, famine, sword*). Sir John Hale has suggested that such sermons assisted in a mental and moral militarisation which made the Civil War possible ('Incitement to violence? English divines on the theme of war, 1578 to 1631', in J. R. Hale, *Renaissance War Studies* [London, 1983], pp. 487–517).

35 The publication history of this work is complex. A unique copy of *The new pollecye of warre* (*Short-Title Catalogue* 1735) is dated 1542, as is an equally unique copy of material soon to be incorporated in *The true defence of peace*: 'A devout and godly prayer for all degree and estates' and 'Blyssynges and curses' (*STC* 1775). The colophon runs: 'Imprinted at London in Botulph Lane at the sygne of the whyte Beare, by John Mayler for John Gough Anno Dni 1542.' *The true defence of peace* (*STC* 1776) has a similar colophon, but dated 1543. *The polecy of warre, wherin is declared, how the enemies of the Christian publique weale maye be overcome and subdued,* devised by Thomas Becon was incorporated in *The worckes of Thomas Becon* in 1564 (*STC* 1710), from whence it was reprinted in Thomas Becon, *Early Works*, ed. J. Ayre, Parker Society (Cambridge, 1843). In his dedication of this work to Sir Thomas Wyatt, Becon wrote: 'I think there is no man so far estranged from civil humanity which knoweth not how much every one of us is indebted to his native country.' And then he quoted from Horace: 'Dulce et decorum est, pro patria mori.'

36 John Milton, *Animadversions*, ed. Harry Morgan Ayres, *The Works of John Milton*, vol. 3, part 1 (New York, 1931), pp. 144–5.

37 Examples of the trope are in Hugh Latimer, 'God of England, or rather the English God'; John Lyly, 'the living God is only the English God'; Archbishop Matthew Parker, 'where Almighty God is as much English as he is' (see Patrick Collinson, *The Birthpangs of Protestant England: Religious and cultural change in the sixteenth and seventeenth centuries* [London, 1988], p. 4). See also Anthony Marten, *An Exhortation, to stirre up the mindes of all her Maiesties faithfull subiects* (London, 1588), sig. B2r. A similar trope could perhaps be found in French and Spanish sources; it is unlikely to have been an English peculiarity.

38 Calamy, 'Englands Looking-Glasse', *Fast Sermons*, vol. 2, p. 19.

39 Hill, *The English Bible*, p. 264.

40 A. K. McHardy, 'Liturgy and propaganda in the diocese of Lincoln during the Hundred Years War', in *Religion and National Identity: Studies in Church History*, 18, ed. Stuart

Mews (Oxford, 1982), pp. 215–27. Only a few of Brinton's sermons have any political resonance (Brinton, *The Sermons of Thomas Brinton, Bishop of Rochester [1373–1389]*, ed. M. A. Devlin, 2 vols, Camden 3rd ser., nos 85, 86 [1954]). But in one of them, Brinton preached on Hosea, and at Paul's Cross, with the warning: 'Deus qui sole-bat esse Anglicus a nobis recedit' ('God who was accustomed to being English will abandon us') ('Timeo', in Brinton, *Sermons*, vol. 1, p. 47). For 'more recent wars', see D. Naphtine and W. A. Speck, 'Clergymen and conflict 1660–1763', in *The Church and War: Studies in Church History*, 20, ed. W. J. Sheils (Oxford, 1983), pp. 231–62; Albert Marvin, *The Last Crusade: The Church of England in the First World War* (Durham, N.C., 1974); Alan Wilkinson, *The Church of England and the First World War* (London, 1978); Stewart Brown, 'A solemn purification by fire': responses to the Great War in the Scottish Presbyterian churches, 1914–19', *Journal of Ecclesiastical History*, 45 (1994): 82–104.

41 See McGiffert, 'God's controversy', for a survey of Jacobean Hoseads, of which the most substantial was John Downame, *Lectures upon the Foure First Chapters of the Prophecie of Hosea* (London, 1608). The forensic glosses are Downame's. See also Thomas Sutton, *Englands First and Second Summons. Two Sermons preached at Paules Crosse* (London, 1616), the first of these preached on Hosea 4:13, p. 2: 'The accusation is laid downe in a legall and iudicall manner of proceeding, wherein the Israelites are summoned to appeare at the bar and tribunall of Gods Judgements, there to answer unto such capitall offences as there should be laid unto their charge.' See also George Webbe, *Gods Controversie with England* (a Paul's Cross sermon, preached 11 June 1609) (London, 1609), in which Hosea 4:1–3 is called 'a lively description of a iudiciall forme of proceeding, or course of law' (p. 9; cf. pp. 14–15).

42 Hill, *The English Bible*, p. 255.

43 William Hampton, *A Proclamation of Warre from the Lord of Hosts. Or Englands warning by Israels ruine ... a sermon at Pauls Crosse Iuly the 23, 1627* (London, 1627), pp. 9–10 and passim.

44 'For, some of our Shires are larger then some of their Tribes were: and yet our Shires are in number foure times more than their Tribes were' (Gouge, *Gods Three Arrowes*, part 3, p. 427). 'Arise, arise, yee *Princes of the tribes of England*, yee members of the *honourable houses of Parliament*' (Matthew Newcomen, 'The craft and cruelty of the Churches adversaries discovered' [preached 5 November 1642; published London, 1643], *Fast Sermons*, vol. 4, p. 273).

45 Richard Cust and Peter Lake, 'Sir Richard Grosvenor and the Rhetoric of Magistracy', *Bulletin of the Institute of Historical Research*, 54 (1981): 40–53; Robert Reyce, *Suffolk in the XVIIth Century. The Breviary of Suffolk by Robert Reyce (1618)*, ed. Lord Frances Harvey (London, 1902), p. 7. That historians were, for a time, persuaded that in the seventeenth century 'country' usually meant 'county', loyalty to which took precedence over national sentiment, was due in large measure to the influence of Alan Everitt's *The Community of Kent and the Great Rebellion* (London, 1966), itself colored by the singular provincial identity of Kent, celebrated in the 1570s as 'one special Countrie, set from great antiquity' (William Lambarde, *A Perambulation of Kent* [London, 1826], p. viii).

46 Shuger, *Habits of Thought*, p. 125.

47 Hill, *The English Bible*, pp. 47–78. For the pressure under which Elizabeth was placed to become a good iconoclast and to punish such royal idolaters as Mary Queen of

Scots, see Margaret Aston, *The King's Bedpost: Reformation and iconography in a Tudor group portrait* (Cambridge, 1994), especially pp. 97–127. See also Patrick Collinson, *Elizabethan Essays* (London, 1994), pp. 31–56, 87–118; and Chapter 2 in this volume.

48 Perry Miller, 'The marrow of puritan divinity', *Publications of the Colonial Society of Massachusetts*, 37 (1935): 247–300, and his *The New England Mind: The seventeenth century* (New York, 1939); McGiffert, 'God's controversy' and 'Covenant, crown, and commons in Elizabethan puritanism', *Journal of British Studies*, 20 (1980): 32–52. Reference is also made to Dr. McGiffert's remarks given at a conference on 'Puritanism in Old and New England' held at Millersville University of Pennsylvania in April 1991.

49 Theodore Bozeman, 'Federal theology and the "national covenant": an Elizabethan Presbyterian case study', *Church History*, 61 (1992): 394–407.

50 So I suggested in a sketchy treatment of the English Hoseads in my *Birthpangs of Protestant England*, pp. 20–3. The advantage of what may well have been deliberately manipulated confusion was that it enabled the preacher to address simultaneously the nation as Israel and as a remnant so 'exceeding small' that it was like 'an unit in *Arithmetique* which cannot make a number' (Webbe, *Gods Controversie*, pp. 51–2).

51 Trevor-Roper, 'The Fast Sermons'. While my essay draws principally upon Paul's Cross Sermons before 1640 and the parliamentary Fast Sermons after 1640, it should be said that for three generations before the Long Parliament, public (if often unauthorised) assemblies for prayer, fasting and humiliation, especially at times of adversity and disaster, had been subjected to similar soul-searching, castigating sermons; see Patrick Collinson, *The Elizabethan Puritan Movement* (London and Berkeley, Calif., 1967), pp. 214–19, and 'The puritan classical movement in the reign of Elizabeth I', Ph.D. thesis (University of London, 1957), pp. 323–46. These remarks predated the appearance of Alexandra Walsham, *Providence in Early Modern England* (Oxford, 1999).

52 John Stockwood, *A Sermon Preached at Paules Crosse on Barthelmew Day Being the 24 of August 1578* (n.d.), p. 20; William Whateley, *Charitable Teares: Or a sermon shewing how needful a thing it is for every godly man to lament the common sinnes of our countrie* (London, 1623), Preface; Edmund Calamy, 'Gods free mercy to England' (preached 23 February 1642; published London, 1642), in *Fast Sermons*, vol. 2, pp. 173, 175.

53 George Wither, *Britains Remembrancer* (London, 1628); Hill, *Collected Essays of Christopher Hill*, vol. 2, p. 29.

54 J. H. Prynne, 'English poetry and emphatical language', *Proceedings of the British Academy*, 74 (1988): 135–69.

55 Whateley, *Charitable Teares*, pp. 244–45.

56 James Bisse, *Two Sermons Preached, the one at Paules Crosse eight of Ianuarie 1580. The other, at Christes Churche in London the same day in the afternoone* (London, 1581), sig. G4.

57 Cambridge University Library, MS. Add. 3117. John Craig, Arnold Hunt and Alex Walsham have all worked on Saxby's commonplace book, and I have benefited from discussing it with them. The passages quoted here are from fos 56v and 5v. The remark about Gouge's sermons occurs in Samuel Clarke, *A Collection of the Lives of Ten Eminent Divines* (London, 1662), p. 105. At some point, Saxby settled in London, so that Gouge's sermons were presumably no longer such a rare treat.

58 A caustic account by Bishop Matthew Wren's visitors of the reception of sermons in Bury St Edmunds in 1636 speaks of 'the weomen's sighes and the mens hauchins'

(Bodleian Library, MS. Tanner 68, fo. 54).

59 Tessa Watt, *Cheap Print and Popular Piety, 1550–1640* (Cambridge, 1991); Peter Lake, 'Deeds against nature: cheap print, Protestantism and murder in early seventeenth-century England', in Sharpe and Lake, *Culture and Politics in Early Modern England*, pp. 257–83. The fullest account of the moral and cultural worlds of, on the one hand, the prophetic sermon, and, on the other, cheap(ish) and sensational print, is in Alexandra Walsham's Ph.D. thesis, 'Aspects of providentialism in early modern England' (now published). Dr Walsham notes that *The Repentance of Nineve that Great Citie* was a ballad kept in print for fifty years, that the Lodge and Greene play about Jonah and Nineveh, *A Looking Glasse for London and England*, was the number one box-office success of 1590, and that the story of the destruction of Jerusalem in A.D. 74 continuously captured the public imagination (*Ibid.*, pp. 267–71).

60 This refers to some of the work of Dr Christopher Haigh. Compare the rather extreme pessimism (if that is the right word) in his 'Puritan evangelism in the reign of Elizabeth I', *English Historical Review*, 92 (1977): 30–58, and 'The Church of England, Catholics and the people', in C. Haigh (ed.), *The Reign of Elizabeth I*, (London, 1984), pp. 195–219, with the more balanced account of Elizabethan Protestantism found in his *English Reformations: Religion, politics, and society under the Tudors* (Oxford, 1993).

61 Adolf Harnack, *What Is Christianity?*, tr. T. B. Saunders (London, 1958), p. 35.

62 Tom Webster, 'The Godly of Goshen scattered: an Essex clerical conference in the 1620s and its diaspora', Ph.D. thesis (Cambridge University, 1993).

63 Calamy, 'Englands Looking-Glasse', in *Fast Sermons*, vol. 2, pp. 63, 20, 21.

64 Thomas Jackson, *Judah Must into Captivitie. Six sermons* (London, 1622).

65 Patrick Collinson, 'The Protestant cathedral, 1541–1660', in P. Collinson, N. Ramsay, and M. Sparks (eds), *A History of Canterbury Cathedral* (Oxford, 1995), pp. 180–3.

66 Calamy, 'Englands Looking-Glasse', in *Fast Sermons*, vol. 2, pp. 34.

67 Hampton, *A Proclamation of Warre*, pp. 6, 13.

68 Stephen Marshall, 'Reformation and desolation' (preached 22 Dec. 1641; published London, 1642), in *Fast Sermons*, vol. 2, pp. 112–13.

69 Calamy, 'Englands Looking-Glasse', in *Fast Sermons*, vol. 2, p. 28; Marshall, 'Reformation and desolation', in *Fast Sermons*, vol. 2, p. 131.

70 William Mewe, 'The robbing and spoiling of Jacob and Israel' (preached 29 Nov. 1643; published London, 1643), in *Fast Sermons*, vol. 9 (London, 1971), p. 60.

71 Calamy, 'Gods free mercy to England', in *Fast Sermons*, vol. 2, pp. 145, 147, 139, 183.

72 Stephen Marshall, 'Meroz cursed' (preached 23 Feb. 1642, published London, 1642), in *Fast Sermons*, vol. 2, pp. 195–253; George Yule, *Puritans in Politics: The religious legislation of the Long Parliament 1640–1647* (Appleford, 1981), pp. 297–304.

73 Jeremiah Whitaker, 'Eirenopoios, Christ the settlement of unsettled time' (preached 25 Jan. 1643; published London, 1643), in *Fast Sermons*, vol. 5 (London, 1971), pp. 163–4.

74 Maria Dowling and Peter Lake (eds), *Protestantism and the National Church in Sixteenth-Century England* (London, 1987); Collinson, *The Birthpangs of Protestant England* and Collinson, 'The cohabitation of the faithful with the unfaithful', in O. P. Grell *et al.* (eds), *From Persecution to Toleration: The glorious revolution in England* (Oxford, 1991), pp. 51–75.

75 Thomas Weld to his old parishioners at Terling, Essex; BL, Sloane MS. 992, fo. 92v; printed in Everett Emerson (ed.), *Letters from New England: The Massachusetts Bay Company, 1629–1638* (Amherst, Mass., 1976), pp. 94–98.

76 Jewel, *The Works of John Jewel*, ed. J. Ayre, Parker Society (Cambridge, 1847), vol. 2, pp. 869–70. Jewel's text was 1 Thessalonians, and it must be admitted that his speculations about 'the number of the faithful' were of a suitably eschatological nature. However, eschatological expectations are always liable to have implications for present perceptions.

77 Carol Z. Wiener, 'The beleaguered isle: a study of Elizabethan and early Jacobean anti-Catholicism', *Past and Present*, 51 (1971): 27–62.

78 John Norden, *A Mirror for the Multitude* (London, 1586), Epistle 'To the Reader', pp. 38–9, 60.

79 Foxe, *Acts and Monuments of John Foxe*, vol. 1, p. 520.

80 Norden, *A Mirror*, pp. 87, 88, 100.

81 Patrick Collinson, 'Ben Jonson's Bartholomew Fair: the theatre constructs puritanism', in David L. Smith, Richard Strier and David Bevington (eds), *The Theatrical City: Culture, theatre and politics in London, 1576–1649* (Cambridge, 1995).

82 Whateley, *Charitable Teares*, p. 217.

83 Thomas Carter, 'Prayers prevalence for Israels safety' (preached 28 June 1643, published London, 1643), in *Fast Sermons*, vol. 7 (London, 1971), p. 123.

84 Marshall, 'Reformation and desolation', in *Fast Sermons*, vol. 2, p. 126.

85 William Perkins, *The Work of William Perkins*, ed. Ian Breward (Appleford, 1970), pp. 279–302.

86 Jackson, *Judah Must into Captivitie*, pp. 64–5.

87 Hill, *The English Bible*, p. 270.

88 William Lamont, *Godly Rule: Politics and religion, 1603–60* (London, 1969), ch. 6.

89 Haigh, *English Reformations*, pp. 279–80; see also John Sommerville, *The Secularisation of Early Modern England: From religious culture to religious faith* (New York and Oxford, 1992).

90 Edmund S. Morgan, *The Puritan Family: Religion and domestic relations in seventeenth-century New England* (New York, 1966).

Chapter 7

John Foxe and national consciousness

We all know what William Haller wrote about John Foxe and national consciousness in *The Elect Nation*, 36 years ago; and we can also rehearse the arguments deployed against his thesis by Katherine Firth, V. Norskov Olsen, and others.[1] We know that Foxe was not a vulgar nationalist but a man of universal vision and ecumenical conviction, who believed himself to be living near the end of time. Reopening Haller after a few years, there is less about the elect nation than one remembered, and one suspects that 'the elect nation' of the title may have been a mistake, since, unless I have read carelessly, the phrase which appears in the text is 'an', not 'the' elect nation. Christopher Hill has written that 'the' and 'an' amount to the same thing, but I beg to disagree.[2] That England, typologically Israel, was 'an' elect nation was a commonplace, in the pulpit and elsewhere, but except as a rhetorical flourish – 'God is English!' – the claim that England was *the* only elect nation, God's exclusive favorite, was rarer. However, Haller does say that Foxe's book was about not just the nation's history but also its 'destiny'. He does say that Foxe and the Elizabethan preachers conceived of the Church as one with the nation, the nation itself a mystical communion of chosen spirits, 'a people set apart from all others'.[3] And that was to misread Foxe's apparent intentions.

Firth believed that Haller had virtually invented an 'apocalyptic nationalism' which she nowhere found in Foxe or in any of his near contemporaries, or that he had read it back from the mid-seventeenth century where, as a Milton scholar, he was more at home. If Haller had read Foxe's huge commentary on the Book of Revelation, the *Eicasmi*, he would have found that Foxe explicitly denied that the Church belonged to any single nation, but was to be found wherever true religion and piety were found. 'Ibi ecclesia est.' Olsen

Originally published in *John Foxe and his World*, edited by Christopher Highley and John N. King (Aldershot, 2002). Reproduced by permission of Ashgate Publishing.

rightly insists that Foxe's *Book of Martyrs* is about that Church, not about the nation. However, Foxe, in 1563, does use the words 'specially in this Realme of England and Scotland' (which is of some constitutional interest), his book 'framed chiefly of the English Church'. That, after all, was where his readers, reading him in English, found themselves to be, in space and time.[4] We may add to these arguments the copious evidence in *Acts and Monuments* of Foxe's interest in non-insular church history, and of his dependence upon continental sources. In 1583, Foxe devoted fifty of his dense columns of print to Luther ('Here beginneth the reformation of the Church of Christ, in the time of Martin Luther'), eighteen to the Reformation in Switzerland and elsewhere; while Wycliffe, proudly called in 1563 'our countryman Wycliffe', 'the valiant champion of the truth', was later demoted from his star role, in 1570 simply part of Foxe's 'orderly' chronology, and not without 'some blemishes'. Even in 1563, Foxe had devoted fifty-seven pages to Jan Hus and Bohemia.[5]

My reason, or excuse, for returning to these perhaps hackneyed issues is twofold. First, there has been an intensification of interest in more recent years in the interlinked subjects of religion and national identity, the product of both a post-Cold War, post-Marxist interest in nationalism and its intellectual origins and of a more general and heightened sensitivity to religion as a social and political force and factor. My second reason is that in this age of the history of the book, and of reading practices, we are now more curious than we used to be about the interaction of discursive texts with the real substance of their subject matter on the one hand and with their readers on the other. Andrew Hadfield provides me with a hook on which to hang much of what follows: sixteenth-century 'writers had both to fashion and authorize their own utterances as literature and imagine the national community they addressed. Neither "literature" nor "nation" could be taken as stable entities and were always in the process of being redefined, partly as a result of their interaction and interdependence'.[6]

The British Academy Foxe Project has a moving target, and has taught us what a very unstable entity *Acts and Monuments* was, the 1583 edition conveying a deceptive stability, for just as Cranmer would, according to Diarmaid MacCulloch, have continued to perfect the Prayer Book if Edward VI had lived to a ripe old age, it is perhaps unlikely that the *Book of Martyrs* would have remained the same if Foxe had been given another 20 years to work on it.[7] And this contingent stability would later be compounded by the barbarous practices of Foxe's nineteenth-century editors, who often failed to detect or understand the significance of successive changes to the text. David Loades and Tom Freeman are currently insisting that we must part company for ever with those corrupt and deceptive Victorian editions.[8]

We – and 'we' can be taken to include both Haller and his critics – used to think that we were dealing with a book, understood in the ordinary sense of that term, written by its author, subject to progressive revision but always the same book. Now Tom Betteridge tells us that each of the four English editions of *Acts and Monuments* produced in Foxe's lifetime must be considered a distinct and different text, each differently motivated and constructed, in response to Catholic criticism and a changing religious environment.[9] Freeman and others have demonstrated to what a considerable extent Foxe's Catholic critics, and especially Nicholas Harpsfield, actually contributed to later recensions of the text.[10] And Damian Nussbaum has taught us that the 1632 edition, published almost a half-century after Foxe's death, with much added material (but otherwise respecting the integrity of 1583), was sent on its way to address a new and threatening set of circumstances, a book which now said not so much 'remember the martyrs' as 'prepare for martyrdom!' To be fair, Haller knew that too, in 1963.[11]

What do we now mean by 'Foxe and his collaborators'? Much more than we would have meant only four or five years ago. Thanks to Freeman, and also to Susan Wabuda, authorities both on that important collaborator Henry Bull, we now share some sense, if not yet quite enough, of how many hands and voices contributed to 'Foxe', and of the extent to which the book almost wrote itself, by some of those who would also be its readers.[12] The godly community, if more problematically the national community (and we shall return to this), was constructing itself by both writing and reading, rehearsing these stories. As Foxe's sources and dependencies are identified, in Freeman's words the text deconstructs itself. We now know that Foxe himself was responsible for almost none of the words of the most famous story of all, the martyrdom of Ridley and Latimer, or perhaps only for the lines beginning 'Be of good comfort Master Ridley', which made their first appearance in 1570. The author was Ridley's brother-in-law, George Shipside, perhaps with some help from Latimer's Swiss servant, Augustine Bernher and other witnesses.[13] John Bale, not Foxe, wrote the story of King John which appears in *Acts and Monuments*, his account 'essentially untouched by Foxe'.[14] Undoubtedly there are numerous other examples to be uncovered. Foxe's part in the enterprise is almost reduced to that of an editor (albeit a highly proactive editor) who went to great pains to obtain and verify his materials. So there is less point than I myself thought, no more than five years ago, in engaging with the ghost of C. S. Lewis on the subject of Foxe's prose, his quality and significance as literary stylist.[15] And insofar as it is John Foxe who is communicating with us, John King and Daniel Woolf tell us that Foxe himself was master of a variety of literary genres: multivocality in a single author.[16]

It is always hard to determine how far a breakthrough in the particularities of a somewhat specialised subject like Foxe should be attributed to the *Zeitgeist* of a more general idea, or nostrum: in this case, the much proclaimed death of the author. Multiple authorship is no longer a stigma, and authorship matters less. We are talking more about composite discursive communities, less about individual genius, or talent. Annabel Patterson has told us more than we once knew about the 'syndicate' which was Holinshed, a 'multivocal' chorus of contributors, and about what she calls the 'protocols' of their 'collaborative agenda'. Not only was 'Holinshed' the product of many authors; it ingested, as Foxe ingested, primary and secondary materials from a variety of sources (including Foxe), while its multivocality included eyewitness accounts of such events as the execution of the duke of Somerset which conveyed, as many of Foxe's stories conveyed, popular crowd reaction, a cast of thousands.[17]

And yet the circumstances in which individual authorship was asserted or conceded in our period represent one of the most fascinating aspects of that defining literary-cum-social process which Hadfield has described. Richard Helgerson has touched on this issue at many points in his *Forms of Nationhood*, discussing, for example, how Shakespeare appropriated the history of fifteenth-century England, partly to advance and elevate the theatrical medium, and with it himself. Helgerson quotes Spenser, writing to Gabriel Harvey: 'Why a God's name may not we, as else the Greeks, have the kingdom of our own language?'[18] Tyndale had said something similar fifty years before: 'For God gave the Children of Israel a law by the hand of Moses in their mother tongue.' Prophets, psalmists and apostles all said what they had to say in the 'mother tongue.' 'Why may we not also?'[19]

According to Helgerson, Spenser asserted a proprietorial interest in demanding to 'have' the kingdom of his own language. His 'we' is the royal we, and he wants to make the English language do what he wants it to do. So Spenser would be described on the title page of the 1611 edition of his collected *Works* as 'England's Arch-Poet'. Similarly, Tyndale in his famous vaunt had boasted that he, Tyndale, would 'cause' the ignorant ploughboy to know more of the scripture than supposedly learned clergy, and he would later provoke Thomas More to say that for Tyndale to require all England to go to school with him to learn their own language was 'a very frantic folly'. Even that master in the Renaissance art of self-fashioning and self-presentation, Erasmus of Rotterdam, had presumed in his Preface to the New Testament to say no more than 'would that' (*utinam*) the ploughman should know the scriptures.[20]

The difference between 'utinam' and 'I will cause' was profound. When Tyndale wrote that God gave his children a law 'by the hand of Moses', he was identifying himself with Moses, to the extent that he intended that God should now give England a law, and a gospel, by the hand of Tyndale. The 1534 edition of the New Testament proclaimed, almost scandalously, that it had been faithfully translated by William Tyndale, the only occasion, I think, when the name of an individual appeared on the title page of scripture.

Yet Tyndale told Stephen Vaughan in that clandestine meeting in a field outside Antwerp that if the king would consent to promulgate the simple text of scripture to his people in their own language, he, Tyndale, would shut up and, as it were, cease to exist, which is what effectively happened. His control over the text of the English Bible was enormous, but for ever afterwards hidden and almost forgotten.[21] On the other hand, if personal authorship was regressive in that case, it progressed in other discursive areas, although not always consistently. There was never any doubt that *Britannia* was William Camden's *Britannia*. Yet in the case of Camden's *Annates* of Elizabeth, the early English translated editions spoke only of 'the author', never once mentioning Camden's name.[22]

Foxe almost became his great book, but there was no question of Foxe being buried in it, as if he had never existed. What we now know about the multiple, collaborative construction of the *Book of Martyrs* was either unknown to his contemporaries, friend and foe alike, or overlooked. Although the *Book of Martyrs* was its commonest designation, not 'Foxe's Book of Martyrs', its status as either a 'book of credit, next to the Bible', or a great farrago of lies from start to finish, was inextricably bound up with the person of Foxe himself.[23] There are few instances in English literary history of a more complete fusion of author and text. In 1563 *Acts and Monuments* was modestly presented as merely 'gathered and collected ... by John Foxe', whose name is printed in a small italic typeface, and no more prominently than the name of the printer, John Day, and it is Day's portrait and *impresa* which appear on the colophon page of the 1570 edition. But later editions proclaimed themselves to have been '*Newly recognised and inlarged by the Authour* JOHN FOXE', now in capitals.

If Spenser, and Tyndale, wanted the English language to do what they wanted it to do, Foxe was no less insistent that the lessons of history were what he wanted them to be. The polite convention of Renaissance historiography whereby authors like Polydore Vergil and, later, William Camden, allowed the reader to be the final judge of controverted and difficult matters had no place in Foxe's rhetorical repertoire. In the Preface addressed 'to the true and faithful congregation of Christ's Universal Church' (1570), which was Foxe's principal essay in the rhetorical form known as the *ars historica*, he wrote that he could not insist that people read his book. But once undertaken, a reading of Foxe had to be according to his rules. 'When I considered this partial dealing and corrupt handling of histories, I thought with myself nothing more lacking in the church than a full and a complete story.' 'I considered', 'I thought with myself.' When it came to church history, there were only two kinds: good and bad. Back me or sack me.[24] Compare Polydore Vergil on the origins of Britain: 'Truly there is nothing more obscure, more uncertain, or unknown.' Or read Camden on the same subject, proceeding by means of conjecture, which he defends as an indispensable historical method. Having reduced the mythical British history to rubble, Camden tells the reader, if you want to believe all that stuff, be my guest.[25]

And then return to Foxe's claim to 'open the plain truth of times lying long hid in obscure darkness of antiquity', which Foxe claimed to present 'as in a glass'. So I think we may have here a rather extreme example of an authorial, and authoritative stamp being placed on what was actually a highly collaborative literary venture. Patterson notes that 'Holinshed' imitated the historiographical practice of Foxe, particularly in the large-scale ingestion of 'monuments', but not his prescriptiveness, since the *Chronicles* adopted a deliberately 'indifferent' stance on religion and other matters. Whether or not Patterson is right about the indifference of Holinshed, there is not the slightest tincture of 'indifference' in Foxe.[26]

Susan Felch's study of Foxe's prefaces draws helpful parallels with the apparatus with which Tyndale put his own Lutheran stamp on what he deceptively presented as a 'plain' text of scripture, and with the 'definitive interpretative framework' in which the Geneva Bible was 'encased'. She calls his 1570 prefaces 'coercive', and the coercion extended far beyond this preliminary matter to running headlines and marginalia. This 'encircling discourse' was an exercise in 'shaping the reader'.[27]

But how could all those fences and signposts control what Foxe's readers made of this huge and unwieldy text? No author can hope for that and no intellectual historian should ever count on it. Glyn Parry has argued that by 1576, the date of the third edition, many readers would have found in *Acts and Monuments* a proto-imperial subtext, and that Foxe himself, who counted Sir Francis Drake, the circumnavigator, among his friends, would not have found that antipathetic, or contrary to half of his authorial intentions.[28]

Haller's elect nation thesis ought to have been about the reception of Foxe, a book not so much about Foxe as about his readers. His subject embraced 'what the book appears to have conveyed to the people of its own time', and was meant 'to suggest what seems to have been its effect on the public mind in that and the immediately succeeding age'.[29] Haller failed to appreciate that such matters could hardly be inferred from the printed text alone. He assumed that what Foxe intended he brought about, and therefore concentrated on what Foxe intended. His critics, Firth and others, tackled Haller on these, his own terms, denying that that was what Foxe intended. That was not to advance the argument very far.

Years later, the reception history of a 'Foxe' I am now inclined to put in quotes has remained almost unexplored, and I am not convinced that an adequate reception history can ever be written. Damian Nussbaum had a good crack at it, and can suggest what different kinds of readers may have made of Foxe. He is very good, for example, as is Tom Freeman, on the subject of the book's hostile and critical Catholic reception, and on Foxe's response to that criticism, a striking example of literary feedback.[30] I have nothing to add but what I think are some of the right questions, and even questions without answers can serve a useful historical purpose.

We are largely ignorant, and likely to remain so, about aspects of the subject such as these: who owned copies? Where were they placed in the home, or public place? How often and how were they read? Were even 'private' readings 'acoustic' and consequently public, within the household? Were readings from Foxe directly linked to Bible reading? Were the dramatic possibilities of large portions of the text exploited in multivocal readings (would the women of a household have read the women's 'parts'?) or was the exercise monotonal? Was the book commonly read systematically, they would have said 'throughly', or more selectively? How far, for some 'readers', were the illustrations a substitute for the text? And, above all, our central question, would 'Foxe' have been heard and understood as having a special application to England? There are either no answers to these questions, or only anecdotal answers: Sir Francis Drake in the Gulf of Mexico, Ignatius Jordan in Exeter, the Ferrars in Little Gidding.[31] But there is the more general evidence of the health warnings which prefaced the abridgments of *Acts and Monuments*. Thomas Mason, who as an abridger would say this, would he not, tells us that 'few that have the Booke reade over it', while both Mason and Timothy Bright suggest that even those able to afford the book were just too busy to read it.[32]

It is also clear that 'reception' is not necessarily the appropriate word, since readings of 'Foxe' may have been active and creative, in many appropriations of the text. Lisa Jardine and Tony Grafton in their seminal study of Gabriel Harvey's marginalia have encouraged us to think in terms of what they call a 'transactional mode of reading', a single text giving rise to 'a plurality of possible responses, not a tidily univocal interpretation'.[33] Deconstructionists more radical than Jardine and Grafton would maintain that it could be read in an infinity of ways, leaving the meaning of the text indeterminate and indeterminable.

There may be a way out of this postmodernist morass into which we are stumbling, and I think that it is along this way that students of, as it were, Foxe in action should be pointed. In a work on eleventh- and twelfth-century reading practices, *The Implications of Literacy*, Brian Stock has introduced the concept of 'textual communities'. Stock's context of early heretical circles and of the Cistercian Order was certainly very different from that of the sixteenth and seventeenth centuries, especially so far as concerned the relation between the literate, subliterate and illiterate, although Stock makes points which are still applicable to our period about the influence of written texts extending far beyond those capable of reading them for themselves.

Nevertheless, these observations from Stock seem relevant. Texts defined groups which distinguished themselves from an outside world 'looked upon as a universe beyond the revelatory text'. The text in question was so far internalised that it no longer needed to be spelt out, interpreted, or reiterated. (Stock is thinking of quite short texts here.) 'The members all knew what it was.' The circulation and use of the sermons of St Bernard of Clairvaux among the Cistercians is called 'the [twelfth] century's outstanding example of a "textual community".' From reading, engaging in dialogue and absorbing texts it was but a short step to the formation of these 'textual communities'. 'The group's members must associate voluntarily; their interaction must take place around an agreed meaning for the text.' 'Above all, they must make the hermeneutical leap from what the text says to what they think it means; the common understanding provides the framework for changing thought and behaviour.' Within Bernard's sermons, 'the experience of the text and the experience of the religious life were intermingled, offering a structure to both at once'. 'Texts gradually acquired the capacity to shape experience itself.'[34]

In an essay on the formation in the 1650s of a Quaker identity, '"The Quakers quaking": print and the spread of a movement', Kate Peters has given us a remarkable case study, in many ways parallel to Stock's cases, of how another religious and textual community was formed, especially by the deliberate exploitation of the opprobrious term 'Quaker', which positively assisted the Quakers in their perception of themselves in relation to a hostile world. There was a 'textual dynamic' and 'a sustained textual development of the term which occurred concurrently with the dissemination of Quaker ideas', amounting to the 'textual construction' of the movement.[35]

The homily 'On the Scripture' of the sixteenth-century Church of England – and it could be Stock or Peters speaking – tells us that the Bible reader who will profit most is the one who is 'turned into it, that is ... in his heart and life altered and changed into that which he readeth'. One might indeed suppose that the Bible above all had the capacity to create a textual community, a rather large textual community. But that, of course, has been persistently denied in the polemic of Catholics and some Anglicans, sensitive to the dangers of releasing the biblical text into the hands of the unlearned and 'rude' laity without ecclesiastical guidance and control. Dryden provides us with the most quotable examples of this trope, the almost postmodernist insistence that in those circumstances the Bible will inevitably have as many meanings as it has readers:

> By Sacred Writ, whose sense your selves decide,
> You said no more, but that your selves must be
> The judges of the Scripture sense, not we.
> You rule the Scripture, not the Scripture you.[36]

Kate Peters's Quakers are almost sufficient evidence that such concerns were not groundless polemic, although they are evidence of, so to speak, molecules and clusters of molecules rather than atoms. Yet I have argued, in an essay called 'The Coherence of the Text: How It Hangeth Together' (a quotation from a Geneva Bible preface), that the vernacular Bible could and did have the opposite effect, centripetal rather than centrifugal, as the ceaseless interaction of pulpit, text and hearers imposed a common sense of the meaning of the Bible, including the conviction that there was indeed a common meaning to be found, by a process of cross-referencing. Needless to say, the supposed unity, or concordance, of the entire biblical canon was not so much ontological as read into it by the textual community of its readers.[37]

As with Bible reading, I think it more likely that Foxe was read in ways that were shared and mutually understood than that he was read in any number of ways, that his book probably did achieve a high degree of what Susan Felch has called 'interpretative coherence.'[38] A search of seventeenth-century correspondence and seventeenth-century godly lives is likely to reveal a quasi-biblical habit of referencing and cross-referencing Foxe which may suggest that the exemplary and typological uses of the text were well understood and consensual.

But if 'Foxe' had the capacity to form a 'textual community', even as the text was itself constructed by that community, we are faced with the question: what kind, or shape, of community, or communities, and, the sharp end of the question: inclusive or exclusive? This is the problem of Foxe and national consciousness, Foxe and the godly community. To address it, we need to begin with the text, in order to establish how the mind of Foxe related godly community to nation – Foxe himself as at once inclusivist and exclusivist. This should not be too difficult. We need also to imagine the communities which his book both addressed and constructed. This will be more difficult. Both investigations can be conducted on the broader basis of what has been recently suggested about the role of religious ideas and stories in inventing or consolidating communities, including nations, and about the more specific role of religion in constructing a Protestant English national identity. This has to embrace questions relating to the divisive as well as uniting potentialities of religious texts and ideologies.

Insofar as modernists, historians, political scientists and anthropologists will allow early modernists to even discuss nationalism – or the weaker construction, national sentiment – in the pre-industrial world, there is some agreement that the essential constituents for a sense of nationhood were a shared language, expressed in a written vernacular literature, and a shared religious identity. There is, of course, a difference of opinion about how much relative importance to attach to those two factors, and some exaggerated claims have been made for the religious factor. Claire McEachern, who tells us that English nationhood was a sixteenth-century phenomenon, believes that the nation itself was founded 'in and by the religious culture and ideology of Elizabethan England'. Conor Cruse O'Brien, in a lecture series called *God Land: Reflections on religion and nationalism*, wrote that it was impossible to conceive a nationalism which was not a holy nationalism, while admitting, as a self-confessed agnostic, that he personally regretted the influence of holy nationalism on his own country, Ireland. The late Ernest Gellner, committed to his own modernist understanding of what constitutes nationalism, was brutal in his review of O'Brien, calling him 'intellectually autistic'.[39]

We shall never know what Gellner would have made of the late Adrian Hastings's book, *The Construction of Nationhood: Ethnicity, religion and nationalism*, which appeared in 1997. Hastings does not go so far as O'Brien, but he leads us vigorously and persuasively in the same direction. In the case of Christian Europe, at least, the idea and ideal of the nation-state and of the world as a society of nations was originally 'imagined' (referring to Benedict Anderson's seminal idea) through the Bible, 'a mirror for national self-imagining'. For Hastings the Bible was 'Europe's primary textbook', providing 'the original model of the nation'.

In the particular case of England, Hastings believes that the 'mass impact' of the English Bible 'in strengthening a common language, installing in all its hearers and readers the idea of nationhood and actually shaping the English of all classes into an awareness of their own nationhood cannot be overstated', although Hastings, unlike McEachern, does not make the mistake of supposing that the English nation was born in the sixteenth century.[40] Across the disciplinary divide, Hastings is supported by Janel Mueller who in her *Native Tongue and the Word* argues that 'scripturalism', which began with the Wycliffite translators but which came to its consummation with Tyndale, was the key which both unlocked an English literary renaissance and led inexorably in a Protestant direction. Thomas More in his endless controversy with Tyndale effectively surrendered any claim to the 'open' biblical sentence for which Purvey had argued in the fourteenth century, and which Tyndale perfected. Mueller writes: 'It is hard to avoid the conclusion that More deliberately resigns to Tyndale and the Protestants generally the exercise of native resources for prose composition. He is conceding that the open, vernacular style is a suitable mode for undermining the authority of the Church, not for defending it.' Would we go too far if we were to add that More was also surrendering to Tyndale and his language the future of the nation?[41]

Foxe, who can be said to have built upon Tyndale, is very helpful to Hastings's argument. He calls the *Book of Martyrs* 'a sort of additional biblical testament' and helpfully describes the hundreds of pages devoted to the Marian martyrs as 'a sort of English Book of Maccabees'.[42] But what about the language of the *Acts and Monuments*? Hastings speaks of the English Bible 'strengthening a common language', which is a commonplace. Can we say the same thing of Foxe? Or does the language of Foxe represent a kind of linguistic subculture, peculiar to what, when he first wrote, was a minority of committed, godly gospellers, something like the *vocabulum secretum* which, as

Anne Hudson has taught us, served to identify and construct the textual community of the Lollards?[43]

If Foxe was not writing the national language but a sectarian dialect of the language, he was not yet writing for the nation. We have hardly begun to account for the origins and rapid maturation of the language of godliness which is resonant in 'Foxe', and especially in the letters of the martyrs, as collected by Henry Bull, and these are prime evidence that we are not talking about the literary style of an individual, John Foxe, but of a shared linguistic resource, a kind of godly argot.[44] John Knott has written on what he calls the 'Apostles' style' of 'Foxe', a style derived most obviously from St Paul, who 'provided much of the language with which the Marian martyrs fortify their writings', a language which, in the words of Wayne Meek applied to the earliest Christians, was one 'of kinship and affection', expressing 'the intimacy of communal life'.[45]

St Paul is an undeniable source, ventriloquised through Tyndale. But does Tyndale's St Paul speak of 'societies' of 'sweet' 'favourers'? Does St Paul write, substantively, of 'the godly'? So far as Tyndale himself is concerned, David Daniell suggests that much more work needs to be done on what he calls Tyndale's 'speech-based language', including the reduction of biblical texts, themselves often proverbial in shape, to the everyday forms of proverbial speech, 'the lively shared speech of independent small groups'.[46] 'Foxe' offers a comparable challenge.

Adrian Hastings admits, at one point, that 'there was nothing inherently nationalist about Protestantism. The linkage was largely fortuitous'.[47] And other cautionary voices have been raised, questioning a too easy assumption that, in Tony Claydon's phrase, 'nationality was a sub-set of Protestantism'. Claydon warns us in his introduction to a collection of essays on *Protestantism and National Identity*:

> It is worth asking whether the reformed faith could ever have been a sound basis for a unifying national identity. The Protestant community's sense of the true church as something mystical rather than human; its appeal to foreigners; its universalist mission to convert all mankind; its tendency to fissure; its easy adoption of the divisive rhetoric of anti-popery in internal disputes; and its suspicion of attempts to impose conformity as popish persecution; all these made Protestantism an unlikely bedrock of nationality in the early modern period.[48]

It is blindingly obvious that in sixteenth- and seventeenth-century Europe religion and nationalism were often opposing forces. Peter Lake, with the assistance of Catharine Davies and Jane Facey, has anatomised English Protestantism as psychologically as well as theologically a religion for elect minorities which supposed themselves to be repressed even if they were not. There was consequently tension within Protestantism between a vision of the Church as a persecuted minority and its equation with 'a commonwealth of

Christians', the whole nation. Lake concludes: 'English Protestantism ... [was] an ideology not well suited ... for a genuinely national church.'[49] Foxe, like Tyndale, held in creative and unresolved tension the Troeltschian categories of church and sect.

Whom did Foxe think he was addressing? For what sort of community was he writing? Haller's perspective was, shall we say, pre-revisionist in all sorts of ways, and we can no longer elide the godly Protestant community with the national community, as if they were one and the same thing. There is a parallel ecclesiological question with respect to Thomas Cranmer and the Book of Common Prayer. Diarmaid MacCulloch is clear about Cranmer's 'Calvinism' and that 'the people' for whom the Prayer Book was intended were God's people, which was not everyone.[50] The Prayer Book was not the utterly inclusionary text which we, assisted by the Act of Uniformity, have often taken it to be. Now there is good reason to believe that Foxe was very much aware of the negative pastoral implications of an excessively experimental Calvinism, and perhaps of its divisive potential. His sponsorship of translations of some of Luther's more practical and 'comfortable' works, which seems to have arisen from his pastoral experience, has that implication.[51] The inclusive unity of the whole Protestant nation was something he chose, or, dare we say, pretended to believe in.

How many people did Foxe expect his book to reach? If it was not a question for him, it is certainly one for us, and to answer it with any confidence requires more knowledge about exposure to such large, expensive and scarce books than we have or perhaps are ever likely to have. We know for a fact that no more than 1,350 copies of the 1596 edition were printed. But the print run on that occasion may have been unusually small, given a number of unpropitious circumstances. But it remains unlikely that a total of as many as 15,000 copies was produced of all five sixteenth-century editions – a figure admittedly plucked from the air. It has to be acknowledged that these almost prohibitively expensive books were highly valued, that they made magnificent gifts, and that they were bequeathed at death, passed down through the generations. If it is an old canard that copies were placed in every parish church, by order (scotched by Leslie Oliver in 1943), Foxe was set up in many other public places, and it is likely that both privately and publicly owned copies were read aloud in a variety of domestic and other settings: our 'textual communities' again. The model of private, silent reading is singularly inapplicable to a text of this kind. And yet, without ignoring the various abridgments – which I shall discuss presently – it is clear that only a minority of the population can ever have been directly exposed to Foxe. A broadcasting model is no less inapplicable.[52]

This is something which Hallerian enthusiasm for this supposedly great national text has persistently chosen to overlook. Warren Wooden guessed that by 1684 no more than 10,000 copies of *Acts and Monuments* had been put into circulation, and yet he seems to have thought that that was a lot. It was a book, he claimed, that cut across social divisions and classes to reach 'all English Protestants', and 'met an enthusiastic response in Protestant England'.[53] Even Oliver believed that 'there could have been few people in England during the century after its publication who did not at least have the opportunity to thumb through it'.[54] Eirwen Nicholson brings us to order by inviting us to compare the c. 135,000 copies of Allestree's *Whole Duty of Man* disseminated between 1660 and 1711, and she makes a very pertinent observation that the widespread dispersal of *Acts and Monuments* in seventeenth- and eighteenth-century households has been assumed rather than demonstrated.[55]

Let us press Foxe on his own intentions and expectations. In 1570 the 'Constantinian' thrust of the argument was modified, for reasons which Betteridge and others have helpfully discussed. The Dedication to the queen remains, but now the great decorated initial 'C' belongs to 'Christ, the Prince of all Princes', not Constantine. The wording of a Preface first used in 1570 is significant. It was addressed to 'the true and faithful Congregation of Christ's Universal Church with all and singular the members thereof, wheresoever congregated or dispersed through the Realm of England', which sounds more like some kind of Congregationalism than an established, hierarchical church under the royal supremacy. Felch has pointed out that this Preface predates the orders to place *Acts and Monuments* in cathedral churches and other public places. It was still a private, or at least a household, book rather than a fully authorised, public text. The 'you' addressed were also defined as 'all well-minded lovers and partakers of Christ's gospel', 'all christian readers', and the book was said to be intended for 'the simple flock of Christ'.[56] To square that kind of ecclesiology with the Constantinian Elizabethan settlement was not easy, and it does not look as if Foxe tries very hard. The 'congregationalism' of the 1570 Preface is at odds with the running headline: 'A Protestation to the whole Church of England', and with a change of gear Foxe is soon talking of a unity which is apparently to be national and inclusive. 'And if there cannot be an end of our disputing and contending one against another, yet let there be a moderation in our affections.'

> Because God hath so placed us Englishmen here in one commonwealth, also in one church, as in one ship together, let us not mangle or divide the ship, which, being divided, perisheth ... No storm so dangerous to a ship on the sea, as is discord and disorder in a weal public.[57]

Now Foxe sounds like Hooker.

Foxe addressed himself separately to 'All the Professed Friends and Followers of the Pope's Proceedings', 'pretending the name of Catholics, commonly termed Papists, wheresoever abiding in the realm of England'. The questions put to these people were followed by four matching 'considerations' addressed to 'the christian gospellers', 'well-beloved'. Christopher Haigh and others of the noble army of revisionists might want to ask Foxe how numerous he thought these two groups, papists and gospellers, to have been in 1570, and whether he allowed for a third element in the population (and how large in his perception it might have been) who did not fit neatly into either of those categories, the 'neuters' of Puritan polemic, or Annabel Patterson's 'indifferent' souls. However, in 1570 Foxe assumes just two kinds of readers – well minded and ill minded – a divisive dichotomy which was to become standard in many Puritan anatomies of the nation. What was Foxe's map of English Christianity in 1563, 1570 and 1583? And how closely did it match what we might suppose to have been reality?

John Knott's *Discourses of Martyrdom* is the best account we have of the tension running through these prefaces, perhaps we may even say the contradiction between the Church as a persecuted little flock, validated in its sufferings, and the Church as established, hierarchical, and royal, validated by the Constantinian figure of Elizabeth.[58] This tension, the cracks in Foxe's attempted synthesis of two almost incompatible ideals, was mirrored in his own rather odd ecclesiastical career under Elizabeth, a kind of semi-detached relationship with the national Church: on the one hand detestation of Presbyterian Puritanism; on the other an abiding prejudice against ecclesiastical vestments and what they symbolised.

Knott's avowed interest lies in the legacy which the exclusivist Foxe left to a long line of sectaries and other religious radicals from the Elizabethan Separatists to Bastwick, Burton and Prynne, Milton, Bunyan and the Quakers, all of whom appropriated the highly affective and rhetorical ecclesiology of suffering – a kind of substance which Foxe distilled and dispensed, as persistently powerful as, say, Liberation Theology in contemporary Latin America. Of course Knott knows – but it was not the subject of his book – that Foxe also had his establishmentarian heirs, for whom the blood of the martyred bishops was the seed of an episcopal, Prayer Book church. According to William Lamont, it was necessary to do something about that version of Foxe, even to ditch it, in older to have a Puritan revolution, just as Archbishop Laud had all but suppressed Foxe in order to promote his own antithetical vision of the Church of England.[59]

But it would be a mistake to suppose that Foxe was confused in his rhetoric or in his ecclesiology. Foxe belonged to an age that needed no lessons in exploiting the advantages of ambiguity, even of contradiction. This was an age of preachers (and Foxe was a great preacher) who knew that they had to make all kinds of scarcely defensible or consistent assumptions as they faced congregations of great diversity. The preachers addressed, even apostrophised, the nation, as if it stood literally and in person before them, especially when they occupied the national pulpit of Paul's Cross.[60] They did not have one exclusionary message for the instructed, the committed and even (it might be thought with a certain presumption) the elect, and another inclusionary message for all the rest. They did not preach two covenants but one, and they elided skillfully from God's dealings with individuals to his dealings with the collectivity of his own dear children, and on to his dealings with the whole Church and Nation.[61] One is reminded of early seventeenth-century orators who spoke of their country and who were the exploiters, not the victims, of an ambiguity which historians of the 1960s and 1970s wrongly supposed to be a choice and a dichotomy. Country was not either nation or county. It was both.[62]

So it was that Foxe played the numbers game. The godly community was at once a remnant and a multitude. It was 'how many thousand' who had never bowed their knees to Baal. The time of Wycliffe saw a 'multitude' of faithful witnesses. The recital of names from those years was 'almost infinite', with 'whole armies and multitudes' withstanding the pope. Foxe's arithmetic skillfully added to the numbers of the Marian martyrs and of the thousand or so Marian exiles he counted an 'infinite number' who had suffered what we should now call internal displacement. This enabled him to write of a persecution which extended from Princess Elizabeth herself to all estates, 'rich men, poor men, woman, wife, widow, virgin, old men, young men, boys, infants, blind, halt and lame' – a representative cross-section of the entire nation.[63]

Foxe's description of the last burnings in Smithfield on 27 June 1558 makes the same point concrete. There was an arrangement among the godly 'there standing together', 'which was a great multitude', that as the prisoners appeared they would go to them to embrace them and comfort them, 'and so they did'. For as the victims came into Smithfield, 'the godly multitude and congregation with a general sway made toward the prisoners' with such irresistible force that the guards were forced back. As the narrative proceeds, Foxe (or rather his informant) executes a subtle change of gear and begins to talk about first 'the godly people' and then simply 'the people'. The minister Thomas Bentham, a future bishop, who may well have been that informant, turns his eyes to 'the people' and assures them that those about to be martyred are 'the people of God'. 'With that all the people, with a whole consent and one voice, followed and said, "Amen, Amen!"' The noise was so great that it was impossible to single out any individuals for retribution. The little flock has now become the people.[64]

Wherever we find populism in sixteenth-century texts, whether it is in the Protector Somerset's extraordinary addresses to the rebels of 1549, or in the pages of Holinshed, especially the remarkable account of the labour force which built Dover Harbour, or in Shakespeare's version of Jack Cade and his rebellion in *Henry VI Part 2*, we are encountering something which went against the natural grain of hierarchy and social prejudice, and we need to ask what is going on, and why.[65] Brett Usher and Tom Freeman suggest good reasons why, especially after events in London in the mid-1560s, Foxe needed to emphasise the size and solidarity of the London congregation rather than its sectarian marginality, equating the godly people with the people at large as a kind of moral majority. Foxe may want us to forget that the highest figure which even he had placed on the membership of the underground Protestant congregation in Marian London was 200 (at a time when the population of London was perhaps 50,000), although he tells us that 'it greatly increased' in the latter time of Queen Mary. And Usher has assured us that there was only one London congregation, not a cluster of congregations. Nevertheless, the godly people are the people of England, or perhaps will be. Whether Foxe's prolepsis would come good remained to be seen.[66]

Christopher Haigh has famously pronounced that by about 1600 England was a Protestant nation, if not yet a nation of Protestants.[67] My first reaction to that statement was that it had been made for the sole benefit of those setting examination papers. 'Discuss.' But no doubt Haigh has a point, perhaps equivalent to saying that England was by then an anti-Catholic nation but not, for the most part, a godly nation. Just as we have somehow to explain how a religion of cells and conventicles became a national church, albeit a church riven with divisions which only time could heal, but did not, so we may have to account for the slow transformation of *Acts and Monuments* from a monstrous tract for the times and for not too many readers into the kind of national text it allegedly became in Linda Colley's long eighteenth century, fostering a patriotic anti-Catholicism and, in Colley's Hallerian phrase, the sense of England's, and Britain's, 'Protestant identity'.[68] I say 'may have to' because I am far from convinced that anything resembling 'Foxe' ever did become a national text. So this may be something which we do not, after all, have to do.

That is not to deny a very far-reaching and more diffuse Foxeian influence, explicit in the case of Samuel Clarke's late seventeenth-century *General Martyrologie*, which was Foxe *redivivus*, but implicitly an influence hard to trace, since Foxe is so often invoked without reference or acknowledgment.[69] And I have not forgotten the cheap print, the ballads, the woodcuts and engravings, and all that embroidery, objects which Tessa Watt and Alex Walsham know about: the Armada crescent, Fawkes with his lantern approaching St Stephen's Chapel, the Fatal Vesper – events living on in the national memory which Foxe did not live to see and which were not read out of 'Foxe' but which interpreted through Foxeian spectacles.[70] Taking us into the long eighteenth century, Eirwen Nicholson believes that the idea that *Acts and Monuments* in its complete form was sufficiently well known to form the rhetorical and iconographical basis of anti-Catholicism is unsubstantiated. But then she substantiates in some detail the prevalence and impact of what she calls 'Foxe's bastards', derivative and more or less debased Foxeiana of which she lists sixty-one titles.[71]

I end by discussing the still neglected subject of the sixteenth- and early seventeenth-century epitomes of Foxe, which I believe contain clues if not answers to our almost unanswerable questions. The abridgments are a funny business. And, as Dr C. E. M. Joad would have said on the BBC Brains Trust many years ago, much depends upon what you mean by an abridgment! *Acts and Monuments* cried out for an affordable and user-friendly summary, and as Timothy Bright wrote, it was a great pity that Foxe had not seen to this himself.

That was in the preface to the best known, and most highly praised, abridgment which Bright, the physician and inventor of shorthand, published in 1589. The motive for Bright's interest in the subject is noteworthy. But for the protection which Sir Francis Walsingham had afforded him and others in Paris in August 1572, he believed that he himself would long ago have been martyred.[72] But Bright's effort was a failure. It had only one edition, and I do not think that the reason for that was that its publication, under royal patent, was (unsuccessfully and at some cost) challenged by the Stationers' Company.[73] Bright is a stout quarto of 792 pages, and apart from a woodcut on the title page it has no pictures, although Henry Denham in 1587 had made the pre-emptive and perhaps preventative move of obtaining a licence to print his own abridgment, 'with the picture'. So here was a fat, indigestible tome in its own right, and one's reaction is to ask how Foxe could ever be made accessible to a popular readership. But, as we shall see, there was a way, which was not Bright's. Haller might have noticed that Bright is the only abridger to blow the nationalistic trumpet. He devotes a whole sheet to what he calls 'A special note of England'. Constantine, the first Christian emperor, was an Englishman, as was Wycliffe, 'that first manifestly discovered the Pope', and so on: 'England, the first that embraced the Gospel, the only establisher of it throughout the world, and the first reformed.'

Christs victorie over Sathans tyrannie, faithfully abstracted out of the Book of Martyrs and divers other books appeared from the press in 1614, the work of Thomas Mason, a Hampshire minister who was the grandson of the Elizabethan Privy Councillor, Sir John Mason. The principles of abridgment were different from Bright's, but this was a folio of 418 pages, and it too enjoyed only one edition. Mason's hope that 'all sorts of people' would be able to buy it 'with little charge' was surely too optimistic.[74] To refer to an instructive and parallel case: Bright and Mason did not bear the same relation to the original 'Foxe' as the little summaries of John Stow's *English Chronicles* bore to the full deluxe version. And of those there were seven editions or issues, followed by no fewer than twelve of the regularly updated *Summarie of Englyshe Chronicles now abridged and continued*. This was an intelligent marketing strategy, and must be rated a success, although it failed to make Stow a rich man.[75]

More comparable to Stow's *Summaries* in price, and perhaps appeal, was a little book you could slip into your hip pocket, *The Mirror of Martyrs*, the work of Clement Cotton, the author of Bible concordances and translator of biblical commentaries from the French. The first edition of *The Mirror* (1613) was a duodecimo of 216 pages, which grew through an enlarged edition of 1615 to a larger format of 525 pages in 1625, but still a much slighter book than those of Bright or Mason. The print run of the first edition was 1,500 copies, and there were five editions before 1640 and a sixth in 1685.[76]

I have little doubt that Clement Cotton's 'Foxe' was the version which 'most people' (which is to say a restricted, godly readership) would have encountered, or at least have been able to afford. It is Foxe without tears, and in literary form it bears distinct affinities to the following genres: jest books, Thomas Beard's *Theatre of Divine Judgments*, funeral sermons and the godly lives that Samuel Clarke extracted from them – and, proleptically, *Readers Digest*. Foxe has now been reduced to a collection of short and improving anecdotes, relatively few of them pre-Marian, with some prayers and short extracts from the letters of the martyrs, little gobbets with appropriate headlines. All the best stories are here, especially in the fuller, 1625 edition: Ridley and Latimer's exchanges at the stake; Rowland Taylor and the worms in Hadleigh churchyard; Alice Binden and the Canterbury coal-hole; the Welsh fisherman, Rawlins White; the horror story of Hooper's burning with his arms dripping fat and falling off into the fire; Bonner scorching Thomas Tomkins's hand; 'Bloody Bonner' with his belly blown and head so swollen; Ridley's letter of reconciliation to Hooper; the 1558 Smithfield scenario; the Bilney–Latimer conversion stories; Widow Bradbridge who asked the bishop to take care of her daughters Patience and Charity: 'Nay', said the bishop, 'I will meddle with neither of them both'. Often, as in that case, the anecdote ends with a humorous punch line. Either these tales were already as well known to the godly as Bible stories, or they soon would be.

Headlines derived improving morals from the stories, letters and prayers: 'The Righteous are as bold as a Lyon'; 'The wicked flie, when none pursueth them'; 'The faithfull count not their lives deare unto them for Christ'; 'The way to Heaven is up the Hill'. Later editions include all that you ever wanted to know about the early Christian martyrs in five or six pages: Justin Martyr; Laurence with his gridiron; Polycarp ('fourscore and six years have I been his servant').[77]

Clement Cotton may have been a hack but he was not a dealer in cheap print in quite the Tessa Watt sense. His first edition was dedicated to Princess Elizabeth, subsequent editions to that great patron and connoisseur the Countess of Bedford. But his *Mirror* is utterly undemanding and, which is very much to the point in a paper on Foxe and national consciousness, not only makes nothing of the Englishness of its subject matter (although nearly all the content is English) but is totally lacking in structure, chronology or argument of any kind. I suspect that this is closer to what 'Foxe' came to represent nationwide, rather than the grand edifice of apocalyptic nationalism proposed by Haller. And I will very tentatively suggest that the significance of Clement Cotton lies beyond his six editions. Cotton may be letting us see what owners of the complete 'Foxe' actually read, or practically knew by heart. Which leads to a final question: what did owners and readers of 'Foxe' use for book marks?

NOTES

1 William Haller, *The Elect Nation* (New York, 1963), entitled, in the English edition (London, 1963), *Foxe's Book of Martyrs and the Elect Nation*; Richard Bauckham, *Tudor Apocalypse* (Appleford, 1978), Katharine R. Firth, *The Apocalyptic Tradition in Reformation Britain 1530–1645* (Oxford, 1979), V. Norskov Olsen, *John Foxe and the Elizabethan Church* (Berkeley and Los Angeles, Calif., 1973).

2 Christopher Hill, *The English Bible and the Seventeenth-Century Revolution* (London, 1993), p. 264; Chapter 6 in this volume; Patrick Collinson, 'The Protestant nation', in his *The Birthpangs of Protestant England: Religious and cultural change in the sixteenth and seventeenth centuries* (Basingstoke, 1988), pp. 1–27.

3 Haller, *The Elect Nation*, pp. 224–5.

4 Olsen, *John Foxe*, pp. 36–7, 43–7; phrases used by Foxe in the title of the 1563 edition of *Actes and Monuments*, and in the 1563 Preface, 'A declaration concerning the utility and profit of this history'.

5 Foxe, *Actes and Monuments* (London, 1563), p. 85 *et seq.*; John Foxe, *The Ecclesiastical History Contaynyng the Actes and Monumentes* (London, 1570), p. 523; Foxe, *Actes and Monuments* (London, 1583), pp. 840–74, 424.

6 Andrew Hadfield, *Literature, Politics and National Identity* (Cambridge, 1994), p. 1.

7 Diarmaid MacCulloch, *Thomas Cranmer: A life* (New Haven, Conn., and London, 1996), p. 618.

8 David Loades, 'Introduction: the new edition', in D. Loades (ed.), *John Foxe: An historical perspective* (Aldershot and Brookfield, Vt., 1999), pp. 1–14; Thomas S. Freeman, 'New perspectives on an old book: the creation and influence of Foxe's *Book of Martyrs*', *Journal of Ecclesiastical History*, 49 (1998): 327; Thomas Freeman, 'Texts, lies, and microfilm: reading and misreading Foxe's *Book of Martyrs*', *Sixteenth-Century Journal*, 30 (1999): 23–46.

9 Tom Betteridge, 'From prophetic to apocalyptic: John Foxe and the writing of history', in D. Loades (ed.), *John Foxe and the English Reformation* (Aldershot and Brookfield, Vt., 1997), pp. 210–32; Thomas Betteridge, 'John Foxe and the writing of history', in his *Tudor Histories of the English Reformations, 1530–83* (Aldershot and Brookfield, Vt., 1999), pp. 161–206.

10 Ceri Sullivan, '"Oppressed by the Force of Truth": Robert Persons edits John Foxe', in D. Loades (ed.), *John Foxe: An historical perspective* (Aldershot and Brookfield, Vt., 1999), pp. 154–66; Thomas S. Freeman, 'Harpsfield, Nicholas (1519–1575)', *Oxford Dictionary of National Biography* (Oxford, 2004).

11 Damian Nussbaum, 'Appropriating martyrdom: fears of renewed persecution and

the 1632 edition of *Acts and Monuments*', in Loades (ed.), *John Foxe and the English Reformation*, pp. 178–91; Haller, *The Elect Nation*, p. 227.

12 Susan Wabuda, 'Henry Bull, Miles Coverdale, and the making of Foxe's *Book of Martyrs*', in Diana Wood (ed.), *Martyrs and Martyrologies: Studies in Church history*, vol. 30 (Oxford, 1993), pp. 245–58. Dr Freeman is preparing for the Church of England Record Society an edition of 'The letters of the martyrs', contained in Emmanuel College, Cambridge, MSS. 260–62, which are now understood to have been collected and prepared for publication in the edition conventionally attributed to Coverdale (*Certaine most godly, fruitful and comfortable letters* [1564]) by Bull. Some of the first fruits of this study are contained in '"The good ministrye of Godlye and vertuouse women": the Elizabethan martyrologists and the female supporters of the Marian martyrs', *Journal of British Studies*, 39 (2000): 8–33.

13 Freeman, 'Texts, lies, and microfilm', 42–5.

14 Tom Freeman, 'John Bale's Book of Martyrs? The account of King John in *Acts and Monuments*', *Reformation*, 3 (1998): 175–223.

15 Chapter 8 in this volume.

16 John King, 'Fiction and fact in Foxe's *Book of Martyrs*', in Loades (ed.), *John Foxe and the English Reformation*, pp. 12–35; D. R. Woolf, 'The rhetoric of martyrdom: generic contradictions and narrative strategy in John Foxe's *Acts and Monuments*', in Thomas F. Mayer and D. R. Woolf (eds), *The Rhetorics of Life Writing in Early Modern Europe: Forms of biography from Canandra Fedde to Louis XIV* (Ann Arbor, Mich., 1995), pp. 243–82.

17 Annabel Patterson, *Reading Holinshed's Chronicles* (Chicago, Ill., and London, 1994).

18 Richard Helgerson, *Forms of Nationhood: The Elizabethan writing of England* (Chicago Ill., and London, 1992), pp. 203, 245, 1.

19 *The Work of William Tyndale*, ed. G. E. Duffield, The Courtenay Library of Reformation Classics, 1 (Appleford, 1964), pp. 324–6.

20 Foxe, *Actes and Monuments* (1563), p. 513; *The Confutacyon of Tyndales Answere*, in *The Complete Works of St. Thomas More*, vol. 8, eds Louis A. Schuster, Richard C. Marius, James P. Lusardi and Richard J. Schoeck (New Haven, Conn., and London, 1973), p. 212; Erasmus, *Paraclesis*, in J. C. Olin (ed.), *Christian Humanism and the Reformation* (New York, 1965), p. 97. Erasmus's *utinam* was an echo of a passage in his beloved St Jerome. See Lily B. Campbell, *Divine Poetry and Drama in Sixteenth-Century England* (Cambridge, 1959), pp. 18, 41–3, 49.

21 David Daniell, *William Tyndale: A biography* (New Haven, Conn., and London, 1994), esp. pp. 210–17; Gerald Hammond, *The Making of the English Bible* (Manchester, 1982); many of the articles in *Reformation*, 1 (1996).

22 Chapter 9 in this volume.

23 Patrick Collinson, 'Truth and legend: the veracity of John Foxe's *Book of Martyrs*', in his *Elizabethan Essays* (London and Rio Grande, Ohio, 1994), 151–77.

24 Foxe, *The ecclesiasticall history* (1570), sigs Fii^r–iiii^v.

25 *Polydore Vergil's English History*, ed. Sir Henry Ellis, Camden Society (1846), pp. 1–3; William Camden, *Britain*, tr. R. Robinson (London, 1610), pp. 8, 10, 22.

26 Patterson, *Reading Holinshed's Chronicles*, esp. pp. vii–xv, 145–7. Not all reviewers have accepted the notion of deliberate 'indifference' in Holinshed, and they have been scep-

tical about the claim that 'something like' the values of political liberalism link the early modern with the modern world (pp. x–xii).

27 Susan Felch, 'Shaping the reader in the *Acts and Monuments*', in Loades (ed.), *John Foxe and the English Reformation*, pp. 52–65.

28 Glyn Parry, 'Elect Church or elect nation? The reception of the *Acts and Monuments*', in Loades (ed.), *John Foxe: An historical perspective*, pp. 167–81.

29 Haller, *The Elect Nation*, p. 15.

30 Damian Nussbaum, 'Appropriating martyrdom'; Damian Nussbaum, 'Whitgift's "Book of Martyrs": Archbishop Whitgift, Timothy Bright and the Elizabethan struggle over John Foxe's legacy', in Loades (ed.), *John Foxe: An historical perspective*, pp. 135–53; Freeman, 'New perspectives on an old book', pp. 327–8.

31 Parry, 'Elect Church or elect nation?' pp. 171–7; Samuel Clarke, *A Collection of the Lives of Ten Eminent Divines ... and of some other eminent Christians* (London, 1662), p. 453; *Nicholas Ferrar. Two lives*, ed. J. E. B. Mayor (Cambridge, 1855), pp. 33–4, 64, 166, 238.

32 Thomas Mason, *Christs Victorie over Sathans Tyrannie* (London, 1615), Preface; Timothy Bright, *An Abridgement of the Booke of Acts and Monumentes of the Church* (London, 1589), Preface.

33 Anthony Grafton and Lisa Jardine, '"Studied for action": How Gabriel Harvey read his Livy', *Past and Present*, 129 (1990): 30–78.

34 Brian Stock, *The Implications of Literacy: Written language and modes of interpretation in the eleventh and twelfth centuries* (Princeton, N.J., 1983), pp. 90–11, 522, 526–7.

35 Kate Peters, '"The Quakers quaking": print and the spread of a movement', in Susan Wabuda and Caroline Litzenberger (eds), *Belief and Practice in Reformation England* (Aldershot and Brookfield, Vt., 1998), pp. 250–67. A fuller statement of the argument will be found in Kate Peters, *Print Culture and the Early Quakers* (Cambridge, 2005).

36 'The hind and the panther', in *The Works of John Dryden*, vol. 3 (Berkeley, Calif., 1972), pp. 144–5.

37 Patrick Collinson, 'The coherence of the text: how it hangeth together: the Bible in Reformation England', in W. P. Stephens (ed.), *The Bible, the Reformation and the Church: Essays in honour of James Atkinson* (Sheffield, 1995), pp. 84–108.

38 Felch, 'Shaping the reader', p. 64.

39 Claire McEachern, *The Poetics of English Nationhood, 1590–1612* (Cambridge, 1996), esp. p. 5; Conor Cruse O'Brien, *God Land: Reflections on religion and nationalism* (Cambridge, Mass., and London, 1988), esp. p. 40; Ernest Gellner, 'The sacred and the national', ch. 5 of his *Encounters with Nationalism* (Oxford and Cambridge, Mass., 1994). For O'Brien's alleged 'intellectual autism', see p. 61 of Gellner.

40 Adrian Hastings, *The Construction of Nationhood: Ethnicity, religion and nationalism* (Cambridge, 1997), pp. 1–65 passim.

41 Janel Mueller, *The Native Tongue and the Word: Developments in English prose style 1380–1580* (Chicago, Ill., and London, 1984), esp. 'More Versus Tyndale', pp. 201–25.

42 Hastings, *The Construction of Nationhood*, pp. 58–9.

43 Anne Hudson, *The Premature Reformation: Wycliffite texts and Lollard history* (Oxford, 1988), pp. 142–3, 168–73.

44 The most copious evidence for this is in the 'Letters of the martyrs' (see above, n. 12), to a great extent subsumed in *Actes and Monuments*, with some cosmetic modifications.

45 John R. Knott, *Discourses of Martyrdom in English Literature 1563–1696* (Cambridge, 1993), pp. 87–91.

46 Daniell, *William Tyndale*, pp. 2–3, 14, 17–18, 21, and *passim*; David Daniell, 'Gold, silver, ivory, apes and peacocks', in John T. Day, Eric Lund and Anne M. O'Donnell, SND (eds), *Word, Church, and State: Tyndale quincentenary essays* (Washington, D.C., 1998), pp. 10, 13.

47 Hastings, *The Construction of Nationhood*, p. 55.

48 Tony Claydon and Ian McBride, 'The trials of the chosen peoples: recent interpretations of Protestantism and national identity in Britain and Ireland', in Tony Claydon and Ian McBride (eds), *Protestantism and National Identity: Britain and Ireland, c.1650–c.1850* (Cambridge, 1998), pp. 10, 14–15.

49 Catharine Davies, '"Poor persecuted little flock" or "Commonwealth of Christians": Edwardian concepts of the Church'; Jane Facey, 'John Foxe and the defence of the English Church'; Peter Lake, 'Presbyterianism, the idea of a national Church and the argument from divine right'. All in Peter Lake and Maria Dowling (eds), *Protestantism and the National Church in Sixteenth Century England* (Beckenham and New York, 1987), pp. 78–102, 162–224, esp. 193.

50 MacCulloch, *Thomas Cranmer*, pp. 615–16.

51 Martin Luther, *A Commentarie vpon the Epistle to the Galatians* (1575); *A Commentarie vpon the Fiftene Psalmes* (1577); *Special and Chosen Sermons* (1578). All printed in London by T. Vautrollier, with evidence if Foxe's interest in the project.

52 Leslie M. Oliver, 'The seventh edition of John Foxe's *Acts and Monuments*', *Papers of the Bibliographical Society of America*, 37 (1943): 243–60. Tom Freeman has helped me with the more speculative parts of this paragraph.

53 Warren W. Wooden, *John Foxe* (Boston, Mass., 1983), unpaginated Preface. The words about an 'enthusiastic response' are those of Arthur Kinney, in his Editor's Foreword.

54 Oliver, 'The seventh edition', p. 243.

55 Eirwen Nicholson, 'Eighteenth-century Foxe: evidence for the impact of *Acts and Monuments* in the "long" eighteenth century', in Loades (ed.), *John Foxe and the English Reformation*, pp. 143–77.

56 Foxe, *The ecclesiasticall history* (1570), sigs Fiiʳ–iiiiᵛ; Felch, 'Shaping the reader', pp. 59–60.

57 Foxe, *The ecclesiasticall history* (1570), sigs Fiiʳ–iiiiᵛ.

58 Knott, *Discourses of Martyrdom*, pp. 107–16.

59 William Lamont, *Marginal Prynne 1600–1669* (London, 1963), pp. 65–9; William Lamont, *Godly Rule: Politics and Religion 1603–60* (London, 1969), pp. 23–4, 78–9.

60 Alexandra Walsham, '"England's Warning by Israel": Paul's Cross Prophecy', ch. 6 of her *Providence in Early Modern England* (Oxford, 1999); Chapter 6 in this volume; Collinson, 'The Protestant nation'.

61 Walsham, *Providence*, 305–6.

62 Richard Cust and Peter G. Lake, 'Sir Richard Grosvenor and the rhetoric of magis-

tracy', *Bulletin of the Institute of Historical Research*, 54 (1981): 40–53.

63 Foxe, *Actes and Monuments* (1563), pp. 85–108, 1679–80.

64 Foxe, *Actes and Monuments* (1583), pp. 2074–5, following Foxe, *The Ecclesiasticall History* (1570), pp. 2278–9, and Foxe, *Actes and Monuments* (1563), p. 1701, where the narrative first appeared, apparently a late acquisition, as the book was being printed. Dr Freeman thinks it likely that Bentham himself supplied Foxe with this material. Bentham's isolation and unpopularity as bishop of Coventry and Lichfield in the early 1560s may explain his desire to emphasise the inclusiveness of the Marian Protestant congregation.

65 E. Shagan, 'Protector Somerset and the 1549 Rebellions: new sources and new perspectives', *English Historical Review*, 64 (1999): 34–63.

66 Brett Usher, '"In a time of persecution": new light on the secret Protestant congregation in Marian London', in Loades (ed.), *John Foxe and the English Reformation*, pp. 233–51; Freeman, 'New perspectives on an old book', pp. 321–3.

67 Christopher Haigh, *English Reformations: Religion, politics, and society under the Tudors* (Oxford, 1993), p. 280.

68 Linda Colley, *Britons: Forging the nation 1707–1837* (New Haven, Conn., and London, 1992), ch. 1 'Protestants', and, esp. pp. 25–9.

69 Patrick Collinson, '"A magazine of religious patterns": an Erasmian topic transposed in English Protestantism', in his *Godly People: Essays on English Protestantism and Puritanism* (London, 1983), pp. 499–526.

70 Tessa Watt, *Cheap Print and Popular Piety, 1550–1640* (Cambridge, 1991); Walsham, *Providence*; Alexandra Walsham, '"The Fatall Vesper": Providentialism and anti-Popery in late Jacobean London', *Past and Present*, 144 (1994): 36–87.

71 Nicholson, 'Eighteenth-century Foxe', pp. 172–7.

72 Bright, 'An abridgement', prefatorial dedication to Walsingham.

73 Oliver, 'The seventh edition'; *Records of the Court of the Stationers' Company 1576 to 1602*, eds W. W. Greg and E. Boswell (London, 1930), pp. 31–2, 51, 55; *A Transcript of the Registers of the Company of Stationers of London 1554–1640 A.D.*, ed. E. Arber (London, 1875), I.534.

74 Mason, *Christs victorie*, Preface.

75 C. L. Kingsford, 'Life of Stow', part of the Introduction to his edition of *A Survey of London by John Stow*, 2 vols (Oxford, 1908), vol I, pp. vii–xxviii.

76 Oliver, 'The seventh edition', p. 253; Clement Cotton, *The Mirror of Martyrs in a Short View* (London, 1613); Clement Cotton, *The Mirror of Martyrs ... newly corrected and amended, with additions by the same author* (London, 1625). The 1615 edition is longer than 1613, shorter than 1625, and contains material peculiar to itself.

77 Cotton, *The mirror* (1625), p. 363.

Chapter 8

Truth, lies and fiction in
sixteenth-century Protestant historiography

I

John Foxe (and notwithstanding some glancing references to John Bale and Miles Coverdale, Foxe will serve on this occasion as shorthand for 'sixteenth-century historiography') had a great deal to say on the subject of 'truth'. In a sense he wrote about nothing else. But he was accused by his religious opponents of telling lies on an unprecedented scale. And if he did not deliberately propagate fictions, in the sense of inventing his stories, he wove his material into forms that were as fictive as they were factual. Like his friend and mentor, Bale, he was a myth-maker, even, it has been said, 'the prince of English historical myth-makers',[1] which is not to say that he was not also a great historian. Jane Austen wondered why history was so dull, considering that so much of it was made up. One could say that what makes Foxe's history so arresting is that it is partly made up, or, given his models and materials, makes itself up.

In introducing a section of his *Acts and Monuments* that consists of little more than a collection of original documents of the early German and Swiss Reformations (presented with a minimum of commentary), Foxe wrote that he was giving readers 'a sight thereof', so that they would not believe the 'smooth talk or pretensed persuasions of men', especially in church matters, 'unless they carry with them the simplicity of plain truth'.[2] That was to denigrate rhetoric and to equate 'plain truth', like some sixteenth-century Ranke, with unadorned documents, to tell the story as it actually (or evidently) was.

Originally published in *The Imagination in Early Modern Britain: History, rhetoric and fiction 1500–1800*, edited by D. R. Kelley and D. H. Sacks (Cambridge, 1997). Reproduced by permission of Cambridge University Press. Among the many scholars who have helped me in my limited understanding of John Foxe and the related matters discussed in this chapter, I should like to single out Damian Nussbaum and Alexandra Walsham.

The anachronism is obvious and intentional. Foxe was not Ranke. So what did sixteenth-century historiography mean by the simple or plain truth?

In approaching the question of truth, and of different orders or kinds of truth, as well as the distinctions to be made between truth and falsehood, fact and fiction, it is as convenient as it is thoroughly unoriginal to begin with Sir Philip Sidney's *Apologie for Poetrie*, a text itself not noted for its originality and greatly indebted to the classic definitional statements of Aristotle and Cicero. Yet Sidney states the issues so neatly that even his intended or unintended misunderstandings and oversimplifications give us the best of all purchases on the subject.[3] According to Sidney, history claimed to stand for truth and the practical and ethical value of historical truth, what Foxe in one of his prefaces called 'The Utility of This Story', a past both true and usable. Aristotle was primarily responsible for the distinction between history, an account of real events, and fiction, and Cicero wrote that according to the somewhat undeveloped capacities of Roman (rather than Greek) historiography, 'it is enough that the man should not be a liar' [satis est, non esse mendacem]. 'For who does not know history's first law to be that an author must not dare to tell anything but the truth? And its second that he must make bold to tell the whole truth?'[4] So William Camden, in the preface to his *Annales of Elizabeth*, which in its 1625 English edition would be called *The true and royall history of Elizabeth Queen of England*, wrote: 'Which Truth to take from History, is nothing else but, as it were, to pluck out the Eyes of the beautifullest Creature in the world; and, in stead of wholesome Liquor, to offer a Draught of Poison to the Readers Minds' – while going on to explain that he was not constrained to tell the whole truth: 'Things secret and abtruse I have not pried into.'[5] Sidney was ironically impressed by Cicero's austere standard of factual accuracy. The lips of historiographers 'sound of things done', Sidney wrote, and 'verity' is 'written in their foreheads'. And Sidney was sceptical withal, for when all was said and done, the historian authorised himself for the most part on other historians (nothing changes!), 'whose greatest authorities are built upon the notable foundation of hearsay'.[6]

When Sidney questioned the usefulness of history, deflating the historian who claimed to be *testis temporum, vita memoriae, nuncia vetustatis*, he was of course repeating for the umpteenth but by no means the last time an old Ciceronian maxim. In 1599, the young John Hayward would introduce his *Life and Raigne of King Henrie IIII* with the familiar words: 'Heereupon Cicero doeth rightly call history the witnesse of times, the light of truth, the life of memory, and the messenger of antiquity ... Neyther is that the least benefit of history, that it preserveth eternally both the glory of good men and shame of evil.'[7] Thomas Blundeville, in his pioneering *The true order and methode of wrytinge and reading histories* (1574), did not know whether to deride or pity the folly of those who, 'having consumed all theyre lyfe tyme in hystories', in the end knew nothing except trivial and useless dates, genealogies, 'and such lyke stuff'.[8]

But so far as Sidney was concerned, the historian could not but be useless, since he was the ineluctable prisoner of his facts, 'tied, not to what should be, but to what is, the particular truth of things and not to the general reason of things'. If it were only a matter of having a story told truly rather than falsely, one would of course choose the truth, as with the commissioning of a portrait. No one prefers a poor likeness. But if the question be one of use or learning, then fictions are 'more doctrinable', for only fiction is free to favour virtue. The historian, 'being captived to the truth of a foolish world, is many times a terror from well-doing, and an encouragement to unbridled wickedness'.[9] Sidney might have been thinking of Sir Thomas More's *History of King Richard III*, and of the doubts about its ethically instructive value that may have inclined More to leave that annal of tyranny and unbridled wickedness incomplete.

Sidney knew full well, if only because Cicero had said it, that the bare distinction between historical fact and poetical fiction misrepresents what historians actually do. Even historiographers, he wrote, 'have been glad to borrow both fashion and perchance weight of poets', especially since, as he suggested in a satirical passage that deliberately confused the distinct functions of antiquarians and historians, authorities and sources are often inadequate and uncertain. So it was that historians put speeches into the mouths of their characters 'which it is certain they never pronounced'. If Sidney had been widely read, more widely than he was, he would have known that the relation of the fictive and non-fictive in the classical discussion of such matters was more complex than his representation of them.[10] Cicero had taught that to tell the truth was indeed the foundation of history, but that the complete structure depended as much on the language of presentation as on material content: 'Ipse autem ex aedificatio posita est in rebus et verbis.' This was said in a treatise whose subject was rhetoric, *De oratore*, where history was classified as none other than a branch of rhetoric. 'Videstine, quantum munus sit oratoris historia?' [Do you not see to what an extent history is the business of the rhetorician?][11]

These commonplaces have a particular resonance with what will concern us in the bulk of this chapter. But the conventions of Sidney's epideictic rhetoric prevented him from noticing how far these considerations, while serving his purpose to disparage history, simultaneously undermined his argument, which depended upon too rigid a distinction between history and fiction. Nevertheless, the two senses of truth with which Sidney dealt are fundamental to my argument. What is factually true, 'the particular truth of things', may be at odds with what is true in another and perhaps higher sense, the sense that the Apostle Paul had in mind when he wrote in Philippians 4.8: 'Whatsoever things are true ... whatsoever things are of good report ... think on these things.'

Thomas Becon, a copious first-generation Protestant writer, defined truth as 'Christ himself, the word of Cod', but added: 'There is also a civil truth or verity ... and that is when with that which is said the thing appeareth, and when we find words agreeing with the thing itself.' Sidney professed to believe that there must be a conflict between these two senses of truth. John Foxe's huge enterprise in its entirety depended upon a denial of any such conflict.[12]

How do we account for Sidney's defensiveness? Was it more than a rhetorical pose? If we understand 'poetry' in its modern sense, it may seem odd that Sidney should write of 'this now scorned skill'. But if he is understood to have written of fiction, then indeed the historian of literary genres, aware of the slow gestation of the English novel through the almost two centuries separating *Beware the Cat* from *Pamela,* may share with Sidney some sense of fiction's arrested development. If Sidney had chosen to consider the problem at the level of customer and readership mentalities, he would have found in his own age ample evidence of the satisfaction derived from stories that were either factual or purported to be factual, over against the unashamedly fictive. This preference may have a deep-seated and perennial quality to it. Ghost stories told in darkened school dormitories lose their point if they are not half believed as true stories; so too with magazines like *True Stories,* the improbable but always 'true' stories I read in my youth in *Wide World Magazine,* and with newspaper columns like 'Strange But True' or 'Ripley's Believe It or Not'. In Britain, the willingly gullible buy a paper (it claims to be a newspaper) with headlines like 'World War II Bomber Found on Moon'. Huge sums are spent on supposedly 'authentic' works of antique art, and sometimes good money is thrown after bad in efforts to prove, or disprove, their authenticity, leading to reflections on 'our obsession with originality and oldness'. The pleasing fiction of a forgery, however cunningly contrived, has a limited value.[13]

One might make a similar point about the resurrection narratives in the New Testament, or about the Book of Mormon, prefaced as it is with the testimonies of witnesses who had seen and 'hefted' with their hands the very gold plates from which Joseph Smith by mysterious means derived the text. There are sophisticated accounts of both Christianity and Mormonism that hold their doctrines and aspirations to be 'true', more or less regardless of the literal truth of the historical events on which they are founded. However, neither Christianity nor Mormonism would be likely to survive the discrediting to universal satisfaction of its historical-factual credentials, for all that Sidney suggests that the New Testament might well be more 'doctrinable' if it were fiction than if it consisted of an accurate, unadorned account of certain historical facts.

The case as it concerns sixteenth-century literary and subliterary tastes and genres can be illustrated at random from the titles of relatively ephemeral products of the Elizabethan and early Stuart press, in which reports, however improbable and unreliable, are presented to the gullible reader as 'true' and fully attested;[14] and, said Ben Jonson (in *The Staple of News*), with 'no syllable of truth in them'. The subject may be wonders and monsters, as with *The true description of two monsterous chyldren born at Herne in Kent*, a ballad of 1565; or remarkable 'providences', such as *A true relation of two most strange accidents lately happening at Chagford* (1618); murders – *A true report of the murther committed in the house of Sir J. Bowes* (1607), *The lamentable and true tragedie of M. Arden of Faversham* (1592); foreign wars – *A brief and true rehearsall of the victory which the protestantes of Holland had against the duke of Alba* (1573); voyages and discoveries – *A true discourse of the late voyage of discoverie: for finding a passage to Cathaya* (1578), *A briefe and true relation of the discoverie of the north Part of Virginia* (1602); even romantic fiction – *The true history of the tragick loves of Hipolito and Isabella, Neapolitans* (1628). Groups of men in the alehouse who greeted new arrivals from London with 'what news?' also validated their own reports with 'if what I say be not true'. This was called for, given the notorious unreliability of 'news'. Joseph Mede of Cambridge, who received and passed on the news on a regular basis, could write of 'the newes of the day among our Speculatives in Pauls' (i.e., the nave or 'walk' of St Paul's Cathedral) and frequently reported that such news as the death of Spinola or the duke of Buckingham's departure for the Ile de Rhé had proved false. But the fear of false rumour implied the high premium placed on accuracy. Preachers who used the 'if what I say be not true' formula in the pulpit were being indecorous and could find themselves reported in jest books, like the 'very ridiculous' minister of Halstead in Essex, William Glibery, who used to say, 'if what I say be not true ye may hang me for the veriest knave in Halstead'. For Scripture was self-authenticating, requiring no such warranties as to its truth. One implication of the utterly authentic scriptural norm was a process of self-censorship that tended to inhibit any publication that, far from being 'true', was unashamedly fictional.[15]

In this broad sense, all histories published in the sixteenth century claimed to be true, even while the distinction between 'history' and 'story' was still blurred, the tales of Arthur being presented as history, even by those who admitted that if not entirely false they contained substantial elements of the mythical.[16] One might suppose that when it was reported, in the early seventeenth century, that men read Foxe's *Book of Martyrs* (as *Acts and Monuments* was popularly called) as 'a book of credit, next to the book of God', that was to accord to Foxe a special, near-scriptural status. But secular chronicles, too, were 'credited' in the same way, Holinshed's *Chronicles* calling itself, and in principle all chronicles, books of 'credit'.[17] Claims to be credited were built into virtually every publication asserting historical status. Thus, George Cavendish, in his *Thomas Wolsey, late Cardinall, his lyffe and deathe*, refers in his preface to the 'malycious ontrowthe of others', and offers to replace untruth with truth.

'Therfore I commyt the treuthe to hym that knowyth all trouthe.' The opening words of the text that follows are: 'Trewthe it ys.' That Cavendish ends his life of Wolsey with the story of how he, the author, lied to the king and the council about the cardinal's last words following the advice of an experienced courtier – 'if ye tell them the treuthe ... you should undo yorself' – is a complicating and enriching circumstance, for it suggests that truth is a thing of onion-like layers.[18]

Was Cavendish telling the truth about his lie? It was unusual to admit to a falsehood. In the first Elizabethan edition of Foxe's *Acts and Monuments* (1563), the Marian martyr John Careless would not admit to his judges that there were any serious doctrinal differences among the heretics confined in the various London prisons. Asked whether he knew the notorious antipredestinarian free-willer Henry Hart, he denied it. 'But yet I lied falsely, for I knew him indeed and his qualities too well.' In all subsequent editions, Careless's frank admission was suppressed, presumably as incompatible with the truth that the martyrs were supposed to have expressed in all their speeches and actions. And that too was a kind of lie.[19] Whether it could ever be lawful to tell a lie in a good cause had been debated by Saints Augustine and Jerome, and the issue was never far away from the religious controversies of the sixteenth century, as Perez Zagorin has shown.[20] Sometimes only a lie could preserve the truth.

How much did truth matter? Daniel Woolf suggests that what was lacking in Tudor and early Stuart historiography was 'a reason for divergent points of view', since 'historical narrative had yet to be firmly tied to the wagon of ideological and political conflict'.[21] That undervalues the passions aroused throughout the sixteenth century by conflicting accounts of national origins, and in particular by the question of the British History. This version of the island's story had been immortalised and to a great extent fabricated in the twelfth century by Geoffrey of Monmouth's *Historia regum Britanniae*, an excellent example, with all its prolific Arthurian progeny and many afterlives, of the difficulty of defining a history as distinct from a romance in anything like modern terms. We cannot even be certain that Geoffrey was not having his joke at the expense of the past, intentionally but covertly writing a kind of fiction. The later Middle Ages and Renaissance would witness many such sportive literary exercises, one of them called *Utopia*. Polydore Vergil said some caustic things about Geoffrey and conjured up the ghost of Gildas to exorcise him. John Leland was duly angry with Polydore, as was the Welsh antiquary Humphrey Llwyd, who also attacked the rival account of Scottish origins purveyed by Hector Boece and later by George Buchanan. But it is true that many of the authors who ventured into this minefield wrote within the polite convention of referring judgment in the matter to the reader and declining to adopt a rigid position in a case so uncertain. Even Camden wrote that he would be the last to stand in the way of anyone who might want to believe in the story of Brutus and his Trojans: 'For mine owne parte, let Brutus be taken for the father, and founder of the British nation. I will not be of a contrarie minde', adding later, 'I refer the matter full and whole to the Senate of Antiquaries, for to be decided.'[22]

In the extensive learned apparatus that he contributed to Michael Drayton's prodigious chorographical and hydrological poem, *Poly-Olbion*, John Selden gently reprehended the credence that the poet still attached to the British History, although he knew full well that part of Drayton's motive was to be as tactful as possible to the Welsh, those 'Cambro-Britons' who certainly had to be allowed to believe such things, whether true or not.[23]

II

Only very occasionally was John Foxe willing in this fashion to defer to the indifferent judgment of his readers. A rare example of his use of this trope concerns the ecclesiastical miracles recorded by the early church historian Eusebius, 'wherof let every reader use his own judgement'.[24] It was fundamental to Foxe's essentially polemical purpose on no account to condescend to historical ignorance or condone false notions about the past. In a preface addressed to the queen, he explained that he wrote in English for the sake of the common reader who was wrapped in blindness, all 'for wanting the light of history'. In another preface he wrote:

> For, first, to see the simple flock of Christ, especially the unlearned sort, so miserably abused, and all for ignorance of history, not knowing the course of times and true descent of the church, it pitied me that this part of diligence had so long been unsupplied in this my-country church of England.[25]

So, relatively speaking, Woolf is not wrong to suggest that the arena of ecclesiastical history represents an exceptional case in sixteenth- and early-seventeenth-century historiography, exceptional that is for involving extreme ideological conflict over competing versions of truth. For in this arena, the question of truth had an urgent life-and-death quality. Indeed, on the distinction between truth and error lay matters beyond life and death and of transcendent importance. So Bishop Latimer spoke of 'peace' as a 'goodly word', and 'unity' as a 'fair thing'. '[But] peace ought not to be redeemed ... with the loss of the truth; that we should seek peace so much, that we should lose the truth of God's word.' The Elizabethan Catholic controversialist Thomas Stapleton was no less willing to pay the price of truth: 'Truth purchaseth hatred.' 'Therefore', Latimer went on,

> whereas ye pray for agreement both in the truth and in uttering of the truth, when shall that he, as long as we will not hear the truth, but disquiet with crafty countenance the preachers of the truth, because they reprove our evilness with the truth.

> And to say the truth, better it were to have a deformity in preaching, so that some would preach the truth of God.[26]

Here were seven 'truth's in seventy words!

Ecclesiastical historiography during this period saw fierce conflicts over truth, not only between parties but within parties and their minds and consciences. Bishop Jewel observed that truth and falsehood were near neighbours: 'The utter porch of the one is like the porch of the other; yet their way is contrary; the one leadeth to life; the other leadeth to death; they differ little to the shew ... Thereby it happeneth that men be deceived; they call evil good, falsehood truth.'[27]

Thomas Harding, the Elizabethan Catholic apologist with whom Jewel had a great controversy, and who attacked Foxe, had begun, like Jewel, as the Protestant disciple of Peter Martyr. Archbishop Cranmer was forever invoking truth. Henry VIII told him, 'For suerlie I reckon that you will tell me the truth.' But in the last hours of his life, Cranmer first recanted the beliefs of his religious maturity as heresies, prefacing his recantation with 'now is time and place to say truth'; he then renounced his recantations, with remorse for having acted 'contrary to my conscience and the truthe'.[28] Foxe wrote to make the distinction between truth and error objective and unmistakable, in the tribunal of history.

The 'plain' or 'simple' truth to which Protestants were attached had a different appearance from the truth professed by Catholic controversialists. It belonged to a set of values that identified purity with simplicity and plainness and rejected what were perceived as Catholicism's elaborate, man-made ritual and theatrical excess. Protestants, as John King has observed, rejected any substitution of artifice for truth.[29] The truth that was simplicity itself was biblical truth, which was held to be literal and self-evident, and which was best articulated in the plain style of Tyndale's biblical mode and Latimer's pulpit voice, as well as in the plain shepherd's tongue that Spenser appropriated from the fourteenth century. Of course the so-called plain style was never artless. *Artis celare artem.* Nicholas Udall wrote of the English version of Erasmus's New Testament *Paraphrases*: 'For divinitie, lyke as it loveth no cloking, but loveth to be simple and playn, so doth it not refuse eloquence, if the same come without injurie or violacion of the truth.' Erasmus's translators had eschewed elegance of speech for 'a plain style', so that 'rude and unlettred people' should nor be deprived of a true understanding.[30]

In Foxe, style and language are inseparable from the populist strategy that aimed the book at the more or less common people who to such a conspicuous extent throng the pages, both as martyrs and spectators of martyrdom. Hence all those extremely vivid illustrations, no fewer than 160 of them in the 1570 edition. Yet there is a tension between this almost 'tabloid' presentation and the extreme bulk, and expense, of the text illustrated, for how many of the 'rude and unlettred' had access to a book costing half a year's wages? The word 'strategy', then, is used advisedly, and to indicate another of Foxe's rhetorical tropes. Whether the English Reformation really enjoyed the popular basis that the trope regularly invokes is a question that has divided recent historians of those events, the so-called revisionists and their allegedly Whiggish opponents. If the revisionists are right in their denial that the Reformation was a demotic affair, then the blame may be laid on Foxe, who, the revisionists say, their opponents follow all too faithfully.[31]

Foxe did not claim inerrancy for his book in every detail (many modern historians have been less modest about their accomplishments), but he did regard the version of ecclesiastical history that it presented as in all essential respects true. His purpose was 'to open the plain truth of times lying long hid in obscure darkness of antiquity'. Foxe's own question, however – 'But what is in this world so ... true that it will not be contraried?' – anticipated his critics. For Foxe's Catholic detractors, his book was not some curate's egg, good and bad in parts. It was all bad, consisting entirely of lies, 'as full of lies as lines'. The Jesuit Robert Parsons claimed to have discovered more than 120 lies in less than three pages. 'As though', Foxe told the queen, 'neither any word in all that story were true, nor any other story false in all the world besides.' Five years earlier, Thomas Stapleton, professing 'zeale to the truth', had assured Elizabeth that the faith of the English Church for nine hundred years had been 'the true and right Christianitie'.[32]

Foxe's claim to embody *testis temporum, lux veritatis* was rooted in his method, a plain but advanced historical method that placed a premium on the testimony of original sources and that pointed forward to the essentially Protestant professionalism of nineteenth-century historical positivists. To quote the title of the 1563 edition in some of its fullness: These were *Acts and monuments ... gathered and collected according to the true copies and wrytinges certificatorie, as wel of the parties themselves that suffered, as also out of the Bishops Registers which were the doers therof.* It has been said that not least among Foxe's merits was that he discovered the Public Record Office.[33] The effect is best described as deceptively authentic, since while some of the sources had the ineluctable objectivity of official court records, others were highly subjective first-person accounts of trials recorded by the martyrs themselves, together with their letters and other remains, carefully edited.

Nevertheless, nobody any longer accuses Foxe of gross manipulation, still less of the fraudulent forging of his evidence of which he stood accused by his nineteenth-century critics. There is no need to spend time defending his basically sound practice as a transcriber and editor of documents. Historians can say that he was one of us. That is not to say that Foxe felt bound to publish all the evidence available to him, nor to deny that he often disregarded history's second law, according to Cicero, to make bold to tell the whole truth. We have already seen that embarrassing evidence – for example John Careless's holy lying – could be suppressed between one edition and the next. Faced with further scandalous details of theological dissension and of prevarication in the letters of the martyr John Philpot, which included a letter to Careless about the free-willers, Foxe and his editorial assistant Henry Bull discussed what to include, what to suppress. Stripped of the merely mundane, the letters of the martyrs appeared all the more sublime in their single-minded scriptural exultation.[34]

Yet Foxe's appetite for historical information 'for its own sake' sometimes took over. Among his papers in the Harleian manuscripts, there are nearly one hundred closely written folios, detailing the scandals, corruptions, and law suits that in the reign of Edward VI tore the Welsh diocese of St David's apart and damaged the reputation of its first Protestant bishop, Robert Ferrar.[35] Ferrar suffered martyrdom under Mary, and his ordeal was hailed (from the safety of exile) by a fellow bishop: 'O most happy Ferrar, more strong than yron!'[36] A correspondent later begged Foxe not to meddle with the St David's case in the 'augmentyng' of his history. 'The controversye was for prophane matters and therfore unmeet for your hystorye. We must be cyrcumspect in owr doyngs that we geev the papysts no occasyon to accuse us for persecutors whych we lay so much to their charge.'[37] Foxe ignored this advice and printed all fifty-six articles indicting Ferrar of worldly-mindedness and gross pastoral neglect. For example, his enemies alleged that the bishop had spent all his time and labour in discovering mines, and that all his conversation had been about such worldly matters as 'baking, brewing, enclosing, ploughing, mining, of mill-stones'.[38]

Foxe's excuse for printing this unsavory stuff was that it would give other bishops warning 'to be more circumspect, whom they should trust and have about them'. He may very well have had in mind the early Elizabethan bishop of Norwich, John Parkhurst, whose lack of worldly wisdom opened up his diocese to sharks and con men.[39] Foxe called Ferrar 'twice a martyr' and printed his replies to the articles of accusation, defending his reputation and, as he moved on to the scene at the stake, freely calling him 'godly Bishop Ferrar'. Ferrar told a sympathiser that 'if he saw him once to stir in the pains of his burning, he should then give no credit to his doctrine'. Foxe added: 'And as he said, so he right well performed the same.'[40] But it is perhaps significant that Foxe placed in immediate juxtaposition to Ferrar's story a much fuller account of the only other Welsh martyr he records, the obscure and elderly Cardiff fisherman Rawlins White, who, as it happens, was burned in the same month as the bishop.[41] The circumstantial details include White's urging the smith to make sure that he was chained fast to the stake, 'for it may be that the flesh would strive mightily' (almost the same words attributed to Bishop Ridley in the same circumstances);[42] his arranging the straw around him to make a little shelf on which to lean to give 'good ear and attention' to the sermon preached over him; and his appearing 'altogether angelical' – a Polycarpian touch – with the white hairs sticking out from under his kerchief.[43] As with Holinshed's *Chronicles*, Foxe's material was not necessarily so haphazardly arranged as it may appear.

There is some rather more damaging evidence to which I among others have drawn attention, that in his efforts to approximate all heretics whatsoever to a model of 'godly' and acceptable Protestant orthodoxy, Foxe deliberately suppressed or glossed over opinions that were beyond the pale as much in Protestant as in Catholic perception. Faced with confessions of gross errors in the doctrine of the Trinity by some of his Kentish martyrs, Foxe merely commented: 'To these articles what their answers were likewise needeth here no great rehearsal'. Some of this material survives in Foxe's papers, not in the form of transcripts but in the very pages roughly torn from the original trial register of Archdeacon Nicholas Harpsfield, effectively removing them from the public domain. Since the foliation is not continuous, it is just possible that other pages, more incriminating still, were actually destroyed, a capital offence for any historian to have committed.[44] We look forward to the shedding of further light on such matters in David Loades's forthcoming critical edition of Foxe, more than a century and a half after that great Victorian editor, J. G. Nichols, first called for one.[45]

III

With the literary studies made by Helen White and William Haller in the 1960s, and more recently by Warren Wooden and John Knott, interest has shifted from the scrutiny of Foxe's accuracy and reliability as a historian, on the narrow terms of the English empirical tradition, to appreciation of the rhetorical and literary accomplishments of *Acts and Monuments*, or to what Wooden calls Foxe's artistry.[46] The year 1963 was a landmark, for it witnessed the publication both of Helen White's *Tudor Books of Saints and Martyrs* and Haller's famous study, *Foxe's Book of Martyrs and the Elect Nation* (published in the United States as *The Elect Nation*).[47]

For Haller, the question was not whether Foxe told the truth as we would have it told, but what he took the truth to be and induced so many of his countrymen at such a critical moment to accept as such: 'Whether the facts and the meaning of the facts were in every respect what he made them out to be, we need not inquire.'[48] Following Haller, and the important corrections in his reading of the text and understanding of its reception by Katherine Firth, Richard Bauckham, and V. Norskov Olsen, much attention has been concentrated on the apocalyptical and chronological framework of *Acts and Monuments*, together with cognate questions of ethnocentricity. Was it either

Foxe's intention or the inadvertent effect of the book to create in what Foxe called 'this my-country church of England' a Miltonic sense of manifest and unique destiny, of England as not only *an* elect nation but *the* elect nation of God?[49] That grand subject lies beyond the scope of this modest essay, with its more limited concern with truth, lies and fiction.

By now we should be thoroughly sensitised to Foxe's literary strategy of validating the Protestant Church and its 'true' faith in the patient yet triumphant witness of the martyrs. We now know that: these martyrs of the Reformation were represented as not only successors but replications of the early Christian martyrs; that Latimer's ever memorable words to Ridley at the stake, 'be of good comfort ... and play the man', were an echo of the heavenly words uttered to St Polycarp as he entered the arena; that the martyred Bishop Hooper was modelled on that same Polycarp in many respects. That spirited, not to say alienated, gentlewoman Anne Askew, victim of a late Henrician episode of persecution, was presented (by John Bale in the first instance) as a kind of protomartyr of this latest age, the counterpart of Blandina, the second-century slave girl martyred in Lyon: a remarkable case not only of Reformation fashioning but of self-fashioning, since Askew herself prepared most of the materials out of which her legend was composed.[50] Foxe himself was, as it were, a reincarnation of the martyrologist and inventor of ecclesiastical history, Eusebius of Caesarea.

The Eusebian quality of Foxe is particularly evident in the preface called 'The Utility of This Story', where the martyrologist contrasts the themes of secular historiography, 'the roar of foughten fields, the sacking of cities, the hurlyburlies of realms and people', with 'the lives, acts, and doings, not of bloody warriors, but of mild and constant martyrs of Christ'. These martyrs, Foxe wrote, 'declare to the world what true Christian fortitude is, and what is the right way to conquer', adding, 'With this valiantness did that most mild Lamb, and invincible Lion of the tribe of Judah first of all go before us'.[51] Eusebius must have been well known to Foxe before the publication of his first English edition in 1563. But in 1579 he was introduced to a wider audience in Meredith Hanmer's translation. Hanmer was an obscure and by no means respectable individual who can have been little more than a functionary in an enterprise guided by Foxe. The printer was the Huguenot Vautrollier, with whom Foxe and a small team of translators were working in the late 1570s to produce a little library of works by Martin Luther in English.[52] Headed by Luther's lectures on Galatians, these books presented Luther at his most 'comfortable', and were perhaps intended as a prophylactic against the pastoral damage thought to be caused by Calvinism, of which Foxe, as a spiritual physician, had first-hand experience.[53] These were the only translations of Luther available to the English-speaking Protestant world for three hundred years to come.

There is no need to restate at any length the many valuable contributions made to our appreciation of Foxe's text by his modern literary critics, though it is worth mentioning John Knott's convincing argument that what distinguishes the Foxeian narrative from those of the early church martyrologists is the combative, contentious behaviour of the Protestant martyrs as they confront their accusers and judges, contrasted with the more passive disposition of the primitive martyrs. Knott's explanation is contextual and circumstantial. Eusebius wrote in the secure enjoyment of the peace of the church, recording martyr victories that had achieved their earthly as well as heavenly vindication. Although there were parallels between the Constantinian peace and the Elizabethan settlement, which Foxe made something of, if only for courtesy's sake, the struggle between Protestantism and Catholicism, which Bale and Foxe constructed apocalyptically and cosmically as the war of the two churches, Christ and Antichrist, was still being fiercely fought, even as Foxe wrote. Even the English persecution was very recent, and some of the persecutors were still alive. So Askew was frankly presented as a resourceful debater and even a scold, not at all like Blandina, except that Blandina as depicted by Bale and Foxe was not a little like Askew.[54] Knott has shown how Foxe edited the account that the protomartyr John Rogers wrote of his own trial to heighten its polemical effect. If Rogers himself recorded not only what he said but what he would have liked to say, Foxe converted his words into what Foxe would have liked him to say, writing some of his lines for him.[55] Although these resourceful, aggressive courtroom performances were succeeded by the constrained passivity of the executions, Foxe's critics were given grounds on which to complain that his so-called martyrs were not in the least martyrlike in their behavior. Where was that humility that adorned the true martyr?

In what is left of this chapter, I shall first pick a couple of bones with literary scholarship and then consider some of the wider implications of what may be called the textualisation of Foxe. We have hardly begun to come to terms with the great generic diversity of this huge, sprawling text, in Wooden's phrase 'a medley of literary forms', embracing comedic and romantic as well as annalistic elements, not to mention the Protestant recension of the medieval literary tradition of the *ars moriendi*, which is such a large part of its rationale, together with copious controversial polemic. Much work remains to be done. In Wooden's words, 'modern critics have taken only the first harvest'.[56]

Both of my bones concern miracles, matters of truth and fiction. An argument of Helen White, reinforced by John Knott, runs like this: When Foxe disavowed, as he did, the name of martyrologist, he was distancing himself from the hagiographical tradition enshrined in *The Golden Legend*, which had been published in English as recently as 1527. When he called himself a mere storyteller, he meant that he did not deal in legends. Helen White remarks that Foxe's book 'is full of the contempt of the sixteenth-century Reformers for the miracle and the miracle-monger'. The miracles of Thomas Becket were 'lying miracles', 'monkish miracles and gross fables'. Knott suggests that Foxe 'minimizes the intrusion of the supernatural', making his martyrs not saints but 'models of Christian heroism', manifesting the invincibility of true faith. They were 'more closely connected to a sustaining human community, and more fully human' than the martyrs and saints of Catholicism.[57]

This is helpful, but it undervalues the marvelous tokens and signs that Foxe occasionally reported, as it were in spite of himself, and that may well have held a more prominent place in popular Protestant memory and imagination than Foxe himself allowed. White acknowledges this: 'Old habits die hard.' Wooden emphasises that the final 'tokens' of the truth and efficacy of the martyrs' faith, which abound in his set-piece scenes, were 'a palpable substitute' for the fantastic and discredited miracles of *The Golden Legend*.[58] When Thomas Stapleton translated and published *Bede's History of the Churche of Englande* (1565), he defended the miraculous in the pages of Bede and asked why, if 'straunge and uneredible miracles and visions' were inadmissible, there was so much material of this kind in Foxe. 'Ar there not also in that donghell heaped a number of miserable miracles to sette forth the glory of their stinking martyrs?' 'Iff the Crosse of saint Oswalde seme a superstitious tale, how much more fonde and fabulous is the tale of one that suffred at Bramford, with a greate white crosse, appearing in his brest?'[59]

But there are miracles, and miracles. In his *Fortresse of the Faith* (1565), Stapleton conceded that 'as for the miracles of Fox in his Actes and monuments, his owne felowes esteme them but as civill thinges, and such as may happen by course of reason. And in dede they are no other, such of them as are true'.[60] White and Knott rightly insist that the ability to withstand an excruciatingly painful and prolonged death was the real miracle, repeatedly witnessed in Foxe's pages. Were these 'civil' things, subject to rational explanation and medical and psychological description, miracles only in the debased and commonplace sense in which we use the word today? Was the courage of the martyrs no more than a simple function of their humanity, albeit a redeemed and elevated humanity, of which any Christian was in principle capable?

We must be careful not to impose our modern way of seeing things on a writer of Foxe's generation. To represent the heroic endurance of his martyrs as a merely human achievement, with 'no sense of being transformed by the presence of Christ', secularises and modernises to excess. Although the miraculous in the perception of Protestants is no simple matter, it may be cautiously defined as occurrences within and not outside the course of nature (no talking heads or bleeding statues), but according to a causation not, on our terms, natural, 'nature' being not the efficient, or sufficient, cause. When Foxe wrote of the preservation of the Princess Elizabeth during her sister's reign as 'a singular miracle of God', he meant just that. In the 1570 edition, the providential presentation of this story was accentuated by suitable marginal notes and running headlines, perhaps with the intention of admonishing both queen and reader. It was not Elizabeth's strength of character that had preserved her but God.[61] Foxe's classical humanism may have disposed him to represent the deaths of his heroes as, at one level, human achievements. But they were achievements inconceivable without the power of a transcendent yet intrusive God, all of whose workings were marvelous.

To say so much and no more is to sell Foxe and his Protestant readers and their age short. After the account of Elizabeth's travails, Foxe entered what Annabel Patterson might want to call his anecdotage, as *Acts and Monuments* peters out in a catalogue of such particular providences as the loathsome, shameful deaths of the persecutors, in the manner of the *De mortibus persecutorum* of Lactantius, paired with the equally remarkable escapes and preservations of many of the godly. It would be hard indeed to exaggerate how all-pervasive is this kind of providentialism in the early modern mentality, not only before the Reformation but after it. To the modern mind, this may appear the ultimate and most comprehensive of superstitions.

Foxe's appendix of cautionary tales was not the end of a lingering and outmoded tradition, but rather the harbinger of a new wave of morally correct credulity, which for more than a century to come would be fostered by sensational broadsheets and pamphlets, and by such substantial and ambitious albums as Thomas Beard's *Theatre of Gods Judgements* (editions in 1597, 1612, 1631) and Samuel Clarke's *Mirrour or looking-glasse both for saints, and sinners, held forth in some thousands of examples* (1657). This material was so traditional in form, content, and moral values that it would not be appropriate to call it a literary genre peculiar or even proper to Protestantism. But it was manifestly compatible with a Protestant worldview, or theodicy. In Beard's stories (some of them centuries old), the earth opens up to swallow its blaspheming victims, Sabbath-breaking hunters father children with dogs' heads, and punishments fit the crime in bizarre ways that manipulate where they do not defy nature. Such tall stories claimed, of course, to be 'true', but in what sense or degree is a nice question.[62] Foxe is by comparison so restrained that the White–Knott argument threatens to re-enter through the back door.

We return from the providential fantasies of God's violent theme park to Foxe's generally more believable stories. Did these things happen very much as Foxe describes them? This is my second bone to pick. Referring less to such improbable tales as the bull of Chipping Sodbury, which was the instrument of divine providence in goring to death a bishop's chancellor, and more to the edifying and apparently authentic scenes of the martyrdom of Rogers, Hooper, Ridley, Latimer, and quaint old Rawlins White: Were these narratives true? A no-nonsense historical positivist like Sir Geoffrey Elton had no doubt that they were. Foxe did not have to invent the persecutions.[63] (But something depends upon what one means by 'invent.') Curiously enough, modern literary scholarship, with which Elton tended to have no truck, seems to agree, perhaps because even so-called new historicists are ultimately indifferent to what actually happened in history. So Knott only once touches on the reliability of Foxe's narratives in this crucial respect. Commenting on the 'apparent serenity' of John Rogers as he broke the ice, washing his hands in the flames 'as one feeling no smart', Knott remarks: 'At least, this is Foxe's interpretation of the scene, one likely to have been shared by the committed Protestants in the crowd.'[64]

But are we really to believe in such scenes as Foxe describes? It stretches our credulity and sensibility that such agonies could have been so stoically borne. The master of 'sheer horror'[65] spares us none of the gory details: Ridley leaping about in a badly laid fire, shouting 'I cannot burn'; Hooper reviving a poor fire with the fat dropping out of his fingers' ends; the young Dartford linen draper Christopher Wade holding out his extended arms as a sign, until he was 'altogether roasted'.[66] If it really was so, then we may have to invoke something like Seymour Byman's rather shaky historical psychology – fitness training, as it were – in the disciplines of sustained asceticism (another paradox, for these were essentially Catholic disciplines).[67]

On the whole, it may be safe to accept Foxe's word for it that these deaths were martyr-like. It is significant that when the Dutch Anabaptists were burned in Smithfield by the Elizabethan government (in spite of Foxe's pleas and protests), their deaths were observed to be not martyr-like. They died 'in great horror with roaring and crieng'.[68] (But the recorded observations are hostile, and we do not know how an Anabaptist source might have represented these deaths.) Many in the crowds who attended the Marian burnings came expressly to observe the manner of the victims' deaths. For example, the seven thousand present at Bishop Hooper's execution, perhaps 15 per cent of the population of Gloucestershire (it was market day, and the boughs of a great elm tree were 'replenished with people'), were there 'to see his behaviour towards death'.[69] The Catholic controversialist Miles Huggarde,[70] as vivid a writer as Foxe himself, quoted against the incinerated Latimer's own words from an Edwardian sermon in which he had dismissed the suggestion that certain Anabaptists were true martyrs because they had gone to their deaths 'intrepid'. Intrepid let them go. Augustine had taught: 'Martyrum non facit poena, sed causa.' Just so, said Huggarde. He scorned the 'brainsick' fools who scrambled for bones and ashes to use as relics and miracle cures. (Were these the same people as Foxe's godly and restrained spectators?) But he never once suggested that the martyrs themselves were not 'intrepid', which surely he would have done if the testimony of thousands of still living observers had allowed him to.[71] Only a tincture of doubt persists. In the early Elizabethan interlude *New Custom*, the vice character Cruelty exults with nostalgic glee as he remembers the burnings over which he had presided. In the fire, the victims had made a noise like a pack of hounds.[72] So we lily-livered moderns would be inclined to expect. Foxe supplies details of only a fraction of around three hundred burnings. Were some of the others deficient in martyr-like edification?

To conclude, in spite of that elusive fragment, that Foxe told it the way it was, is emphatically not to deny that the power of his narrative depended upon the manner in which he told it, upon style and artistry. On the contrary, in spite of Wooden's and Knott's valuable studies, we have only begun to explore the riches of the fictive constituents of *Acts and Monuments*. I can do little more than sketch out some of the lines of enquiry that merit more extensive investigation, such as recent studies, the new critical edition, and even these modest suggestions, may stimulate.

The point from which all such investigations must embark is the consideration that Sidney's distinction between the factual and the fictional, however useful for his rhetorical-polemical purpose, is unhelpful and even false, as Sidney himself admitted when he noted that historians had been glad to borrow both fashion and weight of poets. Judith Anderson, in her study of the representations of historical persons in Tudor literature, *Biographical Truth*, is struck by the convergence rather than the divorce of fiction and history in the texts she treats, fiction being defined not as pure non-factual invention but as 'the deliberate and creative shaping of fact'. Anderson quotes Hayden White's *Tropics of Discourse*: 'Novelists might be dealing only with imaginary events whereas historians are dealing with real ones, but the process of fusing events, whether imaginary or real, into the comprehensible totality ... is a poetic process.' 'In every historical account of the world', White continues, it matters little 'whether the world is conceived to be real or only imagined; the manner of making sense of it is the same.'[73] Wooden comments on Foxe's consciously artistic preference for the descriptive over the hortatory mode, which crowds his narratives with closely observed circumstantial detail. That such minute particulars were caught, that they actually existed, is trivial in comparison with the use to which they were put. Even where they held no emblematic significance (and often they did) circumstantial details lent the appearance of verisimilitude.[74]

Some historians may by now be cross with me for making such large concessions to the textuality of both historical sources and historical compositions, as they would be downright angry with Roland Barthes for describing historical narratives as 'verbal fictions whose fictionality has been forgotten'.[75] Having elsewhere attacked Natalie Davis's *Fiction in the Archives* (with some willful misunderstanding of her intentions), John Bossy writes in the preface to his enthralling *Giordano Bruno and the Embassy Affair* that it reads like a novel, but with this difference: that the events happened. He is a historian and historians tell true stories about the past.[76] For historians it must matter very much whether Foxe, who is our principal and often only source for much of what we know about the English Reformation, wrote true stories or not. If documents, many of them, have a certain textuality, historians need to know they can put their trust in texts as documents.

That being the case, Foxeian studies ought to address a formal question. Do all Foxe's stories enjoy, or even lay claim to, an equal status? Are they all meant to attract the same amount of credence? I would suggest not. In the main body of the text, consisting of great slabs of cumulative, chronological narra-tive, rolled along on their supporting documentation, Foxe expects and for the most part deserves to be believed. He is not inventing his material in the sense of making it up. But the tail end of the book consists of a kind of delta of wan-dering, inconsequential, anecdotal streams. These stories of divine judgment and mercy may be largely fictional and may have been so understood by both Foxe and his readers. The story of the bishop's chancellor and the bull was too good a story to omit for the trivial reason that in reality the chancellor lived on for many more years.[77] Other anecdotes, like the dreadful fate recorded of the twelve-year-old girl, a foolish maiden, who said that God was 'an old doting fool', were told as warning examples and exactly resemble the fabulous contents of Beard's *Theatre*, or the repertory of tales from medieval pulpits and *florilegia* that Beard appropriated.[78] It is not clear that John Myrc's con-gregations or Thomas Beard's readers believed or were expected to believe all these stories, or that they needed to in order to benefit from them. Wooden's comment that Foxe was 'surely unwise' to accept some of the more dubious of his tall stories may underestimate his literary sophistication. Foxe could make use of a story of 'incredible strangeness', but only in what he calls 'some out-corner of the book', not in 'the body of these Acts and Monuments'.[79]

In Foxe's extended, fifteen-thousand word narrative of the miraculous preservation of Queen Elizabeth in her sister's reign,[80] it is certain that some episodes were invented, or willfully falsified. For example, Foxe must have known that when Elizabeth was arrested at her house at Ashridge and taken to London and eventually to the Tower, she was first allowed to recuperate from an illness, and was not summarily removed 'alive or dead', as his account sug-gests. This freestanding piece is evidently not history in the same sense that the main body of the *Book of Martyrs* is history. What should we call it? I do not suppose that I shall be allowed to call it an early version of the novel.

Foxe's account of Princess Elizabeth's ordeal was the source for Thomas Heywood's *If You Know Not Me You Know Nobody* and for other plays. And Shakespeare depended upon Foxe for a whole scene of his *Henry VIII*. So another fruitful line of enquiry will concern the question of theatricality, a question extending well beyond the use of theatrical metaphors, which are as common in *Acts and Monuments* as in Sir Thomas More.[81] Foxe was himself a dramatist, author of an academic comedy, *Titus et Gesippus*, an ambitious apocalyptic drama, *Christus Triumphans*, and of other Latin plays no longer extant. Like his friend and mentor, John Bale, he believed in attacking popery with the full repertoire of the three Ps, which comprised not only preachers and printers, but players.[82]

The trials and executions of heretics were carefully stage-managed affairs, a literally dramatic and richly ritualised demonstration of orthodoxy, which martyrs and martyrologists appropriated and inverted for their own equally dramatic and didactic purpose.[83] And if Foxe's conscious theatricality reflected the inherent theatricality of his material, the production of the text enhanced its dramatic status. Investigations of *The Book of Martyrs* as theater should not neglect those bibliographical insights that Don Mackenzie has characterised as 'the sociology of texts',[84] including the typographical layout of the page, and what may be inferred from the typography about the ways in which the text may have been read. We know that *The Book of Martyrs* was read 'thoroughly', which is to say, systematically, and that it was presumably read aloud, especially in godly Protestant houses. But that by no means exhausts the questions that may be asked about the manner of the reading. The nineteenth-century edition is useless when addressing this question. G. Townsend and S. R. Cattley do not tell us, for example, that in the 1570 edition, the speeches given to Queen Mary and Princess Elizabeth in the encounter marking the climax of Foxe's account of Elizabeth's preservation are for the first time broken up into short paragraphs, one for each interlocutor, so presenting the visual representation of a play text.[85]

The two-way traffic between Foxe's enormous tome and some of the more popular and ephemeral literature of the day, a somewhat incongruous relationship of elephant and gnat, deserves more attention than it has yet received. On the one hand, *Acts and Monuments* incorporates the texts of broadside ballads, such as 'The Fantasie of Idolatry', a song of fifty stanzas on the folly of going on pilgrimage (preserved by Foxe from oblivion), and the very popular 'The Exhortacion of Robert Smith unto his Children', a Marian prison ballad known by its composer as 'Rogers Will'.[86] On the other, it includes a number of essentially Protestant and improving ballads derived from Foxe or from similar texts, such as Bale's account of Anne Askew or Coverdale's *Letters of the Martyrs*. These included *The godly and virtuous song and ballad of John Careless*, sung to the tune of 'Greensleeves', but also to a melody of its own called 'The tune of John Carelesse', evidently popular since in its turn it was appropriated for other purposes. In a little book published in 1577, 'Rogers Will' was accompanied by ballads attributed to other Marian martyrs, including Bradford and Hooper, making what has been called by Tessa Watt 'a miniature book of martyrs', one both affordable and portable. 'The most rare and excellent history of the Dutchesse of Suffolks calamity', adapted from Foxe by

Thomas Delony and set to the tune of 'Queen Dido' (1602), was still in print in 1754.[87] The evidence of this material ought to be prescribed study for those historians who believe that Protestantism and popular culture were incompatible in 1754.

To appreciate Foxe as a living text that recorded performances and invited performance, and that fed on a popular Protestant culture and nourished it in return, is to point to yet another helpful approach, and one suggested both by Knott and by Richard Helgerson in his *Forms of Nationhood*.[88] *Acts and Monuments* was both the product and the possession of a godly community, one of those 'imagined communities' which, according to Benedict Anderson, include modern nations.[89] The 'invisible church' of Foxe and other apocalyptic writers is just such an imagined community. Its members are readers who imagine themselves in invisible fellowship with thousands of other readers and, one may add, with generations of Christians no longer living. Foxe was, as it were, but the amanuensis of this godly community, which both constructed his book and was constructed by it. More materially, Foxe was, at least initially, but one member of a Protestant network actively committed to recovering and recording the history of the Marian persecution and the monuments of its martyrs, a collective that included Edmund Grindal, Miles Coverdale, Latimer's servant Augustine Bernher, and the neglected Henry Bull, Foxe's Magdalen contemporary, whose contribution to the preservation and editing of the all-important 'Letters of the Martyrs' preserved, since the sixteenth century, in Emmanuel College, Cambridge, was very considerable.[90] And we should include in the joint authorship of *The Book of Martyrs* not only its star performers, the highly self-conscious writers of all those letters and examination transcripts – Rogers, Bradford, Careless, and Philpot – but the cast of thousands, that 'godly multitude' in Smithfield and elsewhere that made the imagined myth of the godly community credible.

Foxe's pages are peopled by, on the one hand, large, undifferentiated, uniformly godly crowds, and on the other by remarkable and exemplary individuals, good and bad, called by Wooden 'tent-post figures', and the subject of extended biographical treatment.[91] These elements are made to interact almost cinematically at the scenes of martyrdom. Thus Foxe sets the stage for the last of the Smithfield burnings: 'It was appointed before of the godly there standing together, which was a great multitude, that so soon as the prisoners should be brought, they should go to embrace them and to comfort them; and so they did', with 'the godly multitude and congregation' making 'a general sway toward the prisoners, meeting and embracing, and kissing them'.[92] As for the 'tent-posts', in spite of Judith Anderson's reservations about the formulaic and repetitive limitations of Foxe as biographer, it is precisely the conventions controlling his fashioning of the lives, personalities, and conduct *in extremis* of his martyrs that deserve scrutiny. Whether or not they really cracked jokes on their way to the fire, or fetched great leaps, or clapped their hands in the flames for sheer joy, it was necessary to include such details as manifestations of that *apatheia* which, in the Aristotelian ethical scheme, is true courage, a mean between cowardice and rash self-destruction.[93]

Plutarch depended upon Aristotle, and Foxe was the Plutarch of the sixteenth century. Why has no one commented on the Plutarchan device of the double biography as deployed by Foxe in the most celebrated of all his scenes, the martyrdom of the two bishops, Ridley and Latimer? The point of the device is to employ contrast to illuminate the admirable qualities of two dissimilar individuals (or, in other circumstances and for other purposes, to prefer one to the other). Erasmus used it in his double portrait of John Colet and Jacques Vitrier.[94] So we are shown Ridley, in his handsome fur-trimmed gown and tippet, 'such as he was wont to wear being bishop', a man still physically and intellectually fit, his pockets full of valuable trifles to give away as keepsakes, his watch, his napkin, some nutmegs. And then we catch sight of Latimer, struggling along behind in his poor frieze coat all worn and his comical headgear, 'which at first sight stirred men's hearts to rue upon them, beholding on the one side, the honour they sometimes had, and on the other, the calamity whereunto they were fallen'. And yet Latimer, who while still clothed appeared 'a withered and crooked silly old man', stripped to his shroud 'stood bolt upright, as comely a father as one might lightly behold'.[95] We do not necessarily have to doubt the nutmegs or any other of these circumstantial details. Foxe's informant was probably Latimer's faithful servant Augustine Bernher,[96] who was certainly present and who lived on into the reign of Elizabeth to assist both Foxe and Coverdale with their martyrological labours.

It remains relevant that Foxe, in his carefully balanced presentation of this material, proves himself to be every bit as much a humanist, a product of the Renaissance, as he was a Protestant and a creator of the English Protestant tradition. More attention could well be paid to his Stoicism, which, more than any distinctly Christian ethic, may have sustained that unusual aversion to violence, which, Foxe wrote, made it hard for him to pass by the very slaughter yards without a sense of revulsion and pity for the poor beasts.[97] It may even have been Stoicism that made Foxe a martyrologist.

It mattered that Latimer should be presented as upright and comely, a wholesome old man. In one of his providential anecdotes, Foxe told of a man in a pub in Abingdon who boasted that he had seen 'that ill favoured knave Latimer when he was burnt', and that he had teeth like a horse. In that very hour, the man's son hanged himself, not far away.[98] Disgusting and shameful deaths, gross physical deformities, were reserved for the persecutors, and mainly for the clergy. (The lay officers in Foxe's perception were often only doing their job.) I do not think that we need to believe that Bishop Stephen Gardiner had toenails like claws, any more than that King Richard III was grossly deformed from birth.

All this fashioning, which was indeed a self-fashioning by and of the Protestant community through Foxe, was achieved by means of language. How the English Protestant community contrived within a very few years to invent its own demotic, a language of heightened emotion, warmth, fervent exhortation, and, above all, biblical resonance, is a question not only still to be answered but almost never put, except in a German work of the 1920s, Levin Schücking's *The Puritan Family*.[99] It is Foxe's rhetorical style that above all deserves the serious evaluative study it has never received, and that an earlier generation, C.S. Lewis to particularise, disparaged. In a chapter of his *English Literature in the Sixteenth Century* called 'Drab and transitional prose', Lewis said of Foxe: 'His English style has no high merits. The sentences have not the energy to support their great length.' Foxe was 'an honest man' (as Cicero had written, 'it is enough that the man should not be a liar'), but not 'a great historian'.[100] Warren Wooden helpfully adjudicates. Examples of the lumbering, tottering sentences Lewis describes are not hard to find in a work whose style is plastic rather than uniform. But neither is it difficult to discover sentences that are 'spare, compact, and distinguished by highly functional syntax', the work of 'an impressive prose craftsman'.[101]

Finally, we return to the matter of truth. Insofar as Foxe is to be charged with falsifying on a large and general scale, then it was his language that did the falsifying, and altogether insidiously. Language turned into sweet societies of faithful favourers – into innocent lambs of Christ, decorous and dignified, loving and meek – men and women who in reality were creatures of passion as well as of flesh and blood, whose street language, when Foxe happened to catch the *ipsissima verba*, was robust and abrasive.[102] And yet what a fictive triumph it amounts to! Lewis's judgment can no longer be sustained. We cannot better the verdict of Helen White: 'Foxe proves himself a storyteller of quite remarkable power, one of the greatest of a great age.'[103]

NOTES

1 Leslie P. Fairfield, *John Bale, Mythmaker for the English Reformation* (West Lafayette, Ind., 1976), especially p. 119; Glanmor Williams, *Reformation Views of Church History* (London, 1970), p. 62.

2 *The Acts and Monuments of John Foxe*, ed. G. Townsend and S. R. Cattley (London, vol. 1, 1841; vols 2–4, 1837; vols 5–7, 1838; vol. 8, 1839), vol. 4, p. 295.

3 Sir Philip Sidney, *An Apology for Poetry or the Defence of Poesy*, ed. G. Shepherd (London, 1965), pp. 105–12. For an excellent discussion of the issues traversed by Sidney, but more subtly by a number of other sixteenth-century authors, see William Nelson, *Fact or Fiction, the Dilemma of the Renaissance Storyteller* (Cambridge, Mass., 1973), pp. 49–55.

4 Cicero, *De oratore*, 2.13.62.

5 William Camden, *The History of the Most Renowned and Virtuous Princess Elizabeth Late Queen of England*, ed. and abr. Wallace T. MacCaffrey (Chicago, Ill., 1970), pp. 4–5.

6 Sidney, *Apology*, pp. 97, 105.

7 *The First and Second Parts of John Hayward's* The Life and Raigne of King Henrie IIII, ed. John J. Manning, Camden 4th ser., 42 (London, 1991), p. 63.

8 Cited in D. R. Woolf, *The Idea of History in Early Stuart England: Erudition, ideology and 'the light of truth' from the accession of James I to the Civil War* (Toronto, 1990), pp. 4–5.

9 Sidney, *Apology*, pp. 107, 109–11.

10 Sidney, *Apology*, p. 97. William Nelson comments on 'two conflicting attitudes: on the one hand, the insistence of the Judaeo-Christian tradition on veritable reports, testified to as by witnesses in a courtroom; on the other, a sense that in tales of the past truth mattered little in comparison with edification or even entertainment.' *Fact or Fiction*, p. 27.

11 Cicero *De oratore*, 2.14.62.

12 The passage from Becon refers to *Prayers and Other Pieces of Thomas Becon*, ed. J. Ayre, Parker Society (Cambridge: Cambridge University Press, 1844), p. 604. Michael McKeon draws attention to a passage in Foxe in which 'the two kinds of truth' are 'suddenly severed': 'To express every minute of matter in every story occurent, what story-writer in all the world is able to perform it?' Foxe insisted that he had better and higher things to do. *The Origins of the English Novel* (Baltimore, Md., and London, 1987), p. 93; citing *Acts and Monuments of Foxe*.

13 Marion True *et al.*, *The Getty Kouros Colloquium Athens, 25–27 May 1992* (Malibu, 1993); reviewed, *Times Literary Supplement*, 22 October 1993. On Sidney's defensive attitude toward 'poor Poetry', see *Apology*, pp. 95–6 and *passim*; and on its implications, see Nelson, *Fact or Fiction*.

14 The 'epistemological stance' of ballad texts, in which 'strange but true' almost becomes 'strange, therefore true', is discussed in McKeon, *Origins*, pp. 46–8. See also Lennard J. Davis, *Factual Fictions: The origins of the English novel* (New York, 1983), pp. 47–56.

15 Joseph Mede's news letters are in BL, MSS. Harleian 389, 390, the remark about 'our Speculatives' occurring on fo. 277r of Harleian 390. John Rastell's *A. C Mery Talys* (1526) includes (sigs Dii–Div) the story of the Warwickshire preacher who told his auditory: 'Yf you beleue me not, then for a more suerte & suffycyent auctoryte, go your way to Coventre, and there ye shall se them all played in Corpus Cristi playe.' Preaching in Cambridge in 1627, Thomas Edwards, the future author of *Gangraena*, affirmed: 'If all this be not true, then this book (clapping his hand upon the holy Bible) is full of falsehoods, and God himself is a lyar, and Christ himselfe a deceiver'; *Cambridge University Transactions During the Puritan Controversies of the 15th and 17th Centuries*, ed. J. Heywood and T. Wright (London, 1854), vol. 2, p. 362. Both preachers were in breach of pulpit decorum. For Glibery's preaching, see NA, S.P. 12/159/27. He is called 'a verie ridiculous preacher' in the Puritan survey of the ministry in Essex, *The Seconde Parte of a Register*, ed. Albert Peel (Cambridge, 1915), vol. 2, p. 163. Glibery finished up in the pages of Martin Marprelate and may have given us our word 'glib'. See my essay, 'Ecclesiastical vitriol: satire and the construction of Puritanism', in *The Reign of Elizabeth I*, ed. John Guy (Cambridge, 1995), pp. 150–70. On the Bible as 'the touch-stone by which all other tales of the past must be tested', see Nelson, *Fact or Fiction*, pp. 20–1.

16 See, for example, Christopher Middleton, *The Famous Historie of Chinon of England, with his strange adventures for the love of Celestina daughter to Lewis King of Fraunce* (1597), ed. W. E. Mead, Early English Text Society, o.s. 165 (1925). Michael McKeon points out that as late as the late seventeenth century, not even in the catalogues of the book trade was any clear distinction drawn between (on our terms) 'history' and fiction, 'another sort of Historyes which are called *Romances*'. However, in this state of 'generic chaos', typical of Renaissance literary culture, the distinction was perfectly accessible and just as often made. McKeon, *Origins*, pp. 26–8.

17 'Next unto the holie scripture, chronicles do carry credit.' Raphael Holinshed, *The Firste Volume of the Chronicles of England, Scotlande, and Irelande* (London, 1577), p. 766.

18 *The Life and Death of Cardinal Wolsey by George Cavendish*, ed. R. S. Sylvester, Early English Text Society, 243 (1959), pp. 4, 183–6. Judith H. Anderson comments: 'The meaning of *truth* alters and evolves in this biography.' *Biographical Truth: The representation of historical persons in Tudor-Stuart writing* (New Haven, Conn., 1984), pp. 27–39.

19 *Acts and Monuments of Foxe*, vol. 8, pp. 164–6. See also Patrick Collinson, 'Truth and legend: the veracity of Foxe's *Book of Martyrs*', in *Clio's Mirror: Historiography in Britain and the Netherlands* vol. 8, ed. A. C. Duke and C. A. Tamse (Zutphen, 1985), p. 44; reprinted in Patrick Collinson, *Elizabethan Essays* (London, 1994), p. 169.

20 Perez Zagorin, *Ways of Lying: Dissimulation, persecution and conformity in early modern Europe* (Cambridge, Mass., 1990).

21 Woolf, *The Idea of History*, p. 35.

22 William Camden, *Britain* (London, 1610), pp. 6–8.

23 Michael Drayton, *Poly-Olbion: Or a Chorographical Description of Great Britain ... digested in a poem* (London, 1613–22).

24 *Acts and Monuments of Foxe*, vol. 1, p. 272; cited in John R. Knott, *Discourses of Martyrdom in English Literature, 1563–1694* (Cambridge, 1993), p. 42.

25 *Acts and Monuments of Foxe*, vol. 1, pp. 504, 514.

26 Both passages from Latimer refer to *Sermons of Hugh Latimer*, ed. G. E. Corrie, Parker Society (Cambridge, 1844), p. 487. Stapleton's remark appears in the epistle introducing his translation of *The History of the Church of England Compiled by the Venerable Bede* (Antwerp, 1565). Cited hereafter as Stapleton, epistle.

27 *The Works of John Jewel*, ed. J. Ayre, Parker Society (Cambridge, 1850), vol. 4, p. 1167.

28 See also Patrick Collinson, 'Thomas Cranmer', in *The English Religious Tradition and the Genius of Anglicanism*, ed. G. Rowell (Wantage, 1992), pp. 79–103.

29 John N. King, *English Reformation Literature: The Tudor origins of the Protestant tradition* (Princeton, N.J., 1982), pp. 138–60, and *passim*.

30 *Ibid.*, p. 141.

31 On the use to which some of Foxe's illustrations were put, as well as cheaper products that were a spin-off from Foxe, see Tessa Watt, *Cheap Print and Popular Piety, 1550–1640* (Cambridge, 1991), pp. 90–1, 94, 147, 158–9, 223–4. The revisionists' opponents referred to include A. G. Dickens, *The English Reformation* rev. edn (London, 1989); the revisionists themselves, Eamon Duffy, *The Stripping of the Altars: Traditional religion in England, 1400–1580* (New Haven, Conn., 1992); and Christopher Haigh, *English Reformations: Religion, politics, and society under the Tudors* (Oxford, 1993).

32 *Acts and Monuments of Foxe*, vol. 1, pp. 502–3; Collinson, 'Truth and legend', p. 31; and Stapleton, epistle.

33 I am not sure whether Professor A. G. Dickens ever committed that statement to print, but I have heard him make it verbally more than once.

34 See Susan Wabuda, 'Henry Bull, Miles Coverdale, and the making of Foxe's *Book of Martyrs*', in *Martyrs and Martyrologies: Studies in Church history*, vol. 30, ed. Diana Wood (Oxford, 1993), pp. 256–7.

35 BL, MS. Harleian 420, no. 12, fos 80–178.

36 *An Epistle Wrytten by John Scory the Late Bishop of Chichester... unto all the faythfull that be in pryson in Englande* ('Southwark', *recte* Emden, 1555), sig. A3.

37 Richard Prat to John Foxe, 20 January 1560, BL, MS. Harleian 416, fo. 176.

38 *Acts and Monuments of Foxe*, vol. 7, pp. 4–9.

39 For Foxe's excuse, see *ibid.*, 21. For Parkhurst's incompetence and its consequences, see *The Letter Book of John Parkhurst Bishop of Norwich Compiled During the Years 1571–5*, ed. R. A. Houlbrooke, Norfolk Record Society, 42 (Norwich, 1975); Diarmaid MacCulloch, *Suffolk and the Tudors: Politics and religion in an English county 1500–1600* (Oxford, 1986), pp. 184–7; and Felicity Heal, *Of Prelates and Princes: A study of the economic and social position of the Tudor episcopate* (Cambridge, 1980), pp. 251–2. Foxe's East Anglian connections, especially in the 1560s, make it likely that he had Parkhurst in mind.

40 *Acts and Monuments of Foxe*, vol. 7, p. 26.

41 *Ibid.*, pp. 28–33.

42 *Ibid.*, p. 550.

43 *Ibid.*, p. 33.

44 *Ibid.*, vol. 8, pp. 326, 300. See also p. 254. See Collinson, 'Truth and legend', pp. 41–4.

45 Nichols drew attention to the need for a scholarly edition of Foxe in editing *Narratives of the Days of the Reformation, Chiefly from the Manuscripts of John Foxe the Martyrologist*, Camden Series, o.s. 77 (London, 1859). The British Academy is currently funding a 'Foxe's *Book of Martyrs* Project' under the guidance of Professor Loades. In an appendix to his *John Foxe* (Boston, 1983), pp. 117–19, Warren W. Wooden compares the accounts of a particular episode in the 1563, 1583, and Victorian editions of *Acts and Monuments*, illustrating both the need for such an enterprise and the difficulty that it will inevitably entail.

46 Wooden, *John Foxe*, p. 76.

47 Helen C. White, *Tudor Books of Saints and Martyrs* (Madison, Wis., 1963); William Haller, *Foxe's* Book of Martyrs *and the Elect Nation* (London, 1963); and *The Elect Nation: The meaning and relevance of Foxe's* Book of Martyrs (New York, 1963).

48 Haller, *Foxe's* Book of Martyrs, pp. 15, 187.

49 Richard Bauckham, *Tudor Apocalypse* (Appleford, 1978); Katharine R. Firth, *The Apocalyptic Tradition in Reformation Britain 1530–1645* (Oxford, 1979); and V. Norskov Olsen, *John Foxe and the Elizabethan Church* (Berkeley and Los Angeles, Calif., 1973).

50 *Acts and Monuments of Foxe*, vol. 7, pp. 550. See Collinson, *Elizabethan Essays*, pp. 99–101; and John N. King, *Tudor Royal Iconography: Literature and art in an age of religious*

crisis (Princeton, N.J., 1989), pp. 207–11.

51 *Acts and Monuments of Foxe*, vol. 1, pp. 521–3.

52 The Hanmer translation is *The Auncient Ecclesiasticall Histories Wrytten by Eusebius, Socrates, and Euagrius* (London, 1577, 1577, entered with the Stationers, 1579). For Meredith Hanmer's distinctly spotty reputation, see *Dictionary of National Biography*. The Vautrollier Luther translations (original editions) are *Short-Title Catalogue* nos. 16965, 16975, 16989 and 16993. See G. R. Elton, 'Luther in England', in *Studies in Tudor and Stuart Politics and Government* (Cambridge, 1992), vol. 4, pp. 230–45.

53 Thomas Fuller, in his *Worthies of England*, told the story of the Kentish matriarch Mrs Mary Honywood who suffered from a chronic religious melancholy of the kind for which Calvinism has often been blamed. She told Foxe that she was as sure to be damned as the glass that she hurled to the floor was to be broken. But then there happened a wonder. The glass rebounded entire. Fuller, *The Worthies of England*, ed. J. Freeman (London, 1952), pp. 273–4.

54 Knott, *Discourses of Martyrdom*, pp. 57–8.

55 *Ibid.*, pp. 11–32.

56 Wooden, *John Foxe*, p. 115.

57 White, *Tudor Books of Saints and Martyrs*, pp. 164–7; Knott, *Discourses of Martyrdom*, pp. 33–46.

58 White, *Tudor Books of Saints and Martyrs*, p. 164; Wooden, *John Foxe*, pp. 45–6.

59 Stapleton, epistle, fos 8v–9r.

60 Thomas Stapleton, *A Fortresse of the Faith* (Antwerp, 1565), fo. 99v.

61 I am indebted to the study of this text made by Damian Nussbaum as a bibliographical exercise for the M.Phil. degree in medieval and Renaissance literature at Cambridge University, and to discussions with Mr Nussbaum. See also his M.Phil. dissertation, 'Foxe's *Acts and Monuments:* development and influence. Dramatising contests and contesting dramas: the ritual and representation of Tudor heresy executions' (1993).

62 These suggestions draw freely on Alexandra Walsham's Cambridge Ph.D. thesis, 'Aspects of providentialism in early modern England' (1995) and especially on her chapter on Thomas Beard. See also Peter Lake, 'Deeds against nature: cheap print, Protestantism, and murder in early seventeenth-century England', in *Culture and Politics in Early Stuart England*, ed. Kevin Sharpe and Peter Lake (Basingstoke and London, 1994), pp. 257–83.

63 G. R. Elton, *Reform and Reformation: England 1509–1558* (London, 1977), p. 386.

64 Knott, *Discourses of Martyrdom*, p. 12.

65 White, *Tudor Books of Saints and Martyrs*, pp. 160–2.

66 *Acts and Monuments of Foxe*, vol. 7, p. 551 (Ridley); vol. 6, p. 658 (Hooper); vol. 7, pp. 319–21 (Wade).

67 Seymour Byman, 'Ritualistic acts and compulsive behaviour: the pattern of Tudor martyrdom', *American Historical Review* 83 (1978): 625–43; and Byman, 'Suicide and alienation: martyrdom in Tudor England', *Psychoanalytical Review* 61 (1974): 355–73. Warren Wooden is another student of Foxe who has drawn attention to the painful physical tests to which the martyrs subjected themselves, experimenting with their capacity to bear the pain. *John Foxe*, pp. 44–5.

68 John Stow, *The Annales of England* (London, 1592), p. 1162. Walter Strickland reported to Edward Bacon that they 'died stubernly and nether patiently nor martir like'. Folger Shakespeare Library, MS. L.d.568. In the next century, the Leveler Richard Overton would ask: 'Who writ the Histories of the Anabaptists but their Enemies?' Cited in McKeon, *Origins*, p. 77. However, note also the manner of the death of the radical Arian heretic Francis Kett, who was burned at Norwich on 14 January 1589. The Norwich minister William Burton reported that 'he went leaping and dancing: being in the fire, above twenty times together, clapping his hands, he cried nothing but blessed be God ... and so continued untill the fire had consumed all his neather partes, and untill he was stifled with the smoke'. Cited in *Dictionary of National Biography*, s.v. Kett. The future Bishop Joseph Hall wrote to a Norfolk recusant about the joyful death of a priest, Robert Drewrie, executed at Tyburn on 26 February 1607: 'How many malefactors have we known that have laughed upon their executioners, and jested away their last wind! You might know. It is not long since our Norfolk Arian leaped at his stake.' Cited in F. L. Huntley, *Bishop Joseph Hall, 1574–1656: A biographical and critical study* (Cambridge, 1979), p. 66.

69 *Acts and Monuments of Foxe*, vol. 6, p. 650.

70 See Joseph Martin, 'Miles Hogarde: artisan and aspiring author in sixteenth-century England', in *Religious Radicals in Tudor England* (London, 1989), pp. 83–105.

71 Miles Huggarde, *The Displaying of the Protestants* (London, 1556), fos 36–7, 41.

72 The passage, from *A New Enterlude No Lesse Wittie: then plesant, entituled new Custome* (London, 1573), is worth quoting in full: 'CRUELTIE: By the masse there is one thing makes me laugh hartely ha, ha, ha. AVARICE: I pray thee what is that? CRUELTIE: What? ha, ha, ha, I can not tel for laughing | I would never better pastime desier | Then to here a dosen of them howling together in the fier | Whose noyse as my thinketh I could be compare: | To a crie of houndes folowing after the Hare. | Or a rablement of Bandogges barking at a Bear, | ha, ha, ha.' The copy in the Huntington Library bears the (spurious?) signature of 'Wm Shakespeare'.

73 Hayden White, *Tropics of Discourse: Essays in cultural criticism* (Baltimore, Md., 1978), pp. 97–8, and ch. 3, 'The historical text as literary artifact', *passim*; Anderson, *Biographical Truth*, pp. 1–5. Anderson excludes *Acts and Monuments* from her *Biographical Truth* on the surprising and hardly necessary ground that Foxe's lives are 'formulaic and repetitive'. 'Foxe's book is not about men but about martyrs.' In a sense, the subject is not mankind but the Holy Spirit. Anderson, *Biographical Truth*, pp. 2, 3.

74 Wooden, *John Foxe*, pp. 71–75.

75 Roland Barthes, 'Historical discourse', in *Structuralism: A reader*, ed. Michael Lane (London: Penguin Books, 1970), cited in Keith Thomas, *History and Literature: The Ernest Hughes Memorial Lecture 1988* (Swansea, 1988), p. 23.

76 John Bossy, *Giordano Bruno and the Embassy Affair* (New Haven, Conn., 1991), pp. 1–2. Bossy's attack on Natalie Zemon Davis's *Fiction in the Archives: Pardon tales and their telling in sixteenth-century France* (Princeton, N.J., 1988) appeared in the *Times Literary Supplement*, 7 April 1989.

77 J. F. Mozley, *John Foxe and His Book* (London, 1940), p. 164.

78 According to Foxe, these stories tell of 'The severe punishment of God upon the persecutors of his people and enemies to his word, with such, also, as have been blasphemers, contemners, and mockers of his religion'. *Acts and Monuments of Foxe*

(London, 1839), vol. 8, p. 628. The lamentable story of the twelve-year-old 'wench', Denis Benfield of Walthamstow, supplied to Foxe by William Maldon and his wife, occurs at p. 640.

79 Wooden, *John Foxe*, p. 23; McKeon, *Origins*, p. 92.

80 *Acts and Monuments of Foxe*, vol. 8, pp. 600–25.

81 Nussbaum, 'Dramatising contests and contesting dramas'.

82 Patrick Collinson, *From Iconoclasm to Iconophobia: The cultural impact of the second English Reformation* (Reading, 1986), p. 15; Collinson, *The Birthpangs of Protestant England: Religious and cultural change in the sixteenth and seventeenth centuries* (Basingstoke and London, 1988), pp. 103, 114. See also Paul Whitfield White, *Theatre and Reformation: Protestantism, patronage and playing in Tudor England* (Cambridge, 1993), *passim*.

83 See David Nicholls, 'The theatre of martyrdom in the French Reformation', *Past and Present* 121 (1988): 49–73; and Nussbaum, 'Dramatising contests and contesting dramas.'

84 D. F. McKenzie, *Bibliography and the Sociology of Texts: The Panizzi Lectures 1986* (London, 1986).

85 I owe this information to Damian Nussbaum.

86 Collinson, *Birthpangs*, p. 106; John Foxe, *Acts and Monuments* (London, 1563), sigs 3U2–3U2v.

87 Collinson, *From Iconoclasm to Iconophobia*, pp. 17, 17 n. 67, 35; Tessa Watt, 'Piety in the pedlar's pack: continuity and change, 1578 to 1630', in *The World of Rural Dissenters, 1520–1725*, ed. Margaret Spufford (Cambridge: Cambridge University Press, 1995); Watt, *Cheap Print and Popular Piety*, pp. 100–1, 95, 317–18; 91–4.

88 Knott, 'The Holy Community', ch. 3 in *Discourses of Martyrdom*; Richard Helgerson, *Forms of Nationhood: The Elizabethan writing of England* (Chicago, Ill.: University of Chicago Press, 1992), pp. 265–6.

89 Helgerson, *Forms of Nationhood*, refers to Benedict Anderson, *Imagined Communities: Reflections on the origin and spread of nationalism* (London, 1983).

90 See Wabuda, 'Henry Bull'. Coverdale's *Certain most godly letters* (London, 1564) was more properly the work of Bull.

91 Wooden, *John Foxe*, pp. 51–2.

92 *Acts and Monuments of Foxe*, vo. 8, p. 559.

93 See Collinson, 'Truth and legend', p. 48.

94 Erasmus to Jodocus Jonas, 13 June 1521, *Opus Epistolarum Des. Erasmi Roterodami*, ed. P. S. and H. M. Allen (Oxford, 1906–58), no. 1211, vol. 4, pp. 502–27. An English translation is in *Desiderius Erasmus: Christian Humanism and the Reformation: Selected writings*, ed. John C. Olin (New York, 1965), pp. 164–91. See Jessica Martin, 'Izaak Walton and his precursors: a literary study of the emergence of the ecclesiastical life', Ph.D. thesis, Cambridge (1993), pp. 78–85; and Jessica Martin, *Walton's Lives: Conformist Commemoration and the Rise of Biography* (Oxford, 2004).

95 *Acts and Monuments of Foxe*, vol. 7, pp. 547–9.

96 I owe this suggestion to Dr Susan Wabuda.

97 Mozley, *John Foxe and His Book*, pp. 86–7.

98 *Acts and Monuments of Foxe*, vol. 7, pp. 547–9.

99 Levin L. Schücking, *The Puritan Family: A social study from literary sources*, tr. Brian Battershaw (London, 1969).

100 C. S. Lewis, *English Literature in the Sixteenth Century Excluding Drama* (Oxford, 1954), pp. 299–301.

101 Wooden, *John Foxe*, pp. 62–4, 76.

102 Collinson, 'Truth and Legend', pp. 48–50.

103 White, *Tudor Books of Saints and Martyrs*, p. 160.

Chapter 9

◆

One of us? William Camden and
the making of history

I

The Royal Historical Society will not be startled to learn that one of the best-informed essays on William Camden was written by its quondam president, Sir Maurice Powicke:

> A great book might be written about Camden, his life and his works, his wide circle of friends and correspondents and his humanity. It would be a very difficult book to write, for its author would have to be steeped in the social history of the time and to be familiar with the personal life, the friendships and all the correlated activities of scholars all over the western world in Camden's day. To recapture that society with learning and imaginative amplitude might well engage a fine and patient and sympathetic scholar in the work of a lifetime.[1]

This polymath (who has yet to appear) will also need to share the knowledge of classical antiquity which was in the bloodstream of Camden and his contemporaries, and in particular of the historians, Livy, Polybius and Tacitus.

As Powicke reminds us, Camden was a cosmopolitan. So to ask whether he was one of us is to face a paradox. Camden never crossed the Channel, and Continental Europe was for him only a republic of letters. And yet he wrote in a universal language, primarily for the edification of the learned European rather than English reader.[2] His historiographical model was Jacques-Auguste de Thou, 'historiarum nostri seculi Princeps', author of *Historia sui Temporis*.[3]

Paper read at a Colloquium on William Camden held at Westminster School on 7 October 1997, celebrating the centenary of the sponsorship of the Camden Series by the Royal Historical Society. (On the same occasion there were papers from Dr Pauline Croft on 'Camden, Westminster and the Cecils', Professor Blair Worden on 'William Camden and Ben Jonson', and Dr Tom Birrell on 'William Camden and His European Reading Public'.) Published in *Transactions of the Royal Historical Society (6th Ser.)*, 8 (1998): 139–63, and reproduced by permission of the Royal Historical Society and Cambridge University Press.

So the hundreds of letters to Camden published by Thomas Smith, most of them from foreign correspondents, and Camden's own letters to de Thou, would be only the start of the labours of Powicke's exemplary scholar.[4] We, to speak of 'us', the modern historians of Elizabethan England, are jet-lagged globe-trotters. We equally write in a universal language, but that language is now English, which tends to draw us back into an insular version of our own history.

Yet it was with Camden's works that this insular detachment began. The translations of *Britannia* and of his *Annales* of Elizabeth, not translations which he undertook personally,[5] served to create an educated rather than learned English readership which appropriated his scholarship and turned it into a piece of English apartness, exceptionality, and self-discovery. *Britannia* became Philemon Holland's *Britain*, his *Annales* Robert Norton's *Historic of the most renowned and victorious princesse Elizabeth*.

What of the secondary element in my title, 'us'? Not a lifetime ago, when working as an apprentice under the watchfully indolent eye of Sir John Neale, I knew what was meant by 'us'. We Tudor historians of the London school were empiricists and archival positivists (or so we later learned). Postmodernism had not been invented, and we spent our time in search of the realities which were new sources, new facts; and on that basis we presumed to write history as it really (rather than Ranke's 'evidently') was, a true account of a past which had truly existed, an actual essence which became our property. We were not at fault in our desire not to get it wrong, but we were naive (if not arrogant) in our assumption that we, and we perhaps alone, had actually got it right. Neale used to say that there are no pundits in history, but his colleague Joel Hurstfield told me that he didn't really mean it, or, if he did, he made an exception in his own case. But we were perhaps an extreme case. Lawrence Stone has told us that at Oxford he was taught historical relativism, and has nothing to learn from postmodernism.[6] Be that as it may, to call Camden one of us will be to credit him with writing a history close to its sources, equivalent to the truth as he saw it, and even as it very probably was. But this may prove to be an inappropriate and anachronistic way to judge Camden, or any other historian of his age.

To read Camden's Preface to his *Annales of Elizabeth* is to be persuaded that he was indeed one of the first archival positivists, and that that constituted his achievement. He made much of his dusty exertions among 'great Piles and Heaps of Papers and Writings of all sorts':

> Charters and Grants of Kings and Great Personages, Letters, Consultations in the Council-Chamber, Embassadours Instructions and Epistles, I carefully turned over and over; the Parliamentary Diaries, Acts and Statutes, I thoroughly perused, and read over every Edict or Proclamation.

I am not sure that Sir John Neale ever did as much. On these foundations, Camden erected a history which he could presume to consecrate 'at the Altar of Truth'. 'Which Truth to take from History, is nothing else but, as it were, to pluck out the Eyes of the beautifullest Creature in the World.'[7]

Another former president, Sir Geoffrey Elton, nods approval. Thus it was that Fritz Levy made Camden's *Annales* the logical as well as chronological terminus of his Whiggishly progressive *Tudor Historical Thought* (1967). Camden's *Annales* was 'the greatest accomplishment of the school of politic historians'.[8] Powicke wrote that Camden (by implication alone) grasped the fact that the study of history, if it is to be more than a literary amusement or a branch of the study of conduct, is a very serious business, while Hugh Trevor-Roper's verdict was that Camden had placed historical studies 'on a new base of scientific documentation'.[9] There is, of course, a long tradition, so far as this matter is concerned, of cocking one's ear for the first cuckoo in spring.

Implied in these judgments, and here too Elton would approve, is the doctrine that political history is the last to which the historian-cobbler should stick. History is past politics, and the truth about past politics is discoverable. Ergo, the truest history is political history.[10] When Digory Wheare, the first holder of the chair which Camden endowed at Oxford, found to his dismay that he was expected to lecture on ecclesiastical history, a subject of which he claimed to be ignorant, Camden wrote, reassuringly: 'It ever was and is my intention, that ... he should read a civil history', not the history of churches, except insofar as that impinged on politics.[11]

Nowadays, these are no longer secure certainties. It may be possible to write 'true' history if we define history as high politics, involving the motives, decisions and acts of individuals and committees. Within these limits, the historian may even hope to provide plausible causes for events. As Camden himself wrote, quoting Polybius, history was not history without the why and wherefore and to what end.[12] But the 'truth' about historical questions which are both smaller and larger than the contingencies of high politics, small because they concern what Camden himself called 'small things', which is to say social history; larger because they deal with longer periods and larger chunks of history: this is more elusive. The higher, or at least broader truths and explanations, the master narratives of metahistory, often embodied in the banality of book titles, 'ages' of this and that, exist only in the eye of the beholder and are read into history rather than out of it. Historical positivists are necessarily revisionists, masters of the short to medium term and contingent. Or they write thick descriptive microhistories, *histoires évènementielles*, which through sheer detail are held to contain their own explanatory if anecdotal truth.

This is to defer a little to postmodernists such as Hayden White, who insists on the fictive nature of the historical enterprise, a nature determined by a process of selection and exclusion, and by the attribution of form and shape to what is selected. 'This is essentially a literary, that is to say fiction-making, operation. And to call it that in no way detracts from the status of historical narrative as providing a kind of knowledge.'[13] But what Hayden White might have to tell us about Camden's fictive powers in his *Annales* is limited by the boundaries and shape of a given subject, the reign of Elizabeth, and the fact that Camden adopted an annalistic method, in principle non-intrusive and neutral.

What did Camden's contemporary and admired friend, Sir Philip Sidney,[14] have to say in his *Apology for Poetry*? Contrasting three roads to edifying instruction, Philosophy, History and Poetry (which is to say, imaginative fiction), Sidney took as read the Aristotelian/Ciceronian premiss that the historian deals with the truth in the sense that he does not make up his stories. It is almost sufficient that the man should not be a liar.[15] According to Sidney, the historian 'bringeth you images of true matters, such as indeed were done, and not such as fantastically or falsely may be suggested to have been done'. But this was faint and ambivalent praise indeed. For the historian is the prisoner of 'that was', 'his bare was', and since he deals with particulars, he cannot account for events. Even if history could teach lessons, they would not be edifying or useful. The poet, by contrast, derives edification from what never happened, and perhaps never could happen.[16] Most of this comes straight out of Aristotle[17], who was correcting Plato, who thought fiction pedagogically risky.

However, Sidney torpedoed his own argument with the admission that history itself is more than half fictional. The historian tells of events of which he can yield no cause 'or, if he do, it must be poetical'. For even historians, for all their talk of things done and of absolute verities, have been glad to steal the poet's clothes. Herodotus and all who came after him borrowed from poetry their passionate descriptions, details of battles which they dreamed up; and they put speeches into the mouths of their characters 'which it is certain they never pronounced'.[18] Here Sidney anticipated Hayden White.

At once we have some kind of bench-mark for Camden. For Camden, almost alone among his peers, eschewed the practice of *prosopopoeia*: 'Speeches and Orations unless they be the very same *verbatim*, or else abbreviated, I have not meddled with all, much less coined them of mine own Head.'[19]

We are now ready to consider whether Camden as a historian was one of us, not neglecting the question, what kinds of historian do we aspire to be, in this centennial year of the appropriation of Camden's name by the Royal Historical Society. How would Camden himself have defined 'historian? Most would agree that of Camden's two major literary accomplishments, *Britannia* and the *Annales* (never forgetting the remarkable socio-linguistics of his *Remains Concerning Britain*,[20] and other works) the greater was *Britannia*, both in the range and originality of its learning, and in its seminal importance for the developing study of antiquity on the basis of material artefacts as well as of textual evidence.

Yet, as all commentators on Camden have pointed out, the author of *Britannia*, in his own self-perception, was not a historian at all.[21] The only point of difference is whether Camden's true destiny and ambition was to be a historian, or whether he remained suspicious of history as a pursuit and doubtful about his own fitness to pursue it.[22] John Pocock has drawn our attention to what he calls 'a great divorce' between Renaissance antiquarians and historians. The critical techniques evolved by antiquarians were only slowly and belatedly combined with the literary undertaking of writing history.[23] When Camden disclaimed the role of historian in *Britannia*, it was because this great compilation of antiquity and chorography (rather than of history) lacked rhetorical art; and Cicero had written that history was a branch of rhetoric. 'Do you not see how far history must be a job for the rhetorician?'[24]

To be sure, Pocock's divorce was never an absolute decree nisi, and Sidney deliberately blurred the distinction when he simultaneously mocked the historian as antiquary, 'loaden with old mouse-eaten records', and as rhetorician, 'authorising himself (for the most part) on other histories'.[25] And whatever Camden might want us to think, there is much that we should regard as history in *Britannia*, and even a greater care in the deployment of sound historical method. Camden is more explicit in the use of what is technically conjecture – about, for example, the meaning of place-names (which he often got wrong), or the location of Roman towns, or the distribution of British tribes.[26] There may be conjecture in the *Annales*, but it is formally excluded on Camden's own terms.[27] In *Britannia* we encounter the word 'guess'; not, I think, in the *Annales*. This leads to a paradoxical consequence of the great divorce for historiography and its immediate future, two paradoxes in fact. *Britannia* is a compendium of facts, which Camden's contemporaries with access to the same facts were able to judge and censure. And they did. Some people were made unhappy by the *Annales*, particularly if they were related to the great personages they met in Camden's pages.[28] Francis Bacon was allowed to insert a number of passages helpful to the posthumous reputation of his father, Sir Nicholas Bacon.[29] But there were no savage reviews along the lines of Ralph Brooke's *A discoverie of certain errors published in print in much commended Britannia* (1594). For every letter which Camden received about his *Annales* he got twenty others offering friendly or unfriendly advice on matters of factual detail in *Britannia*.[30] As the historian of the reign of Elizabeth, Camden was on his own. But as antiquary, he was part of an extensive guild of scholars, inside and outside the Society of Antiquaries. Selden praised Bacon's *Reign of Henry VII* and Camden's *Elizabeth* as the only two royal lives written in his own time which came up to the dignity of the subject.[31] But did Selden have any idea how different these two books were, and did he have much interest in how accurate and truthful they were? This was history, and where history was concerned that was hardly the point. But when the poet Michael Drayton turned *Britannia* into verse as *Poly-Olbion*, the same Selden filled the margins with critical censure whenever Drayton played fast and loose with the facts and perpetuated myths.[32]

The fact that antiquarians concerned themselves with the 'small things' for which Camden found little room in his *Annales* makes our second paradox. Insofar as 'us' is not Sir Geoffrey Elton, the early modern springs and roots of history as we know it are to be found almost anywhere but in history as 'politic history'. There is potentially more history in *Britannia* than in the *Annales*, and certainly more social and economic history.[33] Arthur B. Ferguson has argued that Renaissance historical consciousness is to be found in a variety of particular and practical contexts, more so than in 'history', written as an end in itself, as a narrative of deeds done. It follows that what Camden and his contemporaries understood to be history is not necessarily the place to look for the best of Renaissance historiography.[34]

II

The remainder of this chapter will address the subject of Camden's *Annales*, in the context of the 'politic history' of its time. But first we may consider *Britannia*,[35] and its historical and prehistorical prolegomenon, which provides revealing examples of Camden's conduct when it came to confronting dubious historical evidence. Having reduced the British History of Geoffrey of Monmouth to rubble, Camden concludes, to the astonishment, not to say scandal, of 'us', that it was not his intention to 'impeach' this improbable tale. Let Brutus be taken for the father and founder of the British nation. 'I will not be of a contrarie minde.' In things of so great Antiquitie, it is easier to proceed by guesswork than by knowledge.[36] Camden's poem *De Connubis Tamae et Isis* makes similar, conventional gestures towards Brutus as founder of the nation, and to Troy as London's mother.[37] Camden's elusiveness on this delicate subject is best conveyed in his Latin: 'Sin autem Britanni nostri, velit, nolit veritas, origine Troiani esse velint, me sane repugnantem non habebunt.'[38] Philemon Holland's translation loses the irony of 'velit, nolit veritas'.[39] And so with the legendary origins of Cambridge University: 'I will be no dealer in this case ... Howbeit, I feare me, they have builded Castles in the aire'.[40] Yet Camden was prepared to believe that his own university had been founded by King Alfred, and to tamper with the text of Asser to bolster his belief. So it appears that his critical faculties were sharpened more by *parti pris* than by the concerns of disinterested scholarship.[41] Anthony Grafton has taught us that that was how the learned minds of the Renaissance often worked.[42] However, the reign of Elizabeth was not a thing 'of great Antiquitie', and so a different matter.

Three late Elizabethan and Jacobean historians are conventionally bracketed together as representative of the so-called 'new' politic or 'civil' history:
besides Camden, Sir John Hayward, who wrote, amongst other things, a
history of the usurpation and early years of King Henry IV, and Francis Bacon,
for his *Reign of Henry VII*.[43] In fact Camden, Hayward and Bacon have little in
common, beyond a shared appreciation of Cornelius Tacitus, whom they put
to very different uses.[44] But Hayward and Bacon make admirable foils for the
question we are pressing upon Camden: one of us? For clearly they, at least,
were not.

Hayward understood the historian's task to consist of the making of patch-
work quilts: the reworking of moral, psychological and political reflections on
great events and those who shaped them; and why not in the very words of
earlier histories written about other epochs and subjects? Hayward is a subject
which belongs to Lisa Richardson.[45] We have always known that Hayward borrowed from Tacitus. Francis Bacon called it stealing, in a famous exchange
with Queen Elizabeth herself. Hayward could not be had up for treason, as the
queen had hoped. (The first part of his *Life and Raigne of King Henrie IIII*, a sad
story of deposition and death, had been dedicated to the earl of Essex, which,
when it happened, appeared to implicate the author in the Essex revolt.) But,
said Bacon, Hayward was certainly guilty of felony: 'For he had taken most
of the sentences of Cornelius Tacitus ... and put them into his text.'[46] What
Bacon said has not hitherto been understood quite literally, and the full extent
of Hayward's plagiarism, if that is the right word, has not been appreciated.
John Manning, who edited the first and second parts of *Henrie IIII* for the
Camden Series as recently as 1991, supposed, as anyone perhaps would, that
he was dealing with a more or less original literary composition.[47] Hayward
was even credited with inventing a new kind of historiography, 'significant
and enduring'.[48]

But Lisa Richardson will demonstrate that Hayward was a master of scissors
and paste. Of the *First part*, 72 per cent is traceable to its immediate sources,
word for word, and without authorial elaboration, and 18 per cent comes
straight from Sir Henry Saville's 1591 translation of the *Histories* of Tacitus,
including almost all of Hayward's characterisations. Hayward ingested whole
chunks of the relevant medieval chronicles (which could at least be regarded
as legitimate 'sources'); as well as a variety of other more recent texts, such as
the memoirs of Philippe de Commynes and even Sir Philip Sidney's *Arcadia*,
a fictional romance, which makes a distinctly Hayden White-ish point. He also
recycled some of this material in his own later histories, where, for example, a
politician from the reign of Edward VI was made to put on the same Tacitean
costume previously worn in the time of Richard II and Henry IV. Since it has
been hard work, even for Miss Richardson, to cover all of Hayward's traces,
it is perhaps unlikely that as much as 28 per cent of the first part of *The Life*

and Raigne will prove to have been, in the words of the pavement artist, 'all my own work'.

Tacitus is of critical importance.[49] Lisa Richardson can provide hundreds of examples of Hayward's Tacitean shoplifting. Tacitus (in Savile's translation) had written of the ambitious general Antonius Primus: 'peradventure prosperity in a man of that disposition, discovered the secret and inward faultes of his minde, as covetousness, and pride, and other vices that were suppressed before'; and of the unsavoury character of one of the Emperor Galba's minions, Vinius, who, 'carrying an ill minde, and serving in great place a weake master, made open sale of his Princes free grace and favours'.[50] Out of these materials, Hayward invented a pastiche of Michael de la Pole, earl of Suffolk: 'Prosperity laid open the secret faults of his minde, which were suppressed and cloaked before; and serving a weake ruler in great place, with an ill minde, he made open sale of his prince's honour.'[51] The example of Galba provided the commonplace that 'a good prince governed by evil ministers is as dangerous as if he were evil himself'. Of Richard II, Hayward wrote: 'For it is oft times as dangerous to a prince to have evil and odious adherents as to be bee evil and odious himself.'[52]

The irony of this is that Tacitus himself has been exposed as a 'scissors and paste' historian. Tacitus's model was Sallust, and he helped himself freely to Sallust's character sketches. But Tacitus had the talent to transform many of the passages which he ingested.[53] Let us be fair to Hayward. Tacitus, in the perception of the Renaissance, had uttered aphorisms which are eternally true. Peter Burke remarks: 'Men believed that the maxims could be "unlocked", or released from their context, without loss of value.'[54] Hayward was no more than an extreme case. But far from being one of us, he would be denied even a third-class degree in any modern university. However, to judge him by such a standard would involve a monumental misunderstanding of what this early modern rhetorician thought history was about.

Bacon was the only one of our three political historians to have written extensively and originally on the nature of historical knowledge and the practice of history. Bacon wanted history in the broadest sense (for his definition embraced what we should call natural history, that is, all science) to be derived from the study of particulars, from which could be constructed what Bacon called a 'perfect history' of some worthy subject, such as the history of England and Britain from the union of the roses to the union of the crowns. But Bacon thought it beneath the dignity of the historian (himself) to do the work of collecting the particulars. That task belonged to 'factors and merchants', research assistants.[55] So the historian's function was perhaps not essentially different from what it had always been: literary and rhetorical.

Bacon preached better than he practised. In the only 'perfect' history which he ever completed, his *History of the Reign of King Henry VII*, a book which has been described as 'an intellectual anticlimax',[56] he fell below his own exacting standards, effectively dispensing with the primary labour of research. That is not to say that Bacon managed without sources. But he wrote in conditions of enforced rustication, depending upon what the Keeper of Public Records and Selden (some 'factors'!) were able to supply.[57] For his narrative core, he followed earlier accounts of the reign and Speed's *History of Great Britaine*, faithfully reproducing some of Speed's mistakes.[58] Here is a good example of Sidney's historian, authorising himself for the most part on other histories. Bacon's own contribution was to create an at least partly imaginary Henry VII. On the one hand he too wrote under a Tacitean spell, the moral degeneration of Henry Tudor resembling that of the Emperor Tiberius, although Bacon was no crude Haywardian plagiarist.[59] On the other, Bacon's Henry VII resembled James I. Without the example of James and Anne of Denmark, would Bacon have alleged, without any evidence, that Henry neglected his wife?[60] In the funeral oration with which the book ended, Bacon wrote: 'This King (to speak of him in terms equal to his deserving) was one of the best sort of wonders, a wonder for wise men':[61] in short, Solomon redevivus, James Stuart. *Henry VII* was a political treatise, not learning from the past but teaching from it. It was also the autobiography of a statesman, particularly in the hostility the book expresses for courtiers of the kind who had destroyed Bacon's own career.[62] These were further refractions of the Roman historians, with whom it was virtually a convention to deplore the rise of upstarts.[63] This was not what we should call a history at all. And yet Bacon set the reign of Henry VII in a mould which historians have broken only in recent years.[64]

III

Which leaves us with Camden, who set Henry VII's granddaughter in a mould which has endured for at least three hundred years.

For a book acknowledged to partake of a certain greatness, Camden's *Annales* is a strangely neglected text. Hugh Trevor-Roper used the occasion of a Neale Memorial Lecture to talk about it with characteristic brilliance.[65] Neale himself, whom Trevor-Roper flattered as 'our modern Camden', almost never cited his illustrious precursor.[66] Trevor-Roper's lecture was a typical exercise in investigative scholarship, opening the diplomatic bag and listening in to the whispering galleries of European intellectual life in order to discover why and how Camden's book came to be written, and written as it was: a tangled plot concerning the posthumous reputation of Mary Queen of Scots, not least with her son, James VI and I; George Buchanan's account of Scottish affairs which Jacques-Auguste de Thou was all too inclined to incorporate, *faute de mieux*, in the great universal history of his own time; circumstances directly relevant to the publication of the first three books of the *Annales* in 1615; and, according to Trevor-Roper, no less to James's lack of interest in Book 4, which dealt with matters after the death of his mother. There is no need on this occasion to repeat that story.

But, more recently, the respective roles in this literary and diplomatic game of Camden and Camden's friend and sometime Westminster pupil, Sir Robert Cotton, have been re-examined by Kevin Sharpe, to the advantage of Cotton;[67] while Daniel Woolf has suggested that James I's interest in the work was more enduring than Trevor-Roper supposed, since Camden's Elizabeth in her moderate instinct for middle and pacific courses bore a flattering resemblance to James himself.[68]

However, the bibliographical story of the *Annales* has never been told. Trevor-Roper was indifferent to such matters, failing even to explain to his audience that the book was written and originally published in Latin, and that Camden had nothing to do with the various English translations. Here, at some risk of being tedious, is the barest summary of the biography of the book.

Conception was in 1608, when Camden recorded: 'I began to compile my Annals.'[69] Then follows the story of gestation, the book hidden in the womb, as told by Trevor-Roper and Sharpe. The events of birth, wholly neglected in modern scholarship, are documented in ten stout volumes in the British Library, MSS. Cotton Faustina F.[70] These contain not one but the better part of two autograph manuscript copies of the *Annales*, some volumes in the first series authenticated, in Sir Robert Cotton's hand, as 'manu Authoris scripta'.[71] Volume IV of the series is (flamboyantly) headlined with 'Robert Cotton Bruceus' (Cotton claimed descent from Robert the Bruce), 'the first copy after mended'. Camden's Preface is absent from these manuscripts and was presumably supplied at the time of publication. The first series contains many substantial corrections and interpolations. There are excised – and inserted – passages, which are not to be found in any printed edition. It would take a competent Latinist and palaeographer some time to collate this material with the printed text.

Cotton, whose own hand appears at many points, has recorded the progress of his copy-editing of the manuscripts, two or three distinct readings of each part, which began in August and continued until late October 1613. From these notes it is clear that the whole work up to 1603 had been completed by the autumn of 1613, whereas it has been thought that Book 4, from 1589 to 1603, was written later. However, Cotton's notes prefacing Faustina F VI and IX tell us that he was again reviewing Book 4 for publication between November 1618 and May 1620.

Faustina F X contains this intriguing Cotton note: 'The copye of the storye of Queen Elizabeth from 1583 to 1587, not transcribed for my self as yett but sent unto France to Tuanum [de Thou].'[72] There is evidence here and there that these copies were set up for the printer. One important document is endorsed in Camden's hand: 'I praye that this maye be verie fayre wrytten with some golden letters' – presumably for a presentation copy. Another hand, doubtless the printer's, has added: 'it is so done'.[73] It appears only just that the first edition of the *Annales* was licensed to Camden and Cotton jointly.[74] Cotton had supplied much of the source material, either from his own collections or from his privileged access to the state archives,[75] but evidently that was not all that he contributed. It appears that we should be as cautious in referring to the *Annales* as Camden's *Annales* as to the play *Henry VIII* as simply Shakespeare's *Henry VIII*. Joint authorship is now acknowledged to have been commoner than we once thought, and no disparagement to the quality of the work in question.

The first three books of the *Annales*, which took the story as far as 1588, were published in London in 1615: *Annales Rerum Anglicarum, et Hibernicarum Regnante Elizabetha*.[76] This volume was translated into French by Phillipe de Bellegent, a native of Poitou, and printed in London in 1624: *Annales des choses qui se sont passées en Angleterre et Irlande soubs le Regne de Elisabeth*. This was the basis of the first English translation, entered with the Stationers five months later, the hasty and incompetent work of Abraham Darcie, who was born in Geneva and apparently knew no Latin: *Annales: The true and royall history of Elizabeth*.[77] This edition makes no mention of Camden, who is referred to simply as 'the author'; and whereas Camden had rather pointedly dedicated his book not to his sovereign but to the reader, posterity and his country, Darcie's jingoistic dedication was to James as 'Emperour of Great Britanne' (etc) and to Prince Charles. In 1625, soon after Camden's death, the Fourth Book, which he had been reluctant to publish in his lifetime, most of all in English (and his biographer suggests why, 'the censures he met with in the business of *Mary Queen of Scots*'[78]), was for the first time joined to Books 1–3 in an edition published in Leiden.[79] Two years later Book 4 was separately published in London as *Tomus alter annalium, sive pars quarta*. In 1629 a translation of the *Tomus alter* by Thomas Browne was published at Oxford and dedicated to Charles I.[80] Again, Camden was nowhere named. In 1626 a translation of all four books by Robert Norton, presumably from the Latin, was entered with the Stationers, but only appeared from the press in 1630. The title was now altered: *The historie of the most renowned and victorious princesse Elizabeth*, no longer 'Annals'.[81]

We now have three English translations of Camden and they make an odd bunch: Darcie, the expatriate and third-rate man of letters; Browne, learned cleric, student of Christ Church, and chaplain to both Archbishop Laud and Charles I; and Norton, son of the great Elizabethan 'parliament man' Thomas Norton, a military engineer and gunner.[82] Browne, as we might expect, was the most competent of the three. Compare the first sentence of Book 4, taking up from the failure of the Armada, in his version and Norton's:

NORTON:

After that the expedition of the *Spaniards* against *England* had proved so adverse, dishonourable, and fully frustrate, they to repair their glory, and divert the cogitations of the English from fixing upon an invasion of the Countryes of the King of *Spaine* ... [and so on].[83]

BROWNE:

After that so unexpected a successe had blasted the glory of the Spanish Invasion; they to salve their wounded honour, and to forestall in the English the very thought of the like invasion ... [and so on].[84]

Thirty-three words to Norton's forty-three, in better English, and more faithful to Camden's tight, economical Latin.

However, Browne was to disappear without trace and it was Norton's version which became the *textus receptus* in a further edition of 1635 (calling itself the third and amplified and corrected edition).[85] Forty years later, in 1675, a version based on 1630 rather than 1635 claimed to be a third edition and to incorporate radical (but mostly harmless) 'improvements' to the text. We may compare the personal appreciation of Mary Queen of Scots in Camden's epitaph for the poor lady: Darcie (1625) 'of surpassing beauty';[86] Norton (1630) 'and passing beauty' (a subtle variant that);[87] (1675) 'and admirable beauty'.[88] Professor Wallace MacCaffrey employed a further edition of 1688 for his 'selected chapters' of Camden (1970), the only version of any kind to have been made available in this century.[89]

Finally, in 1717, Thomas Hearne published in three volumes a Latin text of the *Annales* based on Bodleian Library MS. Smith 2.[90] This is a printed text (the 1615 London edition), containing the revisions and corrections which Camden intended for a second edition which never materialised. Several of Camden's *addenda* are of interest. For example, under 1559, Camden tells us about Elizabeth's old-fashioned veneration for the cross, the Virgin Mary and the saints. In Hearne's 1717 text, there is an additional sentence otherwise to be found only in Norton 1635. 'And least shee should breake the Ecclesiasticall fast in Lent, shee solemnely asked licence every yeere of the Archbishop of *Canterbury*, for eating of flesh.'[91] Hearne's scholarship is impeccable, and any critical modern edition will have to be based on this text (or MS. Smith 2), collated with MSS. Faustina F I–X.

Camden's Latin is the only text to speak with an authorial voice. In translation, much is lost, although only occasionally the actual sense. It is notorious that Camden detested Puritans, so the following examples are significant. The year is 1564, and Camden is discussing the division of opinion over the succession, and in particular about the claims of Mary Queen of Scots. Camden wrote that 'Protestantes efferuescentes' were hostile to Mary's title; whereas her title was favoured by 'Pontificorum alii, et plerique omnes aequi benique'. 'Protestantes efferuescentes' means the wilder sort of Protestants.

Darcie makes this less polemical: 'Protestants, transported with an ardent zeal'; Norton is closer: 'the hot Protestants'. 'Pontificorum alii' Darcie and Norton render, reasonably enough, as 'papists'. (That Camden brackets these Catholics with 'plerique omnes aequi benique' puts an interesting spin on public opinion, suggesting that animosity to Mary was a sectarian, minority sentiment. Darcie makes this 'those who had reference to that which was just and equall', Norton, 'and the greatest part of all indifferent men'.)[92] In 1603, with Elizabeth on the brink of death, among those posting north to pay their respects to James were both 'Zeloti' and 'Pontifici'. Browne translates 'Zeloti' as 'the more zealous'; Norton, who knew what Camden meant, 'Puritans'.[93] But 'Puritani' is not a word which Camden ever used.

More was lost in translation than such small details. The major casualty, the unavoidable consequence of the act of translation itself, was the intense, epigrammatic, often ironical style and tone of the original. This was the essence of Camden's Tacitism, little in the way of naked plagiarism, but style and tone determining interpretation. For an example, we need look no further than the most famous statement in his Preface. '*Manifesta* non reticui, *dubia* mollius sum interpretatus, *occultiora* non indagavi.' The italicised nouns become rather clumsy constructions in English, 'things manifest and evident', 'things doubtful', 'things secret and abtruse'.[94] A modern authority on Tacitus remarks on the difficulty facing his English translators of 'the intransigence of an uninflected language'.[95]

So much for the problematics of Camden's *Annales* as literary texts. But historians will want to know how faithfully such an influential history depended upon its sources, and is itself dependable. If Camden is to be reckoned 'one of us', and posthumously elected to the fellowship of this learned society, it will be because he, unlike Hayward and Bacon, authorised himself, not on other historians, but on the original archival record, those 'Great Piles and Heapes of Writings of all sorts'.

It is worth asking why Camden went into the archives; not, I think, because he wanted to be one of us, the Whiggish answer. The explanation lies in the doctrine, rooted in the Roman historiographical tradition, that a historian ought to be an experienced politician, or at least an ex-politician, with first-hand knowledge of the arcane mysteries of state. Tacitus, after all, was the son-in-law of his first subject, Agricola, and a senator who served as consul and governed a province, Asia no less. The Elizabethan Member of Parliament Francis Alford was aware of this ancient convention when he suggested that he, Alford, should be allowed and funded to do what Camden later achieved, 'write the storie of her Majestie's reign'. Making what he could of his own not very distinguished public service, Alford remarked: 'To write a storie there apertaineth more then a schollers knowledge.' Lord Burghley himself, if he were not too busy, was the obvious man to do it. But failing that, Alford would take it on, if suitably rewarded.[96] Similarly, Camden represents himself in his Preface as virtually Burghley's *amanuensis*. Sir Henry Saville's dedication of his *Tacitus* to the queen refers to her own 'admirable compositions' and 'excellent translations of Histories (if I can call them Translations, which have so infinitely exceeded the originals).' He wished that she might be her own Tacitus.[97] Camden later assumed the same courtly pose. He would be content if James I were to publish the fourth part of his *Annales* over his own name.[98] Evidently, according to this rhetorical conceit, the most suitable historian of Elizabeth's reign was her first minister, or even the queen herself, or her successor. A second best was the scholar capable of making sense of the state archive, to which Camden had been admitted as a special privilege by Burghley himself, and to which he later had access through Cotton's winning ways with their keeper.

Balancing Camden's desire to please, or at least avoid offence, was his celebrated devotion to truth. 'For the Love of Truth, as it hath been the onely Incitement to me to undertake this Work: so hath it also been my onely Scope and Aim in it ... As for Danger, I feared none, no not from those who think the Memory of succeeding Ages may be extinguished by present Power' – a statement with Tacitean resonances.[99] Trevor-Roper thought that Camden was as good as his word. 'The pressure of King James is reflected not at all' in 'this magnificently uncourtly work'.[100] But a more sceptical reader might take Camden's protestations as a health warning. Trevor-Roper conceded that Camden allowed prejudice to overcome impartiality when it came to the earl of Leicester, but believed this to have been a unique lapse of judgment.[101] However, it has recently been shown that Camden was also capable of stretching a point in the other direction, in order to protect the reputation of his principal patron, Burghley.[102]

Let us not deny Camden a generous measure of impartiality, but rather seek to account for it. If he was to trespass into the quagmire of recent politics, it provided some protection to follow the path of fidelity to the written record. 'Mine owne Judgment I have not delivered according to Prejudice or Affection, whilst writing with an undis-tempered and even Mind'.[103] This may also help to account for Camden's most common, and laconic, rhetorical device: some thought this, some that, which is surely how Burghley himself would have written history. We associate archivally based, ostensibly objective history with the liberal, bourgeois environment of the nineteenth and twentieth centuries, the product of academic freedom. Have we given sufficient thought to the possibility that 'modern', 'scientific' history, was enforced by the hostile environment of the world of Tacitus reborn, a Europe of incipient absolutism?

However 'uncourdy' Camden may have been, he gave James I's mother, Mary Queen of Scots, a good press: 'A Lady fixed and constant in her Religion, of singular Piety towards God, invincible Magnanimity of Mind, Wisedom above her Sex, and admirable [surpassing? passing?] Beauty; a Lady to be reckoned in the List of those Princesses which have changed their Felicity for Misery and Calamity.'[104] It is impossible to say whether this was Camden's own honest appraisal of the lady (we know how much he detested those 'effervescent' Protestants who deserved more of the blame for Mary's downfall than Mary herself); or whether his eulogy took some prudent account of 'present power'.[105]

But Hearne reveals that where Mary Queen of Scots was concerned, Camden made adjustments to the first edition which are significant. In the 1615 text and the translations which derive from it, it is said that Elizabeth, from her heart, as it seemed, 'ut videbatur',[106] misliked the insolency of the Scots in deposing their queen. Camden had second thoughts about 'ut videbatur' and struck it out, leaving Elizabeth's displeasure unqualified.[107] In the text of 1615, it was said that when the news of Mary's execution reached Elizabeth, she 'either conceived or pretended grief and great displeasure', grief about the fate of her cousin, anger directed against William Davison, the under-secretary who was to carry the can for delivering the execution warrant: 'iram ... et dolorem ... conceperit aut praesetulerit'.[108] This sentence is written in Cotton's hand in Cotton MS. Faustina F X.[109] But in his revision of this passage Camden crossed out 'aut praesetulerit'.[110] These were the most important two words which Camden ever wrote, or unwrote. For their implication was that Elizabeth was fully complicit in Mary's death and that her grief and anger were synthetic and diplomatic. Hearne's 1717 edition also contains a paragraph, which follows this passage and which had otherwise only occurred in 1635. This tells how letters, messengers and spies were sent into Scotland to sound out James VI's intentions and to put the best face on what had happened, explaining amongst other things that Leicester's part in the affair had been prompted by his need to placate the Protestants ('Puritans'?) and to protect himself against his enemies among papists and courtiers; and that Walsingham was an honest man 'that bare a *true Romane* spirit'.[111] This passage was not an afterthought but was prudently suppressed in the first edition. The question remains unanswerable, whether these textual adjustments were dictated by the apprehension of 'present power', or by respect for Camden's own declared principles: 'Things doubtful I have interpreted favourably; Things secret and abtruse I have not pried into. "The hidden Meanings of Princes (saith that great Master of History [Polybius]) and what they secretly design to search out, it is unlawful, it is doubtfull and dangerous: pursue not therefore the Search thereof."'[112]

It is now a little late to address the question of what Camden's sources actually were. Camden supplies no references and does not tell us. Was that too a deliberate stratagem? Sometimes he is his own authority. He lived through the whole of Elizabeth's reign, seven years of age when it began, fifty-two when it ended. 'Mine own Cabinets and Writings I also searched into ... ; ... have myself seen and observed many things, and received others from credible Persons that have been before me, men who have been present at the transacting of Matters, and such as have been addicted to the Parties on both sides in the contrariety of Religion.'[113] On Francis Drake, Camden writes: 'to relate no more then I have heard from himselfe'.[114] So as the contemporary of the history he wrote, Camden has a huge advantage over 'us'. We were not there when John Stubbs had his right hand struck off by the executioner for that seditious libel, *The Gaping Gulf.* But Camden was. 'I remember (being there present) that when Stubbs, after his Right hand was cut off, put off his Hat with his Left, and said with a loud voice, "God Save the Queen"'; and he tells us about the reaction of the crowd, silent and shaken.[115] Camden's hostile feelings about Leicester are never disguised. 'In a word, people talked openly in his Commendation, but privately he was ill spoken of by the greater part.'[116] Nevertheless, we prick up our ears when Camden tells us that he himself, 'being then a young man', often heard it said that a clause in the Treason Act of 1571 dealing with the succession, 'except the same bee the Natural issue of [the queen's] body', was put there by Leicester on purpose, 'that he might one day obtrude upon the English some bastard sonne of his, for the Queens naturall issue'. This was no more than a good political joke, and it is evidence not of Leicester's actions or intentions, still less of the queen's sexual history, but of what the chattering classes were heard by the young Camden to be saying.[117]

Camden's account of Queen Elizabeth's deathbed is very famous: how she declared that since her throne was a throne of kings, she would not be succeeded by some vile person; and, asked what she meant, '*Rex*, inquit, *mihi succedat volo, et quis nisi qui cognatus proximus, Rex Scotorum*' – who but my cousin, the king of Scots?[118] This passage is heavily worked over in Cotton's hand in MS. Faustina F III.[119] Was it pure invention? Elizabeth is thought by this stage to have been speechless and only capable of signifying her mind by a hand signal. Yet Camden was, if not an observer, very close to those who were. Nine days before the end, he had written to Cotton about the queen's symptoms and the likely prognosis, evidently from the Court: 'I know you are (as we all here have been) in a melancholy and pensive cogitation.'[120]

But very soon the editor whom Camden deserves will have to penetrate the archives. And he will be wise to begin with the Cotton MSS. According to Smith, 'the Records and Instruments out of which he extracted his *Annales* are most of them, if not all, in *Cotton's* Library'.[121] However the search is unlikely to end there and is certain to take some time.

I end with a vignette. In her first Parliament, Elizabeth was under pressure to marry; and she responded with one of those answerless speeches, famous for its concluding flourish. She would be content if in due course a marble tomb should proclaim that a queen, having reigned such a time, lived and died a virgin. These words come through very well in Camden's taut, sententious Latin: HIC SITA ELIZABETHA, QUAE VIRGO REGNAVIT, VIRGO OBIIT, placed in capitals in the printed text and so corrected in MS. in Faustina F I, Cotton's version of the speech (at least it is in his hand) having been inserted in the earlier version of 1559, in Faustina F IV.[122]

The speech in Camden, while manifestly the same speech, differs from all other known copies.[123] The most interesting variant is a small piece of theatre recorded nowhere else. 'And behold (said she, which I marvell ye have forgotten) the Pledge of this my Wedlock and Marriage with my Kingdom. (And therewith [she stretched forth her finger and shewed the ring of gold] wherewith at her Coronation she had in a set form of words solemnly given her self in Marriage to her Kingdom.)' And then, having made a pause, she said that she should not be upbraided for lack of children: 'for every one of you, and as many as are English-men, are Children and Kinsmen to me'.[124]

Neale and the editor of *Proceedings in the Parliaments of Elizabeth I* deny Camden's version documentary status.[125] The implication is that without further evidence we must regard it as suspect. Did Camden make up the little scene with the ring? Only if he forgot his own declared historiographical principles. Surely he must have received and recorded the little play with the ring as a piece of oral testimony, transmitted by some of those 'credible persons'?

But no doubt this was more than a simple piece of reporting. Elizabeth's strategy had been to declare herself ready both to marry and not to marry, while not concealing her preference for the latter. Camden's version differs from what appears to be the canonical text in suggesting that the transition from a private to a public life had actually strengthened this celibate resolve. 'But now that the publick Care of governing the Kingdom is laid upon me, to draw upon me also the Cares of Marriage may seem a point of inconsiderate Folly.'[126] And then follows the little ring scene. The effect of this, when added to 'Virgo Regnavit, Virgo Obiit' was to strengthen Elizabeth's apparent commitment to virginity, and at the age of twenty-five; indeed to project back into 1559 the legend of the Virgin Queen which, as recent scholarship assures us, was in reality invented, for political purposes, some twenty years later.[127] Is it relevant that Camden himself, as Smith tells us, 'chose a single life'?[128] While historians are not allowed to lie, they cannot help being themselves. But whether Camden tampered with the historical record to achieve this effect, against his own declared principles, we shall never know.

Was Camden one of us? Let Sir Maurice Powicke have the last as well as the first word. We do not read Camden for his learning. The philology of his *Britannia*, for example, is 'pitiful'.[129] But then comes this: 'The foundations of historical criticism were not yet laid. What Camden did was to help to create the atmosphere in which they could be laid.'[130] But that can hardly have been what Camden, the historian, intended to do.

NOTES

1   Maurice Powicke, 'William Camden', *English Studies 1948. Being Volume One of the New Series of Essays and Studies Collected for the English Association* (1948): 67–84; this quotation at p. 81.

2   This was amply demonstrated by Dr Birrell's contribution to the Camden Colloquium. Camden's *Anglica, Hibernica, Normannica, Cambrica* was published at Frankfurt in 1602 and 1603, but never in translation and never in England.

3   William Camden, *Annalium Apparatus, Annales Ab Anno 1603 ad Annum 1623*, bound with Thomas Smith, *Vita Clarrissimi Gulielmi Camdeni et Illustrium Virorum ad Gulielmum Camdenum Epistolae* (1691), p. 25.

4   Smith, *Epistolae*; De Thou correspondence in the Collection Dupuy in the Bibliothèque Nationale, Paris, noted by D. R. Woolf, *The Idea of History in Early Stuart England* (Toronto, 1990), pp. 294, 333. Bodleian Library MS. 15680 (MS. Smith 74) contains Latin letters from Camden, chiefly to foreign scholars, 1587–1620, not included in *Epistolae*.

5   But Thomas Fuller wrote (*The History of the Worthies of England* [1662], vol. 3, p. 128) that Holland's translation of *Britannia* was done not only with Camden's knowledge and consent but with his 'help'. Letters to Camden from Jean Hotman establish that he was kept informed about the French translation of the *Annales* and had some control over it (Smith, *Epistolae*, nos. 161, 163, pp. 201–3).

6   Lawrence Stone, 'History and Postmodernism', *Past and Present*, 135 (1992): 189–94; reprinted, in an adversarial context, in Keith Jenkins, ed., *The Postmodern History Reader* (London, 1997), pp. 255–9.

7   Wallace T. MacCaffrey, ed., *William Camden: The history of the most renowned and victorious Princess Elizabeth Late Queen of England: selected chapters* (Chicago, Ill., and London, 1970), 3–8; hereafter, MacCaffrey.

8   F. J. Levy, *Tudor Historical Thought* (San Marino, Calif., 1967), p. 279.

9   Powicke, 'William Camden', p. 79; Hugh Trevor-Roper, 'Queen Elizabeth's first historian: William Camden', in his *Renaissance Essays* (London, 1985), p. 146. More recently, Daniel Woolf has claimed that the *Annales* is the first English narrative history to have been founded almost entirely on primary sources (*The Idea of History*, p. 120).

10 G. R. Elton, *Political History, Principles and Practice* (London and Aylesbury, 1970).

11 H. Stuart Jones, 'The foundation and history of the Camden Chair', *Oxoniensia*, 8–9 (1943–4): 175.

12 MacCaffrey, p. 6.

13 Hayden White, 'The historical text as literary artefact', in *Tropics of Discourse: Essays in cultural criticism* (Baltimore, Md., 1978), pp. 81–100. For recent responses to the challenge to 'traditional history' of postmodernism, see Keith Windschuttle, *The Killing of History* (Sydney, 1994), and Richard J. Evans, *In Defence of History* (London, 1997). However, as part of what, to coin a phrase, may be called the 'peace process', Evans's book has not succeeded. Patrick Joyce, in *Past and Present*, 158 (1998): 211, asserts that it 'spectacularly fails to meet the real challenges of postmodernist thought'. It appears that the jury is still out.

14 On the Camden–Sidney relationship, see W. A. Ringler, ed., *The Poems of Sir Philip*

Sidney (Oxford, 1962), p. xviii, and G. B. Johnson, ed., 'Poems by William Camden', *Studies in Philology*, 62 (1975), pp. 90–1, 94–5, 102–3. In *Britain*, Camden lauded 'the glorious starre', 'the lovely ioy of all the learned sort', 'a sample of ancient vertues' (William Camden, *Britain* [London, 1610], p. 329).

15 'Satis est, non esse mendacem' (Cicero, *De Oratore*, II. xii. 51).

16 Geoffrey Shepherd, ed., Sir Philip Sidney, *An Apology for Poetry, or, The Defence of Poesy* (London, 1965), pp. 107–14.

17 Plato, *Republic*, II, III; Aristotle, *Poetics*, IX.

18 Sidney, *Apology*, pp. 110, 97.

19 MacCaffrey, p. 6.

20 The best modern edition is R. D. Dunn, ed., *Remains Concerning Britain* (Toronto, 1984).

21 Woolf, *The Idea of History*, p. 22.

22 On the one hand, we know that Camden intended some kind of History of England before being diverted by *Britannia* (Levy, *Tudor Historical Thought*, p. 280); on the other, his correspondence with de Thou suggests antipathy. He could even write: 'History is in the beginning envy, in the continuation labour and in the end hatred' (J. Collinson, *The Life of Thuanus* [London, 1807], p. 173). But this was a highly charged correspondence, the stakes high, the hazards evident.

23 John Pocock, *The Ancient Constitution and the Feudal Law* (Cambridge, 1987), p. 6.

24 'Videstine, quantum munus sit oratoris historia?' (Cicero, *De Oratore*, II. xv. 62). My translation is surely closer to the mark that that found in Loeb: 'Do you not see how great a responsibility the orator has in historical writing?'

25 Sidney, *An Apology*, p. 105.

26 See Camden's Preface (*Britain*): 'Many happily will insult over me for that I have adventured to hunt after the originals of names by conjectures, who if they proceed on to reject all conjectures, I feare me a great part of liberall learning and humane knowledge will be utterly out-cast into banishment.'

27 'Things doubtful I have interpreted favourably; Things secret and abstruse I have not pried into.' (MacCaffrey, p. 5.)

28 The son of the Scottish statesman, Maitland of Lethington, wrote: 'in loca quaedam incidi, in quibus parentis mei mentio non satis honesta facta est' (*Epistolae*, no. 243, pp. 305–6).

29 Peter Beal (*Index of English Literary Manuscripts, vol. 1: 1450–1625*, Part I [New York, 1980], p. 149) reports that the relevant revisions (in Cotton MSS. Faustina F, see n. 70 below) are in the hand of Francis Bacon. But James Spedding, in (*Works of Francis Bacon*, vol. 11, *Letters and Life*, vol. 4. [1868], pp. 211–14) notes that the hand is not Bacon's.

30 For example, a letter from Camden's close friend John Saville (25 December 1589) consists of an endless catalogue of *corrigenda*: 'Taunton in Somersetshire a suffragan see; and had never but one Earl'; 'Sussex *contermine Cantio* as well as Surrey' (was Camden an elder in the Society of Antiquaries and knew not such things?); 'Christ Church in Canterbury hath twelve Prebends'; 'Blithe is not upon the river that goeth to Worksop; but to Scrouby, the Archbishop's Town' (Smith, *Epistolae*, no. 30, pp. 36–9).

31 Quoted by Thomas Hearne in *Guilielmi Camdeni Annales* (1717), vol. 1, sig. a2; and by Thomas Smith in his *Vita* (English translation in Edmund Gibson, ed., *Camden's Britannia* [London, 1695]).

32 Michael Drayton, *Poly-Olbion: Or a chorographical description of Great Britain ... digested in a poem* (London, 1613–22).

33 Take, for example, Camden's account of the crofting lifestyle of the inhabitants of Thanet, 'as if they were *Ampibii, that is both land creatures and sea-creatures* ... as well Husband-men as Mariners ... According to the season of the year, they knit nets, they fish for Cods, Herring, Mackerels etc ... The same again dung and manure their grounds' (*Britain*, p. 340). However, there is enough non-'politic' history in the *Annales* for Trevor-Roper to have accentuated its colourful detail in his account of the book (*Renaissance Essays*, pp. 138–41).

34 Arthur B. Ferguson, *Clio Unbound: Perception of the social and cultural past in Renaissance England* (Durham, N.C., 1979), *passim*.

35 T. D. Kendrick, *British Antiquity* (1950), ch. 8 'Britannia', pp. 134–67; Stuart Piggott, 'William Camden and the *Britannia*', *Proceedings of the British Academy*, 37 (1951): 199–217; F. J. Levy, 'The Making of Camden's *Britannia*', *Bulletin d'Humanisme et Renaissance*, 26 (1964): 70–97.

36 Camden, *Britain*, pp. 8, 10.

37 *Poems by William Camden*, pp. 90–103.

38 William Camden, *Britannia* (1586), p. 160.

39 'But if our Britons will needs be descended from the Trojans, they shall not verily have me to gainsay them' (Camden, *Britain*, p. 22). Does Camden mean by 'Britanni' the Welsh? I think that he does, for deferring to the sensibilities of that nation was a literary *topos* of the time.

40 Camden, *Britain*, p. 488.

41 Powicke, 'William Camden', p. 78.

42 Anthony Grafton, 'Invention of traditions and traditions of invention in Renaissance Europe: the strange case of Annius of Viterbo', in A. Grafton and A. Blair, eds, *The Transmission of Culture in Early Modern Europe* (Philadelphia, Pa. 1990); Anthony Grafton, *Forgers and Critics: Creativity and duplicity in Western scholarship* (London, 1990).

43 John J. Manning, ed., *The First and Second Parts of John Hayward's* 'The Life and Raigne of Henrie IIII', Camden 4th ser. 42 (London, 1991); Brian Vickers, ed., *Francis Bacon: The history of the reign of King Henry VII*, Cambridge Texts in the History of Political Thought (Cambridge, 1998). This leaves out of account the poet-historian Samuel Daniel, who is conventionally regarded as an 'artistic' rather than 'politic' historian: which is somewhat anachronistic and undervalues Daniel.

44 It is also less than clear what was 'new' about these political historians which was self-evidently newer than Thomas More's *History of Richard III*, written a century earlier by a man who had also read his Tacitus; unless it was a further measure of emancipation from 'Providentialism', normally pin-pointed as the essence of 'politic' or 'civil' history.

45 Lisa Richardson's Cambridge Ph.D. thesis (1999) on Hayward ('Sir John Hayward and early Stuart historiography'), includes an 80,000 word appendix which details, remorselessly, all of Hayward's borrowings which she has been able to trace, in *The*

Life and Raigne and in his other historical works. She also corrects the arguments of, e.g., David Womersley, 'Sir John Hayward's Tacitism', *Renaissance Studies*, 6 (1992): 46–59, who tends to exaggerate the subversive topicality of Hayward's use of Tacitus. I am grateful to Miss Richardson for permission to make use of her work.

46 Manning, *The First and Second Parts*, p. 2.

47 Citing another authority, Manning thought that a complete list of Hayward's Tacitean borrowings in *The First Part* might run to a dozen pages. This is a considerable under-estimate. (*Ibid.*, p. 36, n. 121.)

48 *Ibid.*, p. 34. S. L. Goldberg, too, found in Hayward 'a new approach to history', consist-ing in the kind of dispassionate political analysis which substituted 'is' for 'ought'. See S. L. Goldberg, 'Sir John Hayward, "Politic Historian"', *Review of English Studies*, n.s. 6 (1955): 233–4.

49 J. H. M. Salmon, 'Seneca and Tacitus in Jacobean England', in Linda Levy Peck, ed., *The Mental World of the Jacobean Court* (Cambridge, 1991), pp. 169–88; Malcolm Smuts, 'Court-centred politics and the uses of Roman historians, c.1590–1630'; Blair Worden, 'Ben Jonson among the historians', in Kevin Sharpe and Peter Lake, eds, *Culture and Politics in Early Stuart England* (Basingstoke, 1994), pp. 21–43, 67–89.

50 Publius Cornelius Tacitus, tr. Henry Savile, *Histories* (1591): 143; *The End of Nero and the Beginning of Galba* (1591), p. 14.

51 Manning, *The First and Second Parts*, p. 72.

52 Tacitus, *The end of Nero*, p. 1; Manning, *The First and Second Parts*, p. 70.

53 R. H. Martin, 'Tacitus and his predecessors', in T. A. Dorey, ed., *Tacitus* (London, 1969), pp. 131–4.

54 P. Burke, 'Tacitism', in *ibid.*, p. 162.

55 Francis Bacon, 'The dignity and advancement of learning' (translation of Bacon's *De Augmentis*), in J. Spedding *et al.*, eds, *The Works of Francis Bacon*, vol. 4. (1858). On Bacon's rhetoric in his historical writings, see John F. Tinkler, 'The rhetorical method of Francis Bacon's *History of the Reign of King Henry VII*', *History and Theory*, 26 (1987): 32–52, and Brian Vickers' Introduction to his edition of *The History*.

56 Daniel R. Woolf, 'John Selden, John Brough and Francis Bacon's *History of Henry VII* 1621', *Huntington Library Quarterly*, 47 (1984): 47.

57 *Ibid.*, 47–53.

58 Most notoriously, in repeating Speed's perversion of André's account of Henry's en-try into London *laetenter* (happily) as *latenter* (covertly), so that he entered 'in a close chariot'. This fitted Bacon's characterisation of Henry (Vickers, ed., *The History*, p. 11, n. 42).

59 Whatever the truth of the matter, historically (it was debated between G. R. Elton and J. P. Cooper), Bacon's account of the avarice of Henry's later years and of his 'oppor-tune' death, 'in regard of the great hatred of his people' (Vickers, ed., *The History*, pp. 194–5) was Tacitean. Bacon (cf. Thomas More in his *Richard III*) was doubtless aware of the ambivalent hesitation of Tacitus as he approached the reign of Trajan. Would this prove to be a new golden age? Probably not. (Martin, 'Tacitus and his predeces-sors', pp. 126–7; Alistair Fox, 'Thomas More and Tudor historiography: *The History of King Richard III*', in his *Politics and Literature in the Reigns of Henry VII and Henry VIII* (Oxford, 1989), pp. 109–27.) Lisa Richardson informs me that Bacon was very sparing

in directly borrowing from Tacitus.

60 Vickers, ed., *The History*, p. 201; David M. Bergeron, 'Francis Bacon's *Henry VII*: commentary on King James I', *Albion*, 24 (1992): 17–26.

61 Vickers, ed., *The History*, p. 196.

62 S. J. Gunn, 'The courtiers of Henry VII, *English Historical Review*, 108 (1993): 23–49.

63 Martin, 'Tacitus and his predecessors', p. 122.

64 S. B. Chrimes, *Henry VII* (1972). But as an introduction to studies which break the mould, see S. J. Gunn, *Early Tudor Government, 1485–1558* (Basingstoke, 1995).

65 Trevor-Roper, *Renaissance Essays*, pp. 121–48; first published as *Queen Elizabeth's First Historian: William Camden and the beginnings of English 'civil history': Neale Lecture in English History 1971* (London, 1971).

66 And since neither Camden nor Neale (in his *Queen Elizabeth* (London, 1934)) provides any references to sources, it would be a fascinating but difficult task to establish the extent to which Neale was indebted to Camden, not as a substitute for research, but in his adoption of Camden's patterning of the reign.

67 Kevin Sharpe, *Sir Robert Cotton 1586–1631: History and politics in early modern England* (Oxford, 1979), pp. 84–110; Kevin Sharpe, 'Introduction: Rewriting Sir Robert Cotton', in C. J. Wright, ed., *Sir Robert Cotton as Collector: Essays on an early Stuart courtier and his legacy* (London, 1997), pp. 12–13.

68 Woolf, *The Idea of History*, pp. 123–4.

69 'Annales digerere coepi' (William Camden, 'Memorabilia' [Diary], in *Addenda* attached to *Annales ab Anno 1603 ad Annum 1623, Epistolae*, 85).

70 The Faustina manuscripts are not mentioned by Trevor-Roper or Sharpe, nor are they specified by David McKitterick, although he refers in general terms to 'the drafts and the preparatory materials' of the *Annales*, surviving in the Cotton manuscripts. (David McKitterick, 'From Camden to Cambridge: Sir Robert Cotton's Roman inscriptions, and their subsequent treatment', in Wright, ed., *Sir Robert Cotton as Collector*, p. 115.) Nor are they noticed in J. K. Moore, *Primary Materials Relating to Copy and Print in English Books of the Sixteenth to Nineteenth Centuries*, Oxford Bibliographical Society Occasional Publications 24 (Oxford, 1992).

71 BL, Cotton MSS. Faustina F I (1558–72), II (1573–86, 1588–90), III (1593–1603), VI (1589–96), VII (1597–99, 1600–3) comprise what are here called 'the first series', 'a manu Authoris scripta' and, elsewhere 'a prima manu Camdeni' (in Cotton's hand). MSS. Faustina F IV (1558–72), 'the first copy after mended', V (1573–82), VIII (1589–97), IX (1598–1603) are perfected and fair copies. For the nature and contents of MS. Faustina F X, see n. 72 below.

72 This statement occurs on fo. 254, which was evidently originally a cover sheet/title page to the volume. Fos 105–70 of MS. Faustina F X, including this statement, are copied (by Thomas Hearne?) in BL, MS. Add. 6217, which concludes with a list of textual variants, 'deest paragraphus'. Fo. 255 of MS. Faustina F X is a holograph letter from Camden: 'Right worshipfull. I send you by this gent. Mr Quin: the first parte of my Annales of Q. Elizabeth with manifold additions. I praye you playe an Aristarcho therein and note severally what you thinke to be omitted or emended etc. I will follow your directions.' Was this letter written to Cotton?

73 BL, MS. Cotton Faustina F X, fos 247^r–9^4.

74 Trinity College Cambridge, MS. R.5.20, fo. 112ᵛ, dated 25 February 1615.

75 Sharpe, *Sir Robert Cotton*, p. 92, n. 40. Cotton later claimed the credit for conserving many of the Scottish materials for the *Annales*, writing of abstracts 'which Sir Robert Cotton hath compyled into a story of Q Eliz time by mr Camden and published in print' (Nigel Ramsay, 'Sir Robert Cotton's service to the Crown: a paper written in self-defence', in Wright, ed., *Sir Robert Cotton As Collector*, pp. 68–80). See also Woolf, *The Idea of History*, p. 118.

76 And in Frankfort in 1616. Hereafter '*Annales*'.

77 No fewer than three printers were employed in the collation of the ten copies listed in the *Revised Short-Title Catalogue* (no. 4497): a bibliographer's nightmare, or, playground. Hereafter 'Darcie'.

78 Smith, *Vita*, in Gibson, ed., *Britannia*.

79 There was a further Leiden edition in 1639.

80 Hereafter 'Browne'.

81 Hereafter 'Norton 1630'; and Norton's 1635 edition, 'Norton 1635'.

82 *Dictionary of National Biography*, arts Darcie, Browne, Norton; Michael Graves, *Thomas Norton: The Parliament man* (Oxford, 1994). Robert Norton's occupation may explain the delay between the licensing and publication of his translation of the *Annales*. In 1627, as gunnery expert, he took part in the ill-fated expedition to the Ile de Rhé.

83 Norton 1630, bk 4, p. 1.

84 Browne, p. 1.

85 This edition incorporates passages from Camden's amended text, only found otherwise in Hearne's 1717 edition (see below).

86 Darcie, bk 3, p. 206.

87 Norton 1630, bk 3, p. 112.

88 1675, p. 385.

89 See above, n. 7.

90 Thomas Hearne, ed., *Guilielmi Camdeni Annales Rerum Anglicarum et Hibernicarum Regnante Elizabetha, Tribus Voluminibus Comprehensi*; hereafter 'Hearne'. This edition derives from Bodleian Library, MS. 15609 (MS. Smith 2), which is inscribed by Hearne: 'Aprilis 2ᵈᵒ 1717 ... I give this Book to the Bodleian Library when I die as Dr Smith desired me. Tho. Hearne March 28 1719.' MS. Smith 2 is a copy of the printed 1615 (London) edition, with Camden's autograph revisions.

91 Hearne, vol. 1, p. 34; Norton 1635, pp. 7–8.

92 *Annales*, pp. 91–2; Darcie, bk 1, p. 111; Norton 1630, bk 1, p. 73.

93 *Annales, Tomus Alter* (1627), p. 284; Browne; Norton 1630, bk 4, p. 223.

94 *Annales*, Preface; MacCaffrey, p. 5.

95 Norma P. Miller, 'Style and content in Tacitus', in Martin, ed., *Tacitus*, p. 114.

96 Francis Alford to F[rancis] W[alsingham], Inner Temple Library, Petyt MS. 538.10, fo. 11ᵛ; Francis Alford, 'A sute for the writing of the storie of her Ma[jes]ties reigne', *ibid.*, fos 14ᵛ–15ʳ.

97 *The Ende of Nero and Begining of Galba*, Epistle.

98 Camden to 'N.N.', 'Right Honourable', Smith, *Epistolae*, no. 287, p. 351.

99 MacCaffrey, pp. 4–5. Cf. Publius Cornelius Tacitus, tr. R. Grenewey, *The Annales* (1598), p. 101, referring to the error 'of such as thinke with the power and authorities they have in their own time, they can also extinguish the memory of former times' (I owe this reference to Lisa Richardson).

100 Trevor-Roper, *Renaissance Essays*, pp. 134–5.

101 *Ibid.*, p. 142. The reasons for Camden's hatred of Leicester will repay further reflection and investigation, given his friendship with Sir Philip Sidney and others in that connection, including Leicester's secretary Jean Hotman, who was a valuable continental contact (Smith, *Epistolae*, pp. 120–1, 124–6, 174–5, 201–3; Eleanor Rosenberg, *Leicester Patron of Letters* (New York, 1955), pp. 269–70; *Poems by William Camden*, p. 30). Camden's copy of the *Franco-Gallia* by Hotman's father Francis is in the Bodleian Library, with annotations in Camden's hand.

102 Hiram Morgan has shown how Camden composed the history of a murky episode, the political assassination of the Lord Deputy of Ireland, Sir John Perrot, in order to cover up what Morgan calls Burghley's 'despicable behaviour' in this case (Hiram Morgan, 'The fall of Sir John Perrot', in John Guy, ed., *The Reign of Elizabeth I: Court and culture in the last decade* (Cambridge, 1995), pp. 109–25. Comparison of the various editions of the *Annales* suggests that Camden repented of what he had done to Perrot. There are passages in Hearne (vol. 2, pp. 425–6, 456–8, 558–9) which place him in a much more favourable light. It is not clear what motivated these changes.

103 MacCaffrey, p. 6.

104 *Ibid.*, p. 288.

105 But we know, because he tells us, that Camden feared that James I would take exception to his laudatory if barbed obit for his mother's arch-enemy, Sir Francis Walsingham. (*Epistolae*, no. 289, p. 351.) The obit ran: 'A man exceeding wise and industrious, having discharged very honourable Embassies, a most sharpe maintainer of the pure Religion, a most diligent searcher of hidden secrets, who knew excellently well how to winne mens mindes unto him, and to apply them to his own uses' (Norton 1630, bk 4, pp. 20–1).

106 *Annales*, p. 145.

107 Hearne, vol. 1, p. 171, noting the correction 'in Camden's own hand'. Norton 1635, bk. 1, p. 99, retains 'as it seemed', in parentheses.

108 *Annales*, p. 466.

109 BL, MS. Cotton Faustina F X, fo. 80ᵛ.

110 Hearne, vol. 2, p. 546. Norton's edition of 1635, which incorporates many of Camden's changes, retains, for whatever reason, 'either conceived or pretended' (Norton 1635, p. 349).

111 *Ibid.*, p. 550; Norton 1635, p. 352.

112 MacCaffrey, pp. 5–6.

113 *Ibid.*, p. 4. For a 'politic' (*politique?*) historian, Camden is very preoccupied with 'the contrariety of Religion'.

114 Norton 1630, bk. 2, p. 110.

115 MacCaffrey, pp. 138–9.

116 *Ibid.*, p. 330. Cf. Savile's Tacitus, (of Mutianus): 'openly praiseworthy, his secrete actions were ill spoken of' (*The Ende of Nero and Beginning of Galba*, p. 6). I owe this reference to Lisa Richardson.

117 Camden admitted that it was a joke: 'Incredible it is what ieasts lewd catchers of words made amongst themselves' (Norton 1630, bk 2, pp. 28–9.)

118 *Annales, Tomus Alter* (1626), p. 285.

119 BL, MS. Cotton Faustina F III, fos 215ᵛ–216ʳ.

120 Camden to Cotton, 15 March [1603], BL, MS. Cotton Julius C III, fo. 64ʳ; printed, T. Wright, ed., *Queen Elizabeth and Her Times* (1838), vol. 2, p. 494.

121 Smith, *Vita*, in Gibson, ed., *Britannia*.

122 *Annales*, p. 35; BL, MS. Cotton Faustina F I, fos 39–40, MS. Faustina IV, fos 27ʳ–29ᵛ.

123 T. E. Hartley, ed., *Proceedings in the Parliaments of Elizabeth I, vol. 1: 1558–1581* (Leicester, 1981), pp. 44–5.

124 MacCaffrey, pp. 29–30. The passage in square brackets is supplied from Norton 1635, which is more faithful to the original Latin (Helen Hackett, *Virgin Mother, Maiden Queen: Elizabeth I and the cult of the Virgin Mary* [Basingstoke, 1995], p. 274, n. 83).

125 J. E. Neale, *Elizabeth I and her Parliaments 1559–1581* (1953), p. 47, n. 3 ('I Know of no text, I have therefore ignored it'); Hartley, ed., *Proceedings*, p. 44. Susan Doran calls Camden's account 'little more than a myth', and seems to think that the absence of his version in Cecil's papers ('Camden's source') is conclusive evidence of invention (*Monarchy and Matrimony: The courtships of Elizabeth I* (London and New York, 1996), pp. 1–2.

126 MacCaffrey, p. 29.

127 Hackett, *Virgin Mother*, pp. 229–30: Doran, *Monarchy and Matrimony*, pp. 154–209; Susan Doran, 'Juno versus Diana: the treatment of Elizabeth's marriage in plays and entertainments, 1561–81', *Historical Journal*, 38 (1995): 257–74; John N. King, 'Queen Elizabeth I: representations of the virgin queen', *Renaissance Quarterly*, 43 (1990): 30–74.

128 Smith, *Vita*, in Gibson, ed., *Britannia*.

129 Powicke, 'William Camden', p. 75. The greatest eighteenth-century authority on the Welsh language, Lewis Morris, author of *Celtic Remains*, wrote of Camden's 'wild fancies' and 'lame guesses' where matters Welsh were concerned (Geraint H. Jenkins, 'The cultural uses of the Welsh language 1660–1800', in Jenkins, ed., *The Welsh Language Before the Industrial Revolution* [Cardiff, 1997], p. 386).

130 Powicke, 'William Camden', p. 78.

Chapter 10

William Camden and the
anti-myth of Elizabeth: setting the mould?

I

As an apprentice Elizabethan historian I was given discouraging advice by
someone whose identity I have long since forgotten: 'It's all in Camden,
and what's not in Camden won't hurt.' William Camden, a Londoner born in
1551, was educated at Christ's Hospital and St Paul's schools and subsequently
at Oxford. He died at Chislehurst in 1623 and was buried in Westminster Abbey,
having been a man of distinct, if related, parts: schoolmaster (at Westminster),
herald (Clarenceux 'king' of Arms), antiquary, and historian. These last two
roles were considered at the time to be formally distinct. History dealt with
the notable deeds of men and required some first-hand experience of great
affairs. And it was a vehicle for literary invention and elaboration, governed
by the rules of rhetoric, which did not bind in the same degree the often disparaged if perhaps more historically learned compiler of antiquities, who was
merely concerned with things, or the humble compiler of chronicles.[1] It was
as the antiquarian author of *Britannia* (first published in 1586) that Camden
was chiefly famous, particularly in those international scholarly circles which
had encouraged him to undertake this 'chorographical' guidebook to what was
for these luminaries the *terra incognita* of the British Isles, with the emphasis on its very respectable Roman past: witness the bulk of Camden's foreign
correspondence. As Justus Lipsius wrote in 1586: 'Multum patria tibi debet,
multum exteri nos, qui per Te videmus *Britanniam*, cur non videmus.' 'Not
only your own country is indebted to you but us foreigners, who scarcely knew
about Britain until now'.[2] But in Camden's day these boundaries were fluid
and evolving; and Camden was a master both of antiquity and of a history
which still had something of the chronicle in it.

Originally published in *The Myth of Elizabeth*, edited by Susan Doran and Thomas Freeman
(Basingstoke and New York, 2003). Reproduced by permission of Palgrave Macmillan.

There is some evidence that Camden's early ambition was to be a historian, until persuaded by the Dutch scholar Ortelius that the *Britannia* project should have priority.[3] It is rather more certain that Camden had an ambivalent attitude to the near-contemporary history which was his next major undertaking, a history of England, Scotland and Ireland in the reign of Elizabeth I, constructed on the model of the *Annals* of the Roman historian Tacitus, to which we shall refer as his *Annales*.[4] 'History is in the beginning envy, in the continuation labour and in the end hatred.'[5] According to Camden's own testimony, it was in about 1597 that Lord Burghley more or less ordered him to undertake 'an historical account of the first beginning of the reign of Queen Elizabeth', a project which lapsed with Burghley's death but revived, in circumstances which Camden was rather careful not to explain, in about 1606.[6] The earliest edition of the first three portions of a four-part work, telling the story to the end of 1588, appeared in 1615.

II

But should we speak, *tout court*, of 'Camden's *Annales*'? In this postmodernist age, authorship is sometimes questioned, or is held to be a matter of little account, while multi-authorship is no longer a stigma.[7] Camden's strongly first-personal preface ('ego' occurs 71 times in an essay of something over two thousand words) suggests single-mindedness and total authorial control, but this we are entitled at least to question.

We know from characteristic intelligence work on the matter by Hugh Trevor-Roper[8] that the gestation of the work involved political and diplomatic negotiations which criss-crossed the Channel, since the interest of King James VI and I in the undertaking was motivated by his desire to rescue the reputation of his mother from what was being written about her and her unhappy life and reign by Jacques-Auguste de Thou in his internationally celebrated *Historia sui temporis*.[9] De Thou, for want of better sources, had followed the lead of the book which had criminalised the career of Mary Queen of Scots in a radical, quasi-republican ideological context, and which James had put on his own private Index, George Buchanan's *Rerum Scoticarum historia*. This is what Camden failed fully to explain in his preface.

Moreover, in its earlier English versions the book made its way in the world without the authority or backing of Camden's name. Whereas the first (Latin) edition of the *Annales* in 1615 included an engraved portrait and prefatial material which loudly celebrated Camden's fame, his first two translators, Abraham Darcie and Thomas Browne, who, as with the third, Robert Norton, in their presentation were effectively reinventing it, never mention Camden by name, only referring to him as 'the author' of what Darcie calls 'a masterpiece of History'.[10]

And then there is the complicated business of the participation in the project of Camden's close friend and former pupil, Sir Robert Cotton. In his monograph on Cotton, Kevin Sharpe suggested that there was more of Cotton in the *Annales* than meets the eye, while it has long been suspected that Cotton made particular contributions to the handling of Scottish matters, on which Camden was no expert, proud as Cotton was of his supposed descent from Robert the Bruce.[11] In his 'defence of himself and of his services to the crown', Cotton claimed to have conserved many of the documents relating to Mary Queen of Scots and Scottish affairs more generally, to have abstracted them for the benefit of de Thou, and by the king's express order and warrant to have had them 'compiled into a story of Q[ueen] Eliz[abeth's] time by Mr Camden and published in print'.[12]

Cotton's involvement meets the eye very directly in ten volumes in his own manuscript library, MSS. Cotton Faustina F (in the British Library), which contain not one but the better part of two autograph recensions of the *Annales*, the second revised and set up for the printer. Some volumes in the first series are authenticated, in Cotton's hand, as 'manu Authoris scripta',[13] which seems to indicate that Camden was indeed considered to be the prime mover, but MS. Faustina F IV is headlined 'Robert Cotton Bruceus'. The first series contains many substantial corrections and interpolations, and there are passages both excised and inserted which are not to be found in any printed edition. Cotton's hand appears at many points.[14]

Since it was in all probability Camden who first stimulated Cotton's antiquarian interests, we are dealing with a somewhat circular, not to say incestuous, scenario.[15] Camden conserved a letter from the king dated 25 February 1615, ordering the publication of 'so much of the history of England in Latin as we have perused', that is from 1558 to 1588. It is addressed to Sir Robert Cotton, who is named first (but only perhaps because he was a baronet, ranking above Camden as a mere king of Arms), and Camden.[16] Yet on a neighbouring folio of the same manuscript, Camden himself has roughed out the title page for the book in block capitals, much as it would appear in print:[17]

ANNALIVM
RERUM ANGLICARVM
ET HIRERNICARVM
REGNANTE ELIZABETHA
AD
ANNVM SALVTIS
MDLXXXIX
AVTHORE GVILIELMO
CAMDENO

Camden says very clearly in his preface that he was beholden to Cotton 'for the greater part' of his sources; Smith thought 'most of them, if not all',[18] which appears to refer to the renewal of work on the project in the early years of James I, and to postdate earlier researches in which he was given privileged access by Burghley to 'the Queen's rolls, memorials and records', presumably in the Tower.[19] The Faustina manuscripts are evidence of Cotton's very full participation in what was prepared for the printer, but first of all for the benefit of de Thou in Paris, for Cotton MS. Faustina F X contains this enigmatic statement in Cotton's hand: 'The copy of the story of Queen Elizabeth from 1583 to 1587, not transcribed for myself as yet but sent unto France to Tuanum.'[20] And perhaps a letter in Camden's hand, also occurring in Faustina F X, if indeed it was addressed to Cotton (that is not clear), may tell us a little more about his role: 'Right worshipful, I send you by this gent[leman] Mr Quin: the first part of my Annales of Q. Elizabeth with manifold additions. I pray you play an Aristarcho therein and note severally what you think to be omitted or emended etc. I will follow your directions.'[21] That may bring us as close as we are every likely to get to the nature and extent of Camden's and Cotton's collaboration; that and notes in the Faustina manuscripts in Cotton's hand which are evidence of two or three stages of copy-editing for which he was responsible, and which establishes that the whole book to its conclusion in 1603 was complete by October 1613, well before the publication in 1615 of the three books which take us to 1589, and 14 years before the posthumous publication of the fourth part, *Tomus alter annalium rerum Anglicarum et Hibernicarum*.[22]

What soon made Camden's name inseparable from the *Annales*, and from the received memory of Queen Elizabeth herself, was the sense, which Camden himself helped to foster, of his commanding stature as a historian, especially as the historian of her reign. Noting in his Jacobean Annals the death in March 1617 of de Thou, Camden calls him 'historiorum nostri seculi Princeps'.[23] So there was a pecking order of historians, in which Camden intended to stand high. That must have been at least part of his motive in founding a professorship of (ancient) history in the University of Oxford, which ensured that at his death he was celebrated with a lavish collection of speeches and elegies, *Camdeni Insignia*. Oxford's public orator spoke of Elizabeth's and Camden's equal fame, and invited Camden's soul to ascend into heaven and take its place beside the great queen. One of the elegists wrote: 'Quam bene convenierunt *Camdeni* scripta et *Eliza* / Facta? O quis melius scriberet aut faceret'; another, 'Historia in Camdeno obiit, sed bis vice versa / Vivit Camdenus, vivet in Historia'. 'What a perfect match of Camden's writings and Elizabeth's deeds! Who had written better than Camden or who had done better than Elizabeth?' 'History with Camden was no more, but Camden lived in his history.'[24] Digory Wheare, Camden's first professor, naturally added his own tribute, and in 1652, when his next successor but one, Lewis Moulin, delivered his inaugural lecture, there was yet another opportunity to celebrate the memory of this great historian and 'munificentissimus fundator'.[25]

Not even Trevor-Roper thought it necessary to mention that Camden wrote in Latin, not in English, or that two of his three English translators (but not Browne, now sadly forgotten'[26]) were not very competent, including the military engineer Robert Norton, from whose *Historie of the most renowned and victorious Princesse Elizabeth*, a translation of all four books (1630), all subsequent English versions derive.[27] The edition which most deserves to be consulted for any scholarly purpose is Thomas Hearne's Latin text of 1717, based on a copy of the 1615 (London) edition of the first three parts of the book, containing notes and emendations in Camden's hand, some, as we shall see, of significance, and intended by Camden for a second edition which never materialised.[28]

III

How much did Camden's *Annales* (continuing to call it that) contribute to the legendary, even mythical, history of Elizabeth I? Not very much. His book is notably lacking in eulogistical material. The preface is only tangentially concerned with Elizabeth, since it takes the form of the rhetorical essay form known as the *ars historica*. The subject, that is to say, is not Elizabeth but History, and the references to 'that renowned Queen' and 'that incomparable Princess' are minimalist and conventional. At the end of the book, the account of Elizabeth's death is followed by an obituary notice of little more than seventy words, which would be economical for a church monument, and which is barbed by the initial statement (more than twenty-five words of the entire obit): 'The sad desire of her, which her death bequeathed to all *England*, was amply paralleled with the hopes conceived of the virtues of her famous successor.'[29]

We may contrast this with the 'Death and Character' which concludes Francis Bacon's *Historie of the raigne of king Henry the seventh* (1622), containing those memorable assessments, themselves stuff for a partly mythical Henry Tudor: 'one of the best sort of wonders – a wonder for wise men', 'a prince sad, serious, and full of thoughts and secret observations', 'what he minded he compassed'.[30] Wallace MacCaffrey tells us that Camden's book was 'conceived as a monument to the achievement of Queen Elizabeth and her government', but he is bound to admit that that purpose was accomplished 'not by praising her merits but, more obliquely, more delicately, by laying out the record of her reign'.[31] And it is true, as MacCaffrey points out, that the voice we hear in Camden's pages is not so much an authorial voice as what is at least presented as the impersonality of the historical record. The more than merely conventional wisdom is that Camden, true to his declared principles, treated his primary sources with more than ordinary respect. However *ipsissima verba* may have been deployed with the deliberate intent of protecting the author against any charge of partiality. Who can impugn the National Archives? Archivally based objectivity may consequently be the defensive fruit of censorious illiberality as much as of more liberal and modern values.

So whereas it might be assumed by anyone not investigating the matter that Camden, as the queen's pioneering historian, fostered that celebratory history of 'Gloriana' which for the most part has been in the ascendancy ever since, this was not the case. It is the English translations, over which Camden had little or no control, which are responsible for the warm post-Elizabethan glow in which the subject is, so to speak, gift-wrapped, and especially in their prefatial material. Abraham Darcie, who worked from the French of Philippe de Bellegent, *Annales des choses qui se sont passées en Angleterre et Irlande soubs le Regne de Elisabeth* (1624) and who apparently knew no Latin, rechristens the book '*The true and royall history of the famous Empresse Elizabeth ... of ... happy memory*' (1624), and blows a fanfare with a brave and intricate title page which, among other details, depicts Drake's ships off the coast of Peru, the defeat of the Armada, and such slogans as 'THE STRAITS OF GILBALTAR [*sic*]', 'ALBIONS COMFORT IBERIAS TERROR'.[32] Elizabeth was 'this heroic Empress', 'Albion's best Queen', 'the most religious, learned and prudent Empress that ever lived on earth'.[33] Not to be outdone, Norton celebrates the 'halcyon days' of 'our late glorious Sovereign of renowned memory', 'this Queen of Queens', 'an admiration to all the Princes of her time, and a pattern to all that should come after her'. Norton felt it necessary to boost Elizabeth's 'glorious fame' by supplementing Camden with extensive materials of his own, collected out of 'worthy authors'. So it is first in Norton (and not in what Camden himself wrote) that we find what Sir John Neale turned to account in his once standard biography, a legend of spontaneous outpourings of love and devotion from the subjects of this paragon of a queen: the people 'running, flying, flocking to be blessed with the sight of her gracious countenance as oft as ever she came forth in public', a monarch 'thinking it her greatest strength to be fortified with their love, and her greatest happiness to make them happy'. She was 'born to possess the hearts of her subject'.[34] Quite apart from the excesses of these prefaces, the English translators inevitably lose the laconic detachment of Camden's Tacitean Latin style. All this was consistent with the afterlife of Queen Elizabeth, which was intended as a critical yardstick with which to judge and beat her unsatisfactory Stuart successors, but it was not a stick which Camden can be said to have wielded, or even fashioned.[35]

It is not Elizabeth but Mary Queen of Scots, denounced in Holinshed's *Chronicles* in the year of her execution as 'malicious and murderous',[36] who is eulogised by Camden, especially in the succinct pen-portrait which immediately follows a dignified and in every way creditable account of the manner of her death: 'A woman most constant in her religion, of singular piety towards *God*, invincible magnanimity of mind, wisdom above her sex, and passing beauty'.[37] Compare the cameo of Mary at the block recorded by Richard Fletcher, dean of Peterborough: 'somewhat round shouldered, her face broad and fat, double-chinned ...'.[38] Earlier, Camden had told how Mary received the intimation of her trial 'ad Regiam dignitatem composite et animo sedato'; intimation of the sentence against her with 'a stable and steadfast countenance', 'a most patient mind'; and the news that she was to die the next day 'intrepide, mente composita'.[39]

We know, of course, that much of the motivation for writing the *Annales* arose from the offence occasioned by de Thou's over-dependence for his Scottish history on Buchanan. Patrick Young, James I's librarian, in recommending that Camden be commissioned to write the book, spoke of it as 'a complete history of the two queens'.[40] So although written as Annals, his book is at heart an account of the tragedy of Elizabeth and Mary Stuart. No other topic is given as much attention. For the year 1582, Camden included a letter written by Mary to Elizabeth from Sheffield, defending herself from all the charges of the last 15 years and, significantly, defending her son's interest, a document of almost three thousand words.[41] Whether or not, as Trevor-Roper has suggested, James lost interest in the later chapters, as it were a post script to February 1587 – and we cannot say with confidence that he did[42] – Camden's book subsequently descends from the high, dense tension of the climax of that tragedy. The longest, most copiously documented chapters are those which deal with the events of 1586 and 1587. Those of 1586 receive 46 pages in Norton's translation – some 25,000 words – and Mary's trial itself occupies 15 pages with more than 7,000 words, while the account of the early months of 1587 is equally copious. A more literally annalistic history, which gave equal weight to the events of every year, would by this measure have been a million words in length. So I cannot agree with MacCaffrey that 'there is no central matrix of questions' to hold the book together.

Camden's narrative of these events may not have been thickened with the sole motive of satisfying his royal master. And was it all, or essentially, Camden's narrative? It was Cotton who had sent de Thou 'the copy of the story ... from 1583 to 1587'. And at this point Cotton's close relationship with, and dependence on, that shaky lynchpin of Elizabethan conservatism, Henry Howard, under James I earl of Northampton, may assume significance.[43] Camden's account of the execution in 1572 of Northampton's brother, the duke of Norfolk (and Camden was present at both the trial and the execution), could hardly have been more favourable.[44]

Camden's *ars historica* preface, which as so often with Renaissance historiography may have scant bearing on the text which it introduces, has much to say about truth as the only thing of value with which the historian should be concerned, and declares that the author had written without fear of danger from 'present power'. So Trevor-Roper has written of 'this magnificently uncourtly work'.[45] Camden could not be sure that James would be delighted with what he had written. He was afraid that the king would take exception to his favourable obit for his mother's arch-enemy, Walsingham, and in a letter to a foreign correspondent he wrote that the king 'praeter expectationem' had personally ordered the book's publication. He was also very diffident about the publication of the final part, suggesting with a conventionally modest trope that James might like to issue it over his own name.[46]

So Camden's sympathetic treatment of Mary was perhaps a not insincere expression of his own feelings and convictions. It is apparent that he (or Cotton) corrected Buchanan with discreet use of the *Defence of the honour of the right highe, mightye and noble princesse, Marie queene of Scotlande*, written by her servant John Leslie, bishop of Ross, and first published in 1569, a work regarded by a great modern authority as rather more reliable than the 'flagrantly and deliberately mendacious' Buchanan.[47] Moreover, we know how much Camden loathed the earl of Leicester, invariably attributing to him the basest and most self-regarding of motives, giving him a distinctly Tacitean 'character',[48] and above all making him the arch-architect of a virtual conspiracy against the Scottish queen and her title to succeed: Leicester, 'qui credebatur de praevertenda legitima successione cogitare' ('plotting to divert the legitimate line of succession').[49] And Camden, a prominent member of a religiously conservative Westminster circle, detested no less the Puritans who were Leicester's allies and agents, referring to them contemptuously as 'Protestantes effervescentes', 'Zeloti'; and he is critical of the 'declamationes et exclamationes' against Mary of what he calls, ironically, the 'vehement', ecclesiastical sort of persons.[50] The traitor Babington is quoted as referring to Mary's keeper, Sir Amyas Paulet, as a Puritan and a 'mere Leicesterian'.[51] Trevor-Roper suggests that Camden's detestation of Leicester was the exception to prove the rule of his judicious impartiality in all other respects.[52] I would argue that it was an essential component of the conceptual structure of the work.

The 'Leicesterians' were contrasted with wiser and more detached observers, 'aequi boni rerum aestimatores', who thought that Mary had been dealt with too sharply.[53] Although Camden reports the apparently almost universal joy with which the city of London received the news of the arrest of Anthony Babington and his fellow conspirators, he emphasises Mary's utter ignorance of many of these developments, and the centrality of Walsingham's *agent provocateur* role, 'thus far had Walsingham spun this thread himself alone'; and he leaves us with the impression that the destruction of Mary was not something consensual, but a high level stitch-up involving a minority of the political nation.[54] Here Camden, the first Elizabethan historian, comes close to turning conventional Elizabethan history upside down while it was still in the womb.

It appears that Camden could not win. If he was in danger from 'present power' for a not unfavourable account of Walsingham as a kind of English Brutus, 'a true Roman', his appreciative descriptions and characterisations of Mary Queen of Scots may have cost him dear in more popular estimation.[55] Smith in his late seventeenth-century *Vita* reported Camden's reluctance to pursue his history beyond 1588. It was primarily 'the censures he met with in the business of Mary Queen of Scots' which deterred him from proceeding any farther along such a troublesome road.[56] Later, his friend Hearne quoted a critic as reporting that Camden himself had confessed that James I's directions had led him 'rather to vindicate the honour and integrity of the King's mother ... than to do right for a mistress, who had from a schoolmaster made him the first king at arms'. This charge does seem to have some plausibility, although Hearne, who was fairminded but a fairminded Tory and anti-Puritan, denied it. 'This is very unjustly alleged against Mr Camden.'[57]

IV

Let us examine in a little more detail Camden's account of the final act of the Elizabeth–Mary Queen of Scots drama. It will be of particular interest to discover Camden's first and second thoughts about Elizabeth's reaction to the news of the execution, from which generations of historians have attempted to infer her intentions in the matter; and to investigate his account of the role of Lord Burghley in what Camden presented as Leicester's near-conspiracy, but in which the Lord Treasurer, Camden's patron whom he always presented in a favourable light, appears from other sources to have been up to his neck.

Sentence had already been pronounced against the Queen of Scots and confirmed in parliament and announced in a proclamation. (Camden says nothing about the public acclamation with which the proclamation was received.[58]) But execution, in a double sense, was still required, entailing the most painful decision of Elizabeth's life, a decision to be taken in an unfavourable diplomatic limelight. Camden would have us believe that a reluctant Elizabeth was only persuaded to sign Mary's death warrant by rumours of fresh plots, 'scarecrows', spread not only by some courtiers but 'saucily' by preachers and common people.[59] (He could have had in mind the inflammatory speech which the radical Job Throckmorton, alias 'Martin Marprelate', delivered to parliament on 4 November 1586.[60]) So it was that a queen sick with indecision delivered to Secretary William Davison a written instruction to have a warrant drawn up for the execution, merely to be held in reserve against further dangers, charging him to keep the matter secret, an order which she thought better of the very next day: but too late, since the warrant was already drawn and sealed, and the council, 'apt to believe what they desired', had been assured that the queen had commanded it to be executed.[61]

The warrant was accordingly conveyed to Fotheringhay by the clerk of the council, Robert Beale, Mary's 'bitter adversary' (but better described, by a modern historian as the resident expert on the Scottish queen) and on 8 February duly put into execution.[62] Mary's death was martyr-like and full of dignity. With a neat piece of footwork, Camden adds that through her death both queens obtained what they most desired: Mary, posthumously, the English succession, Elizabeth the preservation of true religion.[63]

Camden's account may be compared with versions of events recorded, independently, by Davison and Beale.[64] There are points of agreement. Beale agrees with Camden that it was Leicester who had proposed making Mary 'away by poison', which we know not only Elizabeth but the international community thought would have been the better solution to the problem.[65] But other details differ. For example, Beale insists that it was not he but his servant George Digby who physically conveyed the warrant to Fotheringhay, and Beale supplies details of the itinerary and attendant expenses.[66] That hardly matters, but other differences are significant, and they mostly take the form of tactful omissions and silences on Camden's part. Both Beale and Davison testify to Elizabeth's persistent desire to have Mary secretly murdered, according to the spirit of the Bond of Association of October 1584, 'another course', but an option with doubtful precedents (Edward II, Richard II) which Beale was still forced to ponder when he arrived at Fotheringhay.[67]

Camden prints some of Davison's 'Apologetical Discourse' to Walsingham, but with significant omissions. According to Davison, on 1 February, a pleasant morning, Davison had been called in from a walk in the park by a relaxed queen who told him he should do that more often, and who was perfectly aware that she was signing among other papers the fatal warrant, discussing with the secretary the necessity of an execution and sending him on his way with that famous bit of black humour (which Camden could not resist repeating) that he should tell the news to Walsingham, who was on sick leave, 'because the grief thereof would kill him outright'. From these accounts it is less than clear whether the queen subsequently changed her mind and, even if she did, Beale's and Davison's recollection was that she wanted nothing more to do with the matter, while Davison further recalled that two days later the queen told him about a dream that Mary had been executed, and confirmed with an oath that it should be done; while she still preferred that 'other course', assassination, which is all that we hear about this episode from Camden. On 1 February Davison had gone straight to Burghley (according to one version, finding Burghley in company with Leicester in Burghley's chamber), and to Lord Chancellor Bromley, who had applied the great seal at five o'clock the same day, according to Davison's testimony.[68] Burghley resolved to involve the whole Privy Council, which met at ten or eleven o'clock on 3 February in his own inner chamber at court. In addition to Davison, nine councillors were present to sign the commission and the accompanying letters ordering action to be taken,[69] of which Beale preserved a draft copy, with the additional signature of Walsingham, obtained from his sick-bed; and, according to Beale, 'her Majesty['s] hand was also in the top'.[70] The most important of these circumstances was the central and almost conspiratorial role of Lord Burghley, whom Camden kept out of the picture altogether, except in his digest of Davison's Apologetical Discourse, containing what was no more than Davison's allegation, that Burghley and the rest of the council accepted joint responsibility for hastening the execution.[71]

If Elizabeth's strategy was to exonerate herself in international, and especially Scottish, eyes by shifting the blame for Mary's execution on to other shoulders, which is how we must interpret her various prevarications and pronouncements, the self-preserving concern of Privy Councillors, and of Burghley above all, was in their turn to evade their shared culpability (if culpability it was). Beale and Davison were clear on this, and on the intention to make Davison almost wholly responsible. This is very fully and variously documented, not least in a secret letter from Burghley's own hand in which he appears to bare his soul.[72] Camden was present at Davison's trial in Star Chamber and furnishes a lengthy, if select, account of it (extensively emended in Cotton's hand in MS. Faustina F X, fo. 175). If we had no other account of the proceedings we should know that the nub of the matter was Davison's word against the queen's (did she or did she not tell him to delay the matter?) and against Burghley's (had he or had he not shown Burghley the green light?), and this meant for the unfortunate secretary what we nowadays call a hiding to nothing: imprisonment in the Tower and a fine of 10,000 marks, a sentence later remitted. Camden presents Davison as a naive fall-guy (which he was certainly not), no courtier and brought on stage to play a puppet-like role.[73] That was to incriminate his senior colleagues, Burghley above all, but that is not a moral that Camden chose to draw. Both the very hostile speech at Davison's trial of Lord Lumley and the relatively favourable speech of Lord Grey, both of which Camden shares with us, suggest that it was really the Privy Council, shall we say 'the government', which was in the dock, and for something like *lèse-majesté*, for Grey thought it was Davison's simple duty to have revealed such weighty matters to the council 'whom it specially concerned to know', while Lumley thought it a contempt against the queen for the council to meet in her very palace and to resolve a matter of such consequence without her advice or knowledge.[74] Beale recorded in his own hand: 'After that Mr Davison was thus proceeded with, it was thought that the Lords of the Council that were privy to the sending down of the commission should have been called into Star Chamber. But first the L[ord] Treas[urer] had set to his hand to a writing whereby he confessed he had been abused by Mr Davison, which was perused as evidence against him.' In a separate note, Beale's story was that the Privy Councillors concerned had signed a joint statement, which Elizabeth was able to show to the Scottish ambassador.[75] But Camden, who in Latin always writes of 'Consiliarii' (individual councillors) rather than 'Consilium' (a corporate body) was either unaware of these constitutional implications or not inclined to make anything of them.[76] (But nor, until just the other day, was anyone else.[77])

And what of the queen? In a justly famous passage, Camden describes her displeasure against Davison and her great grief for the death of her cousin as 'either conceived or pretended', 'iram ... et dolorem ... conceperit aut prae-setulerit', a piece of Tacitean history if ever there was one. But in the revised edition which he intended Camden crossed out 'aut praesetulerit' and altered 'conceperit' to 'concepit'. After all, there was to be no doubt about the genu-ineness of Elizabeth's grief and anger.[78] Whose hand are we seeing here, and elsewhere in the narrative of 1587: Camden's or Cotton's? The answer seems to be both. On folio 176v of MS. Faustina F X we find the relevant passage in Cotton's hand, complete with 'aut prae se tulerit'; on folio 177r the same passage in Camden's hand omits 'conceperit'. Elizabeth *only* pretended. But Cotton's hand has erased 'praesetulerit' and has inserted the familiar 'conce-perit, aut prae se tulerit'.[79] What appear to have been Camden's final thoughts on the matter need not have been composed with a timid glance over his shoulder at 'present power'. In his preface he firmly stated the self-denying ordinance (which he did not always remember) that it was wrong to second-guess 'the hidden meanings of Princes'. 'Things secret and abstruse I have not pried into.'[80]

V

The moral? Sir John Neale observed: 'grief and anger: whether genuine or forged, it is for us to judge.'[81] (Did he mean perhaps 'it is *not* for us to judge'?) History is what the historian may choose to make of it, without necessarily perpetrating gross falsification; and the response of the reader is part of it. Not everyone will read Camden's *Annales* as I have read it.[82]

We owe to Camden ample material for both favourable and unfavourable characterisations of Elizabeth. We also owe to her first historian our sense of the absolute centrality to the Elizabethan story of the so long deferred question of Mary Queen of Scots. Camden made sure that Leicester would be vilified for more than 300 years to come, while he did a good job for his patron by setting in a block of concrete, which modern historiography has only very recently broken,[83] a Lord Burghley of utter probity and statesmanship, 'an exceeding wise man' – 'his singular wisdom' – 'who always had a great care for the safety of the commonwealth and religion'.[84] But like Polonius of whom he was the prototype, Camden's Burghley was not always visible behind the arras, one of the more boring characters in Elizabethan history. Camden's *Annales* is, for its

time and perdaps for any time, a remarkable work of history.[85] But it was the
influential first word, not the last word on the subject, and it is definitely not
the case that it's all there and what isn't there won't hurt. And Camden was
certainly not the stuff of which Elizabethan myths of *Gloriana* are made.

NOTES

1 D. R. Woolf, 'Erudition and the idea of history in Renaissance England', *Renaissance Quarterly* 40 (1987): 11–48; D. R. Woolf, *Reading History in Early Modern England* (Cambridge, 2000), p. 23.

2 Thomas Smith, *V. Cl. Gulielmi Camdeni et Illustrium Virorum Epistolae* (1691), p. 31.

3 F. J. Levy, *Tudor Historical Thought* (San Marino, Calif., 1967), p. 280.

4 The following editions are cited in what follows: *Annales Rervm Anglicarvm et Hibernicarvm Regnante Elizabethae ad Annum Salvtis MDLXXXIX* (London, 1615); tr. Abraham Darcie, *Annales: The true and royall history of Elizabeth* (London, 1625), hereafter 'Darcie'; tr. Thomas Browne, *Tomus alter et idem; Or the historie of the life and reigne of Elizabeth* (bk 4, London, 1629), hereafter 'Browne'; tr. Robert Norton, *The Historie of the Most Renowned and Victorious Princesse Elizabeth* (1630), hereafter 'Norton 1630'; a second edition of Norton, 1635, hereafter 'Norton 1635'; Thomas Hearne, ed., *Guilielmi Camdeni Annales Regvm Anglicarvm et Hibernicarvm Regnante Elizabetha*, 3 vols (Oxford, 1717), hereafter 'Hearne'; Wallace T. MacCaffrey, ed., *William Camden: The History of ... Princess Elizabeth Late Queen of England, Selected Chapters* (Chicago, Ill., 1970), hereafter 'MacCaffrey'.

5 'Inchoatio invida, continuatio labor, finis odium'; Camden to Jacques-Auguste de Thou, 10 Aug. 1612, quoted in D. R. Woolf, *The Idea of History in Early Stuart England* (Toronto, 1990), p. 294 n. 50.

6 MacCaffrey, p. 3; Trinity College Cambridge, MS. R. 5. 20, fo. 2.

7 Witness the modern preparedness to acknowledge John Fletcher as the co-author of 'Shakespeare's' *Henry VIII* (*King Henry VIII, or All is True By William Shakespeare and John Fletcher*, ed. Jay L. Halio [Oxford, 1999]).

8 Hugh Trevor-Roper, *Queen Elizabeth's First Historian* (London, 1971) repr., Trevor-Roper, *Renaissance Essays* (London, 1985), pp. 121–48.

9 On the injury done to James's honour by his mother's execution, see Susan Doran, 'Revenge her foul and most unnatural murder? The impact of Mary Stewart's execution on Anglo-Scottish relations', *History*, 85 (2000): 589–612.

10 Browne mentions Camden by name only in his Appendix. The copy in the Cambridge University Library, Syn.6.62.6, bears on its spine the title 'Browne's life of Elizabeth'.

11 Kevin Sharpe, *Sir Robert Cotton, 1586–1631* (Oxford, 1979), pp. 89–95.

12 Woolf, *The Idea of History*, pp. 115–19; Nigel Ramsay, 'Sir Robert Cotton's services to the Crown: a paper written in self-defence', in C. J. Wright, ed., *Sir Robert Cotton as Collector: Essays on an early Stuart courtier and his legacy* (London, 1997), pp. 68–80. In the same collection (pp. 12–13), Kevin Sharpe felt even more confident about the case for Cotton, wondering 'how much of what scholars persist in calling Camden's *Annales* was in fact written, drafted, or corrected by Cotton'.

13 See, for example, fo. 2 of MS. Faustina F III, in Cotton's hand: 'Annales Gulielmi Cambdeni ab Anno 1593 ad An 1603 manu Authoris scripta'. But this volume is in places heavily corrected by Cotton.

14 A particularly notable example is the account of Elizabeth's death, which in MS. Faustina F III, fos 215v–16r, bears much evidence of Cotton's interventions, establishing the printed text of Book 4, *Tomus Alter* (1627).

15 Colin G. C. Tite, *The Manuscript Library of Sir Robert Cotton: The Panizzi Lectures 1993* (London, 1994), pp. 4–5.

16 Trinity College, Cambridge, MS. R.5.20, fo. 112v.

17 *Ibid.*, fo. 114v.

18 MacCaffrey, p. 4; Smith's *Vita*, translated in Edmund Gibson, ed., *Camden's Britannia* (London, 1695), sig. C 2r, col. 2.

19 MacCaffrey, p. 3.

20 BL, MS. Cotton Faustina F X, fo. 254.

21 *Ibid.*, fo. 255. And see a note on fo. 163v of MS. Faustina F X, addressed to 'Mr Taylor' (in the print shop?), which refers to 'Sir R pleasure' about the arrangement of some material: 'I pray know Sir R mind herein.'

22 References to copy-editing readings ('perlegeri', 'regnoscere', 'relegere') in Aug.–Oct. 1613, Oct.–Nov. 1618, Mar.–May 1619, and May–June 1620 are found on the preliminary folios of MSS. Faustina F I, II, III, IV ('the first Copy after mended'), V and VI ('the first Copy corrected and enlarged').

23 Trinity College, Cambridge, MS. R. 5. 20, fo. 20v.

24 *Camdeni Insignia* (Oxford, 1624), sigs 4, 4v, D2, G2v.

25 Oratio auspicalis, cui subjuncta est laudatio clarissimi viri GUL. CAMBDENI DICENTE LUDOVICO MOLINAEO (Oxford, 1652), p. 20.

26 Browne worked in part from 'the original manuscript, which I have perused', 'an Authentic Copy, and under Mr Camden's own hand', presumably some of the Faustina manuscripts, which he would have consulted in Cotton's library. (Browne, sigs Hhh 4r, I iiv, Mmm 3r–4v.)

27 Including the 1675 edition, which claimed to be the third, 'amended' and made more 'agreeable to the modern (though not fantastical) expression'. MacCaffrey used the 1688 edition of this touched-up Norton version, which he supposed to be an independent and anonymous translation.

28 Deposited by Hearne in the Bodleian Library, where it is MS. Smith 2 (Bodleian Catalogue, sub Rawlinson K).

29 Browne, 384. The Latin original reads: 'Tristissimum desiderium, quod Anglis reliquit, lenivit spes optima de Regis Jacobi, successoris virtutibus concepta' (Hearne, vol. 3, p. 912).

30 Francis Bacon, *The History of the Reign of King Henry VII*, ed. Brian Vickers (Cambridge, 1998), pp. 196, 202, 204.

31 MacCaffrey, p. xxxi.

32 In his 'explication' of this frontispiece, Darcie expatiates: 'The Port of Gibaltar's straits, sure can tell, | How that a Spanish Fleet (by DRAKE) there fell ... | To end, the Fleet of Eighty-eight doth show, | England was aided in that overthrow | Given to Spain, by God whose potent hand | Preserved ELIZA'S glory, and her land. | Gainst those that owe true Religion spight, | Both seas and earth, for Albion's cause will fight.'

33 Darcie, prefatory material.

34 Norton 1630, sigs A–A4. Norton's panegyric was extended in the preface to the 1635

edition. See J. E. Neale, *Queen Elizabeth* (1934 and many subsequent editions), ch. 13.

35 The 'critical yardstick' thesis is critically reviewed in John Watkins, '"Old Bess in the Ruff": Remembering Elizabeth I, 1625–1660', *English Literary Renaissance* 30 (2000): 95–116. Darcie addressed dedicatory epistles to both James I and Prince Charles, extolling the latter as 'the fame and honour of this spacious hemisphere, and Great Britain's both help and solace, by your princely valour and constant virtue no less dreaded and admired abroad than feared and loved at home'.

36 *Holinshed's Chronicles* (London, 1808), vol 4, p. 897. Sometimes Mary's virtues, 'femina prudens et provida', are balanced by Camden against those of Elizabeth, 'illa consultrix et provida femina' (Hearne, vol. 1, pp. 85, 111). But elsewhere the weaknesses characteristic of their shared sex are somewhat chauvinistically attributed to both ladies. See, for example, MacCaffrey, p. 178.

37 So in Norton 1630, bk 3, p. 112; in Camden's Latin, 'Femina in Religione sua [note the gently provocative 'in religione sua' – *her* religion, not mine] constantissima, eximia in Deum pietate, invicta animi magnitudine, prudentia supra sexum, formaque venustissima.' (Hearne, vol. 2, p. 537.) Camden's Latin means 'in her appearance most lovely', and Norton's 'of passing beauty' seems to be a backhanded variant on Darcie's 'of surpassing beauty' (bk 3, p. 206)! But 'prudentia supra sexum, formaque venustissima' is absent from MS. Faustina F X, fo. 173r.

38 BL, MS. Add. 48027, fo. 690v.

39 Norton, 1630, bk 3, pp. 103, 109, Hearne, vol 2, p. 533.

40 Woolf, *The Idea of History*, pp. 117–18.

41 Norton 1630, bk 3, pp. 16–19; Hearne, vol 2, pp. 387–93. The original, in Mary's holograph and in French, is in BL, MS. Cotton Caligula C VII, fo. 54 *et seq.*, whence printed, Prince Alexandre Labanoff, *Lettres, Instructions et Mémoires de Marie Stuart* (London, 1844), vol. 4, pp. 318–38: a good example of Cotton's good offices in respect of the correspondence between Mary Queen of Scots and Elizabeth.

42 Trevor-Roper, *Queen Elizabeth's First Historian*, p. 19; Woolf, *The Idea of History*, p. 119.

43 Sharpe, *Sir Robert Cotton*, *passim*; Tite, *The Manuscript Library*, pp. 6–7.

44 Hearne, vol. 2, p. 229: 'qui pro innata bonitate', rendered by Norton 1630 (bk 1, p. 131) 'his innated goodness'.

45 MacCaffrey, p. 5; Trevor-Roper, *Queen Elizabeth's First Historian*, p. 20.

46 Camden to Joannes de Laet, 18 June 1616, Smith, *Vita et Epistolae*, p. 167; Camden to 'N.N.', *ibid.*, p. 351.

47 Gordon Donaldson, *Mary Queen of Scots* (London, 1974), pp. 148, 182, 185.

48 'In a word, people talked openly in his Commendation, but privately he was ill spoken of by the greater part' (MacCaffrey, p. 330). Cf. the characterisation of Mutianus in Tacitus, tr. Henry Savile, *The Ende of Nero and the Beginning of Galba* (1591): 'openly praiseworthy, his secret actions were ill spoken of' (I owe this to Lisa Richardson). The motive which Camden attributed to Leicester in helping to entrap the duke of Norfolk is no less Tacitean: 'ex titillante imperii et gloriae cupiditate' (Hearne, vol. 2, p. 458).

49 *Ibid.*, vol. 2, p. 423.

50 *Ibid.*, vol. 1, p.110; vol. 3, p. 911; vol. 2, p. 517.

51 Norton 1630, bk 3, p. 74. In Camden's Latin, quoting Babington (Hearne, vol. 2, p. 475), Mary was 'in custodiam Amicii Powletti Puritani, mere Leicestriani'.

52 Trevor-Roper, *Queen Elizabeth's First Historian*, pp. 28–30.

53 Hearne, vol. 2, p. 517; elsewhere characterised as 'prudentiores autem et opulentiores' (*ibid.*, vol. 1, p. 110).

54 Norton 1630, bk 3, p. 78.

55 An entire paragraph, missing from all previous editions with the exception of Norton 1635, and supplied by Hearne (vol. 2, p. 550), tells how after the execution of Mary Queen of Scots, messengers and spies were sent to Scotland to sound out James VI's intentions and to put the best face on what had happened. They were to explain Leicester's motivation and characterise Walsingham as 'a man that bare a true *Roman* spirit'. (Norton 1635, p. 352.)

56 'The Life of Mr Camden', in Gibson, *Camden's Britannia*, sig. c2r, col. 1.

57 Hearne, vol. 1, sig. a2.

58 John Stow in successive editions of his *Annales* and *Summarie of Chronicles* recorded 'the great and wonderful rejoicing of the people of all sorts, as manifestly appeared by the ringing of bells, making of bonfires, and singing of Psalms in every of the streets and lanes of the City [scil., of London].' (*Annales* [1592], p. 1260).

59 *Ibid.*, vol. 2, p. 529: 'terriculamentis et formidolosis argumentis'.

60 T. E. Hartley (ed.), *Proceedings in the Parliaments of Elizabeth I, vol. 2: 1584–1589* (Leicester, 1995), pp. 228–32. But Camden did not have to invent this atmosphere of panic. See J. E. Neale, *Elizabeth I and her Parliaments, 1584–1601* (London, 1957), p. 136. William Davison's nineteenth-century biographer, who imputed 'personal hatred' of Mary to Elizabeth, thought this purported danger 'chimerical', and that the rumours were deliberately spread by the queen's 'agents'. (H. N. Nicolas, *Life of William Davison* (London, 1823), pp. 108–9.) Father John Morris S.J., as one might expect, has a similar interpretation, printing evidence from the Lansdowne MSS. (no. 51) that as far away as Devon there was a 'hue and cry for the Queen of Scots, who is fled' (*The Letter-Books of Sir Amias Poulet* [London, 1874], 354–6).

61 In the edition of 1615, Camden wrote that it was those who were sworn to the lynch-law of the Bond of Association of October 1584, 'illisque in Associationem juratis', who were 'prone quod voluerunt credentibus'. In his revisions (Hearne, vol. 2, p. 532), they became 'Regiis consiliariisque'.

62 MacCaffrey, p. 284; Mark Taviner, 'Robert Beale and the Elizabethan polity', unpublished Ph.D. thesis, University of St Andrews (2000), p. 209.

63 This passage is absent from MS. Faustina F X, fo. 174.

64 Beale's record is in BL, MS. Add. 48027. Davison's most valuable testimony is contained in his letter to Walsingham written from the Tower on 20 February 1587, of which a number of versions survive, cited here from BL, MS. Harleian 290, fos 218–21. Three versions were printed by Nicolas, *Davison*, pp. 231–85.

65 BL, MS. Add. 48027, fos 402v, 640v.

66 *Ibid.*, fo. 636v.

67 *Ibid.*, fos 639v–40r. Morris prints from a copy originally made by Thomas Hearne (*Letter-Books of Sir Amias Poulet*, pp. 359–62) the letter to Paulet which Walsingham and Davison were obliged to write on 1 February, in effect proposing the option of assassination, together with Paulet's indignant response: 'But God forbid that I should make so foul a shipwreck of my conscience.'

68 Nicolas, *Davison*, pp. 261, 300.

69 Burghley, the earl of Derby, Leicester, the Lord Admiral Charles Howard, the Lord

Chamberlain Hunsdon, Lord Cobham, Sir Francis Knollys, Sir Christopher Hatton, John Wolley (whose signature to the commission, however, is lacking) – hardly a cabal of 'Leicesterians'.

70 BL, MS. Add. 48027, fos 642r–6r. In the earl of Kent's copy of the commission, acquired by Lambeth Palace Library in 1996, Beale has entered an imitation of the queen's signature in the top left-hand corner.

71 MacCaffrey, p. 296.

72 BL, MS. Lansdowne 108, fo. 90. See Neale, *Elizabeth I and her Parliaments*, pp. 141–2.

73 MacCaffrey, p. 295; in Camden's Latin (Hearne, vol. 2, pp. 544–5) Davison was 'vir ingenue bonus, in aulicis artibus minus versatus'.

74 MacCaffrey, pp. 293–5; for a full transcript of the trial, one of four amongst Beale's papers, see BL, MS. Add. 48027, fos 666–74; Davison's own copy is in BL, MS. Harleian 290, fos 224–39.

75 MS. Add. 48027, fos 675, 690v.

76 For example (in the context of Davison's trial) 'nisi Consiliariis', 'Consiliaros omnes' (Hearne, vol. 2, p. 541.) Note that one of the documents in the case speaks of the sending down of the sentence as 'the general act of her Majesty's Council' (Nicolas, *Davison*, p. 289).

77 John Guy, 'Monarchy and counsel: models of the state', in Patrick Collinson, ed., *Short Oxford History of the British Isles: The sixteenth century* (Oxford, 2001); Taviner, 'Robert Beale'.

78 Hearne, vol. 2, p. 546. 'Aut prae se tulerit' appeared in the 1615 edition, but not in the Leiden edition of 1625, which (p. 501) has simply 'concepit'. Norton 1630 has 'or, pretended' (bk 3, p. 120), but Darcie (bk 3, p. 217) omits it.

79 Similarly, Camden had written of the beginning of the story, in 1568, that Elizabeth had, as it seemed, 'ut videbatur', misliked the insolence of the Scots in deposing their queen. But among his revisions, Camden later struck out 'ut videbatur' (Hearne, vol. 1, p. 171).

80 MacCaffrey, pp. 5–6.

81 Neale, *Elizabeth I and her Parliaments*, p. 137.

82 Woolf, *Reading History in Early Modern England*.

83 Stephen Alford, *The Early Elizabethan Polity: William Cecil and the British succession crisis, 1558–1569* (Cambridge, 1998).

84 MacCaffrey, pp. 11, 40, 116.

85 Chapter 9 in this volume; Patrick Collinson, 'History', in Michael Hattaway, ed., *A Companion to English Renaissance Literature and Culture* (Oxford, 2000), pp. 58–70.

Chapter 11

John Stow and nostalgic antiquarianism

John Stow might have anticipated Peter Laslett by 350 years, calling his *Survey of London The World We Have Lost*. While Stow never employed the expression 'Merry England', his preoccupation with 'that declining time of charity'[1] makes his book the most extended treatment of the Merry England refrain in all English literature: a mythical story about a world enjoying plenty, but attentive to want, a socially harmonious world consolidated and sweetened by charity, a festive world, in which generosity spilled over freely from the full cup of seasonal pastimes, an open world, and, above all, a religious world. Stow's *Survey* poses on almost every page the questions which all Merry England studies are bound to address.[2] Did Merry England ever exist? And if it did, are selective memories of its fall, or demise, to be trusted? For the myth of the life of Merry England depends upon the companion myth of its death. Later ages placed Merry England in the very years in which Stow lived and constructed his partly mythical London, while still later generations located it in epochs which Stow never lived to see. As Sir Keith Thomas has explained, Merry England was always the day before yesterday.[3] In Victorian fiction, it was associated with the stage coach in its last days, before steam put an end to it, as, for example, in Thackeray's *The Newcomes*: 'The island rang, as yet, with the tooting horns and rattling teams of mail-coaches; a gay sight was the road in merry England in those days.'[4]

Ian Archer has written on the Elizabethan London which Stow somehow failed to notice in his chapter, 'The nostalgia of John Stow'.[5] But it is not my intention to compare Stow's nostalgic perceptions with reality. This essay has the more limited aim of scrutinising and nuancing what might be called

Originally published in *Imagining Early Modern London: Perceptions and portrayals of the City from Stow to Strype*, edited by J. Merritt (Cambridge, 2001). Reproduced by permission of Cambridge University Press.

Stow's selective nostalgia, relating it to a religious position and religious attitudes which were evidently in a process of evolution throughout the forty years of his antiquarian activity. To this I shall add two contrasted points of contemporary reference: Richard Carew's *Survey of Cornwall*, where present-tenseness contrasts with the past-tenseness of Stow's constantly reiterated 'of old time'; and William Lambarde's *Perambulation of Kent*, where the crudest anti-Romanism stands in stark contrast to Stow's religious conservatism. And yet, not only did Lambarde's *Perambulation* provide Stow with the model for his *Survey*. Stow referred to Lambarde as 'my loving friend': a touching tribute to the latitude of shared antiquarian enthusiasm.[6]

I

Although Stow's nostalgia is suffused throughout his text, including the ward-by-ward itinerary of the city which accounts for its bulk, its most explicit and intense expression comes in his descriptions of 'Orders and Customes', 'Sports and Pastimes', the military musters held at midsummer (the Standing and Marching Watches), and the section headed 'Honor of Citizens, and worthinesse of men in the same'. These self-contained cultural-historical essays depended on the *Descriptio Nobilissimae Civitatis Londoniae* which prefaced William Fitzstephen's life of Thomas Becket, which Stow also prints in full as an appendix, 'the said Author being rare'.

Stow's Fitzstephen was not only 'rare'. He wrote in the late twelfth century, so that while we are distanced from the first edition of Stow's *Survey* by four centuries, rather more than four hundred years separated Stow from Fitzstephen. Yet Stow compresses the centuries. Having quoted Fitzstephen at length on orders and customs, 'the estate of things in his time', Stow writes: 'whereunto may be added the present, by conference whereof, the alteration will easily appeare'. The implication is of a world which had remained more or less static until a vaguely defined moment which seems to correspond to the years of Stow's own childhood, the 1530s. The great changes which he alleges, and regrets, had all or mostly happened in his own lifetime, not in the four centuries which distanced him from his rare author. Now, no more than Stow was Fitzstephen a kind of historical camera, recording a series of accurate images of the real London of his day. His *Descriptio* was an early rhetorical exercise in praise of famous cities, a long tradition culminating in the many cartographical and literary descriptions of Renaissance cities, of which Stow appears to have had no knowledge, or none which he discloses.[7] So Stow's principal source is itself an unrealistic, rose-tinted picture of the London he thought he had lost.

Fitzstephen's London is made the occasion for some of Stow's sharpest complaints about the new London. According to Fitzstephen, the only plagues to afflict the city, 'solae pestes', were immoderate drinking and frequent house fires. Stow thought that in these respects there had been some improvement, since the poor could no longer afford strong beers and wines and most new building was in stone and tile. But now there were new 'enormities', especially encroachments on highways, lanes, and common ground, and the problem of heavy, uncontrolled traffic: 'for the world runs on wheeles with many, whose parents were glad to goe on foote'.[8] What Fitzstephen recorded, or alleged, about the great men of his time keeping house in the city, 'as if they were Citizens and free men of London', provoked Stow's lament for the decline of that charity 'of olde time given', recalling what he himself had seen as a child, over the garden wall: Thomas Cromwell's servants doling out bread, meat and drink to as many as two hundred persons every day, 'for he observed that auncient and charitable custome as all prelates, noble men, or men of honour and worship his predecessors had done before him'.[9]

Above all, it was Fitzstephen who inspired Stow's fervently nostalgic calendrical rehearsal of traditional customs and pastimes, all supplied in the past tense. This festive calendar was more civic, less religious and liturgical, than the structure of the festive half of the year described by Hutton in his *Rise and Fall of Merry England*, or by Eamon Duffy in *The Stripping of the Altars*.[10] But it began with Christmas, lords of misrule in every great house, presiding over 'fine and subtle disguisinges, Maskes and Mummeries', everyone's house and the parish churches decked with holly, ivy, bays, and 'whatsoever the season of the yeare aforded to be greene'. This sort of thing went on until Candlemas. The only springtime custom which Stow described was the practice of fetching twisted trees or withies out of the woods into people's houses, which must have been what in other parts of the country was called 'palming'. Then to Mayday and Maytime, a wholly secular celebration.

> I find also that in the moneth of May, the Citizens of London of all estates, lightly in every Parish, or sometimes two or three parishes ioyning together, had their severall mayings, and did fetch in Maypoles, with diuerse warlike shewes, with good Archers, Morice daunsers, and other deuices for pastime all the day long, and towards the Euening they had stage playes, and Bonefiers in the streets.[11]

Midsummer was marked by standing and marching watches, as many as two thousand men and more processing through the streets 'all in bright harnes', with drums and fifes, trumpeters on horseback, together with pageants and morris dancers. Here Stow's chronology is more exact. The Midsummer Watch came to its historical climax on 8 May 1539, when as many as fifteen thousand citizens dressed up and marched from London to Westminster 'in three great battailes'. But boom was followed by bust. Henry VIII – ostensibly considering the heavy cost to the citizens, but also security – suppressed the watch, which was briefly but abortively revived in 1548. This was a matter close to Stow's heart. In his *Summarie of Englyshe Chronicles* he had recorded that in 1564, 'through the earnest suite of the armourers', a standing watch was held at midsummer (no marching), which he implied was a poor show, but as chargeable as the marching watches of the past. This was repeated in 1565 and 1567, but Stow has no reference to the watches after that; nor, as Ian Archer has pointed out, to the lord mayor's inaugural show which filled the vacuum left by the midsummer watches, leaving the quite misleading impression that now there were no more costly and spectacular shows to liven up London's streets.[12]

One thing conspicuously missing from Stow's mostly secular London calendar is the feast of Corpus Christi. Corpus Christi celebrations in provincial towns and cities such as Coventry, Beverley and York, and the great play cycles performed in the context of the feast, were a cultural manifestation of a manufacturing and trading society composed of crafts, which were in competition, the plays serving, in Mervyn James's words, to defuse the 'tension between social wholeness and social differentiation', while sometimes occasioning the very conflict they were intended to prevent.[13] Stow's silence on the subject is a reminder that while the economic fabric of London, no less than that of provincial towns, was one of crafts and guilds, its political structure was composed of wards; and that the great London play cycles (now sadly lost) had no basis in the city guilds and no connection with Corpus Christi, but were organised and controlled by the city fathers, and performed by professional actors, often for the entertainment of royalty.[14] Stow reproduces Fitzstephen's account of summer and winter sports and pastimes, including skating, and merely adds 'these or the like exercises haue beene continued till our time', specifying stage plays, with a few meagre details. 'Of late time in place of those Stage playes, hath beene vsed Comedies, Tragedies, Enterludes, and Histories, both true and fayned: For the acting whereof certaine publike places haue beene erected': which, notoriously, is all that Stow tells us about the theatre of Shakespeare's early and triumphant years. In 1598 he had mentioned two of those 'public places': the Theatre and the Curtain. But in 1603 even those names were deleted.[15]

Stow's nostalgia reached its apogee in his account of the festivities associated with two other religious feasts of the dog days of high summer, St John the Baptist's Day and St Peter's Day, together with their preceding vigils, when

in the Euenings after the Sunne setting, there were vsually made Bonefiers in the streetes, euery man bestowing wood or labour towards them: the wealthier sort also before their doores neare to the said Bonefiers, would set out Tables on the Vigiles, furnished with sweete breade, and good drinke, and on the Festiuall dayes with meates and drinks plentifully, whereunto they would inuite their neighbours and passengers also to sit, and bee merrie with them in great familiaritie, praysing God for his benefites bestowed on them. These were called Bonefiers aswell of good amitie amongest neighbours that, being before at controuersie, were there by the labour of others, reconciled, and made of bitter enemies, louing friendes, as also for the vertue that a great fire hath to purge the infectyon of the ayre.[16]

The doorways of houses were festooned with green branches and flowers, while glass lamps with oil in them burning all night hung on branches of iron curiously wrought, each carrying hundreds of lights. Here was the ever seductive myth of community.

We may notice some other striking examples of nostalgic memory in the walkabout chapters of the *Survey*. There is a memorable description of Houndsditch, a row of almshouses for poor bedridden folk, each with a little garden plot behind, the sick old pensioners as visible through their windows as a rather different class of person in modern Amsterdam, 'a clean linnen cloth lying in their window, and a payre of Beades to shew that there lay a bedred body, vnable but to pray onely'. And there devout men and women would go on Fridays, to bestow their charitable alms. But more recently the whole area had been taken over by brokers and dealers in second-hand clothes, which, remarked C. L. Kingsford, was what the district was still known for in 1908.[17]

There is a horror story of what happened to the Priory of Christ Church, called Holy Trinity, in Aldgate, which had come into the possession of Sir Thomas Audley. The great church was demolished, and there was such a glut of stone that any man in the city could have a cartload brought to his door for sixpence or sevenpence, carriage included. The church of the Crutched Friars had become a carpenter's yard, a tennis court, and a glass factory. St Mary Spittle in Bishopsgate Ward had been 'an Hospitall of great reliefe'. But now, in its place, were 'many faire houses builded, for receipt and lodging of worshipfull persons'. Much of the great complex of buildings which made up the Austin Friars had been demolished, and the marquess of Winchester had sold the monuments of noblemen and the paving, which had cost thousands of pounds, for a hundred, 'and in place thereof made fayre stabling for horses'.[18] It looks as if Margaret Aston's essay on 'The Dissolution and the sense of the past' could well have been written without reference to any text other than Stow's *Survey*.[19]

A strong moral is drawn from the strange story of Moorfields in the sixteenth century, first drained and enclosed, then opened up again for archery practice and other forms of recreation, but then re-enclosed, with gardens and summer houses, 'in worse case than euer ... not so much for vse or profite, as for shewe and pleasure, bewraying the vanity of mens mindes, much vnlike to the disposition of the ancient Cittizens, who delighted in the building of Hospitals, and Almes houses for the poore, and therein both imployed their wits, and spent their wealthes in preferment of the common commoditie of this our Citie'.[20]

But as Stow walked from ward to ward, parish to parish, it was the wanton destruction of tomb monuments which made a constant, distressing refrain. At St Michael's Cornhill, where Stow's father and grandfather were buried, the tombs of two notable citizens having been pulled down, 'no monument remayneth of them', 'notwithstanding their liberality to that Church and Parrish'. St Botolph's in Billingsgate once had 'many fayre monuments', now 'al destroyed by bad and greedy men of spoyle'. The tombs in St Magnus the Martyr at the foot of London Bridge were 'for the most part utterly defaced'. The Franciscan church of the Grey Friars, rechristened Christ Church by Henry VIII, was stuffed with notable burials, of which Stow lists no fewer than 138, including that of the foundress, Edward I's queen, Queen Isabel, the consort of Edward II, a daughter of Edward III, the wife of Robert the Bruce, and Sir Thomas Mallory. 'All these and fiue times so many more haue bin buried there, whose Monuments are wholly defaced.' In Shoreditch church the vicar had stripped all the memorial brasses from the graves, the action either of 'a preposterous zeale, or of a greedy mind'.[21] Stow told John Manningham that he had omitted many new monuments from his *Survey*, 'because those men have bin the defacers of the monumentes of others, and soe thinkes them worthy to be deprived of that memory whereof they have injuriously robbed others'.[22]

II

If we attempt to dissect Stow's nostalgic antiquarianism, what do we find? First, and most simply, the values of an old man, seventy-three years of age when the *Survey* was first published, someone who lived in the past, had no enthusiasm for the present, and no words for the future. Stow had spoken with 'some ancient men' who had seen King Richard III and who could describe his physical appearance, 'comely enough, onely of low stature', and he passed this on to Sir George Buck in the seventeenth century, just as in the twenty-first century I may tell my grandchildren about the tiny and nearly globular Queen Victoria whom my father saw with his own eyes, riding in a coach in Hyde Park in the late nineteenth century.[23] As a child, Stow had walked every day to the fields beside the Tower to buy a halfpenny-worth of milk, which was three pints in summer, a quart in winter, 'always hot from the Kine, as the same was milked and strained'.[24] By the time he wrote, the countryside had retreated far down the Mile End Road, beyond Whitechapel. I myself grew up on a Suffolk farm where I rode on the backs of gentle carthorses, fed the pigs, and took part in the harvest with everyone else in the village. That farm no longer exists. The ponds in which I used to fish and catch newts have long since dried up. Old men hate change.

Stow was an historical ecologist before his time. All the old open spaces were filling up, the fields where the Stow family's milk had come from 'let out for Garden plots, Carpenters yardes, Bowling Allies, and diuerse houses thereon builded'. No more than forty years before he wrote, Hog Lane, which ran to the north towards Bethlehem Hospital (and nowadays Liverpool Street Station), had been lined with elm trees, 'with Bridges and easie stiles to passe ouer into the pleasant fieldes, very commodious for Citizens therein to walke, shoote, and otherwise to recreate and refresh their dulled spirites in the sweete and wholesome ayre', which was now 'made a continuall building throughout'.[25]

Such nostalgia for the raped and now distant countryside is a potent urban myth, symbolised by all that greenery allegedly brought in at Christmas and in the month of May, and it is impossible to say how many sixteenth-century Londoners were consciously moved by it. As for Stow's account of May morning, partly suggested by Fitzstephen's lyrical description of twelfth-century London's rural setting, and perhaps by the poets whom Stow knew so well, from Chaucer to Lydgate, this certainly reads like a pleasant fiction: 'Euery man, except impediment, would walke into the sweete meadowes and greene woods, there to reioyce their spirites with the beauty and sauour of sweete flowers, and with the harmony of birds.'[26]

Stow took particular exception to the creation of the East End. He objected to the encroachment of 'filthy cottages' and other 'purprestures' on what had once been open and common fields, making an 'unsauery and unseemly' passage into the city from that direction.[27] And he was equally disturbed by the abandonment of the great houses within the walls on the east side of the city, creating more slums and equally destructive of old-style community. For example, Northumberland House, two minutes' walk from Stow's own house by Aldgate pump, and once the town house of the Percies, had first been converted into a complex of bowling alleys and dicing houses, but then, when the competition of other unlawful gaming houses proved too severe, it was opportunistically developed as small cottages, 'for strangers and others'.[28] But it was none of Stow's business to tell us how the underlying problem of immigration and overcrowding was being created, addressed and managed, which is the contested preoccupation of our modern historians of early modern London: Pearl, Foster, Rappaport, Archer, Boulton.[29]

Stow was less exercised by ribbon development along the roads leading towards Hoxton and Hackney, and thoroughly complacent about the growth of the newly fashionable London to the west, beyond Temple Bar and along the Strand into Westminster. The expressions used in those passages are 'faire buildings', 'diuers fayre houses', 'diuers fayre Tenements lately builded'.[30] But as we gather from some of the most spine-chilling passages in Defoe's *Journal of the Plague Year*, inhabitants of Aldgate were not necessarily well informed about what went on in St Martin's Lane.

The ecological strand in Stow's *Survey* weaves its way in and out of three related themes and preoccupations: open and enclosed, public and private, innocence and sophisticated corruption. 'Of olde time', on holy days, and after evening prayer, the youths of the city had exercised themselves at their masters' doors with cudgel play, while their sisters danced for garlands 'hanged thwart the streetes': 'which open pastimes in my youth, being now suppressed, worser practises within doores are to be feared'. What, asked Stow, should be said about the daily exercises in the long bow, 'now almost cleane left off and forsaken? I ouerpass it: for by the meane of closing in the common grounds, our Archers for want of roome to shoote abroad, creepe into bowling Allies, and ordinarie dicing houses, nearer home, where they have roome enough to hazard their money at vnlawfull games: and there I leaue them to take their pleasures.'[31]

The development of part of the churchyard of St Botulph's Bishopsgate to create Petty France, a collection of houses let out to French immigrants, was, reported Stow, the work of some citizens 'that more regarded their owne priuate gaine, then the common good of the Cittie'. And then, much closer to home, there was the shocking story of how Thomas Cromwell, without a by-your-leave, had encroached twenty-two feet into Stow's father's garden, in the course of the operation of moving a garden house out of the way on rollers 'ere my father heard thereof, no warning was given him'. A symbol of the new age was the ambitious house built in Bishopsgate and known for generations as 'Fishers Folly', about which 'men haue not letted to speake their pleasure'.[32]

What all this added up to was a catastrophic collapse of age-old and traditional charity, which in Stow's perception seems to have been equivalent to the end of citizenship and community as he had known it. Ian Archer has dealt thoroughly with this matter. Hospitality, together with face-to-face, informal, charity may have been in decline in Stow's lifetime. It is impossible to say. But 'there can be no doubting the huge surge in philanthropic giving in the sixteenth century', a 'massively increased participation in giving to the poor', and this is a finding which could never be inferred from Stow.[33]

III

Was the taproot of Stow's nostalgic antiquarianism religious, the attitude of an essentially unreconstructed English Catholic, as it were a denizen of the pages of Duffy's *Stripping of the Altars*? A good case can be made for a strong link between antipathy to the Reformation and all that flowed from it and what might be called the antiquarian bug, and it is made by Richard Cust for certain Midland antiquarians, such as the Leicestershire gentleman Sir Thomas Shirley, and the Staffordshire chorographer Sampson Erdeswicke, Stow's exact contemporary. Catholic antiquarians compensated for their exclusion from many areas of public life by celebrating their ancient lineage with elaborate armorial displays, in their houses and parish churches, where they erected tombs which were assertive genealogical and heraldic statements. Here was the summoning up of the ghost of a past world to redress the unequal balance of the new. Lord Lumley up in County Durham is another good example of the same phenomenon.[34]

Stow, as a London citizen, whose trade was tailoring, and whose greatest adventure into public life was as a conner of ale, was not, to be sure, moved by the same grandiose motives as an Erdeswicke or a Lumley. His friend William Camden makes a more relevant point of reference. Camden's dislike of what he once called 'protestantes effervescentes' runs through his *Annales* of Elizabeth like bindweed.[35] And the Preface to his *Britain* contains this affirmation:

> There are certaine, as I heare who take it impatiently that I have mentioned some of the most famous Monasteries and their founders. I am sory to heare it, and with their good favour will say thus much, They may take it as impatiently, and peradventure would have us forget that our ancestoures were, and we are of the Christian profession when as there are not extant any other more conspicuous, and certaine Monuments, of their piety, and zealous devotion toward God. Neither were there any other seed-gardens from whence Christian Religion, and good learning were propagated over this isle, howbeit in corrupt ages some weeds grew out over-ranckly.[36]

The 'weeds' were not some polite deference to Protestant prejudice. Camden was some kind of Protestant, who had suffered for his convictions in Catholic Oxford, not to be sure at the stake but perhaps by what some would regard as a worse fate, failure to gain a fellowship at All Souls, which, in a letter to Archbishop Ussher, he attributed to 'defending the religion established'.[37] This takes us into the problematical, and perhaps unprofitable, business of determining what religious labels it may or may not be appropriate to pin on representatives of the generation whose lives were intercepted and diverted by the Protestant Reformation.

An exception to prove the rule of the linkage between antiquarianism and a conservative religious outlook is the very unproblematical William Lambarde. But if Sir Thomas Shirley was compensating for a present which had deprived him of his past, Lambarde as a newcomer to Kent was creating for himself his own instant heritage. In what has been written about his *Perambulation of Kent*,[38] not enough has been made of Lambarde's virulent and even, in Camden's phrase, effervescent, Protestantism, no doubt because attention has been concentrated on his Anglo-Saxon interests and learning, evidenced, for example, in Lambarde's extensive discussion of the Kentish law of gavelkind, and in the extent of his indebtedness to other Anglo-Saxon scholars, and especially to the mysterious Laurence Nowell.[39] But anti-popery is a very conspicuous feature of the *Perambulation*, apparent in such small details as a comment on the foundation of the nunnery of Minster in Thanet, with the foundress 'instructed belike by some Monkish counsellor'.[40]

Lambarde's longest continuous narratives were accounts of gross popish superstition. Such was the sensational story of the Maid (or Nun) of Kent, whose exploits had been engineered by 'the enimie of mankinde and Prince of darknesse', the bishops, priests, and monks with closed eyes winking, the Devil and his agents 'with open mouth laughing at it' (more than a thousand words); the conjuring Rood of Boxley (1,500 words): 'if I should thus leave Boxley, the favourers of false and feyned Religion would laugh in their sleeves, and the followers of Gods trueth might iustly cry out and blame me'.[41] John Bale, who also combined a genuine and learned passion for antiquity with an Ian Paisley-like hatred of all forms of monkery and popish superstition, could hardly have done better.

Lambarde pulled all the stops out when his chorographical itinerary brought him to Canterbury and to the great monasteries of Christ Church and St Augustine, 'two irreligious Synagogues' 'harborowes of the Devil and the Pope'. It was no wonder that Canterbury, like Walsingham, was now 'in a maner waste', since that was where God in times past had been blasphemed most. Lambarde's attitude to ruined abbeys differs from Camden's:

> In which part, as I cannot on the one side, but in respecte of the places them-
> selves pitie and lament this generall decay, not onely in this Shyre, but in all other
> places of the Realme also: So on the other side, considering the maine Seas of sinne
> and iniquitie, wherein the worlde (at those daies) was almost wholy drenched, I
> must needes take cause, highly to praise God that hath thus mercifully in our age
> delivered us, disclosed Satan, unmasked these Idoles, dissolved their Synagogs, and
> raced to the grounde all monuments of building erected to superstition, and ungod-
> lynesse.[42]

Lambarde's 'pitie and lament' were not crocodile tears. Paradoxically, he, and that hot Protestant Bale, bitterly regretted the dispersal of the monastic libraries and the loss of their manuscripts, an aspect of the religious alteration which the conservative Stow never mentions.[43] But it appears that Lambarde would have been the last to complain if Canterbury Cathedral had been turned into a quarry: which is what happened to St Augustine's. The flip-side, as it were, of Lambarde's fierce anti-popery was the account, in his second edition, of the fleet riding at anchor at Chatham, 'these most stately and valiant vessels', 'such excellent ornaments of peace, and trustie aides in warre', 'this triumphant spectacle'.[44]

Lambarde regarded the murder of Thomas Becket as an unlawful crime, but asked 'whether such a life deserved not such a death'.[45] In stark contrast, John Stow's interest in Becket was as a person of honour, wisdom, and virtue, a local boy made good, following Fitzstephen with the marginal comment: 'A

Shiriffes clarke of London became Chancellor of England, and Archbishop of Canterburie.'[46]

This brings us back to Stow's religion. There is not any doubt that he regretted the 'preposterous' zeal which had made a holocaust of so much of London's past, and that he deplored all acts of iconoclasm, especially when they were as senseless as the decapitation of the images of Lud and other ancient kings which had 'beautified' Ludgate, the act of those who 'iudged every Image to be an Idoll'.[47] Stow's detailed account of the regularly repeated acts of unlawful violence perpetrated against the images on the cross in Cheapside leave us in no doubt where he stood on that matter. In 1581 the target was 'the image of the blessed virgin, at that time robbed of her son, and her armes broken, by which she staid him on her knees: her whole body also was haled with ropes and left likely to fall'. In 1595 repairs were carried out, and in the year following 'a new misshapen son, as borne out of time, all naked was laid in her armes, the other images broke as afore'. But then, in 1600, between the two editions of the *Survey*, the image of Our Lady was yet again defaced 'by plucking off her Crowne, and almost her head, taking from her her naked child, and stabbing her in the breast etc.'. 'Thus much for the crosse in west Cheape.'[48]

What mordant pleasure Stow derived from the story of St Andrew Undershaft, the church round the corner from his home! The shaft after which the church was named was the principal maypole of the city which had not been set up since the racial riots of the 'evil' May Day of 1517, and it hung on iron hooks under the eaves of neighbouring houses. In 1549, the curate of the parish of St Katherine Christ Church, a certain 'Sir Stephen', preaching at Paul's Cross, denounced the shaft as an idol and demanded that the quaint and in his perception superstitious names of such churches be altered. According to Stow's account, this man was a fanatical extremist who had once preached out of an elm tree in his churchyard. The effect of the sermon was that the neighbours over whose doors the shaft had hung for thirty-two years, after a good dinner, hauled the thing down and sawed it up for firewood. 'Thus was this Idoll (as he tearmed it) mangled, and after burned.' Soon afterwards there happened the 'commotions' of the summer of 1549, in the midst of which, with martial law in force, a man from Romford, the local bailiff, was hanged for incautious words spoken to the same curate. The summary execution happened on Stow's very doorstep. This was a gross miscarriage of justice and the victim was a popular figure. Stow tells us that the villain of the piece immediately left London and was never heard of again.[49]

All this was consistent with the views of a non-effervescent Protestant, which is what Hugh Trevor-Roper supposed Stow to have been. But had that always been the case? C. L. Kingsford knew that there was more to it than that, but was swayed by a somewhat anachronistic view of Elizabethan religion typical of the time in which he wrote: 'Whatever lurking sympathy he might have felt for the old faith was lost in the deep loyalty of a true Elizabethan.'[50] That sounds more like Lambarde.

We must deal with another, and still more questionable reading of Stow. Barrett Beer, in an article based on a reading of successive editions of Stow's *Chronicles*, regarded Stow as a representative and detached layman, the man in the street, who viewed the Reformation 'from the outside'. Beer even suggested that Stow 'never really grasped the significance of the religious revolution through which he lived'.[51]

There is no need to make things up. There is some evidence. In February 1569, Stow came under suspicion as a closet Catholic. The circumstances are obscure but had to do with Stow's possession of a manifesto circulated by the Spanish ambassador on behalf of the duke of Alva. Although Stow was called to answer before the lord mayor, this would probably not have happened if he had not been shopped by his younger brother Thomas, with whom Stow was on the worst possible terms. Thomas knew about his brother's books and papers and suspected him of dabbling in witchcraft. 'I will make all the world know what artes he practysythe.'[52] A few days after Stow's court appearance, he was visited by what might be called the bishop of London's thought police, and his library and papers were searched. After his chaplain had reported on what was found, Bishop Grindal sent a report to the Privy Council and wrote to William Cecil in his own hand, which suggests that the matter was taken seriously.[53]

Historians have not made very much of this episode. There has been a tendency to focus on Stow's collections of chronicles and other papers, and what Grindal's chaplain chose to call 'phantasticall popishe bokes prynted in the old tyme', pretty harmless stuff. But the chaplain paid little or no attention to this material, whereas he prepared a catalogue of 'such bokes as have been lately sett furth in this realme or beyonde the seas for defense of papistrye'. These, he claimed, declared Stow to be 'a great fautor of papistrye'. The chaplain was quite right. The books in question were not old and fantastical but a fairly complete library of the up-to-date Catholic literature of the English Counter-Reformation. There were over thirty titles, including Bishop Bonner's Catechism and *Homilies*, Richard Smith's *A Bouclier of the Catholike Fayth* (1554) and his *Defence of the Blessed Mass* and *Assertion and Defence of the Sacramente of the Alter* (both 1546), Bishop Stephen Gardiner's *Explication and Assertion of the True Catholique Fayth Touchyng the Sacrament of the Aulter* (Rouen, 1551), Bishop Thomas White's sermon on the real presence (1554), Miles Hogarde's *Displaying of the Protestants* (1556), and two much more recent imports from Catholic presses overseas, Thomas Stapleton's translation of Bede (1565), in effect a retort to Foxe's *Book of Martyrs*, and Thomas Dorman's book against Bishop Jewel, *A Proufe of Certeyne Articles in Religion* (1564). This does not sound like the bedside reading of a man who never really grasped the significance of what was going on in the Reformation. These were apologetical and polemical works, not books of devotion. What made Stow such a dedicated student of the doctrine of the real presence?

If Bishop Grindal's chaplain had paid closer attention to Stow's own papers and manuscripts, he might have been alerted to a kind of diary which finished up in a Lambeth Palace Library manuscript, a document of considerable interest if we are trying to pin Stow down, religiously, and a source of the utmost importance for the religious history of London in the 1560s.[54]

This piece of contemporary history suggests a fascination with religious weirdos, of whom early Elizabethan London afforded several examples, including two inmates of Bedlam, John More, who claimed to be Christ; and William Jefferey, who had appointed himself More's apostle, Saint Peter; and the self-confessed usurer, Richard Allington, who recounted on his deathbed many strange visions, with devils 'lyke puppets, they came up and downe my chamber'. 'And maisters, I can not tell of what religion you be that heare, nor I care not': 1,600 words of this.[55] For the year 1562, Stow records the summary arrest of a priest for preparing to say mass in Lady Cary's house in Fetter Lane, the hauling of the priest to prison with the crowd baying for his blood, 'mokynge, derydynge, cursynge, and wyshynge evyll to hym', 'well was he or she that cowld get a plucke at hym or gyve hym a thumpe with theyr fyst or spyt in his face' – and note, says Stow, the priest had not actually said mass but was only dressed and ready for it; the ladies of quality who had been present themselves arraigned 'amongeste theves and mowderars'.[56] Here Stow's sympathies are not in much doubt. When, in the following year, the Marian bishops were removed from their imprisonment in the Tower to more comfortable quarters, Stow records that the preachers at Paul's Cross and other places fed the flames of popular prejudice, preaching 'as it was thowght of many wysse men' 'very sedyssyowsly', and he particularly mentions William Baldwin, the author of the satire *Beware the Cat*, whose sermon had demanded that the bishops 'and othar papestis' be hanged in Smithfield. Although he had assisted him in early work on his abridgement of the *Chronicles*, Stow seems to have taken pleasure in the fact that Baldwin died of the plague a week after this provocative sermon. When Sir Thomas Lodge as lord mayor grew a beard, the first to have done so, it was thought of 'mayny people very strange':[57] beards were Protestant things. By now we begin to appreciate that Stow's 'all men', 'mayny people', 'many wise men', are confessionally loaded rhetorical devices, resembling Camden's use of similar expressions in his *Annales* of Elizabeth.

Stow's account of the Paul's Cross sermons of these years is strikingly mordant. A lengthy report of a robustly anti-Catholic performance by William Cole, the archdeacon of Essex, is ironically prefaced 'Poynts of Devinitie'; another of Cole's sermons, which likened priests to apes – for both were bald, the priests before, the apes behind – was headlined 'A Noate of Divinitye'.[58]

Then comes Stow's invaluable and colourful account of the vestiarian disturbances of 1566 which launched the Elizabethan Puritan movement: Robert Crowley barring the entry of a funeral into St Giles Cripplegate, 'saynge the churche was his ... whereof he wold rule that place and wold not soffer eny suche superstycious rages of Rome ther to entre'; a radical sermon preached at St Magnus the Martyr by a Scot, 'wyth very byter and vehement words agaynst the quene not here to be named'; the same Scot's conformist capitulation, appearing in a surplice, whereupon 'a sertayne nombar of wyves threw stons at hym and pullyd hym forthe of the pulpyt, rentyng his syrplice and scrattyng his face'; the women of St Margaret's Fish Street shouting 'ware horns!' at the bishop; women (again) loading the non-conformist preachers with bags and bottles, sugar and spice, as they passed over London Bridge to custody in the country. It is significant that this narrative puts centre stage the gross and radical disorder of 'womanish brabbles'.

And then follows Stow's spin on the actions of those radical Protestants whose response to the vestments crisis was to reinvent the secret, privy churches of Mary's reign: 'About that tyme were many congregations of the Anabaptysts in London, who cawlyd themselves Puritans or Unspottyd Lambs of the Lord.'[59] We know about these people from other sources.[60] They did not call themselves Puritans, and they were certainly not Anabaptists.

There is no more informative account of the divided religious scene which was the sequel to the fires of Smithfield, and it is clear on which side of the fence Stow stood in these still inchoate 1560s. His religion was probably not very different from that of the undertaker and diarist, Henry Machyn, whose Catholic sympathies have never been in doubt.[61] But he was the religious opposite of the great Protestant chronicler John Foxe, who gloried in the repudiation of the religious past, and who suppressed evidence of religious division among Protestants and of those radical tendencies which Stow gleefully exposed. Were Stow's memoranda intended as a riposte to the *Acts and Monuments*?[62]

In the years which followed, if Stow did not become a Protestant, he learned to be discreet. His *Summarie of Englyshe Chronicles*, which began to appear from the press in 1565, contains none of the tendentious observations on the religious events of the mid-1560s which he had privately recorded. His practice in recounting for public consumption events close to his own time was, as with his use of Fitzstephen in the *Survey*, to incorporate other chronicles in his possession, and one of these, now contained in MS. Harley 540, was conservative in outlook.[63] It characterised Katherine of Aragon as 'a blysyd lady and a good', and told the story of the punishment of two women who had said that she and not Anne Boleyn was rightfully queen.[64] Stow omitted these details from his *Summarie*. The early editions of the *Summarie* gave an upbeat account of the accession of Mary Tudor, and of her restoration of the old religion. 'In this tyme the people shewed themselves so ready to receive their old religion, that in many places of the realme, understandyng the quenes plesure, before any law was made for the same, they erected agayne theyr aultars, and used the Masse and latin service, in such sorte as was wont to be in kyng Henries tyme.' These passages too were dropped from later editions.[65]

There is further self-censorship in the *Survey* itself. When Stow quotes the epitaphs inscribed on pre-Reformation tombs, he turns them into theologically innocuous statements, mere monuments, omitting the lines which invite prayers for the dead or refer to the doctrine of purgatory. The full texts can be found in the original manuscript of the *Survey* (MS. Harley 538). Thus, the nine lines quoted from the tomb of John Rainwell, fishmonger, in St Botolph's Billingsgate (1446) end with an 'etc.', omitting five more, where we find: 'Wherfore now agre | To pray unto God that reynethe eternally | His soule to embrace and take to his mercy'. Only in MS. Harley 538 do we find these words from the epitaph for Robert Dalusse and his wife, buried in St Martin in the Vintry in the days of Edward IV: 'Pray for us, we yow pray. | Lyke as you would be prayed for another day'; and, from the lengthy epitaph in St Anthony's Budge Row for Thomas Knowles, a former mayor, and his family, the formula: 'We may not pray, hartely pray ye | For our sowles pater noster et ave; | The sonner owre paynes lessed may be, | Graunt vs the Holy Trinitie.'[66]

If there is any sense in which John Stow was converted, if not exactly to a religion known as Protestantism, to the Protestant Church of England, he doubtless underwent, as with so many of his generation, a process of conversion by conformity. There is no evidence that he was ever a recusant and copious evidence appears on almost every page of the *Survey* to continuing commitment to the fabric and the social and mystical community of London's parishes. But when Stow refers, as he sometimes does, to churches having been recently rebuilt or refurbished, one should not be misled. In every case it appears that the improvements to which he refers were not at all recent, and had been carried out before the Reformation, a watershed which he probably never ceased to regret.[67] Later editions of his *Summarie of Chronicles* included laudatory obits for Archbishop Parker, whom he calls 'my especiall benefactor', and for Bishop Jewel, 'a most eloquent and diligent preacher, but a farre more painfull and studious writer, as his workes remaining witness'.[68] It sounds as if Stow's library had been reconstructed since Bishop Grindal's chaplain visited it in 1569. However, one is bound to conclude from this investigation of religious opinions and attitudes, expressed and suppressed, that John Stow's *Survey of London* was born out of the old religion and its values, roughly adapted to fit the new suit of clothes which we almost have to call, however anachronistically, Anglicanism.

IV

In 1602, one year before Stow's second edition, another survey was published by a fellow member of the Society of Antiquaries, Richard Carew: *The Survey of Cornwall*.[69] Carew was not unaware that the world is a changeable place. In his Preface he wrote: 'the state of our countrie hath vndergone so manie alterations, since I first began these scriblings, that in the reviewing, I was driuen either likewise to varie my report, or else to speake against my knowledge'. Given what he called 'the ceaselesse revolution of the Vniverse' it would be marvellous if any part of it 'should retain a stedfast constitution'. But having stated the problem, Carew immediately put it behind him, declaring that what he called, significantly, his '*Eulogies*' would plot Cornwall 'as it now standeth'.[70]

So Carew provided a huge present-tense snapshot of his native county. There is a great deal of historical material in his *Survey*, much more than one would suspect if one relied only on F. E. Halliday's modern abridgement. In particular, Carew's pages are stuffed with genealogy. But for anything in the past Carew was reliant on other authorities, many of whom were of the most shaky kind, and his amateurishness as an antiquarian was an embarrassment even to himself. Making what he confessed to be 'a great leap' from King Arthur and his knights to a man who died in 1507, he admitted: 'which conuinceth me an vnworthy associat of the antiquary Colledge'. He tells us about Conan who conquered Brittany and, having settled it, wrote to Dionethus, king and duke of Cornwall, asking him to send over 'some Maidens' to marry with his people. The result was that St Ursula and her 11,000 virgins were shipped over but on the way miscarried, 'as their wel known history reporteth'. Not that Carew was incapable of the sceptical irony with which the Tudor antiquarians often presented historical myths. Another doubtful detail of Cornish history was not to be questioned 'unlesse you will, withall, shake the irrefragable authoritie of the round tables Romants'.[71]

So there is a past as well as a present tense in Carew, as misty as the seafret around Tintagel, which excited him with as much romantic awe as any traveller might have felt in the age of Wordsworth and Walter Scott. But the difference with Stow is that the past was not brought critically to bear on the present, as a better time. Carew too was a nostalgic writer, but his nostalgia was one of celebration of the present, of which he paints a very rosy picture. Take, as an emblem of this upbeat writer, his description of the view from the coastal path at Fowey, well supplied with seats for tired walkers and summerhouses 'for their more priuate retrait and recreation': 'In passing along, your eyes shall be called away from guiding your feete, to descry by their fardest kenning, the vast Ocean sparkled with ships, that continually this way trade forth and backe to most quarters of the world', nearer to home the fishing boats 'houering on the coast', and closer still 'the faire and commodious hauen'.[72] Actuarially speaking, there was no better place to live than Carew's Cornwall. 'For health, 80 and 90 yeres age is ordinary in euery place, and in most persons, accompanied with an able vse of the body and his sences.'[73] He does tell us that Cornish houses were infested with rats, 'a brood very hurtful for deuouring of meat, clothes and writings', but he romanticises even this nastiness, describing 'their crying and ratling, while they daunce their gallop gallyards in the roofe at night' – from which we gather that these were plague-carrying black rats.[74]

One would never suspect that Cornwall, especially in the 1590s, was full of grinding poverty. To be sure there comes the moment when Carew says: 'We must also spare a roome in this Suruey to the poore', but he then tells us that if it were not for the whole shiploads of Irish poor brought over 'yeerley, yea and daly', there would be no problem. Carew, who was a magistrate and had been sheriff, launches into a conventional diatribe against rogues and vagabonds, complaining that what was given to them was 'robberie of the needy impotent', but on the subject of what he calls honest poor parishioners he has nothing else to say, except that no-one in Cornwall needed to starve, since there was always plenty of shellfish available for the gathering.[75]

Rather, 'let me lead you from these impleasing matters, to refresh yourselues with taking view of the *Cornish* mens recreations, which consist principally in feastes and pastimes'. And there follows, after a contrived debate about church ales and feasts, whether allowable or not (and Carew clearly approved of these things), the richest description of the sporting life which we have for any part of early modern England: miracle plays and what are called 'three men's songs', 'cunningly contriued for the ditty and pleasantly for the note', football – or rather hurling and of two different kinds, one peculiar to east Cornwall, the other to the west – and Cornish wrestling, 'more delightful, and less dangerous' than hurling, which, when ended, 'you shall see them retiryng home, as from a pitched battaile, with bloody pates, bones broken, and out of ioynt, and such bruses as serue to shorten their daies; yet al is good play, and neuer Attourney nor Crowner troubled for the matter'.[76]

John Stow would have set all this in the past and would have lamented the passing of so much honest manliness. But Carew puts it in the present, which causes problems for the historian of traditional culture. His account of the Cornish miracle play, or 'gwary', to which 'the Country people flock from all sides, many miles off' is not only the best, it is the only description we have before more modern times of any play in performance, with the actor followed around the stage by the prompter, or ordinary, who tells him his lines.[77] But was the old drama still alive and well in Cornwall in 1600, when it had been suppressed almost everywhere else? The leading authority on the Cornish play text known as the *Ordinalia* finds it remarkable that in a county which only forty years earlier had been in active rebellion against the new religion, the high sheriff should record the performance of the old religious plays, with all their 'devils and devices', to be sure without much sympathy, but with perfect equanimity.[78]

The problem of the gwary and its fortunes as the sixteenth century turned into the seventeenth is tied up with the fact that the plays were written and performed in the Cornish language, which was itself in terminal decline. Carew's somewhat distant and condescending attitude towards the common people was accentuated by the fact that he himself seems to have known little Cornish (whereas he wrote an essay for his friend Camden on 'The excellencie of the English tongue'),[79] and was not sympathetic towards it, alleging that if a stranger who was lost were to ask the way, he would be told, in Cornish, 'I can speak no Saxonage', which was perhaps all the Cornish the man knew. Carew's Cornish phrase book knows nothing about postillions struck by lightning, but does include the Cornish for 'ten thousand mischiefs in thy guts'.[80]

Yet this did not prevent Carew from supplying the most detailed and knowledgeable accounts of how the Cornish people made their living, including 6,000 expert words on the subject of tin-mining. While the men were down the mine, 'the women and children in the West part of *Cornwall*, doe vse to make Mats ... which for their warmthe and well wearing, are carried by sea to *London* and other parts of the Realme, and serue to couer floores and wals'.[81] And there were no barriers between Carew and his subject, either linguistic or social, when it came to fish and fishing, which he loved. His model may have been Pliny, but he also wrote from the richest personal experience, from digging lugworms for bait to the netting of pilchards. The particular taking of divers kinds of fishes (and he lists more than thirty), is almost as divers as themselves. 'I will ... shew you, what they are, when they come, where they haunt, with what baite they may be trayned, with what engine taken, and with what dressing saued.' Fourteen pages on: 'But you are tired, the day is spent; and it is high time that I draw to harbour.'[82]

Carew does not tell us, but a report drawn up in the same decade does, that in many places in west Cornwall the clergy, Protestant preaching ministers, were often the victims of physical assault, afraid to poke their noses out of doors.[83] On matters of religion, Carew was to the right of Lambarde, but a little to the left of Stow, and perhaps close to where Camden stood. It was not from the pope that Cornwall had received its Christianity. Vicarages had been created by the impropriation of benefices by the religious houses 'in more corrupt ages'. If the English bishops would only keep fast to their first institution, they would easily close the mouths of those 'who would thrust vpon vs their often varying discipline'.[84] On the whole, Cornwall, church as well as state, worked very well, and there was no better place to live, especially beside Carew's delightful and ingeniously devised fish pond at his ancestral Antony.

Is it possible to be nostalgic about the present, as well as about the past? The proof that it is is in Carew's *Survey of Cornwall*, which covers its subject with a thick, rich gloss which is just as deceptive as the regretful, nostalgic varnish which Stow applied to London. My exploration of these works of late Tudor antiquarianism, Stow, Lambarde and Carew, suggests that we should not trust any one of them as a simple description of its subject. All three need to be taken with a healthy pinch of postmodernist salt. But that should not in any way diminish our enjoyment of what Hayden White would assure us are three charming fictions. And if that appears too large a concession to make to postmodernism, perhaps we are entitled to say that Kent, Cornwall and, above all, John Stow's London were, in Benedict Anderson's phrase, so many imagined communities, the product of three very different imaginations.

NOTES

1 Stow, *Survey of London*, vol. 2, p. 89.

2 Ronald Hutton, *The Rise and Fall of Merry England: The Ritual Year 1400–1700* (Oxford, 1994).

3 Keith Thomas, *The Perception of the Past in Early Modern England*, The Creighton Trust Lecture 1983 (London, 1983).

4 W. M. Thackeray, *The Newcomes*, ed. D. Pascoe (Oxford, 1996), p. 108.

5 Ian Archer, 'The nostalgia of John Stow', in David L. Smith, Richard Strier, and David Bevington (eds), *The Theatrical City: Culture, theatre and politics in London, 1576–1649* (Cambridge, 1995), pp. 17–34.

6 Stow, *Survey*, vol. 1, p. 1; vol. 2, p. 253.

7 Xavier Baron, 'Medieval traditions in the English Renaissance: John Stow's portrayal of London in 1603', in Rhoda Schnur (ed.), *Acta Conventus Neo-Latini Hafniensis: Proceedings of the Eighth International Congress of Neo-Latin Studies*, Medieval & Renaissance Texts & Studies 120 (Binghamton, N.Y., 1994), pp. 133–41.

8 Stow, *Survey*, vol. 1, pp. 83–4.

9 *Ibid.*, vol. 1, pp. 84–9.

10 Eamon Duffy, *The Stripping of the Altars: Traditional religion in England, c.1400–c.1580* (New Haven, Conn., and London, 1992).

11 Stow, *Survey*, vol. 1, pp. 91–9.

12 *Ibid.*, vol. 1, pp. 99–104; John Stow, *A Summarie of Englyshe Chronicles* (1570 edn), fos 402r, 405v; (1587 edn), pp. 327, 330, 334; Archer, 'The nostalgia of John Stow', pp. 24–5. But see Lawrence Manley's essay on Stow accompanying Ian Archer's 'Of sites and rites' in *The Theatrical City*, pp. 47–8. There is a lavish description of an early seventeenth-century lord mayor's show in Thomas Middleton, *The Triumphs of Truth: A Solemnity Vnparalleld for Cost, Art, and Magnificence, at the Confirmation and Establishment of that Worthy and true Nobly-minded Gentleman, Sir Thomas Middleton, Knight; in the Honorable Office of his Maiesties Lieuetenant, the Lord Maior of the thrice Famous Citty of London* (London, 1613).

13 Mervyn James, 'Ritual, drama and social body in the late medieval English town', in M. James, *Society, Politics and Culture: Studies in early modern England* (Cambridge, 1986), pp. 16–47; Charles Phythian-Adams, 'Ceremony and the citizen: the communal year at Coventry, 1450–1550', in Peter Clark and Paul Slack (eds), *Crisis and Order in English Towns 1500–1700: Essays in urban history* (Cambridge, 1972), pp. 57–85.

14 This point was clarified for me by Professor Caroline Barron.

15 Stow, *Survey*, vol. 1, p. 93; vol. 2, p. 236.

16 *Ibid.*, vol. 1, p. 101.

17 *Ibid.*, vol. 1, p. 128; vol. 2, p. 289.

18 *Ibid.*, vol. 1, pp. 143–4, 148, 166–7, 176–7.

19 Margaret Aston, 'English ruins and English history, the Dissolution and the sense of the past', in M. Aston, *Lollards and Reformers: Images and literacy in late medieval religion* (1984), pp. 313–37.

20 Stow, *Survey*, vol. 2, pp. 76–8.

21 *Ibid.*, vol. 1, pp. 197, 207–8, 212, 319–22; vol. 2, p. 75.

22 R. P. Sorlien (ed.), *The Diary of John Manningham* (Hanover, N.H., 1976), p. 154.

23 George Buck, *The History of the Life and Reigne of Richard the Third* (1647), p. 79.

24 Stow, *Survey*, vol. 1, p. 126.

25 *Ibid.*, vol. 1, pp. 126–7.

26 *Ibid.*, vol. 1, p. 98.

27 *Ibid.*, vol. 2, p. 72.

28 *Ibid.*, vol. 1, p. 149.

29 Valerie Pearl, 'Social policy in early modern London', in H. Lloyd-Jones, B. Worden, and V. Pearl (eds), *History and Imagination: Essays in honour of H. R. Trevor-Roper* (London, 1981), pp. 115–31; F. F. Foster, *The Politics of Stability. A portrait of the rulers in Elizabethan London* (London, 1977); Steve Rappaport, *Worlds Within Worlds: Structures of life in sixteenth-century London* (Cambridge, 1989); Ian W. Archer, *The Pursuit of Stability: Social Relations in Elizabethan London* (Cambridge, 1991); Jeremy Boulton, *Neighbourhood and Society: A London suburb in the seventeenth century* (Cambridge, 1987).

30 Stow, *Survey*, vol. 2, pp. 74, 98, 101–2.

31 *Ibid.*, vol. 1, pp. 95, 104.

32 *Ibid.*, vol. 1, pp. 164, 179, 165–6.

33 Archer, 'The nostalgia of John Stow', p. 27.

34 Richard Cust, 'Catholicism, antiquarianism and gentry honour: the writings of Sir Thomas Shirley', *Midland History* 23 (1998): 40–70; Mervyn James, *Family, Lineage and Civil Society: A Study of Society, Politics and Mentality in the Durham Region, 1500–1640* (Oxford, 1974), pp. 108–10.

35 Chapter 9 in this volume.

36 William Camden, tr. Philemon Holland, *Britain* (1610), 'The Author to the Reader'. This preface, including this statement, addressed to an English rather than a continental readership, appeared for the first time in 1610.

37 Thomas Smith (ed.), *V. Cl. Gulielmi Camdeni et Illustrium Virorum and G. Camdenum Epistolae* (London, 1691), pp. 246–8.

38 I cite the 1596 edition of *A Perambulation of Kent: Conteining the Description, Hystorie and Customes of that Shyre*, first published in a limited edition of 600 copies (intended for the Kentish gentry?) in 1576. Lambarde was republished in 1826, an edition reprinted in facsimile and edited by Richard Church (Bath, 1970).

39 Robin Flower, 'Laurence Nowell and the discovery of England in Tudor times', *Proceedings of the British Academy* 21 (1935): 47–74. Flower's misidentification of Nowell is corrected in Retha Warnicke, 'Notes on a Court of Requests case of 1571', *English Language Notes* (Boulder, Colo., 1973), and in her *William Lambarde; Elizabethan Antiquary 1536–1601* (Chichester, 1973). See ch. 4, 'The antiquary'.

40 *A Perambulation*, p. 99.

41 *Ibid.*, pp. 187–94, 227.

42 *Ibid.*, pp. 296–8.

43 I owe this point to Dr Thomas Freeman.

44 *A Perambulation*, pp. 346–50. Lambarde provides a list of all ships present in December 1596, the 'Estate of the Navie Royall', forty vessels.

45 *A Perambulation*, p. 305.

46 Stow, *Survey*, vol. 1, p. 105.

47 *Ibid.*, vol. 1, p. 38.

48 *Ibid.*, vol. 1, pp. 266–7.

49 *Ibid.*, vol. 1, pp. 143–5.

50 H. R. Trevor-Roper, 'John Stow' in *Renaissance Essays* (1985), pp. 94–102; Kingsford's Introduction to the *Survey*, vol. 1, p. xxx.

51 Barrett L. Beer, 'John Stow and the English Reformation, 1547–1559', *The Sixteenth-Century Journal* 16 (1985): 257–71.

52 Stow, *Survey*, vol. 1, pp. xvi–xviii, lvi.

53 Bishop Edmund Grindal to Sir William Cecil, 24 February 1568(9), enclosing a letter from Thomas Wattes to Grindal, 21 February 1568(9), together with 'A Catalog of such unnlawfull bookes as were founde in the studye of John Stowe of London'; BL, MS. Lansdowne 11, fos. 4–8. The catalogue was printed by John Strype in his *Life of Edmund Grindal* (Oxford, 1821), pp. 516–19.

54 James Gairdner (ed.), *Three Fifteenth-Century Chronicles With Historical Memoranda by John Stow the Antiquary, And Contemporary Notes of Occurrences Written by Him in the Reign of Queen Elizabeth*, Camden Society, n.s. 28 (1880).

55 *Ibid.*, pp. 115, 117–21.

56 *Ibid.*, pp. 121–2.

57 *Ibid.*, pp. 126, 127.

58 *Ibid.*, pp. 128, 133.

59 *Ibid.*, pp. 135–44.

60 Patrick Collinson, *The Elizabethan Puritan Movement* (London and Berkeley, Calif., 1967; Oxford, 1990), part 2, ch. 3, 'London's Protestant underworld'.

61 J. G. Nichols (ed.), *The Diary of Henry Machyn Citizen and Merchant-Taylor of London, From A.D. 1550 to A.D. 1563*, Camden Society, 42 (1848).

62 I owe this point to Dr Thomas Freeman.

63 C. L. Kingsford (ed.), *Two London Chronicles From the Collections of John Stow*, Camden Miscellany 12, Camden Society, 3rd ser. 18 (1910). Stow also employed a chronicle, more Protestant in tone, MS. Harley 530, together with MS. Harley 194, edited by

J. G. Nichols as *The Chronicles of Queen Jane and of Two Years of Queen Mary*, Camden Society, 48 (1850).

64 Kingsford, *Two London Chronicles*, pp. 7–8.

65 Stow, *A Summarie of Englyshe Chronicles* (1565), fos 222v, 224. Stow's version of the spontaneous return of Catholic practice under Mary can be compared with the Yorkshire story told in A. G. Dickens (ed.), 'Robert Parkyn's narrative of the Reformation', *English Historical Review* 62 (1947): 58–83, reprinted in Dickens, *Reformation Studies* (1982), pp. 287–312. It may be no less indicative of where his sympathies lay. Compare later editions of the *Summarie*.

66 These omissions were noted by Kingsford: Stow, *Survey*, vol. 2, pp. 309, 326, 327.

67 Examples in *ibid.*, vol. 1, p. 194 (St Peter Cornhill, 'lately repayred, if not all new builded'), 202 (All Hallows Lombard Street, 'lately new builded'), 297 (St Michael Wood Street, 'a proper thing, and lately well repayred'), 314 (St Peter in Cheap, 'a proper Church lately new builded'). I have been helped with this point by Dr Julia Merritt.

68 Stow, *Summarie of Chronicles* (1587 edn), pp. 370, 350; John Stow, *The Annales of England* (1592), dedicatory epistle addressed to Archbishop Whitgift. The 1601 edition of the *Annales* included for the first time a generous obit for Archbishop Grindal (pp. 1174–5).

69 Richard Carew, *The Survey of Cornwall. Written by R. Carew of Antonie, Esquire* (London, 1602). There is a modern, somewhat abridged, edition by F. E. Halliday (1953, repr. 1969). All references here are to the original edition.

70 Carew, *The Survey*, 'To the Reader'.

71 *Ibid.*, fos 61v, 77.

72 *Ibid.*, fo. 133r.

73 *Ibid.*, fo. 63r.

74 *Ibid.*, fo. 22r.

75 *Ibid.*, fos 67, 68r, 31r.

76 *Ibid.*, fos 68r–76r.

77 *Ibid.*, fos 71v–2r.

78 Jane A. Bakere, *The Cornish Ordinalia: A critical study* (Cardiff, 1980), p. 14. Bakere suspects (p. 13) that Carew had not himself witnessed the 'gwary' in performance, and that his story is apocryphal. But she draws on town records for evidence of plays (unidentified) in performance in several places (pp. 15–22), as does A. L. Rowse, *Tudor Cornwall, Portrait of a Society* (London, 1941), pp. 435–6. See also Roger Longsworth, *The Cornish Ordinalia: Religion and dramaturgy* (Cambridge, Mass., 1967), Brian Murdoch, *Cornish Literature* (Cambridge, 1993).

79 The best modern edition of William Camden's *Remaines of a Greater Worke, concerning Britaine* (1605) is by R. D. Dunn (Toronto, 1984).

80 Carew, *The Survey*, fos 55r–56v.

81 *Ibid.*, fos 7v–19r.

82 *Ibid.*, fos 28r–35r.

83 'The lamentable estate of the mynystry in Cornewall', Westminster Abbey Muniments, Muniment Book 15, fo. 84.

84 Carew, *The Survey*, fos. 81r–82r.

Index

Index